Democratization and Constitutional Reform in Thailand

Has Constitutionalism Saved Democracy?

Democratization and Constitutional Reform in Thailand

Has Constitutionalism Saved Democracy?

Ayako Toyama

TRANS PACIFIC PRESS

Democratization and Constitutional Reform in Thailand:
Has Constitutionalism Saved Democracy?
© Ayako Toyama, 2024
Originally published in 2020, *Tai minshuka to kenpō kaikaku: Rikken shugi wa minshu shugi wo sukutta ka* [*Democratization and Constitutional Reform in Thailand: Has Constitutionalism Saved Democracy?*] by Kyoto University Press, Japan.
This English edition published in 2024 by Trans Pacific Press Co., Ltd.

Trans Pacific Press Co., Ltd.
PO Box 8547
#19682
Boston, MA, 02114, United States
Telephone: +1-6178610545
Email: info@transpacificpress.com
Web: http://www.transpacificpress.com

Copyedited by Miriam Riley, Armidale, NSW, Australia
Designed and set by Ryo Kuroda, Tsukuba-city, Ibaraki, Japan

Distributors

World
Independent Publishers Group (IPG)
814 N. Franklin Street
Chicago, IL 60610, USA
Telephone inquiries: +1-312-337-0747
Order placement: 800-888-4741
(domestic only)
Fax: +1-312-337-5985
Email: frontdesk@ipgbook.com
Web: http://www.ipgbook.com

Japan
MHM Limited
3-2-3F, Kanda-Ogawamachi, Chiyoda-ku,
Tokyo 101-0052
Email: sales@mhmlimited.co.jp
Web: http://www.mhmlimited.co.jp

China
China Publishers Services Ltd.
718, 7/F., Fortune Commercial Building,
362 Sha Tsui Road, Tsuen Wan, N.T.
Hong Kong
Email: edwin@cps-hk.com

Southeast Asia
Alkem Company Pte Ltd.
1, Sunview Road #01-27, Eco-Tech@
Sunview
Singapore 627615
Email: enquiry@alkem.com.sg

The publication of this book was supported by a Grant-in-Aid for Publication of Scientific Research Results (Grant Number 21HP6005), provided by the Japan Society for the Promotion of Science, to which we express our sincere appreciation.

All rights reserved. No reproduction of any part of this book may take place without the written permission of Trans Pacific Press.

ISBN: 978-1-920850-12-8 (paperback)
ISBN: 978-1-920850-11-1 (eBook)

Contents

List of Figures vi
List of Tables vi
List of Photographs vii
About the Author viii
Preface ix
Introduction: Investigating Constitutionalism in Thailand
– Academic Significance 1

**Part I: Constitutional Reform in the 1990s and Beyond
– Cause and Intent** 37
   1 The History of Politics and Constitutions in Thailand 39
   2 Revisiting the Political Reform Movement:
      What Is Thai 'Constitutionalism'? 81

Part II: Constitutional Reform and Power Elected by the People 143
   3 Constitutional Reform and Administrative Power: The Political
      Implications of 'Directive Principles of Fundamental State Policies' 145
   4 Constitutional Reform and Legislative Power:
      An Analysis of Electoral System Reforms 179

Part III: Constitutional Reform and Power Not Elected by the People 221
   5 Constitutional Reform and Anti-Corruption – The Creation of
      Corruption: Legal Provisions and Criticism of Politicians 223
   6 Constitutional Reform and the Judiciary: Institutional Problems of
      the Constitutional Court and Independent Agencies 263
   7 Constitutional Reform and 'Non-Elected' Legislative Power:
      The 2007 Constitution and a New Mission for the Senate 295

Conclusion: Constitutional Reform – What Has It Achieved? 331
Bibliography 363
Index 381

List of Figures

Figure 5.1 The structure of a legal definition of corruption (1) 242
Figure 5.2 The structure of a legal definition of corruption (2) 242

List of Tables

Table 0.1 Summary of Thai Government administrations 8
Table 1.1 Provisions relating to cabinet and the parliament
in constitutions between 1932 and 1978 43
Table 1.2 Democracy and the constitutions of Thailand, 1932–1978 44
Table 3.1 Changes in 'Directive Principles of State Policies' or
'Directive Principles of Fundamental State Policies' of
Thai constitutions 152
Table 3.2 Abhisit Cabinet Policy Speech Appendix (partial excerpt) 164
Table 3.3 List of laws to be enacted or amended according to
Article 303 of the 2007 Thai Constitution 166
Table 3.4 Laws made compulsory under Section 304 of
the 2007 Constitution 167
Table 4.1 Comparison of provisions related to political parties (1) 188
Table 4.2 Comparison of provisions related to political parties (2) 192
Table 4.3 Chapter divisions of the 1981, 1998 and 2007
political party laws 196
Table 4.4 Chapter divisions of the 1979, 1998 and 2007 election laws 206
Table 5.1 Chronology of the implementation of major laws regulating
corruption and relevant political incidents 227
Table 5.2 Restrictions on the eligibility to be elected for the House of
Representatives (partial extract – summary) 230
Table 5.3 Matters forbidden to members of the House of
Representatives 234
Table 5.4 Matters prohibited to members of cabinet 235
Table 5.5 List of cases related to false statement of assets and
liabilities and violation of the upper limit of shareholdings 244

Table 6.1	Membership of the Constitutional Court and independent agencies (the 1997 Constitution)	270
Table 6.2	Membership of the Constitutional Court and independent agencies (the 2007 Constitution)	276
Table 6.3	List of lawsuits related to the overthrow of popularly elected governments	284
Table 7.1	Occupational classification of candidates and elected senators in the 2008 upper house election	304
Table 7.2	Occupational breakdown of 2008 upper house nominees for Senate appointment and for appointed Senate members	307
Table 7.3	Brief summary of political rulings since 2013	329
Table C.1	Survey period and sample numbers	332
Table C.2	Satisfaction rating towards democracy and the government	332
Table C.3	Level of trust in the prime minister	332
Table C.4	Approval of non-democratic government	332
Table C.5	Disapproval of non-democratic government: entire nation	332
Table C.6	Disapproval of non-democratic government: Bangkok	333
Table C.7	Disapproval of non-democratic government: Central Region	333
Table C.8	Disapproval of non-democratic government: Northern Region	333
Table C.9	Disapproval of non-democratic government: Northeastern Region	333
Table C.10	Disapproval of non-democratic government: Southern Region	334

List of Photographs

Photo 6.1	Red Shirts	291

About the Author

Ayako Toyama is an associate professor of the Institute of Humanities and Social Sciences at the University of Tsukuba specializing in Thai politics and comparative politics. After graduating from the Department of Political Science in the Faculty of Political Science and Economics at Waseda University and the Graduate School of International Cooperation Studies at Kobe University, she worked as a civil servant before completing her PhD in 2013 at Kyoto University's Graduate School of Asian and African Area Studies.

Preface

The purpose of this book is to investigate the relationship between democratization and constitutional reform in Thailand mainly from 1992 through to the 2014 staging of the nineteenth coup d'etat of the modern Thai era. During the 1990s, when prospects for Thai democratization were positive, many scholars and Thai people believed that the coup era had come to an end. This changed, however, as the country entered the twenty-first century and state power was once again seized by means of a coup d'etat from a popularly elected government. For a long time after the so-called 'Siamese Revolution' of 1932, the military was an impediment to the democratization of Thailand. In the twenty-first century, the judiciary, however, played a crucial role in the demise of the three popularly elected governments installed between 2001 and 2008 – the Thaksin administration (2001–2006), the Samak administration (2008) and the Somchai administration (2008) – and also in the fall of the Yingluck administration (2011–2014) that held power until just prior to the 2014 coup d'etat. Given that there were no previous examples of this kind of judicial intervention in the history of governance in Thailand, how are we to understand the impact of such intervention on Thai democratization? The common factor in the overthrow of the Samak, Somchai and then Yingluck administrations was the Constitutional Court, an institution established under the 1997 Constitution and continued in the 2007 Constitution. We might therefore reasonably assume that the design blueprint of the 1997 and 2007 constitutions was a factor contributing to the judicial removal of popularly elected governments. With a focus on the political reform movement initiated following the 1992 Bloody May Incident and also on the design blueprints of the 1997 and 2007 constitutions that embodied the ideals of that movement, this book attempts to clarify the following three points: 1. What triggered the start of the political reform movement advocating constitutionalism? 2. What were the characteristics of the constitutions enacted after the political reform movement (especially the 1997 and 2007 constitutions)? 3. What kind of impact did the constitutions based on constitutionalism have on democratization?

The contents of this book are largely based on research conducted from 2008 to 2012 when I was a doctoral student at the Graduate School of Asian and African Area Studies, Kyoto University, and from 2013 to 2017 when I was a researcher in the United States and Thailand with support from the Japan Society for the Promotion of Science. My doctoral dissertation was submitted to Kyoto University in November 2012. After that, my overseas research material was added and the book based on the dissertation was published in Japan in January 2020 by Kyoto University Press with the support of the Japan Society for the Promotion of Science. The book won the nineteenth Japan Society for Southeast Asian Studies Award in October 2021.

This English version of the book is a translation of the Japanese original. More than three years have passed since the publication of the Japanese version. In the introductory chapter and the first chapter of this book, I brought in some new research by other scholars that appeared after my Japanese version was published, but the arguments and analysis contained in the English version are the same as those in the Japanese version.

I would like to thank the many people who have supported me over the years in publishing this book. First of all, I would like to thank Professor Yoshifumi Tamada, who served as my supervisor in the doctoral course at Kyoto University. When I entered the doctoral course, I was working as a civil servant and was pregnant with my daughter. From the beginning of my research life, my situation was more difficult than that of a normal student, but thanks to the patient guidance of Professor Tamada, I was able to complete my doctoral dissertation. As for my overseas research, I got a precious opportunity to become a visiting researcher at the Southeast Asia Program of Cornell University, the Faculty of Political Science of Chulalongkorn University, and the Faculty of Political Science of Thammasat University. At Cornell University, Professor Thak Chaloemtiarana accepted me as an advisee. I am very grateful to have had the opportunity to study under such a wonderful professor. At Chulalongkorn University, Professor Siripan Nogsuan Sawasdee kindly accepted me. In addition, I would like to thank professors Pandit Chanrochanakit, Pornson Liengboonlertchai, Puangthong R. Pawakapan, Viengrat Nethipo and

Pitch Pongsawat. I am also indebted to many professors at Thammasat University. I am especially indebted to those of the Faculty of Political Science and the Faculty of Law. In the Faculty of Political Science, I was kindly accepted by Professor Supasawad Chardchawarn. The other professors who helped me, too many to mention all by name, include professors Nakharin Mektrairat, Wasan Luangprapat, Virot Ali, Puli Fuwongcharoen, Vannapar Tirasangka, Amporn Tamronglak, Prajak Kongkirati, Kasian Tejapira and Chai Chaiyachi. I also had the opportunity to attend classes in the Faculty of Law, where I learned a lot from talking with professors Teera Suteevarangkul, Prinya Thaewanarumitkul, Piyabutr Saengkanokkul, Worachet Pakeerut and Suraphol Nitikraipot. I am also deeply grateful to other researchers and friends not named here who have helped me along the way.

As mentioned above, this book has received a publication grant from the Japan Society for the Promotion of Science (21HP6005). I would like to thank Trans Pacific Press for all the arrangements for the publication of the English version. Finally, I am grateful to my family for supporting my research life over the years. My husband and daughter were very patient and supportive during my research abroad in the United States and Thailand. More than anyone else, I would like to express my deepest gratitude to my mother, Michiko Toyama, who has supported me since I was born.

Introduction: Investigating Constitutionalism in Thailand – Academic Significance

Why we need to examine constitutionalism now

Democratization in the twenty-first-century world

The politics of developing countries has long been viewed as progressing democratization along with economic and social growth. This is the analytical framework of the famous theory of modernization. In fact, after the end of the Cold War, it seemed that democratization began to progress worldwide. In many places, however, this trend almost immediately appeared to reverse as, from the mid-1990s, one emerging nation after another encountered problems in democratizing, against expectations (Edles 1995: 355). Of the close to 100 places regarded at the time as transitioning to democracy, it is likely that less than twenty followed the process through to the end. Thus, the majority of sites that appeared to be riding Huntington's 'third wave' (1991) were unable either to achieve an effectively functioning democracy or to ensure that their democratic processes functioned at a deep level. In some of these countries, moreover, authoritarian regimes re-emerged. However, it has also been pointed out that most of the countries considered to be in transition are in an ambiguous situation, neither clearly progressing toward dictatorships nor democratization (Carothers 2002: 9). Under these circumstances, democratization theory must now be reconsidered.

It was in this global context that Ottaway's concept of 'semi-authoritarianism' (2003) came to the fore. According to her, 'semi-authoritarianism' is a hybrid system characterized by 'ambivalence' which, while deploying liberal democratic rhetoric and functioning by means of more or less democratic mechanisms that permit a level of civil and political freedom, simultaneously displays illiberal and authoritarian traits (Ottaway 2003: 3). Furthermore, rather than being a failed or transitioning democracy, a semi-authoritarian system is carefully constructed and well-entrenched, with the following characteristics: 1. limits to the transition of power; 2. a weak systemization (that is, there is reliance on a leader); 3. no appetite for reform; and 4. limits on civil society (Ottaway 2003: 6–7, 14–19). Ottaway also noted that, while such regimes had existed in the past, the democratic guise assumed a greater importance in the post-Cold War era when there was an increase in the number of nations whose governance systems could be classified as 'semi-authoritarian' (Ottaway 2003: 4).

Indicators of global country-by-country political rights and civil liberty rankings are published annually by Freedom House. These rankings involve three categories: free, partly free and not free. Indicators from 2022 suggest that 45% of countries surveyed are free, 30% are partly free and 25% are not free.[1] There are, however, huge regional differences. In contrast to the 86% of European countries classified as 'free', with the remainder as 'partly free', 67% of Middle Eastern and African countries are classified as 'not free'. In the Asia Pacific region, 46% are 'free' and 33% are 'partly free', while 21% are 'not free'. As for Southeast Asia, none of the ASEAN member states are regarded as free. The Philippines, Malaysia, Indonesia and Singapore are categorized as 'partly free', while the remainder fall into the category of 'not free'. It can thus be said that a special political characteristic of Southeast Asian countries is that the proportion of countries with an intermediate position that are classified as 'partly free' is higher than in other regions.

It will be useful to examine the special characteristics of the 'ambivalent' political systems of the countries of Southeast Asia. From about the 1960s, Thailand, Indonesia and Myanmar were under the control of military dictatorships. In Indonesia, the 1998 fall of the Suharto regime saw democratization progress relatively smoothly without a military coup d'état. In Myanmar, a military dictatorship held power continuously even through the 1990s until, in accordance with the 2008 Constitution, elections were held in 2010 and 2015. The world was shocked, however, when a coup was staged in February 2021 and the military seized control once more. Thailand's case is interesting.

---

1 https://freedomhouse.org/report/freedom-world/2022/global-expansion-authoritarian-rule

Although a military dictatorship was toppled in 1973 and some degree of democratization briefly occurred, a coup in 1977 saw the military again take power. Following this, however, regular elections were held with a lower house chosen by popular vote. Although there was a democratically elected government with representatives chosen by the people during the fifteen years between 1992 and 2006, in September 2006, the military staged a coup d'état. General elections were conducted at regular intervals again between 2007 and 2014, although another military coup was staged in May 2014. For about five years until the March 2019 general election, Thailand was governed by an interim military administration. In the 2019 election, the military-aligned Palang Pracharat Party claimed victory with former Army Commander-in-Chief and leader of the previous military junta, Prayut Chan-o-cha, returning triumphant as prime minister.

Thailand is thus a country in which democratization has been repeatedly interrupted. Yet, the system of government cannot be classified unambiguously as either authoritarian or democratic. While during the 1980s Thailand had a military prime minister and an appointed upper house, lower house membership was by popular election. With the exception of the interim military regime that took power after the 1991 coup d'état, a democratic system subsequently operated. This was based on the conduct of regular elections and the appointment of a prime minister chosen from the lower house. Accordingly, there was a sense that democratization was under way. From 2006 to 2014, however, a completely new phenomenon emerged. While those governing the country were chosen through elections by the people, their administrations were overthrown either by the non-elected agency of the Constitutional Court or a military coup d'état. This became a cycle that was repeated on four occasions. We might consider how best to assess democratization in Thailand when viewed from this perspective.

Thailand is not the only country in which the political role of the judiciary has expanded. A similar phenomenon has occurred in developed nations such as the United States and various European countries, and also in several Asian countries such as Korea. However, it is in countries with emerging democracies that the non-elected aspect of judicial rulings has particularly gathered attention. One Southeast Asian example is Thailand's neighbor, Cambodia. Although Cambodia held a general election in July 2018, there was widespread criticism from international agencies that the country's supreme court had the previous year ruled to dissolve the largest opposition group, the Cambodia National Rescue Party. Furthermore, a five-year court-imposed political activity ban on 100 politicians led to the highly irregular result of the ruling Cambodian People's Party, led by Prime Minister Hun Sen, winning every contested seat. This is one example of how, parallel to the emergence of strongmen, the defeat of elected governments and the dissolution of opposition parties by the judiciary has become an important topic in the context of twenty-first-century democracy.

Thailand: From the progress of institutional democratization to a judicial change of government

As the country democratized through the 1990s, Thai politics underwent ongoing rapid change. While the point of contention in Thai politics at the beginning of that decade was the democratization of governance systems, the ordinary people, with a focus on the media and Bangkok residents, were demanding a popularly elected prime minister who had been chosen by election and opposed the military's long-time grip on government power. After a coup d'état was staged in February 1991, a general election was held in March the following year under the auspices of an interim military administration. However, following the appointment of former General Suchinda, also a leader of the coup d'état, as prime minister, a strong resistance movement centered in Bangkok protested that the country's newly appointed head had not come to power through popular election. The resulting 1992 Bloody May Incident (*pruetsapakhom tamin*) occurred when clashes broke out between the military and those involved in resistance demonstrations. Following a huge loss of life, the 1991 Constitution was revised in the same year to newly ensure that 'the prime minister should be a member of the Lower House'. This constitutional revision gave strong impetus towards institutional democratization in Thailand. Strong criticism of the Bloody May Incident resulted in a decline in the political influence of the military, which had long held power in Thailand, with some arguing that it was now impossible for another coup to ever be staged (Murray 1996: 262; Chai-Anan 1997: 55).

The 1992 Bloody May Incident, which led to the tragic loss of many lives, should have been the starting point of genuine democratization in Thailand. Following the incident, the demand for democracy became even greater and a political reform movement emerged centered on Bangkok. Accordingly, the 1997 'People's Constitution' (*ratthathammanun chabap prachachon*) was born making Thailand the model democratization student among ASEAN members of the time. It thus appeared as though the country was finally farewelling the 'vicious cycle of Thai politics' (Chai-Anan 1982: 1–5) which, since the time of the Siamese Revolution of 1932, had seen the cycle of coup d'état followed by a new constitutional system repeated many times.

Now, however, four decades or more after 1992, we must ask to what extent has Thai democratization progressed? We might consider whether, during that time, governing administrations have been selected by the will of the people, whether voters have been the ones who determined policy, whether political parties criticized as underdeveloped have been able or willing to develop favorably, and whether the military has been regulated and kept in check by politicians. It is actually not possible to say 'yes' to any of these questions. In September 2006, approximately fifteen years after February 1991, the military staged a coup d'état. This was the revival of the vicious cycle of Thai politics. After the coup, the 1997 Constitution was abolished and an interim military administration installed. This administration embraced a prime minister who was not popularly elected. Under the 2006 Interim Constitution, the 2007 document was drafted and implemented as a new permanent constitution. A general election was held in December 2007, so that, after a year or so, a transfer took place from military rule back to democratic government. Under the 2007 Constitution, however, further setbacks to democratization occurred. With frequent mass demonstrations against those holding political power, violent clashes between protestors and the military broke out in central Bangkok in May 2010 resulting once more in significant loss of life. This time, close to 100 people died. In May 2015, the country's nineteenth coup d'état was staged and the Prayut Chan-o-cha interim military administration took power.

How did this series of events occur in Thailand, a country with a reputation in the 1990s as a model student of democracy? What was the fate of the democratization trend of that time? One particularly dramatic change evident over the twenty years has been the emergence of regime change through the judiciary. From around the time of the September 2006 coup d'état, it was rulings by agencies such as the Constitutional Court, rather than actions by the military, that led to the repeated fall of popularly elected governments. Firstly, the court handed down a decision declaring the April 2006 general election to be invalid. A May 2007 court ruling dissolved the Thai Rak Thai Party that had previously held power and 111 individuals with party leadership roles were stripped for five years of the right to vote. In 2008, the popularly elected Samak and Somchai administrations fell, and once more the party holding power – the People's Power Party, a successor to the Thai Rak Thai Party – was dissolved. Following the July 2011 general election, the Yingluck administration took power on behalf of the Pheu Thai Party, also a successor to Thai Rak Thai. In May 2014, however, the Yingluck government was overthrown by, predictably, a ruling of the court. In total, the Thai Constitutional Court purged four popularly elected governments from office. That is to say, each of the general elections conducted in 2006, 2007 and 2011 had the outcome quashed by the court. All rulings, with the exception of the May 2007 dissolution of the Thai Rak Thai Party, were handed down by the Constitutional Court which had been established in accordance with the provisions of the 1997 Constitution.

This was the first time in the history of Thai politics that such a situation had occurred. In other words, now it was not only the military that overthrew popularly elected governments. With many members of Thai society strongly opposed to this series of Constitutional Court rulings, violent protest demonstrations repeatedly broke out. When looking for factors involved in the developments discussed, it is apparent that the common thread that connects Thai political activity from 1992 to 2014 resides in the two new constitutions enacted since the 1990s. The first of these was the 1997 Constitution which, emerging from the political reform movement of the 1990s, was lauded as the most democratic in Thai history. The second was the 2007 Constitution, enacted under the influence of the Council for Democratic Reform Under the Constitutional Monarch (*khana patirup kanpokkhrong nai rabop prachathipatai an mi phramahakasat song pen pramuk*; later the Council for Democratic Reform and then Council for National Security) that had carried out the September 2006 coup. Surely it is these two constitutions that are the key to making sense of the chaos associated with democratization in Thailand today.

Constitutionalism and the judicialization of politics

Trends of democratization theories: from transition to consolidation, and then to 'quality'

This section will provide an overview on trends in theories of democratization while also seeking to clarify the theoretical background behind the global upsurge in the political role of the judiciary. This is a phenomenon also observed in Thailand.

In theories of democratic transitions, the assumption is a progression from transition to consolidation. Transition theories derive from Lipset's discussion (1959) of modernization which notes the interconnectedness between economic and political modernization, and the O'Donnell and Schmitter so-called transition theory (1986) which assumes organizational change as a product of decision-making by a country's elite. When countries from the previous Communist bloc hurriedly democratized once the Cold War came to an end in 1989, a trend towards democratization by emerging nations came to be regarded as established procedure. Against that global background, the main point of interest in terms of democratization theory shifted from transition to consolidation. An important factor during the transition era was democratization from an organizational perspective. Crucial to this was the systemization of government changes through popular election. During the consolidation phase, on the other hand, a wide

Table 0.1 Summary of Thai Government administrations

No.	Term of Office	Name of Leader	Political Party	Background
1	10 December 1932 to 20 June 1933	Phraya Manopakorn Nitithada		Legal official (judge)
2	21 June 1933 to 15 December 1938	Phraya Phahon Phonphayuhasena	People's Party	Military officer
3	20 December 1938 to 1 August 1944	Plaek Phibunsongkhram (first and second terms)	People's Party	Military officer
4	1 August 1944 to 31 August 1945	Khuang Aphaiwong (first term)	People's Party	Civil official
5	31 August 1945 to 17 September 1945	Thawi Bunyaket	People's Party	Civil official
6	17 September 1945 to 13 January 1946	MR (His Excellency) Seni Pramoj (first term)		Legal and civil official
7	31 January 1946 to 24 March 1946	Khuang Aphaiwong (second term)	People's Party	Civil official
8	24 March 1946 to 23 August 1946	Pridi Banomyong	People's Party	Civil official (legal qualifications)
9	23 August 1946 to 8 November 1947	Thawan Thamrongnawasawat	People's Party	Military officer
10	10 November 1947 to 8 April 1948	Khuang Aphaiwong (third term)	Democrat Party	Civil official
11	8 April 1948 to 16 September 1957	Plaek Phibunsongkhram (third to eighth terms)	People's Party	Military officer
12	21 September 1957 to 26 December 1957	Pote Sarasin		Legal official
13	1 January 1958 to 20 October 1958	Thanom Kittikachorn (first term)		Military officer
14	9 February 1959 to 8 December 1963	Sarit Thanarat		Military officer
15	9 December 1963 to 14 October 1973	Thanom Kittikachorn (second term)		Military officer
16	14 October 1973 to 26 February 1975	Sanya Dharmasakti		Legal official (judge)
17	26 February 1975 to 14 March 1975	MR (His Excellency) Seni Pramoj (second term)	Democrat Party	Legal and civil official
18	14 March 1975 to 12 January 1976	MR (His Excellency) Kukrit Pramoj	Social Action Party	Writer (younger brother of sixth, seventeenth and nineteenth prime minister)
19	20 April 1976 to 6 October 1976	MR (His Excellency) Seni Pramoj (third term)	Democrat Party	Legal and civil official
20	8 October 1976 to 19 October 1977	Thanin Kravichien		Legal official (judge)

No.	Term of Office	Name of Leader	Political Party	Background
21	11 November 1977 to 3 March 1980	Kriangsak Chomanan		Military officer
22	3 March 1980 to 4 August 1988	Prem Tinsulanonda		Military officer
23	4 August 1988 to 23 February 1991	Chatchai Choonhavan	Thai Nation Party (Chart Thai Party)	Military officer
24	2 March 1991 to 23 March 1992	Anand Panyarachun (first term)		Civil official
25	7 April 1992 to 24 May 1992	Suchinda Kraprayoon		Military officer
26	10 June 1992 to 23 September 1992	Anand Panyarachun (second term)		Civil official
27	23 September 1992 to 24 May 1995	Chuan Leekpai (first term)	Democrat Party	Legal official
28	24 May 1995 to 1 December 1996	Banharn Silpa-archa	Thai Nation Party (Chart Thai Party)	Businessman
29	1 December 1996 to 9 November 1997	Chavalit Yongchaiyudh	New Aspiration Party	Military official
30	9 November 1997 to 9 February 2001	Chuan Leekpai (second term)	Democrat Party	Legal official
31	9 February 2001 to 19 September 2006	Thaksin Shinawatra	Thai Rak Thai Party	Businessman (former police officer)
32	1 October 2006 to 29 January 2008	Surayud Chulanont		Military officer
33	29 January 2008 to 9 November 2008	Samak Sundaravej	People's Power Party	Media identity
34	17 November 2008 to 2 December 2008	Somchai Wongsawat	People's Power Party	Legal and civil official (judge; brother-in-law of thirty-first prime minister)
35	15 December 2008 to 5 August 2011	Abhisit Vejjajiva	Democrat Party	University professor
36	5 August 2011 to 7 May 2014	Yingluck Shinawatra	Pheu Thai Party	Businesswoman (younger sister of thirty-first prime minister)
37	22 May 2014 to present time	Prayut Chan-o-cha		Military officer

Source: Compiled by the author.
Note: Shaded areas denote administrations overthrown by the judiciary.

variety of factors came to the fore. Attention was firstly given to whether elections were free and fair, with major points under consideration being the extent to which governments were efficient and accountable, and the extent to which politicians and bureaucrats were corrupt. This was necessary because, even in cases in which it appeared that system changes had occurred and that those responsible for governance were chosen by election, examples of unfair elections emerged. As a result, there was a return to the same authoritarian structure that had previously operated, albeit equipped with a democratic exterior. Such a system came to be called 'competitive authoritarianism' (Levitsky and Way 2010).

The notion of 'quality' has also featured in recent democratization theories. In order to assess the quality of a democracy, Larry Diamond and others have listed the following eight points: 1. rule of law, 2. participation, 3. competition, 4. vertical accountability, 5. horizontal accountability, 6. freedom, 7. equality, and 8. political policy responsiveness (Diamond and Morlino 2005). The first point, rule of law, is a concept designed to eliminate autocratic control of national power and to constrain this by legal means. In this context we might also consider constitutionalism which, by restricting government power through various laws with the constitution at the apex, has the objective of guarding the rights and freedoms of the people. This, too, is a system of thought based on the principle of rule of law. Both (rule of law and constitutionalism) are classic notions that arose and developed in Europe and the US several centuries ago. In the 1990s, when many countries seemed to have ended their transition stage and sought to implement substantive forms of democratization, these classic notions were once more in the spotlight.

Constitutionalism regards a constitution as the ultimate piece of legislation. A constitution based on theories of constitutionalism acts as a restraint on the power of a national government and draws on the framework provided by such a document to protect against abuse of power. The nucleus of such a system is the process of judicial review through the courts and the mutual checks and balances operating on the three powers: administrative/executive, legislative and judicial. Trends in democratization theory have shifted from a focus on institutional democratization to what is necessary to guarantee the quality of these systems. In that context, attention has centered on the role of constitutions, legal systems and the judiciary.[2]

---

2   As elements operating in the likely democratization of authoritarian systems, attention has focused on the role of elites in addition to social structures and political systems. One point of view argues that stable democratization depends largely on the consensual unity of a country's elite, and that government systems remain unstable in the absence of agreement among elites (Higley and Burton 1989). This theory developed from research related to breakdowns in democracy (democratic breakdowns) which saw various governments in Latin America and other places that had democratized from the 1950s until the early 1960s revert by the mid-1960s to authoritarian regimes (Higley and Burton 1989: 28). This position was confirmed by further research into the role of elites in system change. Recent work has closely examined how elite influence can destabilize democratization. Acemoglu and Robinson (2001) put forward a very simple theory of system change based on the experiences of various Western and Latin American countries. They argue that the threat of revolution and social instability leads to democratization, while the desire to redistribute the wealth of the elites results in a change of course to a non-democratic system. Furthermore, because democratization is not consolidated through wealth redistribution, elites have a motive to stage a coup d'état. It is therefore difficult to consolidate democracy in a society in which a huge economic disparity exists, with the writers pointing out that the political systems in such places oscillate unstably between democratic and authoritarian processes (Acemoglu and Robinson 2001). Albertus and Menaldo (2013) also discuss the relationship between the redistribution of elite wealth and democratization based on an analysis of cases in which, under democratic systems that should have redistributed wealth, the huge economic disparity of the past remained. These scholars argue that economic elites prefer a democracy to an autocracy as long as they can resist pressure – even under democratic systems – for wealth redistribution. They further point out that there are many cases in which there is pressure from below to move towards democratization, and as long as economic elites are able to protect their own interests, the shift to democratization occurs easily. They suggest that the key for economic elites is a constitution, stressing that a smooth shift to democratization occurs when the interests of economic elites can be protected through a constitution that continues the pre-democratization legacy or heritage. These commentators further point out a constitution's influence on whether or not democratization is a success (Albertus and Menaldo 2013).

The judicialization of politics in emerging democracies

We will now confirm the nature of the relationship between rule of law, constitutionalism and democracy in emerging democracies. Since the 1990s, increasing attention has been given globally to the phenomenon known as the 'judicialization of politics'. This expression refers to the increasing reliance on the courts and legal measures to find solutions to core ethical dilemmas, public policy problems and political disputes (Hirschl 2006: 721). It has been pointed out that, having exceeded the role with which they were traditionally endowed and shifted towards being agencies that hand down important political decisions, various supreme courts have become active political players that exert considerable influence in various dimensions of governance (Dressel 2014: 262). This phenomenon has been apparent in North America, South America, Europe and the Indian subcontinent. At the outset of the 1990s, however, it was believed that it would generally be difficult for such a phenomenon to operate in Southeast Asian countries, because it was assumed that the countries where the judicialization of politics was likely to occur were those with political regimes that adopted the systems and norms of liberal democracy and accepted the principle of judicial independence (Tate 1994: 187–188).

However, developments different to expectations subsequently occurred. Over the past two decades, the courts have become major players in Asian politics, including in the various countries of Southeast Asia. Thus, proactive intervention into political matters by the Filipino Supreme Court is no longer a special case. It was the Indonesian Constitutional Court that opened a path to competitive and stable presidential elections and also to elections for the country's parliament, while the High Court in Malaysia has been embroiled in a range of political lawsuits. In Thailand, also, the Constitutional Court continues to hand down decisions that dramatically alter the political landscape (Dressel 2014: 259).

The background to these post-1990s changes in Southeast Asian countries was said to be an emphasis on the rule of law and constitutionalism as a prescription for solving political problems. At present, the rule of law has come to occupy a central position in political debates not only in China and South Korea, but also in Southeast Asian countries. It has been pointed out that many Southeast Asian countries, including Thailand, have grappled with the process of consolidating democratization because of problems, related to the constitution, concerning the structural balance between fundamental rights and a wide range of powers (Peerenboom 2004: 13–14). During the third wave of democratization, newly democratized countries held a range of expectations concerning constitutionalism and the rule of law. In addition, the expressions 'good governance' and 'accountability' were imported for local use from international agencies. These terms were then glorified as a panacea for solving multiple problems without much distinction between their meanings.[3] It has also been pointed out that behind these movements there is an idea that in a democratic political process, voters and politicians are not necessarily devoted to democratic values, and that it is instead the guardians of the constitution and the judiciary that protect these values (Bellamy 2007: 1–2).

Currently, scholarly opinion is divided concerning the influence exerted on governance by the judicialization of politics. According to Bjorn Dressel's analysis, scholars working at the traditional macro-level enthusiastically welcomed the rise of global constitutionalism and sang the praises of broadened territory for judicial review as protecting citizens and furthering democratization. Other researchers have been skeptical of the implications in the current trend to hand down judicial rulings on governance matters and have misgivings about the possibility of this tendency ultimately sliding downward into a 'juristocracy' (Dressel 2014: 262–263).

There is a long history of discussion around the problem of conflict and balance between majoritarian rule based on election results on the one hand and protecting the principles of a constitution through

---

3 From the 1990s, in order to guarantee aid effectiveness, international agencies demanded that developing democracies achieve rule of law and good governance. In 1992, the World Bank released a strategy paper related to governance that argued for the necessity of public sector reform, devolution of power from the center and improvements in legal systems. Furthermore, from 1996 the IMF also made use of the expression 'good governance' in economic and political reform plans. In Thailand, powerful opinion-leaders promoted the circulation of this sort of discourse which became official Thai government policy in 1999 (Callahan 2005: 498–499).

the courts on the other. However, the problem in recent years related to the judicialization of politics concerns the court now handing down rulings with high political cachet, such as system changes of election results or even matters of war and peace, rather than on traditional issues such as rights problems and international cooperation. Ran Hirschl (2008) refers to the new fields in which courts have handed down judgments as 'mega-politics' and emphasizes that we should consider these as separate from traditional areas of judicial review. Hirschl furthermore points out that it was insufficient to merely adopt the legal studies approach of the past when analyzing the reality of this sort of political judicialization and that it was therefore necessary to supplement this with a political approach also. There is a growing body of case-based country-specific research regarding the role of the judiciary in governance system changes. Ginsburg summation suggests that, while it was rare for the courts to take a lead in democratization during the transition period, a court could give a ruling that became a focal point for mobilizing a comprehensive anti-establishment coalition that indeed became an opportunity for system change (Ginsburg 2012). On the other hand, he pointed to cases in which, when an authoritarian system was being dispensed with, the courts assumed the role of protector of the interests of old political power-brokers. Ginsburg referred to this as 'hegemonic preservation' (Ginsburg 2012).

Research is only now beginning on the glorification of rule of law and constitutionalism in newly emerging democracies, and also on the judicialization of politics that recently developed in those sites. It has already been noted that it is insufficient to merely apply existing research from developed countries on their constitutions and processes of judicial review. Important questions to be clarified in future research into democratization include: Why has there been an enthusiastic adoption of rule of law and constitutionalism immediately after the democratization of various countries? Why has the judicialization of politics occurred? And what influences do these sorts of phenomena exert on democratization?

Reliance on constitutionalism: warnings from previous research

In opposition to the political trends of emerging democracies, recent research into and investigation of the situation in developed nations has identified the threat of excessive reliance on constitutionalism and rule of law. The common factor in constitutionalism and rule of law is the expectation that each has towards judicial review. It has been pointed out, however, that the relationship between judicial review and democracy is fraught with various problems.

Martin Shapiro (2004) argues that the success of judicial review in the United States is a function of the country's federal system of government. According to Shapiro, while the judiciary there achieved success with strong authority in order to maintain a federal system, the United States Supreme Court has almost never handed down a decision related to the separation of powers. This, he points out, is because that court formulated a fundamental theory associated with the separation of powers that was grounded in constitutionalism and that required each of the three powers to refrain from excessively interfering with or intervening in the others. He states that, because there is a clear tendency toward anti-majoritarianism especially in matters related to rights, the judiciary's high-level political strategy skills are questioned and criticized, and compromise and trade-offs around these skills occur (Shapiro 2004). Roberto Gargarella (2004) suggests that, from the experience of Latin America with a focus on Argentina, the fundamental problem concerning judicial reform relates not to any political predisposition on the part of judges, but to factors such as the measures grounded in an overly powerful constitution that have been granted to the courts and the inducements to judges these provide. He notes the danger, in situations in which there is no shared interpretation of the law, of the courts holding wide-ranging discretionary powers and of judges lacking incentives to protect democracy or those from minority groups who suffer disadvantage (Gargarella 2004).

There is also debate over interpretations of constitutionalism. Richard Bellamy refers to attempts to regulate democracy through the judiciary and counter-majoritarian remedy and reform measures as 'legal constitutionalism', pointing out that in a worst-case scenario these restraints are quite capable of overturning the democratic foundations of constitutional assets and, in fact, corrupting the legality and validity of the law and the courts (Bellamy 2007: 2). Comparing democratic and judicial procedures, he points out that both have advantages and disadvantages and that the two are essentially mutually complementary (Bellamy 2007: 27). Bellamy himself favors 'political constitutionalism', and, emphasizing that democratic procedures themselves are in fact the constitution, gives weight to these (Bellamy 2007: 4–5). Tom Ginsburg identifies the importance of facilitating constitutional dialogue between the stakeholders involved in judicial review. He emphasizes that, rather than being subject to clarification and declaration by special persons of virtue, the contents of a constitution should clearly be interpreted through the ongoing interactions of the various powers involved. Ginsburg further argues that when courts challenging political forces provokes a backlash there is the possibility that consolidated democracy can be reversed (Ginsburg 2003: 72–73).

The boundary between law and politics

We might consider the degree to which the restrictions imposed on the operation of political power through constitutionalism are favorable to democracy. This issue speaks to whether or not a minority group (the judiciary) should exert control over the majority group (a parliament and government) and classic theories on the necessity or otherwise of clear divisions between a legal system and the state. Constitutionalism is a multi-faceted and ambivalent concept with a long history, and it can be interpreted differently depending on the country and the time. I will here provide a basic definition of constitutionalism while also offering information on the historical development and arguments related to this term.

While modern constitutionalism developed in the nineteenth century in both the United States and France, the understanding of this concept differed in each place. The United States interpretation came to favor equilibrium through checks and balances of the three powers (administrative/executive, legislative and the judiciary). This separation of powers was enacted in the country's 1788 Constitution and the people's deep distrust of power there operated against the background of that same constitution. James Madison Jr., a central figure in the drafting of the Constitution of the United States who is even referred to as the 'father of the Constitution', proposed the division and restraint of the powers. In this sense, he advocated that, with each power firmly based, there be a system of checks and balances that ensured mutual regulation (Sato 2015: 90–93). This differed from the system of constitutionalism that arose in France where, following the French Revolution and the overthrow of the absolute power of the monarchy, the absolute sovereignty of the people came to the fore. Prominent politicians at the time of the French Revolution argued that while the constitution might constrain the powers constructed through that document, it could not constrain the citizens so created. They emphasized that not only could citizens change the constitution, but that they need not accept the form that any changes might take. It was furthermore believed that statute law should not grant the judiciary the power to review whether or not a citizen must comply with higher forms of law. Any judgment on the constitutionality of a law was to be entrusted to the legislative authorities rather than the judiciary. The background to this, it was argued, was a deep distrust of the courts (Sato 2015: 107–120).

As demonstrated above, the design blueprint of a governance system based on constitutionalism differs according to country and is not a one-size-fits-all proposition. However, while the United States might give precedence to equitable restraints and balances operating on the three powers, with France cautioning against judicial restraints on the legislative arm, neither assumes that the judiciary should dominate and have the strongest authority of the three. Each, rather, acknowledges the need for a line to be drawn between a legal system and a government.

A key moment for courts to step into what was once largely the territory of government came with the Fundamental Law for the Federal Republic of Germany that was implemented in 1949 after the end of the Second World War. The German Constitutional Court was established under that law. The first constitutional court was founded in Austria in 1920 following a proposal to that effect by prominent Austrian public law scholar, Hans Kelsen. With the Austrian Court given the power of judicial review, it was decided that any law ruled unconstitutional would be declared invalid. Underpinning this decision was a desire to protect minority groups against the majority oppression that might occur under a democratic government. However, there was an awareness, as noted above, of the need for caution in terms of courts stepping into the governance sphere. Kelsen, too, pointed out how judicial review should occur only in terms of what was permitted by the constitution and drew attention to problematic aspects of the abstract general principles of justice, freedom and impartiality (Sato 2015: 208–209).

Following the end of the Second World War, the German Fundamental Law saw the establishment of a constitutional court that was granted wide-ranging powers. Not confined merely to determining the constitutionality of laws, these powers included the authority to rule on constitutional violations (those who were harmed by the Fundamental Law itself could appeal to the Constitutional Court). The special characteristics of post-Second World War German democracy, which resided in the stipulations of articles 18 and 21, came to be known as 'fortified democracy'. Article 18 stipulated that any entity that abused the fundamental rights of freedom of speech and association in order to oppose free and democratic fundamental order would lose its own fundamental rights. Article 21 stipulated that any act that damaged or removed free and democratic fundamental order or that aimed to endanger the German Republic was a violation of the constitution. Rulings concerning both articles became the province of the Constitutional Court.[4]

Originally, European nations tended to exercise caution against the judiciary expanding its powers into the political realm. It goes without saying, however, that justification for the granting of strong political powers to the Constitutional Court in Germany after the end of the Second World War was a desire to prevent a repeat of the

---

4 Regarding the German Basic Law, I referred to the English translation found at this site: https://www.gesetze-im-internet.de/englisch_gg/

profound human rights violations, historically almost unprecedented, of the Nazi administration (1933–1945) under the leadership of Adolph Hitler. Jan-Werner Müller presents an interesting theory of what he terms 'constitutional patriotism' regarding a link between German reflection on Nazi atrocities and the present and future stance of the German people towards democracy. Müller's constitutional patriotism is 'an idea in which the focus of political attachment should be located within the context of the various norms and values, and indirectly in the various processes that operate in a liberal democratic Constitution' (2017: 2–15). The roles of 'memory' and 'combativeness' are key to ensuring that constitutional patriotism functions as political attachment. 'Memory' here refers to a self-critical retrospection on the Holocaust and the former Nazi regime, while 'combativeness' is the stance taken towards the enemies of democracy. Both are often expressed through judicial processes that might, for example, forbid political parties and limit free speech. Müller nevertheless points out that at the same time memory and combativeness can have an undeniably anti-liberal dimension (Müller 2017: 2–15).

The German experience influenced all of Europe. Even France, which traditionally has a strong sense of distrust towards the courts, introduced amendments that gradually heightened the judiciary's political role. Historically, the higher court of France, the Parlement of the Ancien Régime, took an anti-revolutionary position with the judiciary accepting the mission of safeguarding vested rights and interests. As a result, there has been a long-standing veto on the notion that the courts should interfere with legislative and/or administrative (executive) government powers. This resulted in judicial review being regarded as a major assault that defied the axiom, 'the law = an expression of the common will' (Yamamoto 2017: 45). However, with the 1958 implementation of the current Constitution of France – also known as the Constitution of the Fifth Republic – during the presidency of General Charles de Gaulle, it was conceded that the former parliamentary focus made the formation of a national unified purpose difficult. As a result, constitutional amendments were made, giving preeminence among the three powers to executive government. This search for a constitutional format that reined in the power of the parliament, weakening the authority of the parliament, was called 'rationalisation du parlement' or the 'rationalization of parliament'. There was, nonetheless, an awareness of the need for the parliament to monitor any deviation from the powers that were strictly stipulated in the constitution. This task was assigned to the Conseil Constitutionnel, or Constitutional Council. The Constitution of the Fifth Republic stipulated the jurisdiction of matters to be implemented by the parliament. The judicial review role given to the Constitutional Council involved monitoring the laws presented, amended and then adopted by the parliament to ensure that these did not overlook constitutional stipulations or violate the government's rule-making powers. Following De Gaulle's death, however, the role of the Constitutional Council was broadened so that, after the 1970s, judicial review also came to be invoked as a means of strengthening human rights guarantees. Furthermore, as European integration progressed, France, too, overtly acknowledged the important value of human rights. As a result, comprehensive constitutional revision occurred in 2008 which enabled even the average citizen whose rights and freedoms were violated to lodge a case with the Constitutional Council demanding judicial review (Yamamoto 2017: 61–65).

As outlined above, 'advanced' nations such as the United States, Germany and France with long histories of constitutionalism and democracy developed careful arguments concerning the advisability or otherwise of the legal sphere intervening in the political realm. That is to say, there was acknowledgement of the need for a dividing line between the law and politics. In European countries, one pressing reason for the expansion in the role of the judiciary following the end of the Second World War, including the courts plunging into the political realm, was 'memory' of the tragic human rights violations committed by the Nazis. The intention, however, in each of the three nations whose circumstances have been outlined above was to protect human rights, not to give the judiciary preeminence among the three powers. Aware of the dangers inherent in the judiciary stepping into government realms, newer nations were on the alert and changed course.

Definition and requirements of the rule of law

Before considering the specifics of Thailand, it will be useful to provide a definition of the 'rule of law' and to clarify the necessary conditions that apply to the operation of this concept. This includes understanding the conditions that must be met when a constitution or set of laws are applied through a court. The concept of the 'rule of law' has a long and continuous history from Ancient Greece and Rome through to medieval and later European eras. As with constitutionalism, various definitions apply in various European countries. Generally, there are a range of theories which, drawing on the nineteenth century work of Albert Venn Dicey as a starting point, are divided into the 'thin theories' of twentieth century thinkers such as Friedrich August von Hayek, Lon Luvois Fuller and Joseph Raz, and the 'thick theories' promoted by the International Congress of Jurists. We will here draw on the overview provided by Charles Sampford to clarify the meaning of this key concept.

Albert Venn Dicey's definition of the rule of law comprises three elements: 1. that the regular court system only has the authority to enforce general law, 2. that all people will follow the law equally, and 3. that rights are guaranteed not in the text but in the practical application of the law. This interpretation was nevertheless subject to widespread criticism which can be summed up as follows: 1. although Dicey opposed a government having comprehensive discretionary powers, he nevertheless argued that this was sometimes necessary; 2. notions of equality before the law disregarded the special privileges and powers conferred upon government officials; and 3. it was not useful to overlook the role of documentation as a means of guaranteeing rights when maintaining and preserving rule of law (Sampford 2006: 42–43). The so-called 'thin theories' that emerged in the twentieth century suggested a narrow meaning of the rule of law. There are, furthermore, slight differences even among Hayek, Fullar and Raz, the three scholars who are representative of this field. Nevertheless, each agrees as necessary 'rule of law' conditions that law is universal, that it is declared publicly, that it is predictable, that it is clear and precise, that it encompasses no contradictions and that it applies equally to all people. In terms of the need for 'principled predictability' in the rule of law, Ronald A. Cass stressed the following five points: 1. that principled predictability be grounded in rules or regulations, 2. that there be adequate clarity of principled predictability, 3. that there be access to the law, 4. that there be validity and reparations (clarity and access were not without compensation), and 5. that there be universality (Sampford 2006: 45–49).

In thin theories of the rule of law, the values of democracy and human rights are not adopted so that rule of law stands alone from other values. In other words, according to this paradigm, the rule of law can operate even under an absolutist or authoritarian regime that practices wholesale abuse of rights. Strong dissatisfaction with this approach led to the rise of a movement that sought to take account of social, economic and cultural conditions, and thus the so-called 'thick theory' of the rule of law emerged. In this theory, enlightenment values such as democracy and human rights were adopted into definitions of the rule of law. In terms of thick theory, however, Geoffrey de Q. Walker pointed out the danger of including special political preferences into the rule of law. Walker thus expanded the definition by including structures that guaranteed judicial independence, universality, harmonious legal and social values, and an absence of conflict between the law and public sentiment (Sampford 2006: 51–52).

While various debates contrast thin and thick theories of the rule of law, we can ultimately say that consensus exists with respect to the necessary conditions that must apply. A key element of the rule of law from Ancient Greece to the present has been 'guidance' and, in order that the law be publicly announced in a way that makes it possible for citizens to comply, it must be clearly articulated in addition to being imbued with stability, consistency and universality. Regarding factors that, in contrast, work against the legal guidance function, Sampford referred to the 'question of degree' approach. This, he explained, involved ambivalence, a 'closed-class' attitude (that is, one that aimed to target specific groups) and retrospectivity (Sampford 2006: 56). From the above, we can conclude that the rule of law refers to order being maintained in a country by a legal system that has clarity, stability, consistency and universality.

It is useful to consider the points of difference that emerge when we compare the system blueprint and actual implementation of newly democratized nations with the theories and norms associated with the experiences of developed countries as outlined above. These differences offer valuable foci of analysis.

Constitutionalism and democracy: a discussion of Thai researchers

The debate among Thai legal scholars

Thai legal scholars came to have significant political leverage, particularly since the 1990s, through for example involvement in constitutional drafting processes. We might therefore consider their responses to heightened criticisms of constitutionalism and ideas concerning the rule of law.

Representative of the public law scholars who had strong connections to politics and who were involved in activities such as the drafting of constitutions are Meechai Ruchuphan, Amon Chantharasombun, Bowonsak Uwanno, Wissanu Krea-ngam and Somkit Lertpaithoon. Born in February 1938, Meechai graduated from the Law Faculty of Thammasat University before completing master's qualifications in Texas in the United States. Upon returning to Thailand, he began his career in 1973 as a legal advisor to the Sanya administration and was then appointed as minister to the Office of the Prime Minister in the Prem administration. He acted as a caretaker prime minister after the outbreak of the 1992 Bloody May Incident. Active even in his senior years, he served as president of the National Legislative Assembly of Thailand convened by the post-coup military administration following the 2006 coup d'état. Meechai has been closely involved in a number of constitutional drafts and, in addition to acting as chair of the 1991 Constitution Drafting Committee, he headed the 2017 Constitution Drafting Committee following the 2014 coup d'état.[5] Amon, whose

---

5 There were two iterations of a constitutional draft that occurred under the Interim Military Administration installed following the 2014 coup d'état. The first was compiled under the chairpersonship of Bowonsak, the second under Meechai. The current 2017 Thai Constitution is the Meechai version.

ideas are examined in detail in Chapter 2, is the scholar who exerted the greatest influence on the 1990s political reform movement. Born in July 1930, he graduated from the Law Faculty of Thammasat University after which he obtained his doctoral degree in France. Upon returning to Thailand, he held a long-term post from 1976 as a member of the Council of State. In addition, he has been an Education Committee member of the Thammasat University Faculty of Law and has held teaching posts at both Chulalongkorn and Ramkhamhaeng universities. He is still respected even today by many young public law scholars in Thailand.

Considerably younger that the two scholars referred to above, Bowonsak was born in October 1954. A graduate of Chulalongkorn University, he obtained his doctorate in France. After accepting a teaching post at Chulalongkorn, he became dean of the university's law faculty in 1995. At the same time, he was a member of both the Constitutional Reform Committee and the Committee on Developing Democracy and was closely associated with the political reform movement. In addition, he was appointed the secretary-general of the 1997 Constitution Drafting Committee and played a central role in the drafting process of the 1997 Constitution. He was also the cabinet general-secretary in the Thaksin government that took power in 2003 but had distanced himself from that administration by the time of its final months in 2006. After the 2014 coup d'état, he was appointed chair of the Constitution Drafting Committee by the Interim Military Regime and supervised the compilation of the first constitutional draft under that administration.[6]

Born in September 1951, Wissanu is Bowonsak's cousin. Upon graduating from the law faculty at Thammasat University, he completed his doctoral studies in the United States. After taking a teaching post at Chulalongkorn University, he was secretary-general to the cabinet from 1993 until 2002 and then from 2002 until 2006. Together with Bowonsak,

---

6 Heavily criticized as undemocratic, the constitutional draft compiled under Bowonsak's chairpersonship was rejected in September 2015 by a vote of the National Legislative Assembly. This led to Meechai being appointed as second chair of the Constitution Drafting Committee which made the new draft.

Wissanu was associated with the draft of the Interim Constitution following the 2006 coup d'état. He was furthermore appointed by the Interim Military Regime as a member of the National Legislative Assembly of Thailand. He was involved also in drafting the Interim Constitution following the 2014 coup and is deputy prime minister in the Prayut Chan-o-cha administration.

Somkit was born in July 1959 and is a former dean of the Thammasat University Faculty of Law. Graduating from Thammasat, he completed his doctoral studies in France. While working in teaching positions at institutions such as Thammasat University, he served as a member of the Legislation Committee. After the 2006 coup d'état, he was appointed secretary to the 2007 Constitution Draft Committee and the Draft Sub-Committee. He thus became a key figure involved in the production of the draft of the 2007 Constitution. Following the 2014 coup d'état he became a member of the National Legislative Assembly of Thailand under the Interim Military Regime, and in 2017 was appointed as advisor to the National Strategy Committee of the same regime.

There have been twenty constitutions in Thailand up to the present time and, as previously noted, almost all were drafted and implemented following a military coup d'état. We might therefore say that among the specific conditions operating in Thailand is the fact that many prominent public law scholars, such as those above, regardless of receiving doctoral qualifications in either France or the United States where government systems are based on constitutionalism and democracy, have had involvement in one or another of the military regimes formed following the staging of a coup d'état.

In addition to those Thai public law identities who have had strong links to successive military regimes, there are scholars who have distanced themselves from those regimes and who, since 2010 when criticism of the judiciary by the Red Shirts began to gather force, have themselves spoken out against the 2007 Constitution and the rulings of the Constitutional Court. The group calling itself 'Nitirat', for example, is comprised of reformist public law scholars centered around Worachet Pakeerut from the law faculty of Thammasat University. The group drew media attention by holding a seminar at the Thammasat Law Faculty on 19 September 2010, the fourth anniversary of the

2006 coup d'état.[7] Including Worachet, the five founding members of the group who were also Thammasat Law Faculty staff, were Prasit Pivavatnapanich, Teera Suteewarangkurn, Thapanan Nipithakul and Piyabutr Saengkanokkul. Even the oldest, Worachet, who was born in August 1969, was relatively young, and the group represented a new generation of public law scholars. Each has a degree conferred by a university in the West, with Worachat studying in Germany, Thapanan, Teera and Piyabutr in France, and Prasit in the United States. The group was later joined by two even younger members, Poonthep Sirinupong and Sawatree Suksri, bringing the total number to seven.

The Nitirat declaration – effectively a mission statement – was first made at the time of the September 2010 seminar when the group also created a website. Worachet set out the reasons for founding Nitirat in the declaration's opening paragraph as provided below:[8]

> The founding members of Nitirat decided to establish a small-scale academic community to promote the knowledge and understanding of proper and right law, to construct democracy, and to provide Thai society with information about the rule of law and the seeds of justice. We also considered a name for the website we intended to create. Ultimately, we decided upon "The Enlightened Jurists". What made us chose this name? Over the past few years, especially since the 19 September 2006 coup d'état, law has been used as a tool to legitimate power and we cannot deny that this power ultimately has subverted democracy. This process of constructing and then destroying legitimation in the name of law and justice has not merely left a deep wound on Thai law and the world of legal scholarship, it has resulted in violently imposing "legitimation" on the whole of Thai society. Through the exchange

---

7 See the article in Prachathai News on 20 September 2010. Available at: https://prachatai.com/journal/2010/09/31162 (accessed 14 August 2018).

8 The first declaration that explained the Nitirat mission was taken down from their homepage by the authorities on 13 December 2021 and is no longer available. See Prachathai, 13 December 2012: https://prachatai.com/journal/2012/12/44204 (accessed 15 August 2018). After the Nitirat site was disabled in April 2016, it briefly reappeared but was once again closed by the authorities.

of views, we agreed that what has created this state of affairs in Thai society is that some people who play a role in guiding society and upper-class lawyers take away beliefs in fairness and tradition to cover up people's thinking and turned them into a prison built with reason and wisdom.

Worachat's declaration confirms how Nitirat members believed that the law had been used as a tool of those in power since the 2006 coup d'état with no protections for the rule of law since that time. Furthermore, the very people who had created the conditions enabling this were the prominent public law scholars referred to above. Many were graduates of Thammasat Law Faculty, as were most members of the Nitirat group. Many from both sides, furthermore, had studied in Western countries. It is interesting then to consider the differences between the thought of the scholarly heavyweights who had participated in the drafting of a number of constitutions and the younger scholars who were the nucleus of the Nitirat group.

In 2009, there was a difference of opinion between Amon who had given theoretical support to the 1990s political reform movement and Nitirat's Worachet concerning an order given by the Central Administrative Court. The dispute involved a case lodged with the court in June 2008 requesting the repeal of a planned joint statement by the Thai and Cambodian governments regarding the Preah Vihear Temple, situated in the Thai/Cambodian borderlands. The case also requested that a temporary protection order be put in place prior to a final judgment being handed down and that an order be made forbidding action of any kind on the issue by either the Minister for Foreign Affairs or the cabinet. The case was based on the fact that, while sovereignty over Preah Vihear Temple lay with Cambodia, the territorial rights of the land surrounding the site were unclear. There had been a 1950s dispute between Thailand and Cambodia concerning the jurisdiction in which the temple was situated. There have been no major clashes since the International Court of Justice ruled in 1962 in favor of the Cambodian side. However, although Cambodia registered the temple as a World Heritage Site, there was strong opposition from Thai citizens' groups over this matter. At the time, the pro-Thaksin

Samak administration held power and a 17 June 2008 cabinet decision was supportive of the Cambodian move. Accordingly, those opposed to the government lodged a case with the Central Administrative Court. After initial deliberations, the court ruled that, until the case concluded and final decisions concerning the Ministry of Foreign Affairs and the cabinet were handed down, there was to be no Thai government action related to the decision to support a joint Thai/Cambodian declaration.

The fact that the Central Administrative Court handed down a temporary stop order that vetoed a political decision by the cabinet led to conflict among Thai public law scholars. Firstly, Nitirat announced a position contrary to the order made by the court. With respect to the cessation of the joint Thai/Cambodian declaration, the Nitirat group stated that: 'Under rule of law, the implementation of power should accord with the law and the judiciary should exert control through lawfulness'. The group further pointed out that 'There are generally categories of action that are outside the control of the judiciary including, for example, political actions and actions associated with government designated policy'. The Nitirat critique included the fact that: 'This sort of order creates the possibility that, without taking any political responsibility whatsoever, the Administrative Court itself will now make decisions about matters related to governance and political policy' (Thiradet and Ram 2008: 55–58). The problem from the Nitirat perspective related to the pros and cons of judiciary intervention into political matters. In other words, the group had concerns about the dividing line between the law and the operation of the three powers, and politics.

Amon, on the other hand, declared his support for the order of the Central Administrative Court. Concerning the 'actions associated with government designated policy' which Nitirat had referenced, he argued that: 'When those carrying out an action are "officials of the nation" [*chao nathi khong rat*] as stipulated by the Administrative Court Establishment Law, the matter in question and the exertion of authority by those in question, regardless of whether through the legal system or the Constitution, is understood to fall within the jurisdiction of the Administrative Court'. He furthermore dismissed the explanation provided by Nitirat concerning 'actions associated with government designated policy' as merely that group's own opinion (Thiradet and Ram 2008: 121–126).

Worachet, in turn, disputed Amon's interpretation, declaring that: 'A decision concerning a national political problem involving the cabinet, or the parliament, which is related to international relations is highly political in nature. Such politically complicated actions should be excluded from the sphere examined by the court'. Touching on matters in France, Germany and Japan, he further explained that the courts in those places did not hand down decisions related to actions of a political nature (Thiradet and Ram 2008: 142–145). In response to Worachet's argument, Amon stated that: 'I don't like the notion of the division of sovereignty into three powers. In actuality there are only two political institutions – the government and the parliament, and these exercise the greatest powers on behalf of the people. They have administrative and legislative powers and, through judicial agencies, have the power to resolve constitutional problems. Accordingly, there is no evenly distributed balance between these powers'. He went on to say that: 'Nitirat refers to the equality of the three powers, but is this what we see in Thailand?' Noting that: 'Political parties are the political institutions that hold the greatest political power in the country', he critiqued his country's system as follows: 'The Thai Constitution gives rise to 1. political party affiliation among lower house politicians, 2. political parties having the power to strip the standing of an affiliated lower house member, 3. the prime minister being selected only from the lower house, and 4. political party dictatorship [*rabop phadetkan doi phakkanmuaeng*] through the regulation stating that the political party that commands a majority in the parliament forms the government' (Thiradet and Ram 2008: 183–197).

The points of the debate between these scholars concern the pros and cons of intervention by the judiciary into the political realm, the relationship of politics to the principle of the division of the three powers, and the dividing line between the law and politics. Making assertions that were understood as complying with Western-style constitutionalism, Worachet offered examples of international constitutions and the precedent of the Supreme Court of Japan. He also emphasized that Thailand should protect the principle of the division of powers. Amon, in contrast, argued that the separation of powers did not exist in Thailand. One main cause was the nature of Thai political parties, which had been created as 'super-organs' by the constitution. The nature of the debate between these two scholars suggests that obstruction to democratization in Thailand cannot be understood by merely examining the behavior of elites. It is evident that close attention also needs to be given to Thai constitutionalism and the operation of the rule of law in that country. Both have been factors in changes that have occurred to the political role of the Thai judiciary.

The debate among political science scholars

Political science scholars also responded with strong interest to the heightened role of the judiciary in Thai politics. It was previously noted that the 'judicialization of politics' is not a problem confined to Thailand. The past several decades have seen a global shift in power from elected officials to the judiciary, with judicial agencies increasingly being required to provide solutions for ethical disagreements, policy differences and political disputes. There is an argument, however, that this judicialization can emerge with the support of politicians, so that system revision takes place with political pressure operating on the courts (Hirschl 2006: 746–747). That is to say, heightening the influence of judicial agencies creates a situation in which the courts can be being made to run risks for others, in which sense they might be used to preserve the interests of powerful political actors (Hirschl 2006: 744–745).

There are a number of insightful published studies on the judicialization of politics in Thailand. We might first consider research that focuses on the design blueprint of the constitutional courts and independent agencies (Dressel and Mietzner 2012; Dressel and Khemtong 2019). A comparison of the design blueprints of the Constitutional Court and independent agencies of Thailand and Indonesia points out that the judiciary in Thailand now considers cases with political elements, such as appointments to the upper house and even legislative proposals, to the point that many judges are unable to resolve them. The judiciary in Indonesia, on the other hand, has never been given that sort of clear political role. There was also a difference in the process of judicial appointments. In contrast to the Indonesian context in which the independence of the judiciary was guaranteed, the executive government in Thailand intervened. The fact that some judges were unable to complete their terms of office was seen as damaging the independence of the courts (Dressel and Mietzner 2012: 404–405).

Saichon Sattayanurak's study (2021), in contrast, conducted a historically positioned in-depth analysis, spanning a long period of time, of the emergence of the judicialization of Thai politics. Saichon points out that, when disputing with autocrats, the middle classes who did not have the power or influence to control or rein in political leaders relied on the moral virtue (*phrabarami*) of the king. She further notes that the background to this is the notion that 'A political leader who is not a "good person" should be replaced'. Saichon asserts that this is related to the emergence in Thailand of a particular style of democracy that has the monarchy as the apogee and that is referred to variously as 'Thai-style democracy' or 'democratic regime of government with the King as Head of State' (hereafter DKHS) (Saichon 2021: 188–194). She goes on to argue that support from the middle-classes for the judicialization of Thai politics is grounded in DKHS ideas that include the sense that, in the face of 'political danger', the king will intervene to resolve political disputes. In the twenty-first century, this has been interpreted as the courts handing down decisions as the representative of the king (Saichon 2021: 211–214). In the history of the past several decades, Thai democracy and the DKHS discursive ideal that 'the king is endowed with a high level of virtue with bad politicians who lack virtue being placed in opposition to the virtuous king' has been fermented by many intellectuals and the media. These ideas were emphasized in the 1990s political reform movement and were repeatedly referenced by the 2005–2006 anti-Thaksin political movement (Saichon 2021: 208). Saichon points out that, from around 2005, the meaning of DKHS was being passionately reproduced and circulated by intellectuals (Saichon 2021: 211–214).

The above discussion suggests that DKHS is an important concept in any analysis of the judicialization of Thai politics. DKHS is a central political concept and appears as a basis in the constitution and in legal discourse. The first use of DKHS-related language in a constitution was in the 1949 Constitution. While there were subsequently several modifications to the terminology, from the time of Section 2 of the 1991 Constitution to the current 2017 document, there has been no change in the wording 'Thailand has a democratic regime of government with the King as Head of State' (*Prathetthai mi kan pokkhrong rabob prachathipatai an mi phramahakasat thong pen pramuk*) (Toyama 2016). It will therefore be useful to clarify how judicialization and DKHS have been examined in research related to the Constitution of Thailand. Somchai Preechasilpakul, the eminent Thai public law scholar, notes that DKHS is the political system by means of which the various powers of the parliament, the bureaucracy, the military and the monarchy co-exist. Somchai refers to this system, which is seen as designating the direction of changes to Thai constitutions in contemporary politics, as 'supra-constitution', that is, as being above the constitution (Somchai 2021: 63). Recently, many Thailand researchers have turned their attention to the relationship between the constitution and the authority of the king, with Eugénie Mérieau also conducting an analysis of the authority of the king in the history of the Thai Constitution (Mérieau 2021). Duncan McCargo notes that while the Thai Constitution might have been revised any number of times, there has been no change to the central objectives of the various legal and political projects that the constitution sets out to embody. The changes made have rather been a codification of governance based on virtue, a notion that is inseparable from theories of the authority of the king during the era of absolutist monarchical rule (McCargo 2019: 2).

Following the political reform movement, constitutions were newly enacted in 1997 and 2007, and then again in 2017. Nevertheless, DKHS discourse was apparent not merely in these constitutions themselves but also in the wording of the so-called 'organic laws' – laws that derive from stipulations made in a constitution. Although DKHS has patently become increasingly important even in the wording of Thailand's constitutions and laws, we are unable to say with any certainty exactly what this discourse means in terms of its application as a provision in either of those realms. Tom Ginsburg points out that the importance of constitutional norms is not specified in the text of the Thai Constitution. This is particularly the case in terms of matters related to King Bhumibol which are difficult to deduce merely from the wording of the text. The king shares power with politicians, bureaucrats and the military and is positioned as having the final decision on political disputes. It has been pointed out that the political intervention exercised by the king indicates that Thai governance is constrained not only formally but informally as well (Ginsburg 2009: 86–89). McCargo points to the existence of a 'network monarchy' that supports informal rule, while also exerting a huge influence on Thai political research. This 'network monarchy' refers to a sub-system in which the privy council and the military support the king, who is the final arbiter, while at times compromising and co-existing with elected politicians also. McCargo was one of the first to note that the objective of the political reform movement of the 1990s, which came to strengthen the political role of the judiciary, was related to the desire of the people – anticipating the switch from King Bhumibol to the unpopular King Vajiralongkorn – to eliminate the importance of the king's intervention into political disputes in order to protect 'social order' in the case of political crisis (McCargo 2005; McCargo 2019: 9). Furthermore, drawing on the idea of 'network monarchy', Mérieau suggests the frame of the 'deep state' (hereafter DS), which became famous when used in an analysis of the American military industrial complex and the Turkish government. DS refers to an anti-democratic alliance between security arms, such as the military and/or police, and the judiciary. Furthermore, while it is organized, disciplined and, at times, appropriates democratic discourse to manipulate public opinion, it is nevertheless an entity that is hidden and unable to be seen (Mérieau 2016: 2). Mérieau argues that, in the case of Thailand, DS was constructed from national agencies that reacted against the rise of popularly elected politicians and that these sought to maintain the social, political and economic order, with the king as symbolic touchstone, that they themselves preferred. She points out, however, that as King Bhumibol aged there was concern about a weakening of 'virtue' (*barami*). This led to the judiciary being selected as the new source of DS legitimacy. Accordingly, the 1997 Constitution was the beginning of a strengthening of the relationship between the king and the judiciary (Mérieau 2016).

McCargo, however, disputes the notion of DS as proposed by Mérieau. Having conducted a detailed survey of judges and their ideas, McCargo concluded that different judges have different attitudes towards judicialization. Furthermore, judges themselves tended to evade political decisions, fearful of criticism from the people. He further argues that it is not possible through DS to understand the confusion, complexities and imprecisions within the Constitutional Court, and that, in reality and in spite of the theories that abound about judicialization, it is rare for judges of the Constitutional Court to be leading actors in the chaos of the Thai political world (McCargo 2019: 209).

This section of the chapter has provided an outline of arguments presented by Thailand researchers concerning the judicialization of the Constitution of Thailand and Thai politics, with three key elements profiled, namely DKHS, governance based on virtue (with the bad politician representing the discursive opposite) and the king's political intervention into crises. While these points are closely interrelated, many aspects of the research referred to above call for further investigation. While the political reform movement was supported by the discourse of the 'bad politician', which emphasizes the importance of virtue in governance and which refers to the popularly elected politician who lacks virtue, it has been argued that this discourse was circulated more visibly from around 2005 when the anti-Thaksin movement gathered force. It was further pointed out that, as this happened, DKHS discourse was also being enthusiastically reproduced. We might consider why that occurred. As Saichon noted, 'bad politician' discourse has a long history. It remains unclear, however, why this discourse exercised the degree of legitimacy necessary to drive many ordinary people into the anti-Thaksin camp at that time.

Furthermore, McCargo and Mérieau stress that the political reform movement and political judicialization arose from concerns regarding the change of king. In other words, the political role of the judiciary was heightened as a means of dealing with the chaos and crisis that might arise after the transfer of the monarchy's power occurred. Certainly, governance based on virtue relied on the personal qualities of King Bhumibol as an individual and there was no guarantee that this would continue with the accession of the new monarch, his son. However, even if the crown prince was unpopular among the people in the 1990s, why did intellectuals of the time harbor such strong fears concerning the possibility of future political crisis. It is unclear precisely what sort of crisis they feared. It is necessary to try to provide answers to both these questions. Both questions – those relating to the power of DKHS and the 'bad politician' discourse and to the sort of crisis feared by intellectuals – require ongoing investigation.

This book aims to answer three questions: 1. What was the impetus that gave rise to the political reform movement that championed constitutionalism? 2. What were the special characteristics of the constitutions – especially those of 1997 and 2007 – that were implemented following the campaigns of the political reform movement? and 3. What sort of influence did these Thai constitutions, based on constitutionalism, exert on democratization in Thailand? The first question is covered in Part I of the book comprised of chapters 1 and 2, the second is covered in Part II comprised of chapters 3 to 7, and the third is addressed in the book's final chapter. The main sources used in this research include written material related to the political reform movement, documents related to the drafting of the 1997 and 2007 constitutions, the texts of both constitutions and of the various organic laws that derive from these, and interviews with a number of those involved. Not all the documentation related to the drafting of Thai constitutions is available to the public. Documentation examined for the book thus includes booklets published in 1995 by the Committee on Democracy Development (*khana kammakan phattana prachathipatai*) which conducted a survey of overseas constitutions in preparation for the drafting of the 1997 Thai document; the meeting records of the 1997 Constitution Drafting Committee which are available to the public; the meeting records of the 2007 Constitution Drafting Committee and Drafting Sub-Committees; and the instruction handbooks for both constitutions. In addition, documentation related to court rulings and various cases was consulted.

PART I

Constitutional Reform in the 1990s and Beyond – Cause and Intent

1 The History of Politics and Constitutions in Thailand

This chapter will examine the history of politics and constitutions in Thailand. After providing an overview of political history and constitutional changes from the time of the 1932 Siamese Revolution to the implementation of the 2007 Constitution, attention will turn to shifts that occurred in points of dispute over democratization since the 1990s. After that, the chapter will also address changes to the nature of the popular demonstrations that created an appetite for system reforms.

From the 1932 Siamese Revolution to the 1980s

A special characteristic of Thai political history is the continuous cycle of military coup d'état followed by elections. During the period from the 1932 constitutional revolution to the 1991 coup, one revolution (*patiwat*) and ten coups (*ratthaprahan*) were carried out. There have also been eleven failed coups (*kabots*). Coups d'état occur frequently, but general elections were also held fourteen times during this period. With the exception of the 1960s military regime, elections have been held regularly.[1] Until 1991, furthermore, eight permanent and five interim constitutions were enacted.[2] The term 'interim constitution' refers to documents compiled immediately following a revolution or coup that operate until a permanent constitution is enacted. The coup process, it will become clear, led to the production of many

---

1   Until the 1991 coup, the military overthrow of a government occurred in 1933, 1947, 1948, 1951, 1957, 1958, 1971, 1976 and 1977. Including the 1991 coup, this is a total of ten times. Lower house elections were held fourteen times, in 1933, 1938, 1946, 1948, 1952, February 1957, December 1957, 1969, 1975, 1976, 1979, 1983, 1986 and 1988.
2   The implementation of permanent constitutions occurred in 1932, 1946, 1949, 1952, 1968, 1974, 1976 and 1978. The 1976 document, however, comprised a mere twenty-nine sections and was thus similar to an interim constitution in form (Kochu 2010: 64).

constitutions. After providing a brief overview of Thai political history, this chapter considers the specifics of the successive constitutions implemented across various eras in Thailand.

Democratization has a long history in Thailand and began with the Siamese Revolution of 1932. This was an uprising against the absolute monarchy, which had ruled since the nineteenth century, carried out by the People's Party (*khana rat*) whose members were young military officers and bureaucrats calling for a constitution and change to the constitutional monarchy. It has been argued, however, that rather than democracy, the Siamese Revolution created a 'bureaucratic polity' whereby the military and bureaucracy monopolized central political power (Riggs 1966). Under the bureaucratic system, parliamentary democracy did not take hold for a long period, and the change of government through elections was not institutionalized. A change of government often takes the form of a coup d'état, and Thailand has experienced an unprecedented number of coups. From the constitutional revolution of 1932 to the coup d'état of 1957, there were repeated power struggles between the military, bureaucrats and royalists. From the coup d'état of 1957 until 14 October 1973 when the military government was overthrown by popular demonstrations called the 'Student uprising', the country was ruled by a military dictatorship for about fifteen years. Since the political influence of the military has operated in Thailand over a long period of time, there has been a tendency in scholarship on Thailand to focus on the mechanism of repeated coups d'état.

Economic development in the 1970s resulted in the gradual expansion in largely urban areas of the middle-classes, and this period also saw the emergence of a pro-democracy movement. This led to student uprisings opposing the military regime and for a brief time the military exited the political domain. Although a popularly elected government was installed, several years later with the claim of fighting communism, the military staged successive coups d'état in 1976 and 1977. The military successfully seized power once more and, with its staunch support for a non-elected prime minister, exerted strong influence in the political sphere between 1977, the year of the coup, and 1988. In Thailand, this political system was referred to as a 'semi-democracy' (*prachatipatai khrueng bai*). In his analysis of the semi-democratic system of government (1978–1988), William Case points out that, while the military as political elites sought alliances with politicians who represented the business world and economic development, with the new middle classes and with their own interests, these were ultimately uneven agreements in which the military held total ascendency (Case 1996: 455). Case furthermore suggests that, from the 1970s until the early years of the 1990s, when the relationship between the military and the elites that followed changed to a more equal one, politics would become unstable, and when the military had the upper hand, it would become stable. That is, the stability of the time was a result of the military being the dominant political force (Case 1966: 457).

During the 1980s, Thailand researchers explained these events using a cyclical model first proposed by Chai-Anan Samudavanija. Chai-Anan argued that the 'vicious cycle of Thai politics' involved the following five stages: 1. the staging of a successful military coup d'état, the rescinding of a constitution, the suspension of parliament and a ban on political activity; 2. the proclamation of an interim constitution and the legitimation of control by the military; 3. the proclamation of a permanent constitution and the conduct of elections; 4. confrontation between the parliament and the military; and 5. the staging once more of a coup (Chai-Anan 1982). Murashima's 'cyclic turnover of the Thai political system' proposes the same basic structure (Murashima 1987). According to Murashima's explanation, until the student revolution of October 1973, regime change, be it toward democratization or authoritarianism, was under the leadership of the military and bureaucrats with no other power group taking effective initiative. In this sense, the theory of the vicious cycle of Thai politics is based on the understanding of the aforementioned bureaucratic system theory. When the Chatchai administration took power as a popularly elected government in 1988, there was optimism for possible change. In 1991, however, the National Peace-Keeping Council (NPKC; *khana raksa khwamsagopriaproi haeng chat*) overthrew the popular government by staging a coup d'état.

The following provides an overview of the specifics of the constitutions enacted during the period under consideration. The items listed, closely related to democratization, impinged on the stipulations of these constitutions: 1. whether the post of prime minister should be restricted to popularly elected members of parliament; 2. whether a serving member of the military or bureaucrat should hold a cabinet position; 3. whether upper house members should be appointed or elected; and 4. whether the chair of the upper or lower house should also be chair of the parliament. Looking at the overview presented in Table 1.1 of the provisions of each of the constitutions involved, it is apparent that provisions have been changed many times.

While the 1932 Constitution required the prime minister to be a member of parliament, this condition was removed in later iterations. Although the 1974 Constitution stipulated that the prime minister be a member of the popularly elected lower house, this was no longer the case by 1978. Furthermore, while almost all constitutions prohibited full-time civil servants from taking a seat in the parliament, this did not apply to cabinet appointments. The 1978 Constitution included transitional provisions concerning the appointment of full-time civil servants to cabinet, which were not immediately prohibited. Except for the 1932 Constitution, all constitutions required a bicameral system and, excluding the provisions laid down in 1946, membership of the upper house by appointment. All, excepting 1974, stipulated that the chair of the upper house also be the chair of the parliament. It is evident from the above that, until the 1978 Constitution, there were disputes concerning: 1. whether the prime minister should be chosen from popularly elected members of the house; 2. whether serving civil servants should hold cabinet appointments; and 3. the power relationship between the upper and lower houses. Based on those three points, Table 1.2 categorizes the relevant Thai Constitutions as democratic, semi-democratic or non-democratic.

Table 1.2 demonstrates that between 1932 and 1978 there were extended periods of time during which Thailand was subject to either a semi- or non-democratic constitution. This is because it was, in fact, the military that seized political power following the overthrow of a monarchical system by the Siamese Revolution of 1932. The bureaucratic powers of the military and civil servants, in addition to being in charge of the government as non-popularly elected prime ministers,

Table 1.1 Provisions relating to cabinet and the parliament in constitutions between 1932 and 1978

Year	Major Provisions
1932	• The prime minister and 14 ministers of the cabinet must be chosen from members of the parliament. Other ministers need not be parliament members (Section 47) • Unicameral system (popular election)
1946	• No member of the upper house to be a full-time civil servant (Section 24) • No member of the lower house to be a full-time civil servant (Section 29) • No member of cabinet to be a full-time civil servant (Section 66) • Bicameral system (upper house chosen by popular vote)* • The chair of the upper house to be chair of the parliament (Section 63)
1947	• No member of the lower house to be a full-time civil servant (Section 37) • No member of cabinet to be a full-time civil servant (Section 74) • Bicameral system (upper house membership by appointment) • The chair of the upper house to be the chair of the parliament (Section 71)
1949	• No member of the Upper or the Lower House to be a full-time civil servant (Section 79) • No member of the cabinet to be a full-time civil servant (Section 142) • Bicameral system (upper house membership by appointment) • The chair of the upper house to be the chair of the parliament (Section 74)
1968	• No member of the lower house to be a full-time civil servant (with the exception of political official) (Section 89) • Bicameral system (upper house membership by appointment) • The chair of the upper house to be the chair of the parliament (Section 72)
1974	• No member of the upper or lower houses to be a full-time civil servant (with the exception of political officials) (Section 102) • The prime minister must be a member of the lower house (Section 177) • The majority of cabinet ministers to be members of the upper or lower houses (Section 177) • No member of the cabinet to be full-time civil servant (with the exception of political officials) (Section 179) • Bicameral system (upper house membership by appointment) • The chair of the lower house to be the chair of the parliament (Section 96)
1978	• Members of political parties may not be appointed to the upper house (Section 87) • Full-time civil servants and local employees cannot run for house of representatives elections (with the exception of political officials) (Section 96) • No member of the cabinet to be a full-time civil servant (with the exception of political officials) (Section 148) – transitional provisions applied • Bicameral system (upper house membership by appointment) • The chair of the upper house to be the chair of the parliament (Section 75)

Note: *Popularly elected lower house members elected upper house members. This upper house was dissolved following the 1947 coup (Tamada 2003: 224). An upper house with members chosen by direct popular elections emerged from the 1997 Constitution. The percentage of popularly elected members holding cabinet positions was zero from 1932 to 1945, 35% from 1946 to 1957, and then non-existent for over fourteen years after 1958. Following the collapse of the military regime in the mid-1970s, the figure exceeded 96%. While numbers once again fell to zero after the 1976 coup d'état, between 1980 and 1988 they rose from 40 to 80% and were 98% in the 1988 popularly elected Chatchai administration (Tamada 2003: 16).

Source: Compiled by the author.

Table 1.2 Democracy and the constitutions of Thailand, 1932–1978

Constitution	Democratic	Semi-democratic	Non-democratic
1932 Interim		5 months	
1932 Permanent		13 years 5 months	
1946 Permanent	1 year 6 months		
1947 Interim		1 year 4 months	
1949 Permanent	2 years 8 months		
1952 (Amended version of the 1932 document)		6 years 7 months	
1959 Interim			9 years 4 months
1968 Permanent		3 years 4 months	
1972 Interim			1 year 9 months
1974 Permanent	2 years		
1976 Interim			1 year
1977 Interim			1 year 1 month
1978 Permanent		12 years 2 months	

Source: Compiled by the author.

have maintained their political influence through the appointed senate. Of the twenty-three prime ministers who held the post from 1932 until immediately before the 1991 coup d'état, there were ten current or former military officers, five former civil officials and seven members of the legal profession. Furthermore, based on the research aggregating appointments to the upper house between 1932 and 1996, and in spite of differences operating at different times, approximately 50–100% of these positions were monopolized by those in positions of government authority, including military officials (Tamada 2003: 225).[3]

In any analysis of the constitutions of Thailand, the influence of the monarchy is as important as that of the military or bureaucracy. While

---

3 Chai-Anan categorizes Thai constitutions as 'democratic', 'semi-democratic' or 'non-democratic', and analyzes these in terms of power-struggles between the non-elected members of both the upper and lower houses (military and bureaucrats) and the popularly elected members of political

the 1932 Siamese Revolution changed the country from an absolute monarchy to a constitutional monarchy, the political influence of the monarchy was revived between the 1960s and 1970s during the reign of King Bhumibol who held the throne from 1946–2016. The authority of the king was particularly enhanced during the 14 October 1973 student uprising. The students, led by Thirayuth Boonmee as secretary-general of the National Student Center of Thailand (NSCT), opposed the long-term military control imposed since the late 1950s, and on 6 October 1973 distributed leaflets throughout central Bangkok demanding an enactment of the constitution. When thirteen students were arrested, protestors gathered at Thammasat University. As discussed in further detail below, these demonstrators dispersed late at night. However, casualties occurred when they were obstructed by the police en route. As news of this spread, clashes in Bangkok between the students and security forces resulted in significant loss of life. With the situation at crisis point, King Bhumibol made a television appearance at 7 pm on 14 October requesting a return to normal. An announcement was made the following day that interim Prime Minister Thanom had departed Thailand. Royal intervention calmed the unrest and, with military dictator Thanom's support faction banished overseas, King Bhumibol's roles assumed 'myth' status among the Thai people. According to this myth, political discord in Thailand could be resolved by the 'virtue' (*Barami*) of the king who could furthermore appoint an interim prime minister. This is one basis for the authority of King Bhumibol and for the respect the people of Thailand hold for the king.

Due to the political situation described above, much of the existing research on the constitutions of Thailand has been carried out from three perspectives: 1. the role of the king; 2. conflicts between bureaucratic forces, including the military, and civilian forces; and 3. the

---

parties (Chai-Anan 2002). Saneh Chamarik furthermore examines the relationship between the constitutions and politics through the lens of disputes between bureaucrats and party politicians, and the power relations between the upper and lower houses (Saneh 2006). The prominent public law scholar, Khanin Bunsuwan, conducts a similar analysis focusing on the relationship between the upper and lower houses and the possibility or otherwise of full-time civil servants being appointed as members of the lower house (Khanin 1999).

ongoing repetition of military coups d'état. Kobkua Suwannathat-Pian (2004) declared the Thai Constitution to be an authority designed to sustain power struggles among the elite and that the purpose of the document was largely to shore up the power and interests of those contributing to the draft. Kobkua accordingly divided the Thai constitutions into four categories: constitutions for politicians (the People's Party), constitutions for the military, constitutions post-1972 and constitutions for the royalists. She argues that constitutions drawn up by the People's Party (1932, 1946 and 1952) were designed to usurp the authority of the monarchy. Regarding the royalist versions of the constitutions (1947 [interim] and 1949), she argues, although there were differences in the interpretation of the 'constitutional monarchy' between the royalists and the People's Party, the royalists generally favored democracy. According to Kobkua, both royalist constitutions gave a royalist faction's interpretation of the constitutional monarchy by advocating some active involvement by the king in the country's governance. She argued that the royalist faction regarded the king's role in a constitutional monarchy as exercising power to maintain a balance between the various interests until democracy could be perfectly implemented.

On the other hand, Kobkua insisted that the military version (1959 [interim] and 1968) showed the interpretation of the constitutional monarchy by the military. She pointed out that under these constitutions, the king would be guaranteed absolute liberty in the private sphere, would be expected to strike a balance between government and parliament in the public sphere, and would be guaranteed traditional rights. She argued that the post-1972 constitutions (194, 1976, 1977 [interim], 1977, 1991 and 1998) resulted from negotiations between multiple power stake-holders – including royalists, the military, politicians and liberals – and reflected the political instability in the country at the time. According to Kobkua, the monarchy was regarded in this context as the foundation of stability and all who drafted these constitutions agreed to preserve the special rights that the king and other royals had enjoyed since 1959. Kobkua further argued that, between 1973 to 1990, King Bhumibol provided Thailand with a version of constitutional monarchy that was most suited to Thailand.

Pointing out that this involved the monarchy actively contributing to the running of the country, she concluded that the king transcended the role of constitutional monarch through the 'power of love' (Kobkua 2004). This accords with a large body of research on Thai politics and the Thai Constitution that favorably assesses the value of King Bhumibol as a stabilizing presence (Kato 1995; Shimojo 2010; Suchit and Prudhisan 2012).

The 1990s political reform movement: shifting points of dispute

Amendments of the 1991 Constitution – towards institutional democratization

The constitutional provisions that have supported the system in which political power is seized by the military and bureaucrats, centered on the monarchy, were the subject of intense debate over the 1991 Constitution. These were as follows: 1. the prime minister does not need to be elected from among the members of the House of Representatives who are elected by the people, and 2. the chair of the upper house can also be the chair of the parliament (an expression of the power of the upper vis-à-vis the lower house). The background to these issues is examined below.

The 1978 Constitution legitimized a prime minister who had not been subject to the popular vote. As a result, Thailand was governed for the eight years from 1980 to 1988 by a non-elected prime minister, Prem Tinsulanonda, a former army commander-in-chief who held the confidence of King Bhumibol. Following growing domestic criticism of his administration's excessively long grasp on power, however, Prem stepped down from the prime ministership of his own accord when a general election was held in 1988. The position was then assumed by Chatchai Choonhavan, also a former army officer. Notwithstanding this background, Chatchai was nevertheless a popularly elected prime minister in the sense that he had run in the 1988 election as a party politician. With investment from both Japan and Korea, 1980s Thailand experienced remarkable economic growth. Furthermore, while many coups d'état had been staged since the 1932 Siamese Revolution, there was no successful coup between 1977 and February 1991. This was seen as evidence that, unlike previous years, the military was directing its interests to professionalization and as a result many Thai people believed that the military coup was 'a thing of the past'.

This position, however, proved misguided when yet another coup d'état was staged in February 1991. The National Peace-Keeping Council (NPKC) (*khana raksa khwamsagopriaproi haeng chat*) gave five reasons for instigating this coup: 1. intensifying pursuit of interests by politicians; 2. cabinet intervention in bureaucratic appointments; 3. 'parliamentary dictatorship' (*phadetkan thang ratthasapa*);[4] 4. sabotage of the military by the government; and 5. a need to respond to the failed assassinations of prominent figures. With any communist threat a thing of the past, 'political corruption' was emphasized as the justification for the coup. As the miliary predicted, their actions were greeted favorably and received the general support of Bangkok citizens who felt a deepening dissatisfaction towards dishonest dealings by politicians.

Problems emerged, however, in the events that followed. The 1991 coup leaders emulated the previous model by repealing the existing constitution. An interim constitution, drawn up by a twenty-member draft committee, was adopted by the National Legislative Assembly whose members were appointed by the leaders of the coup (Khien 1997: 63). Thai society, however, had undergone extensive change that was well beyond the military's expectations and what may have previously been viable no longer applied. Thus, when a draft of the new constitution was released in November 1991, large-scale protests organized by NGOs and others broke out.[5] The three key points of

---

4   'parliamentary dictatorship' (*phadetkan thang ratthasapa*) is a specific term used in Thailand that refers to the will of the majority coming to govern when the cabinet is formed by the majority party in the parliament. While majority governance is a natural consequence of democracy, in Thailand this is referred to as autocracy or dictatorship and used to justify a coup d'état (Chada 2009: 323). This general term is also used by some researchers who regard it as a problem to be addressed in Thai politics (Chumphon 2002: 107).

5   The 'Campaign for Popular Democracy', comprised of nineteen different NGOs and other groups, played a major role in April 1991 (Callahan 1998:

contention were: 1. the authorization of a non-elected prime minister, 2. the appointment of the chair of the upper house as chair of the parliament, and 3. the surfeit of power granted to the appointed (that is, not popularly elected) upper house (Khien 1997: 65).[6] While the coup group promised an early general election, this was interpreted as the intention to retain power regardless of the election outcome (Cooper 1995: 344). As tensions rose, the coup leaders held a press conference where they were forced to explain that there was no plan for Suchinda, the head of the leaders, to assume the role of prime minister. With the help of a 'royal statement' from the king, the 1991 Constitution was eventually enacted in December that year retaining the provision that legitimized a non-elected prime minister.[7]

In March 1992, a general election was held. The military indirectly contested the election by forming the Justice Unity Party (Sammakkhitham Party) which championed values identical to its own. They also dispatched sympathizers to the Thai Nation and Social Action parties. Through these three parties, the military successfully gained a total of 184 seats in the 360-seat house and effectively won the election. Through the coup and then the election, a 'military dictatorship' replaced a 'parliamentary dictatorship' (Murray 1996: 118). The election was followed by the nomination of a prime minister. Concerns were expressed by the media, NGOs and student organizations that Suchinda, the coup leader, might assume the post. Media outlets stressed that 'The next prime minister must be appointed from the popularly elected Lower House' (Murray 1996: 120). Although initially making repeated denials, Suchinda went back on his word and, on 7 April 1992, announced that he would accept the prime ministership. This was the return to a non-popularly elected prime minister who was a former army commander for the first time since 1988.[8]

---

114).

6 The surfeit of powers granted to the upper house in the first draft of the constitution of the time included nominating the prime minister and participating in deliberations on the budget and other important bills (Cooper 1995: 344).

7 The king declared that 'Any stipulation that is clearly not accepted by the people can be amended'.

8 Following the coup, the coup group (NPKC) appointed Anand Panyarachun,

Calls for Suchinda's resignation came from the parliamentary opposition, the media and student groups. The opposition firmed-up the case for constitutional revisions designed to reduce upper house power by calling for the chair of the parliament to come from the lower rather than upper house. Further evidence of a burgeoning protest movement came when former members of the lower house embarked on hunger strikes. The first large-scale demonstration was held on 20 April. According to mass media estimates, there were 70,000 participants, and according to police estimates, there were as many as 36,000 participants. Anti-Suchinda banners mocked the leader's words with slogans that read, 'I will not accept the post of prime minister' (Murray 1996: 133). On 8 May, 150,000 people gathered for the largest protest held to that time. The considerable diversity among protestor is well-known, yet there was common agreement on demands related to the constitution. The demonstration leader and former mayor of Bangkok, Chamlong Srimuang, as well as the opposition, demanded the insertion into the constitution of a stipulation to the following effect: 'The Prime Minister must be an elected member of the Lower House' (Murray 1996: 142). The same call came from the media, NGOs and students. Below, we will revisit newspaper reports of the time.

Although Suchinda had declared many times that he would not accept the role, the five parties forming the government coalition recommended him as prime minister. This was criticized by opposition Democrat Party member, Chuan Leekpai, who argued that 'A prime minister should be subject to a process of popular election and the governing coalition should abide by democratic principles'. Newspaper columns also criticized government politicians, pointing out that 'Thai democracy is different to that of other countries. That is because Lower House members give no thought to the national interest' (*Sayam Rat*, 6 April 1992). Four opposition parties and the Student Federation of Thailand were strongly opposed to appointing a prime minister who had not been popularly elected. They publicly declared, 'The prime

---

a former diplomat, as the leader of the interim government. After leaving the civil service, Anand had been active in the business world as a company CEO and also as chair of the Thai Industry Association. He led an administration that was not chosen by popular election.

minister must be an elected member of the parliament. All members of the lower house must respect the people who are their rulers' (*Sayam Rat*, 7 April 1992). Although the protest emphasis was on Suchinda as prime minister, the real targets of criticism were the governing coalition members who recommended him for the role. Media disappointment also implicated the governing administration on the grounds that, among the five heads of the coalition parties, no-one was suited to the prime-ministerial role (*Sayam Rat* 9 April 1992). Notwithstanding despondency at coalition incompetence, debate inexorably converged on the political need for the prime minister to be 'selected from the popularly elected members of the lower house'.[9]

At a press conference held on 15 April, the New Aspiration Party (an opposition party) public relations spokesperson, Chaturon Chaisan, announced that a party executive meeting, chaired by party leader Chawalit Yongchaiyut, would convene a gathering on 17 April to enhance the understanding of constitutional amendment. According to Chaturon, the points being considered were 1. whether the chair of the parliament should be the chair of the lower house, 2. whether member numbers in the upper house should be reduced, and 3. whether the prime minister should be chosen from members elected to the assembly (*Sayam Rat*, 16 April 1992). By May, Prinya Thaewanarumitkul and other members of the student movement were driving through Bangkok City calling for people to take part in large-

---

9   Because the movement was made up of such a diversity of organizations, the extent to which participants held the same points of view remains uncertain. For example, Sant Hathirat, a medical doctor who also held a teaching post at Mahidol University, mounted a biting criticism in ethical terms of the bad faith shown by Suchinda in going back on his word (*Sayam Rat*, 13 May 1992). Sant repeated this position in an interview with the author conducted on 21 May 2017. According to student leader Prinya Thaewanarumitkul, the movement calling for the prime minister to be subject to popular election primarily sought to prevent the ongoing succession to power by military figures including Suchinda. Prinya had furthermore planned to arrange regular meetings at Thammasat University with other NGOs to decide a common position. However, by early May 1992 and without consultation, Chamlong had assumed leadership of the movement. Chamlong's organization of protest marches, moreover, was done without publicly announcing the march destination beforehand. This caused considerable concern about where and when a clash with the military might occur (interview conducted by the author on 13 June 2017).

scale demonstrations to ensure a return to democracy. The message by Prinya and student movement participants included the demand that 'The prime minister be chosen from members elected by popular vote' (*Sayam Rat*, 3 May 1992).

On 4 May, many NGOs and ordinary people joined opposition party members who gathered to protest under the slogan 'We oppose a non-elected prime minister' (*Sayam Rat*, 5 May 1992). On 11 May, the four opposition parties presented a draft of a revised constitution to the chair of the parliament. The four points for revision were as follows: 1. appointing the chair of the lower house as chair of the parliament; 2. the parliament will be in session for two terms, and all matters can be deliberated in both terms; 3. limiting the power of the upper house; and 4. selecting the prime minister from among members of the lower house. With protests peaking after 17 May at 200,000 people, military intervention on 18 to 19 May resulted in the tragic loss of many lives. Although a government statement issued immediately after the clashes put the death-toll at forty, it is believed that many more Thai people died in the fray.

After the 1992 Bloody May Incident, the following constitutional reforms occurred: 1. prime-ministerial candidates were limited to members of the popularly elected lower house, and 2. the chair of the parliament became the chair of the lower rather than upper house. The general election held in September that year saw the formation of the popularly elected Chuan Leekpai administration. Clearly, the main point of dispute driving the protest movement between 1991 and May 1992 was the procedural legitimacy of the country's democratic structure. In a sense, it was these protests that enabled Thailand to make huge organizational advances in democratization. Following the 1991 constitutional reforms, for example, it was no longer possible for the military to nominate a prime minister who had not been elected by popular vote.

The political reform movement – tackling corruption and democratization

Until May 1992, the primary focus of constitutional amendments was prohibiting the appointment of a prime minister who had not been subject to popular election. With this objective achieved through the 1991 constitutional revisions, political corruption and 'vote buying' (*khai sitthi sue siang*) at election time emerged as new points of concern. In other words, 'tackling corruption' became the political problem to be addressed. With legal scholars leading the way, there was a groundswell of sometimes excessive criticism of corrupt politicians. In reality, however, it also had the aspect of a manufactured movement. The movement's development is examined below.

Particularly from the 1980s, the military initiated what became repeated condemnation of corrupt politicians in Thailand (Tamada 1988). The target was vote-buying during elections.[10] The appointment by the Chatchai Choonhavan administration, which assumed power in 1988, of a prime minister from the popularly elected lower house was seen as a democratic shift. However, charges of corruption gave this administration an extremely bad name. Regarded as a striking example of how corruption developed in Thailand (Suchit 2002: 193), the Chatchai government was ridiculed as a 'parliamentary dictatorship' with a 'buffet [self-serving] cabinet'. As previously noted, the 1991 coup d'état was justified by a need to address cabinet corruption by overthrowing the Chatchai administration.

Although the September 1992 general election was a return to democracy, the 1990s was a decade of distrust of politicians. It has been argued that the media and intellectuals came to exercise considerable power during this decade (McCargo 2000), with intellectuals particularly making trenchant criticisms of the procedural legitimacy

---

10 It has been pointed out that, after the 1979 election, election campaigns became more adversarial. On the other hand, it was said that the person who undertook to collect votes (*hua khanen*) played a very important role. Those expected to act in this capacity included ward heads (*kamnan*), village heads (*phuyaiban*), priests, teachers and merchants. While the 1978 Election Law forbade a ward or village head from supporting a specific candidate or party, it was natural that they took the role of collecting votes when an election was held.

of the elections that brought politicians to power. They asserted that, since these politicians had been 'elected through vote-buying', there was 'no true democratic legitimacy to their being elected'. Comments by prominent public law scholar Bowonsak, for example, were reported as follows: 'The sophisticated voters of Bangkok desire effective politicians who formulate efficient political policy without being overly corrupt. Many others, however, both vote for those who promise to benefit their regions and accept payment at ballot-time' (*Bangkok Post*, 26 October 1995). From a different perspective, it was also claimed that 'Election results not only fail to reflect the will of the people, but political parties fail to function for the people's advantage or benefit.[11] Corrupt politicians insist on benefiting themselves only and there is ultimately no change to autocratic power' (Suchit 2002: 189).

On the other hand, the two interim Anand administrations of 1991 and 1992 conveyed an image of being capable, clean and technocratic and therefore superior to administrations comprised of popularly elected politicians (Girling 1997: 150–152; Callahan 2005: 103–106). There was a strong degree of trust in former diplomat Prime Minister Anand and his cabinet members, many of the whom had technocratic backgrounds. The high opinion in which the media and intellectuals held technocrats meant that, when regional businessman turned politician Banharn Silpa-archa became prime minister in 1995, his administration was criticized on the gounds that 'Over half the Cabinet members are politicians, not technocrats' (*Bangkok Post*, 27 July 1995). That is, theoretical ascendency was given to specialist ability rather than democratic principles. Against this background, political scientist Seksan Prasertkun argued as follows: 'Many people were satisfied with the Anand administration although it did not come to power through popular election. Yet, when Suchinda formed a government with the approval of a lower house chosen at the March 1992 elections, the people rebelled. The middle-classes sought efficiency and accountability

---

11 When conservative intellectuals referred to the 'people', they did not use the usual term '*prachachon*'. Rather, they chose the word '*puangchon*'. The former referred to particular groups while the latter referred to all groups. Underlying the latter was inclusion of the wealthy who did not take part in protests. The expression of the will of the '*puangchon*' asserted what was understood through a national referendum (Wichitwong 2010: 47–50).

rather than democracy' (Seksan 2005: 97–99). Furthermore, rather than the fact that those involved had not been elected, Seksan regarded corruption resulting from the military's sustained grasp on power as the source of the anger directed at Suchinda's administration and the resultant mass revolt. Gradually, the conservative elite who included bureaucrats and intellectuals came to the consensus that 'There is no necessity for a prime minister to be a politician (a popularly elected member of the Lower House)' (Connors 2003: 154).

With revisions to the 1991 Constitution concluded, a political reform movement emerged calling for anti-corruption measures. This campaign, centered around Bangkok intellectuals, offered the adoption of a new constitution grounded in 'constitutionalism' as a measure for political reform. Constitutionalism in this context was introduced by Amon, a pivotal identity in the Thai public law scholarship world. Amon's central interest was in limiting the power of the parliament (in fact, the lower house). He advocated reform with a focus on measures regarded as neutral, such as accountability, checks and balances, and the division of administrative (executive) and legislative powers. Once introduced, these ideas immediately monopolized political discourse. The Committee on Developing Democracy (*khanakammakan phatthana prachathipatai*) was established in June 1994 to promote study into future directions for constitutional reform, and in 1995 formulated a proposal based on Amon's recommendations. Included among these recommendations were the following: support for appointing a prime minister from outside the popularly elected members of the Lower House; limits on the submission of no-confidence motions; the heightening of government accountability through for example the appointment of an ombudsman; strengthening the parliament committee system; and ensuring the power to intervene in parliamentary matters that were critical to the wellbeing of the country through a national advisory council. These recommendations clearly incorporated advice that turned back the clock by reversing the need for a prime minister to be chosen from popularly elected members of parliament, a right hard won through the Bloody May Incident of 1992. Nevertheless, the committee's ideas ultimately received support from the media and NGOs (Connors 2003: 158).

We might consider changes in the nature of media reports from the mid-1990s. The principal factor driving these appeared to be the emergence of the political reform movement. The leaders of this movement were Amon, as noted above, Bowonsak, Prawase Wasi, formerly a royal doctor, and Anan Phanyarachun, a former prime minister.[12] The Committee on Developing Democracy (June 1994 – April 1995), referred to above, played a central role early in the movement by advocating a strategy of social 'empowerment' and also acknowledging the need for information to be disseminated through the media. To capture the hearts and minds of the people, it was seen as essential that this information be clear, firm and easy to understand (Prawase 2002). With Amon's material published in 1994, by 1995 media momentum had gathered in support of a discourse that denied the value of democracy and particularly of a 'popularly elected prime minister'. Overseas news outlets reported that Thai intellectuals and people generally were suspicious of a parliamentary style democratic system, such as the following representative example: 'People have grown tired of democracy [...]. While popular opinion previously called for democratic leadership, there has been an abrupt about-face in attitude toward a Parliamentary system. One prominent political scientist stated that a government chosen by election lacks legitimacy and that, to reinvigorate the ailing economy, the country must be administered by people of talent' (*Far Eastern Economic Review*, 19 September 1996).

The 1997 and 2007 constitutions: ideals and background

The 1997 Constitution: drafting process

We will now briefly recap existing research on the drafting process of the 1997 Constitution that was designed to realize the principles of

---

12 Scholars and intellectuals did not have a monolithic view of democracy. Political scientist, Khien Theeravit, stressed the fact that scholars did not give support to the anti-Suchinda movement to the degree that they had supported the October 1973 student uprising. He stated that this was because, while they agreed in principle with the need for an elected prime minister, they believed that a more flexible response was necessary (Khien 1997: 27–28).

the political reform movement. Responsibility for drawing up a draft constitution lay with the Constitution Drafting Assembly (*sapha rang ratthathammanu*). The parliament lacked power to review the document or to make revisions of any kind. The only capacity permitted to assembly members was a vote on whether or not to accept the draft as presented in total (Bowonsak 2001: 26). While there were no members of parliament on the Constitution Drafting Assembly, members were selected through an indirect assembly vote. Membership prerequisites were education to university graduate level or above and being thirty-five years of age or above. It has been suggested that a constitutional drafting process that was so disadvantageous to politicians resulted from pressure for political reform and suspicions of cabinet corruption by the media (Tamada 2003: 166–169). With the new constitution drafted between 26 December 1996 and 15 August 1997, the assembly voted to accept the document just over one month later on 27 September. Producing the draft was a complicated process involving a total of seven committees. The key roles, however, lay with the Constitution Drafting Committee (*khanakammathikan yokrang ratthathammanun*) and the Draft Amendment Committee (*khanakammathikan phitcharana rang ratthathammanun*).

The Constitution Drafting Committee functioned from 14 January to 8 May 1997. The Committee, which had twenty-nine members and former prime minister Anand as chair, determined a three-point framework for the draft. This involved: 1. the rights and obligations of and participation by the people; 2. checks on the power of the state; and 3. review of relationships between political institutions. The Draft Amendment Committee had thirty-three members and operated from 9 May to 15 August 1997. Anand also chaired this committee, the role of which was to revise the draft in light of the feedback provided by the people at the second reading meeting of the Constitution Drafting Assembly. Not only did this work have to be complete in less than one month, the plenary session review was held over twenty-one days and the second reading concluded on 30 July.

In addition to the above, there was the Public Comment and Hearing Committee (*khanakammathikan rapfang khwamkhithen lae prachaphichan*) and also a committee tasked with gathering commentary from those resident in the seventy-six *changwat* (states) (*khanakammathikan rapfang khwamkhithen lae prachaphichan pracham changwat ruam 76 changwat*). The former had thirty-eight members and the latter fifteen. This was the first time in history that such a wide cross-section of people had commented on a constitutional draft and was largely the reason that the Constitution Drafting Assembly patted themselves on the back by referring to the 1997 Constitution as a 'Constitution of "the people"'. The number of people involved in first stage consultations was 629,232, while 122,584 attended public meetings at the *changwat* level, 3,838 at the regional level and 87,912 through other mechanisms. This made a total of 843,556 people involved in the constitutional draft. In addition, over 300 groups and organizations provided feedback. These included business, industry, agriculture and media groups, as well as professional organizations, environment groups, educational institutions, political parties and groups advocating democracy (Bowonsak 2001: 29). Nevertheless, primary responsibility for the draft clearly lay with the thirty or so members of each of the two major committees. Former prime minister Anand chaired both committees, with an overlap of a significant number of other members (Tamada 2003: 172). In addition, the time given for revision in response to public feedback was only a little less than two months in total, including the plenary session. The 1997 Constitution, a product of the political reform movement, was officially proclaimed on 11 October 1997.

The 1997 Constitution: principles

The explanatory handbook accompanying the 1997 Constitution clearly stated that the aim (*chettana*) of those drafting the document was the advancement of political reform through the creation of various agencies and regulations (Bowonsak 2001: 26). According to members of the Constitution Drafting Assembly, there were three problems undermining contemporary Thai politics: 1. power plays by politicians that made it impossible for the people to truly participate in politics; 2. corruption and a lack of transparency in political governance; and 3. an ineffective political system related to lack of freedom by the government. The need to reform 'politics for politicians' into 'politics for the people' was seen as crucial. Various objectives were regarded as necessary for this to occur, including the advancement of new rights, liberties and equalities for the people and broadening the participation of the people in all the stages of political governance. Drafting Assembly members referred to the representative democracies that operated all around the world as examples of 'politics for politicians' (*kanmueang khong nakkanmueang*) and dismissed these as besieged by power play. In order to improve politics and to ensure participatory democracy at all stages and from national to regional levels, efforts were made to have the new constitution advocate political participation by the people (Bowonsak 2001: 38–42). This suggests that Constitution Drafting Assembly members did not recognize politicians chosen by popular election as the people's representatives.

To legitimate political reform, intellectuals imported a range of new keywords from overseas. In addition to constitutionalism, these were 'rule of law', 'accountability' and 'transparency'. The history of each lay in Europe and all were promoted by international agencies as objectives for newly emerging nations. While the impetus of the political reform movement had launched public law scholar Amon's notion of 'constitutionalism', the term 'good governance' also featured repeatedly in the media prior to the enactment of the 1997 Constitution. This expression accordingly became a reform movement catchphrase. While 'good governance' often appeared during the Anand administration in the context of the need for 'transparency', the term's use became even more frequent by the time of the Banharn administration (1995). With Anand himself often referencing 'good governance', the term gradually spread throughout Thai society. There were various interpretations of this term. Democracy activist Thirayuth Boonmee suggested that good governance was the equivalent of the Thai word '*thammarat*', a term influenced by Buddhism that encompassed notions of righteousness, moral virtue and justice. On the other hand, Saneh Chamarik, who was also a community activist, saw this as elitist and revised the meaning to include grassroots participation. Prawase Wasi furthermore emphasized that the term implied an economy and society that satisfied community needs. Anand and other conservatives, in contrast, understood constitutional reform and good governance as implying a strengthened state and improvements to efficiency, as well as a greater profile for 'good people' (*khon di*) like themselves in national governance (Pasuk and Baker 2000: 124–127). In other words, a gap existed between the interpretation of good governance by liberal reformists and conservatives. While for conservatives, including technocrats, good governance meant an efficient and powerful state, for the reformist faction, including NGO activists, the term implied the empowerment of civil society.

The third concept, 'rule of law', had a particular meaning in Thailand. Here, it referred to governance in terms of laws, determined by the king on the advice and approval of the parliament, which aimed to prevent the violation of individual rights by the arbitrary government of an individual (Bowonsak 2001: 59). This interpretation insisted that rule of law did not permit an entity of whatever kind to monopolize power. Furthermore, an objective advocated by the political reform movement was the need to prevent the 'bad man' (*khon chua khon leu*) from grasping political power (Suraphon 2006: 209). Put another way, whether in terms of good governance or rule of law, there was a tendency in Thailand to emphasize moral virtue. From the viewpoint of political reformists, moreover, politicians were regarded as unsuitable to hold power or to govern. Thus, while concepts of both rule of law and good governance developed in the west, the Thai intellectuals who borrowed these reconstructed each to suit their own perception of local conditions.

The Thaksin administration and the end of the 1997 Constitution

The 1997 Constitution was adopted on 27 September of that year by an overwhelming majority of the parliament. While some politicians voiced opposition, pressure from many quarters made it difficult to vote against the bill. In addition, while the Constitution Drafting Assembly declared the document to be the 'people's constitution', many researchers also expected positive democratization outcomes from this new, most democratic constitution in the history of Thailand (Klein 1998). Ten years later, however, the document was rendered null and void by yet another coup d'état. This coup, it is said, was a response to the Thaksin administration (2001–2006) which came to power with victory in the 2001 general election. A typical assertion is that Thaksin abused the 1997 Constitution and that his administration's use of regulatory loopholes led to the failure of political reform (Mutebi 2008). A representative critique by former diplomat Kasit Piromya proceeded as follows:

> Recognizing rights and freedoms, and also enhancing transparency, the 1997 Constitution was superior to previous documents. It particularly opened political processes to broad participation by civil society. [...] This Constitution halted the cycle of politicians tainted by corruption exploiting the State for their own benefits and had the potential to achieve far-reaching democratic reforms in Thailand. After the 2001 victory of his Thai Rak Thai Party, however, Thaksin heaped scorn, both in word and spirit, on the 1997 Constitution and altered the fundamental structure of Thai politics with his single-party dictatorship. (Kasit 2012: 162–163).

The Thaksin administration remained in power across two terms from 2001 to 2006. The key to its electoral success lay in various stipulations of the 1997 Constitution and in the Thai Rak Thai Party's sophisticated economic and social policies. With Thaksin implementing a raft of electoral promises upon becoming prime minister, many people in Thailand acknowledged his capabilities. After his administration was firmly in place, however, he was criticized for attempts to regulate all aspects of social activity. Important missions proposed by Thaksin were anti-corruption measures and the elimination of drugs, and from May 2003 he did indeed commence a war on the drug-trade with the aim of suppressing influential figures in the Thai equivalent of the mafia. Directing government officials to stand firm in the face of influential politicians at the national and regional levels, he set his sights on drug dealers, gangs, dealers in illegal contraband, owners of gambling premises and illicit arms dealers. The actual crackdown, however, seemed more like a mission to remove or weaken politically influential people in the regions. In this sense, there was a strong impression that Thaksin was eliminating his political rivals (Prajak 2016). Various other criticisms of the Thaksin administration concerned corruption, tax evasion, the conclusion of free trade agreements, infringements of press freedoms, disrespecting the king, violence in the south, abuse of the powers of office, intervention into systems of political monitoring, violating human rights and subverting the unity of the state (Kasit 2012: 165). Thaksin was also harshly condemned for intervening in bureaucratic appointments. In addition, his introduction of ideas and procedures from the business world, with the expectation that even diplomats and state governors would comply with these, was resisted by bureaucrats concerned at the introduction of a CEO-style top-down chain of command into the bureaucratic apparatus (Pasuk and Baker 2009: 184–188). Although many people supported his economic and social policies, Thaksin won the votes of regional powerbrokers with election promises that included programs providing low-cost health care for the poor, programs to expand village subsidies, offers of cheap loans and the provision of job training. Scholars and the media criticized these as populist (Sripan 2009: 7–8).

While the popularity of his administration among the people remained high, an anti-Thaksin movement began to gather force among certain sections of the community well before the February 2005 general election. This is notwithstanding the fact that opinion polls, even in early 2003 when drug-traffickers were being killed one after another, gave a 90% approval rating for the administration's crackdown on drugs. There was nevertheless also strong anger towards this policy, with repeated criticisms both from people who lived in the country's south and human rights activists. This was the catalyst for what eventually became a huge anti-Thaksin movement, with NGOs joining those opposing the prime minister. Initially, the nucleus of activity was a group called the 'Campaign for Popular Democracy', which had also pushed for political reform through the 1997 Constitution. After the involvement of human rights activists, students, workers and various NGOs, a campaign was mounted in January 2005 in cities throughout each region to prevent Thaksin's Thai Rak Thai Party from regaining control of the parliament. Although Thai Rak Thai enjoyed a sweeping victory in the February 2005 general elections, even in early 2006 the anti-Thaksin groundswell showed no sign of subsiding. During a television program broadcast on 9 September 2005, media mogul Sondhi Limthongkul was one of several people who repeatedly criticized Thaksin for, among other things, 'failing to pledge loyalty to the King'. It was as if politics had come out of the parliament to be fought on the streets. This was particularly the case when, after his program's broadcast was halted because of the 9 September content, Sondhi began to hold a weekly talkshow in Bangkok's Lumphini Park. Here, tens of thousands gathered to hear Sondhi criticize Thanksin each week and to repeatedly declare that his ultimate aim was to be 'Free of Thaksin'.

On the other hand, various voices were raised in support of the Thaksin administration. These came, for example, from motorcycle taxi drivers who declared, 'We once had to pay protection money to regional power brokers to be able to work. But an investigation by the Thaksin administration stopped all that and we now do our job without worry'. Many Bangkok taxi drivers, the majority of whom came from the northeast, also supported Thaksin. Regional farm workers, too, began to rally in Bangkok to show support for the prime minister. In March, over 30,000 people from groups such as 'the Caravan of the Poor' and the 'North-East Farm Workers' Network' gathered in Chatuchak Park. This heralded the emergence of a new protestor versus protestor (that is, anti-Thaksin and pro-Thaksin) structure to events. The prime minister's response was to dissolve the lower house and declare a general election for 2 April. The situation nevertheless became precarious through sabotage by anti-Thaksin forces and a boycott by the opposition parties. On 25 April, King Bhumibol declared single party control to be undemocratic and, although declining as monarch to intervene directly, instructed the benches of the Supreme Court and Administrative Court to 'solve the political problem under the leadership of the Supreme Court'. This directive from the king resulted in an eleven-hour joint deliberation of the supreme, administrative and constitutional courts, after which the Constitutional Court ruled the 2 April general election invalid. On 19 September 2006, the military staged the first coup d'état in approximately fifteen years. As a result, the anti-Thaksin movement temporarily came to an end.

Enacting the 2007 Constitution

Among the proclamations made post-19 September 2006 by the group that staged the coup d'état were the following mission objectives: 1. appointing a new (interim) prime minister to undertake political reform, 2. remediating divisions among the people, 3. mounting legal proceedings against people suspected of corruption, and 4. implementing reforms to ensure the independence of civil servants (*Matichon*, 22 September 2006). It is interesting to note that one point involved 'political reform'. Following past models, the coup group set about enacting a new constitution. The 1997 Constitution, regarded as a democratic document with various elitist stipulations, was drafted and enacted by a democratic administration after several years of consultation and discussion. In contrast, the 2007 Constitution was drafted and enacted under an interim military administration. It was accordingly criticized as undemocratic in terms of both enactment and the stipulated content (Dressel 2009).

Following the 19 September coup d'état staged by the Council for Democratic Reform Under a Constitutional Monarchy (*khana pathirup kanpokkhrong nai rapob prachathipatai anmi phramahakasat thong pen pramuk*), an interim constitution was adopted on 1 October. The coup group then exercised political control as the Council of National Security (CNS; *khana montri kwammankhong heang chat*). The interim document stipulated the establishment of an independent Constitution Drafting Assembly to lead the drafting of what became the 2007 document, with a people's vote after six months to approve a new permanent constitution. In the event of the draft being rejected, the military would choose to implement one of Thailand's constitutions from the past. On 14 December 2006, a National People's Assembly of 1,982 members was appointed by order of the king. From these, 200 candidates were selected on 18 December for membership of the Constitution Drafting Assembly. While these included bureaucrats, members of the private sector, and the urban elite, there was not a single farm worker or laborer representative. On 2 January 2007, the Council for National Security whittled the names down to 100, with the first meeting held on 8 January (Dressel 2009: 303). The Constitution Drafting Assembly met on forty-three occasions from 8 January to 20 August, while a

Constitution Drafting Committee was also established. The latter met on sixty-two occasions between 25 January and 17 August. Although the Constitution Drafting Assembly selected twenty-five members of the Constitution Drafting Committee, a further ten members were military appointments. There were also three sub-committees to the Constitution Drafting Committee (*khana anukammathikan rang ratthathammanun*). These examined: 1. the freedom of the people to exercise rights and the division of powers, 2. political agencies, and 3. independent agencies and the courts. On 19 August the document was eventually put to a national vote, with 56.69% in favor and 41.37% against.

Although the 2007 Constitution drafting process was clearly a far cry from that of the 1997 document, both excluded politicians. The 1997 draft was constructed under a democratic administration, although the intellectual leaders of the political reform movement were adamant that 'Politicians cannot conduct reforms to restrain their own powers'. As a result, politician-led intervention in the drafting process was taboo. While several politicians voiced dissatisfaction with the content of the draft, pressure from the media and intellectuals resulted in its acceptance through a vote in parliament. It has been argued that the vote accepting the 1997 Constitution also had the backing of the military. The 2007 Constitution was drafted under an interim constitution and also enacted with military backing. This fundamentally ensured that politicians were unable to exercise any influence on the process at all. In addition to these common restrictions, both constitutions emphasized enhanced participation opportunities for the people (Somkit 2008: 5).

The 2007 Constitution: unchanging ideals

It will be useful to examine the ideals that informed the 2007 Constitution. The introduction to 'Interpreting the 2007 Constitution', a document produced by legal scholars involved in its drafting, explained that this 2007 document was 'round two of political reforms' inherited from 1997. According to Somkit, a member of the Constitution Drafting Assembly, the 2007 Constitution was intended to resolve problems associated with the 1997 Constitution. These included constraints on the free expression of rights by the people, monopolization of and unfair use of national power, lack of moral virtue or ethics among political office holders, and the undermining – by intervention in the monitoring agencies involved – of the systems designed to check the misuse of power (Somkit 2007: 11–13). The most pressing problem was seen as Thaksin's Thai Rak Thai Party having total control in the parliament. This had distorted the checks and balances that operated between the administrative (executive) and legislative arms of government, resulting in a 'parliamentary dictatorship'. Those drafting the 2007 Constitution stressed that this misuse of power by political leaders (Thaksin) distorted the spirit and intent of the 'People's Constitution' (Somkit 2008: 18).

The 1997 Constitution was born of the political reform movement which championed the elimination of political corruption. Immediately after the adoption of the document, the new constitution's desired outcomes were reported as: 1. honest and sincere politicians, 2. impartial voting activity, and 3. the reform of the political system with an intention to eradicate money politics (*Far Eastern Economic Review*, 18 September 1997). Furthermore, the fundamental principles of the 2007 Constitution as the product of a coup d'état were determined as: 1. protecting, promoting and broadening rights and freedoms, 2. eliminating the restraints and misuse of state authoritarian power, 3. guaranteeing transparency, moral virtue and ethical responsibility in political participation, and 4. strengthening the efficiency of surveillance and monitoring systems (Somkit 2008: 29). The two constitutions thus ultimately had the same objectives. Overseas media saw the 1997 and 2007 documents very differently and therefore criticized the 2007 Constitution as 'undemocratic' and 'reactionary'. Although they therefore concluded that Thai politics had reversed its former democratic advances, we will see in Chapter 3 that there were in fact few differences in the fundamental structures of the two.

Furthermore, committees with carriage of the 2007 constitutional draft were required to accord with the following general framework: 1. Thailand is a single and always indivisible nation; 2. Thailand is ruled through a democratic regime of government with the king as military commander-in-chief and head of state; 3. the position of the king will be respected and praised, and no entity may violate this or lodge any kind of legal action against the king; 4. Thailand is governed by rule of law; 5. Thailand is governed by a parliament; 6. the principle power lies with the people of Thailand, while the king as the head of state will use legislative, administrative (executive) and judicial powers; 7. the constitution is the supreme law of the land and there will be no provision in any law or regulation that is inconsistent with the constitution; 8. cases not covered by the provisions of the constitution shall accord with the traditions of the democratic regime of government with the king as head of state; 9. the dignity, rights, responsibilities, freedom and equality of the people, their participation and the power of communities shall be naturally guaranteed and protected; and 10. judges in all courts will conduct their investigations independently and, in the name of the king, will hand down just rulings that accord with the constitution and other laws. This framework was determined in the text of chapters 1 ('General Provisions') and 2 ('The King') of the 2007 Constitution. The expression, 'a democratic regime of government with the King as Head of State', appeared repeatedly in both the constitution itself and in the so-called 'organic' laws deriving from the constitution and was a feature shared with the 1997 document.

Although the 2007 Constitution was enacted following a coup d'état, when compared to the 1997 document, there were ultimately no major differences in ideals and background. Both constitutions included many references to the king and the monarchy, and, while drafted under the auspices of the military, like its predecessor, the 2007 Constitution stressed constitutionalism and rule of law. It is therefore possible to conclude that the ideals informing the enactment of both were unchanged.

The intensification of mass protest and the crisis of a 'myth'

Mass protest and political change: the student uprising of October 1973

In the context of important reforms to the political system and the constitutions discussed above, it is useful to consider the nature of large-scale mass demonstrations that have occurred in Thailand. Three protests were particularly important as turning points in terms of democratization, namely, the 14 October 1973 student uprising, the 1992 Bloody May Incident and the 2006 anti-Thaksin movement. This section will examine the special features of each in addition to changes in modes of mass demonstration that occurred during the period.

Before considering the October 1973 student uprising in detail, it will be useful to provide historical background to the event. Following the seizure of power by Sarit Thanarat in the 1958 coup, Thailand experienced an extended period of military dictatorship. Thanom Kittikachorn, who took over as military ruler following Sanit's death, implemented a constitution in 1968 and held a general election the following year. In 1971, however, he found himself unable to control the politicians of the lower house. As a result, he staged a coup against his own government. Students, led by Thirayuth Boonmee as general-secretary of the National Student Center of Thailand (NSCT), were opposed to this move and on 6 October distributed leaflets throughout central Bangkok demanding that a new permanent constitution be enacted. When thirteen were arrested, their supporters gathered at Thammasat University. Although NSCT representatives commenced negotiations with the government on 13 October, tensions ran high when the protest moved from the Thammasat campus to Democracy Monument. Following King Bhumibol's intercession, the government met with student representatives and both sides agreed on the unconditional release of the thirteen who had been arrested and the enactment of a constitution within a year. However, this information was not immediately conveyed to protestors at the monument. Opinion was also divided among student representatives on the point of constitutional enactment taking a full year. When protestors eventually made their way home late at night, some were injured when stopped en route by the police. As news of these confrontations spread, clashes broke out in central Bangkok leading to a number of fatalities. With a state of emergency declared, King Bhumibol appeared on television at 7 pm on 14 October to appeal for a return to normal. Calm was eventually restored the following day with the announcement that interim Prime Minister Thanon had left the country (Tamada 2014: 241). Once the interim military government was gone, King Bhumibol stepped in to appoint Chief Justice of the Supreme Court and Dean of Thammasat University Faculty of Law Sanya Dharmasakti as prime minister. The king entrusted Sanya with enacting a new constitution and transitioning to civilian rule.

We might distil the four aspects of the student uprising as follows. Firstly, the duration of the protests was brief, lasting a mere ten days from 6 October 1973, when twenty students from Thammasat University began handing out leaflets in the university grounds calling on the Thai people to fight for their rights and freedom, until the situation normalized between 14 and 15 October. Secondly, the movement was led by students with the protests managed by the National Student Center of Thailand (NSCT; *Sunklang nisitnakusueksa haeng chat*). Thirdly, at their peak, protest numbers topped half a million with most participants either university or technical college students. Fourth and finally, there was immediate intervention by King Bhumibol once clashes with the police resulted in deaths (*Sarakhadi Future Magazine*, 1998: 22–51). Furthermore, many scholars observe that this unrest was a turning point that heightened the political influence of the king.

The Siamese Revolution of 1932 saw the king lose the right to absolute rule. Forced to accept a constitutional monarchy, King Prajadhipok (Rama VII) fled to England on the pretext of convalescing due to ill health. In 1935, in protest against the Phraya Phahon Phonphayuhasena administration, the king abdicated of his own volition. Although King Ananta (Rama VIII) was enthroned as his successor, he was still a minor, and because he was continuing his studies in Switzerland, the absence of a king was ongoing in Thailand. King Ananta returned to Thailand in 1945 but was found dead in June of the following year. This incident remains a mystery today with uncertainty surrounding who was responsible. The next in line was King Ananda's younger brother, King Bhumibol (Rama IX), who was also an adolescent at the time of succession and who immediately left for Switzerland to continue his schooling. Upon his return in 1952, Thailand had a resident king for the first time in twenty years. While there was no immediate surge in the popularity of the monarchy when King Bhumibol ascended the throne, royal intervention on 14 October 1973 into the student uprising mythologized the role of the king among many Thai people. Some were in awe of the fact that King Bhumibol had, according to the myth, driven Prime Minister Thanom's military autocratic faction overseas and quelled the violence that had erupted. There was a sense that, even in the face of violence, the solution to political difference lay in the 'virtue' (*barami*) of the monarch. This was one foundation supporting royal authority and the respect of the Thai people for King Bhumibol himself. Even from the mid-1970s, with the military involving itself in political matters, confidence in King Bhumibol based on this 'myth' endured.

The Bloody May Incident of 1992

There is a large body of scholarship in Thai and other languages on the Bloody May Incident of 1992. A key point examined is who played the major role in this tragedy (Ji 1997; Tamada 2001). In addition, protestor savagery is often expressed in the term 'mob' (Callahan 1998). While the media lauded 'the new highly educated middle classes who, with their mobile phones, pushed for democracy', this view has been questioned in terms of responsibility for the incident. Regarding protestor violence, understanding background events might clarify how clashes resulting in so much bloodshed and so many deaths could occur. I will consider that background in detail below.

I noted above how, at the time of the Bloody May Incident, protestors made two demands. These were: 1. that the 1991 coup d'état leaders relinquish their hold on power, and 2. that the undemocratic aspects of the 1991 Constitution be reformed. When an anti-Suchinda movement began, the media expected a repeat of October 1973. However, there were major differences in events leading up to the incident compared to those that led to the student unrest of October 1973. Firstly, the protests took place over a much longer timeframe. Approximately six weeks elapsed from the proclamation of Suchinda's appointment as prime minister on 7 April 1992 until King Bhumibol's mediation on the night of 20 May. If, in fact, we calculate the duration from the emergence in November the previous year of opposition to the draft of the 1991 Constitution, we can argue that the movement lasted for more than six months. The second point of difference is the very large number of protestors. At the time of the student uprising, there were also large numbers, with a peak gathering of 500,000 on the day before clashes with police. In terms of Bloody May, however, 100,000 had already attended a gathering convened on 20 April (*Sarakhadi Future Magazine*, 1998: 192). In addition, there were various events with ongoing numbers of 10–30,000 while, as the situation came to a climax, 300,000 protestors assembled during the afternoon to form a crowd that reached 500,000 by 7.30 at night (*Sarakhadi Future Magazine*, 1998: 222). Some news outlets, in fact, reported numbers of 1,000,000.[13]

The third point to consider is the large number of participant organizations involved. Unlike the 1973 student uprising which was a student-led movement centered on Thammasat University, the Bloody May protests involved civil society groups such as NGOs, students, ordinary citizens and opposition politicians. As a result, in contrast to the NSCT's central role in coordinating the 1973 protests, there was no specific party organizing the gatherings of May 1992. While there were ongoing meetings between NGOs, students and opposition politicians at Thammasat University, communication between these groups was not necessarily effective. This was especially the case after 9 May when Chamlong Srimuang assumed a leadership role and a kind of paralysis set in among the protest organization chain of command.[14] The fourth

---

13 Media outlets report hugely different numbers in terms of protestors involved in the 1973 student uprising and the 1992 Bloody May Incident. These figures often give a maximum of 500,000 for the former and 1,000,000 for the latter. However, since the latter was a protest movement that lasted longer, the total number of participants was definitely higher than the former.
14 Much existing research points out that, compared to the 1973 student movement that drove out the autocratic military regime of the time, the protest movement that culminated in the 1992 Bloody May Incident grew

point relates to the existence of a democratically elected lower house. The 1973 gatherings protested a military regime. This was in marked contrast to the events of Bloody May which occurred with a functioning lower house chosen at the March 1992 general election. It was these very lower house members, however, who nominated Suchinda as a non-elected prime minister. The 1991 Constitution included various undemocratic stipulations, and Suchinda's appointment had complied with provisions laid out in the constitution. When anti-Suchinda protests began, therefore, government politicians dismissed opposition involvement as resentment at 'not being part of the government' (*Sarakhadi Future Magazine*, 1998: 192).[15] The fifth point was protestor violence. Unlike the student uprising protests, which organizers took care to ensure were 'disciplined', protestor-initiated violence often erupted during Bloody May. There was, for example, the occupation of a fire and rescue station, the destruction of a firetruck and the destruction of police vehicles. In terms of this violence, it was observed that Chamlong, who by mid-May was inciting the protests, was a former member of the military with experience in psychological tactics against the masses (Callahan 1998: 68). Even after Chamlong's

---

in participant diversity from 1991 (Khien 1997; Callahan 1998). Examining key individuals involved in the protests confirms that this was a large-scale movement which included the Students Federation of Thailand, largely represented by Prinya Thaewanarumitkul who at the time was a student in the law faculty of Thammasat University, and activists from various NGOs. There were also large numbers of opposition politicians such as leader of the Palang Dharma Party Chamlong Srimuang and former politician Chalard Vorachart who began hunger strikes. The print press of the time repeatedly reported that, in addition to ordinary citizens, the protest movement included the first expression of politics outside parliament through the participation of opposition party identities. Suchinda also regarded the involvement of opposition members in the protest movement as an expression of non-parliamentary politics and was critical of the opposition's actions (*Sayam Rat*, 5 May 1992). The precise impact on democratization in Thailand of this new aspect of the movement must be the subject of a different study.

15 Student leader Prinya Thaewanarumitkul gave the names of Democrat Party members Chuan Leekpai and Abhisit Vejjajiva as politicians who repeatedly made appearances at the 1992 protests. However, he had few memories of speaking directly to either of them (personal interview, 13 June 2017). Abihisit was prime minister in May 2010 when close to 100 protestors were shot and killed in central Bangkok.

arrest on 18 May, however, violent protestor attacks continued. Points four and five above suggest that there is a certain ambiguity around notions of 'justice' in the context of Bloody May compared to the 1973 student uprising.

The final point to consider is the delay in intervention by King Bhumibol. Many in Thailand at the time, from university students to members of the general public, thought that King Bhumibol's late intervention was 'strangely curious'. There was a death toll during the initial clashes of 17 May, with many also losing their lives the following day. In marked difference to the less than one day taken for intervention to occur following the 1973 clashes between police and students, however, King Bhumibol did not summon Chamlong and Suchinda to mediation until the evening of 20 May. Furthermore, by announcing the resignation of Prime Minister Thanom who led the military administration in 1973, the king clearly indicated his own political position. During Bloody May, however, after merely observing to Suchinda and Chamlong that the situation was 'having a negative impact on the country's politics, economy and society', King Bhumibol instructed the pair to 'come together in mutual support to create a situation benefitting the people of the Thai nation' (*Sarakhadi Future Magazine*, 1998: 235).

In terms of the 'moral virtue' (*barami*) of the king, Thai scholarship on the Thai Constitution and politics highly commends King Bhumibol's mediation during Bloody May, assessing this as equivalent to the royal intervention in the 1973 student uprising. When we compare these 'interventions', however, it becomes clear that quite different circumstances prevailed. The 'myth' that was constructed during the student uprisings seemed to face a crisis during the incident of 1992.

The 2006 anti-Thaksin movement

The third example is the anti-Thaksin movement which ultimately resulted in the 2006 coup d'état. Although the popularity of the Thaksin administration among the people remained as high as when it first assumed power in 2001, agitation by an anti-Thaksin movement began prior to the February 2005 general election. While the 1992 anti-

Suchinda demonstrations protested an administration headed by a non-elected prime minister, the anti-Thaksin movement was opposed to a leader who had assumed power after an overwhelming electoral victory. It will be useful to consider the differences between these movements.

Two points stand out when comparing the 2006 anti-Thaksin campaign with previous mass protests in Thailand: the diversity among participants and the high level of violence displayed. We could also add the large numbers of protestors in provincial cities and the extended period of time involved. As noted above, the catalyst for the formation of the movement was the crackdown on drugs in the country's south where, in spite of strong voter support generally, this was regarded as a huge human rights violation. The strong anger voiced by both residents of Thailand's southern regions and human rights activists eventually expanded to become a huge anti-Thaksin movement as NGOs, too, joined the campaign. In January 2005, a push began in many regional cities to prevent the Thai Rak Thai Party from taking control of the parliament once more. Those involved included human rights activists, students, workers and a variety of NGOs.

While the Thai Rak Thai Party enjoyed a sweeping victory in the February 2005 elections, even in early 2006 the anti-Thaksin groundswell showed no sign of subsiding. In January 2006, an NGO that monitored corruption announced the construction of a website exposing government fraud and dishonesty. The group told the media that former bureaucrats supporting the site belonged to a network of more than 3,000 former and present bureaucrats who, it was reported, had uncovered historically unprecedented levels of corruption by the Thaksin administration. Site operation was shared by Democrat Party members of parliament, members of the upper house, former Thai Board of Audit members, a former head of the secretariat to the National Counter-Corruption Commission and university teaching staff. Many politicians and intellectuals who were former bureaucrats were also involved. In January 2006, the anti-Thaksin movement turned to insurgency, with protestors storming the prime minister's office in the middle of the month. A previous upper house member and Anek Laothamatas, a previous lower house member known as a prominent political researcher, were indicted on charges by the police as the protest leaders. The former demanded the resignation of Thaksin for disrespecting the king.

Thaksin's response was to dissolve the lower house and declare a general election for 2 April. The situation nevertheless became precarious through sabotage by anti-Thaksin forces and a boycott by the opposition parties. When on 19 September 2006 the military staged the first coup d'état in approximately fifteen years, the anti-Thaksin movement momentarily came to an end. The movement had operated for an extended period over one year and nine months from January 2005 until September 2006. Participants were extremely diverse and featured NGOs, students and opposition party politicians, in addition to industrialists, former bureaucrats and scholars. Furthermore, even prior to clashes with the police and the military, protestors engaged in a level of violence, such as storming the prime minister's office, previously unseen in Thailand.[16]

Differences also included demands made by the anti-Thaksin movement. In 1973, students campaigned for early enactment of a permanent constitution and the unconditional release of thirteen students who had been interned. The demands of Bloody May participants were revisions to the 1991 Constitution to remove the possibility of appointing a non-elected prime minister and the resignation of Prime Minister Suchinda. The anti-Thaksin movement, in contrast, called for Thaksin's resignation and for revisions to the 1997 Constitution, the provisions of which (to be examined in Chapter 4) were seen as a factor in the huge election victory of the Thai Rak Thai Party. While the aim of constitutional reform was shared with the 1992 Bloody May Incident protestors, as is clear from Sondhi's commentary, the demand to force Thaksin's resignation was especially strong. A further important point is that, while Suchinda faced charges of democratic illegitimacy for becoming prime minister without a

---

16 The People's Alliance for Democracy (PAD), the focus of the anti-Thaksin movement, was a coalition of diverse groups. While there were five central leaders, there was a general sense of distance between each group and its leadership, with significant turnover in participating members (Sinpeng 2021: 108–113).

popular vote, Thaksin was a democratically elected prime minister chosen by an authentic vote of the people. In contrast to both the student movement, which opposed a military regime, and the Bloody May gatherings, which protested a prime minister not elected by the people, the anti-Thaksin movement railed against the popularly elected leader of the land.

The most significant difference, however, was the absence of intervention by King Bhumibol. This is in spite of the fact that the royal 'myth' remained active among the Thai people. The general election scheduled for 2 April 2006 was opposed by the anti-Thaksin movement including opposition parties who expected to lose. Opposition forces such as the Democrat Party announced an election boycott. Furthermore, anti-Thaksin forces proposed the 'appointment of an interim government by the king'. Although this was opposed by serving judiciary, legal scholars and activists, the idea repeatedly surfaced in anti-Thaksin discourse. In other words, those opposed to Thaksin constructed themselves in terms of both the students of 1973 and the protestors of Bloody May 1992 by seeking King Bhumibol's intervention.

On this occasion, however, King Bhumibol's response was quite different. In a 'Royal Statement' released on 3 February 2006, the day before Sondhi planned a large-scale protest, King Bhumibol declared as follows: 'Justice is the very key to harmony and happiness and is the conduct of that which is right and proper. Protecting justice is the duty of the judiciary and, when that occurs, peace will surely lie across the land'. Furthermore, at an administration of oath ceremony held on 25 April for judges of the supreme and administrative courts, the king stated that, while one-party control was undemocratic, a monarch could not intervene in political matters. He thereupon directed that: 'The Supreme Court will take the lead in the resolution of political problems'. Responding to this statement, the Supreme Court, Supreme Administrative Court and Constitutional Court convened a joint sitting that lasted for eleven hours. Eventually, the Constitutional Court handed down a ruling declaring the 2 April general election invalid. As a result, a general election was to be conducted once more from scratch (Toyama 2018: 61–75). Thus, while King Bhumibol may have issued a directive to the courts, he did not intervene directly to mediate as he had at the time of the 1973 student uprising or at the time of the 1992 Bloody May Incident.

We might also consider differences in media reports. As previously noted, the Bloody May Incident emphasized the importance of democratic legitimacy. However, a comparison of the press coverage of this event and the September 2006 coup d'état confirms huge differences in both media reports and arguments presented by intellectuals. In commentary in *Matichon*, published in February 2006 as the anti-Thaksin movement gathered momentum, Professor Wuttisak, the Dean of the Political Science Faculty at Ramkhamhaeng University, supported calls for Thaksin's resignation. He noted that the current system of democracy made it difficult to oust a leader (prime minister) and lamented that there had been no previous successful removal of a Thai leader without violence (*Matichon*, 16 February 2006). A column published in the same newspaper analyzed the clashes between the Thaksin administration and the protesting masses as between 'competency', that is the specialist ability to govern by setting goals, and the 'dishonesty' and 'corruption' that seized authority through high level power and force. The current clashes were constructed as the Thai people confronting the question of which to choose. There were also claims of pressure from elements arguing that those supporting the Thaksin administration chose 'competence', while those opposed chose 'dishonesty' and 'corruption' (*Matichon*, 30 April 2006).

News reports that followed the coup are also significant. A column in the 23 September 2006 edition of *Matichon* claimed that 'The coup d'état has decisively wiped-out the Thaksin system [...]'. Failing to mention that the military itself had brought down a democratically elected government, the column presented the September 2006 coup as having demolished the 'Thaksin system' (*Rabop Thaksin*) (*Matichon*, 23 September 2006). Although a popularly elected administration had been toppled by a coup, reporting on the interim constitution promulgated after that event was largely favorable, with one-sided commentary making claims such as 'Scholars have judged any autocratic tint [...] as limited'. While the 1992 movement profiled democratic legitimacy, an emphasis in 2006 on 'integrity' led to general acceptance of the coup.

When we compare the anti-Thaksin movement to the 1992 Bloody May Incident, it is apparent that the media, intellectuals and even some ordinary people supported the shift in points of political dispute that operated.[17]

There were many changes to the constitutions of Thailand arising from the 1990s political reform movement. Both the 1997 and 2007 constitutions were presented in the name of constitutionalism as necessary to fight corruption and achieve good governance. Post-2006, however, this led to the demise of democratically elected administrations through rulings by the courts.

Some scholarship assesses the 1997 and 2007 constitutions positively. Harding and Leyland (2011), for example, argue that the 1997 Constitution was the most democratic ever adopted in Thailand, declaring that the document bestowed much greater authority on the Thai people than any experienced in the past. As examples, they note that over 50,000 voters were given the right to submit draft laws to the parliament and that over 10,000 voters were given the right to demand the impeachment of those working in politics. They also refer to the devolution of authority to regions and the expansion and enhancement of fundamental rights. The 2007 Constitution made changes to stipulations regarding, for example, the parliament, the upper house, the election system, and the Constitutional Court. These were presented in terms of preventing any type of future political intervention, such as that practiced by Thaksin, into those institutions. As points for commendation in both the 1997 and 2007 constitutions, furthermore, Harding and Leyland pointed to stipulations that enhanced human rights and introduced systems of corruption control. These scholars ultimately deliver a very favorable evaluation of progress in Thailand over the past twenty years in terms of an effective constitutional order (Harding and Leyland 2011: 18–26, 256–257).

---

17 A similar trend emerged even in interviews conducted by the author. Pramot Piphatana, a professor at Rangsit University, stated as follows: 'Initially I supported Thaksin because I believed he was extremely talented. However, when a multitude of problems related to corruption arose, I came to oppose his views because I thought that he was no longer acting for the good of Thailand. There is no change in my position today' (interview conducted by the author on 26 March 2017).

In contrast, Worachet, a Thammasat University scholar of public law, published material after the 2006 coup d'état expressing concern that the law had become a tool of politics. He noted the inadequacy of the system of monitoring independent agencies and the inappropriateness of some court rulings from a legal studies point of view (Worachet 2015). While Worachet made strong and repeated criticism of both constitutions, he had particular concerns about the 2007 document. He pointed out that the system blueprint of the Constitutional Court and independent agencies in Thailand contradicted what should be a fundamental principle of the division of powers. Noting that Thailand possibly operated the largest number of independent agencies based on any constitution in the world, he argued that, with the exception of the Election Commission, these should either be dissolved or merged. On the other hand, he saw no fundamental problem with constitutional stipulations on rights and freedoms, arguing that any problem that did exist in these respects lay in the system blueprint of the machinery of state (Worachet 2009: 87–116, 162–169). Other critics of the public law aspects of the Thai Constitutional Court and independent agencies included Piyabutr and Poonthep, also on the staff of Thammasat University (Piyabutr 2016; Poonthep 2016).

The institutional design of the constitution since the 1990s has been criticized extensively. The forces that promoted the political reform movement included not only technocrats and intellectuals, but also the Bangkok capitalists, who disliked the involvement of local businessmen and members of the House of Representatives with their support in the process of formulating economic policy (Connors 2002: 46). Activists and NGOs who tried to reflect grassroots voices in national politics were also often mentioned. Furthermore, McCargo's discussion of the political reform movement in the previous chapter notes concerns felt by Prawase Wasi, King Bhumibol's court physician, that a violent crisis would arise once the king's reign came to an end and attempts to prevent anarchy would be needed before it occurred. McCargo further argues that all political reform discourse in Thailand can be read as designed by conservatives (or those connected to the monarchy) to protect against social unrest. He interprets the central objective of such discourse as to both stabilize the political system and protect the monarchy from violent instability (McCargo 1998: 97–98). The preparatory process for the enactment of a new constitution supports McCargo's assertions. In comprehensively revising the 1991 Constitution and enacting a new document, the government of the time began with the amendment of Section 211. There were four main revisions proposed to Section 211 as presented by the government to the parliament on 17 May 1996: 1. establishing a Constitution Drafting Assembly comprised of specialists and scholars, 2. strengthening the stability and efficiency of politics, 3. conducting a vote of the people to seek approval for the draft of a new constitution, and 4. retaining and adhering to a democratic regime of government with the king as head of state (Tamada 2003: 166–167).

As outlined in this chapter, changes in the political system and constitutional reforms have been accompanied by changes in the scale and violence of mass demonstrations and protests since the 1970s. Research by McCargo also highlights how 'crisis' and 'social unrest' were the keys that encouraged political reform. In this context, there is clearly value in closely investigating the relationship between the emergence of the 1990s political reform movement and the heightened violence of mass protests. The chapter that follows draws on interviews with law scholars who were involved in committees charged with constitutional drafts to consider the nature of the constitutionalism, promoted by Amon, that drove the political reform movement in Thailand. It also considers why there was a perceived need to introduce constitutionalism into Thailand in the drafts of the 1997 and 2007 constitutions.

2 | Revisiting the Political Reform Movement: What Is Thai 'Constitutionalism'?

Consitutionalism: Amon Chantharasombun's version

When considering the aim of the political reform movement in Thailand, it is useful to step back from abstract notions of cleaning up politics to determine instead the concrete objectives and design blueprint proposed. As previously noted, one of the leading ideological leaders of Thai political reform was the prominent jurist, Amon Chantharasombun. While Amon's thought does not fully explain every aspect of the movement, such as the details of the system blueprint offered in the 1997 Constitution, familiarity with this scholar's argument is essential to understand the details of the two constitutions introduced since the 1990s, namely those of 1997 and 2007. By scrutinizing Amon's position, this chapter will seek to uncover and elucidate Thailand's political reform goals.

The direct catalyst for political reform was the 1992 'Bloody May' Incident. Although the non-elected Prime Minister Suchinda stepped down following this tragedy, there was still deep dissatisfaction among people because the lower house, elected just two months earlier in March of the same year, was not dissolved immediately and little change was evident, furthermore, in the line-up of members of parliament returned to office in the follow-up election held several months later in September.[1] According to Amon, the situation in rural areas, which accounted for more than half the country, including the ignorance of rural voters and the presence of vote brokers (*hua khanaen*), exercised a negative influence over Thai politics as a whole (Amon 1994a: 52).

---

1 After Suchinda left office, the five-party government tried to form a new cabinet. While then President of the Lower House Arthit recommended Somboon, the leader of the Chart Thai Party, for the role, he withdrew support after conferring with the Privy Council. With most parliament members reluctant to undergo an election, the media, business world and pro-democracy groups increasingly called for an election to be held. To defuse this fraught situation, Arthit recommended Anand as the prime minister in accordance with the desire of the king (Murray 1996: 183–187).

The problem lay in the failure to dissolve the parliament according to the will of the people – or, to be more precise, of Bangkok intellectuals. Furthermore, representatives towards whom these intellectuals were hostile were re-elected. At the end of the day, the driving force creating momentum for political reform was the desire of intellectuals to control both the parliament and the election process.[2]

The power to dissolve the lower house

Following the 1992 Bloody May Incident, the chief concern of intellectuals such as Amon was the dissolution of the parliament. According to Amon, general discord around the issue arose at that time. Declaring that 'The ruling parties in the Suchinda administration must take responsibility for the events of Bloody May', intellectuals and the business sector called for a follow-up election. They argued that 'Given the current situation, the parliament should be dissolved, and an election held to allow the people to decide the country's future direction'. Politicians and political parties, on the other hand, asserted as follows: 'It is inappropriate to dissolve the parliament [because there was an election in March that year]. The person who receives the most votes in the parliament should be nominated as prime minister and fulfil their responsibility by forming a cabinet. This is democracy' (Amon 1994b: 41). Opposition to the dissolution of parliament came from both government and opposition members of parliament.

Although intellectuals called for dissolution of the parliament (or the house of representatives), that action could not be forced by an external body. This led to debate over who, in fact, held such power. Amon argued that, historically, only the king held the right to decree the parliament's dissolution. That was because in the operation of

---

2   While not comprehensively discussed in this book, there are clear divisions in Thailand between the center and the regions and between Bangkok and rural areas. Politically, also, the interest groups that have exerted ongoing control are centered on Bangkok. These include the Royal House, bureaucrats and the military (Toyama et al., eds., 2018: 43–46). However, the majority of the population came from regional areas, particularly the impoverished northeast. Since the basis of parliamentary democracy is the number of political representatives, democratization saw greater influence flow to politicians from regional electorates.

the very first parliamentary system in Thailand, the king was the head of state with administrative powers. Amon further asserted that appointment of the cabinet by the king and election of house members by the people created a system of mutual checks. Nevertheless, in terms of whether the king or the prime minister had the contemporary authority to dissolve the parliament, Amon declared that it was possible for both (Amon 1994b: 45). He further asserted that 'Since it is desirable that a monarch's powers differ from country to country, how the Thai monarch exercises power is solely an issue for Thailand. The Thai Constitution devotes successive sections to the royal prerogative (*Praratcha-amnat*). The neutral authority exercised by the king as head of state was necessary in terms of striking a balance with respect to the majority faction in the parliament' (Amon 1994b: 47). While we might read this as Amon's attempt to determine a legal basis for dissolving the parliament, he was certainly uneasy about dissolution by the members themselves. From this perspective, he argued that members dissolving the parliament could be a measure to change the combination of the majority faction group involved in the establishment of a coalition government (Amon 1994a: 71). That point was also related to Amon's dissatisfaction with the result of the election that had been conducted following a dissolution of the parliament.

Amon expected that there would be a dramatic change in lower house membership when representatives from rural electorates who had been members of the Suchinda Cabinet at the time of the Bloody May Incident lost their seats in the September 1992 election. This, however, was a miscalculation by the intellectual camp. What the people in fact called for was procedural legitimacy based on democracy, which 1. opposed a continuation of the political power of the military that had staged the coup d'état, and 2. upheld the selection of the prime minister by members of parliament voted for by the people. Accordingly, intellectuals such as Amon were dissatisfied with the outcome of the September 1992 election.[3]

---

3 In the September election, 64% of the successful candidates were members who were re-elected.

Regarding the result of the election, Amon asserted that whether 'bad politicians' could be returned to the parliament or not depended on rural voters who made up the majority of those with voting rights in Thailand. His post-September 1992 analysis proceeded as follows. The citizens of Thailand could be divided into two groups. The first had a stable way of life and voted according to free will. The second, from the regions and countryside, were constrained by social circumstances when voting. Since this group felt a strong sense of obligation towards regional voter brokers, their votes were easily bought. Such voters had elected many current parliament members (Amon 1994b: 48–49). For that reason, Amon declared, no matter how many times an election was held, the outcome would be the same. He accordingly concluded that vote-buying in the rural areas was the main crime that obstructed the entry of people of 'ability' and 'virtue' into the political world. The strong opposition to dissolution among parliament members, he reasoned, was because they had spent money buying votes. Amon further argued that 'parliamentary dictatorship' itself was the problem that had led to both an intensification of election campaigning and the concentration of political power in the hands of politicians. This argument profiles a uniquely Thai understanding of parliamentary democracy, a point examined below.

Amon and the meanings of 'parliamentary dictatorship' and 'constitutionalism'

Since Amon repeatedly uses the term, 'parliamentary dictatorship' (*phadetkan thang ratthasapa*) when critiquing parliamentary democracy, we might consider the meaning he gave to it. We should also consider what was meant by the 'constitutionalism' he proposed as a strategy to address Thailand's problems. This section will examine Amon's interpretation of these concepts.

Amon himself did not coin the term 'parliamentary dictatorship'. Among the five reasons for initiating the 1991 coup d'état as issued by the coup group in 'Revolutionary Proclamation No. 1', the third was parliamentary dictatorship. This was the term used by the military when critiquing government by popular election. Since Amon, however, theorized the term in detail, we might consider precisely the type of parliamentary dictatorship that this scholar had in mind.

Amon compared and contrasted three different political systems of state. The first was the presidential system, the second the single party system and the third the parliamentary system of government. He explained that the presidential system operates through a single political leader as determined by those who draft a constitution, the single party system operates through governance by an elite, and the parliamentary system operates through the members of a parliament whom the voters elect. Although he explained that, currently, many advanced nations favor parliamentary democracy,[4] he critiqued this system as the most problematic. In particular, he noted two weak points, namely a lack of clear leadership and a consequent jostling for power (Amon 1994a: 20).

Amon's argument began with the observation that the initial stages of a parliamentary system of governance were dualist, comprised of the two authorities of a cabinet appointed by a monarch and a parliament elected by the people. As the power of the king diminishes, however, the system shifts towards monism whereby a majority political party forms government. In a monist administration, the same group forms the cabinet (the administrative power) and the parliament (the legislative power). The negative outcome, Amon concluded, was that power checks and balances fail to function. Thus, an autocratic parliament dominated by a majority political party emerged.

Any ideal that assumed an electorate able to choose 'good people' (*khon di*) of benevolence and virtue willing to devote themselves to a higher cause was absent from Amon's interpretation. Nor did he believe that the representatives of the people would select capable people as ministers. Matters before a parliament are determined by majority decision, with a government also dependent on an election result. To Amon, this made the exercise of leadership impossible (Amon

---

4   Among the thirty-four member countries of the OECD, twenty-two have a president. In many cases, however, this role is merely ceremonial. Accordingly, four have actual presidential systems, one has a half-presidential system, and twenty-nine have parliamentary democracies.

1994a: 25). We can conclude that, for Amon, parliamentary dictatorship refers to the fact that majority parties, which receive many votes in an election, form a government. These, however, are the natural characteristics of a parliamentary system of government. By limiting his understanding of such an arrangement to its being 'authoritarian', Amon demonstrates a potent lack of trust in politicians and those who hold power. While democracy is fundamentally a system based on majority decision-making, the term 'parliamentary dictatorship' is a form of expression that denies the democratic processes on which majority decision-making is based.

The solution to the problem of parliamentary dictatorship, Amon argued, was constitutionalism. This was a concept that regulated the power of a parliament through a constitution involving a system of checks and balances that separated the three arms of legislative, executive and judicial powers. When the end of the Cold War saw democratization become widespread across many countries, constitutionalism also expanded.[5] Its introduction in Thailand was accepted as progressing in accordance with global trends. Was such an interpretation nevertheless valid in the Thai case? Amon's pitch for political reform based on constitutionalism began with a proposal made at the 'Constitution: Legal Structure and Apparatus' seminar held by the Policy Research Institute (*Sathaban nayobai sueksa*) at the Asia Hotel in Bangkok. The institute proposed a project entitled 'Research into Constitutional Reform in Thailand' (*Kansueksa phuea kanpatirup ratthathammanun samrap prathet thai*) and appointed Amon as project committee chair. In June 1995, the project hosted a political reform seminar that saw growing interest in reform by the media and also by politicians such as Prime Minister Banharn and his ministers. That was the beginning of a reform movement with constitutional revision as its fundamental goal (Thiraphat 2010: 217–220).

---

5 As noted in the Introduction, constitutionalism originally developed as a means of limiting the sovereignty of an absolute monarch and protecting individual rights and freedoms. The Constitution of the United States of America was the first to clearly espouse a constitutionalism that accorded with a constitutional draft. When the Cold War ended and many countries democratized, they made contemporary revisions that once again turned the focus to constitutionalism.

Amon advocated a very specific kind of constitutionalism. He argued that political reform required the enactment of a constitution that was based on constitutionalism. This, he explained, would 'lay down a process that would completely eliminate weaknesses arising from the dishonesty and illegal activities, including profit seeking, of politicians and various interest groups. Such an approach ensured that, once a constitution was drafted, a policy position was put in place to guide the formation of a political system and a country's governance apparatus' (Amon 1994a: 25). For Amon, the constitution operating at that time – prior to 1997 – as the highest law in Thailand was not grounded in constitutionalism. As a result, reform was required.

In relation to democracy and the constitution, Amon declared as follows:

> For elected politicians, drafting a constitution that accords with democracy is likely to imply conferring supreme authority on the lower house, having a prime minister chosen from the lower house and having the president of the lower house appoint the president of the parliament. There is no certainty, however, that others would agree with these politicians' ideas. (Amon 1994a: 33)

In the context of drafting a constitution based on constitutionalism, Amon considered the impact of ideas raised during recent discussion. These ideas included the relationship between democracy and elections, the lower house as comprised of representatives of the people, the ceding of high authority to the lower house such as the right to conduct constitutional reform or enact legislation, and only lower house members having the right to choose the prime minister (Amon 1994a: 37). While he found the principle of democracy requiring elections to be correct, he rejected the notion that the lower house represented the people. He argued that, although this was often assumed, individual lower house members were in reality elected by the people of their own electorates and not by the whole country. On conferring high authority on the lower house, Amon found this was a conclusion drawn from the assumption that the lower house represented the people. This, however, was not the case so that what benefited an individual politician did not benefit the people as a whole. Amon accordingly concluded that the exercise of power by lower house members was not generally used to benefit the people. He further expressed the view that a constitution based on policies grounded in constitutionalism would determine the various measures and agencies necessary to monitor and regulate the political activities and use of power by the lower house and the cabinet to realize benefits for the whole nation. The provisions of such a constitution would be the supreme law of the land (Amon 1994a: 38).

Amon proposed three factors as necessary for constitutional reform, namely, 1. reducing vote-buying, 2. creating pathways for able people and those with moral fiber to participate in the political world, and 3. auditing the illegal exercise of power by politicians (Amon 1994a: 30). He specifically proposed four concrete initiatives: 1. a parliamentary system with a strong prime minister (something similar to a semi-presidential system), 2. a system of impeachment, 3. a body to oversee the exercise of power by politicians and civil servants, and 4. a legislative framework enabling the enactment of important laws related to the provisions of the constitution – the so-called 'organic laws' (Amon 1994b: 8). He further argued the necessity of a constitutional court. On the other hand, Amon asserted that even changes to the election laws would be ineffective in reforming elections and that only an audit of the illegal exercise of power would address the problem of vote-buying (Amon 1994b: 8–16). We can thus conclude that Amon's constitutionalism sought to curtail not only the illegal exercise of power by politicians at the national level, but also to regulate voting behavior and the qualities of those chosen by election for political office. We might in fact conclude that Amon supported intervention in the outcome of elections.

Amon's constitutionalism and the three powers

Having flagged the aims outlined above with respect to the three powers that are central to national governance, what problems did Amon foresee and what solutions did he offer? We will examine these matters individually below.

Legislative power

To Amon, vote-buying in elections was the root of manifold evils. Particularly virulent in this respect was members of the lower house elected to represent a provincial electorate. Amon was frustrated at the large population numbers in the provinces where vote-buying was rampant.[6] He was also highly critical of political parties and saw the intensification of electoral wars as a function of the duties of party members as stipulated in the 1978 and 1991 constitutions. To Amon, these duties as outlined in the 1978 Constitution contributed to the power monopolies of political parties. This, he asserted, was a factor in the emergence of a system that lacked a means to balance the exercise of power by political parties which in turn created the current flawed election system. As a result, people with moral fiber had no interest in participating in election campaigns (Amon 1994b: 50–52). Amon argued for a ban on bad politicians returning for a second parliamentary term and proposed a number of strategies to achieve this end. These included restrictions on candidate campaign activities, the establishment of a central body to oversee elections (the Election Commission), a strengthening of the law, and the regulation of political party funds (Amon 1994c: 6).

Administrative power

Amon believed that political reform grounded in constitutionalism required a strong prime minister with the ability to lead. His ideal leader (prime minister) was a person with a national profile and a long-term vision prioritizing the country's good. Rather than bulwarking the 'independence of the position within the parliamentary system itself', Amon argued for the prime minister's standing and power to be strengthened 'as a means of opposing the decisions of the majority party to which he himself was attached' (Amon 1994b: 9). We might deduce from Amon's account of a presidential system as 'control by a

---

6 The distribution of the 375 available seats according to regions in the 2011 Lower House elections saw the central region including Bangkok gain ninety-eight, the northern region seventy-eight, the north-east 126, the east twenty-seven, and the south fifty-three. The most seats were held by the north-east which had the largest population.

leader' and the one-party system as 'control by an elite' that his ideal governance model was control from the top by a strong leader or elite group. It is worth pointing out once more that what Amon criticized most was the simultaneous control of the administrative – or executive – and legislative arms of government by the majority political parties. This, he argued, was parliamentary dictatorship. He essentially planned to bring this under control through separating the prime minister (executive or administrative power) from the lower house (legislative power) and ensuring that the executive power of an extremely strong prime minister had the capacity to keep the lower house's legislative authority in check. Thus, rather than an entity that promoted policies based on the will of the people, Amon regarded a strong prime minister as playing the role of an opposing force that checked the power of the majority.

Judicial power

In Amon's model, the Constitutional Court and various independent agencies were expected to play a crucial role in monitoring the exercise of power at the national level. Although a constitutional review committee existed in Thailand at the time that Amon was writing, it in reality barely functioned. Amon therefore advocated for improvements in areas such as personnel structures, legal procedures and the organization of the justices of the bench in order to heighten specialization (Amon 1994b: 17). As a means of curtailing the power of the state, he proposed four bodies as agencies performing quasi-legal functions: a board of audit (*sathaban kiaokap kantruatgoenphendin*), a council of state, a Counter Corruption Commission (*khanakanmakan po po po*) and a constitutional court. In addition, he referred to the need for a civil service commission and an ombudsman. With regard to the organic laws – laws deriving from the provisions of the constitution – that would determine the specifics of each agency, he emphasized the necessity of clearly determining review methods and structures, the characteristics and specialized knowledge required by candidates being considered for agency appointment, the administrative authority of each agency, the stipulations necessary to guarantee independence or semi-independence and a process of auditing the exercise of power of each agency member to permit the expeditious performance of agency functions (Amon 1994b: 18). He stressed the necessity of clearly determining both the audit processes and organization of each agency (Amon 1994b: 18).

Each of Amon's proposals was reflected in the 1997 Constitution. Furthermore, the strong prime minister appeared in the form of Thaksin Shinawatra, while the creation of an election commission, a constitutional court and an upper house introduced the type of structure advocated by Amon to monitor state power. Nevertheless, rather than the mutual checks and balances necessary for the independent operation of each of the three powers, there was a strong sense that the administrative or executive arm together with the judiciary dominated the legislative arm. While cabinet government assumed control by a majority, an extremely ingenious structure emerged in which the administrative and judicial powers worked in opposition to the majority group in the lower house.

There is a further point of note in Amon's thinking. This was his interpretation of democracy. Amon believed that the biggest issue in Thai politics was corruption among politicians. For this reason, he was extremely cool toward the 1991 constitutional reforms, implemented in 1992, which determined that the 'prime minister be a member of the lower house'. While this was a significant innovation from the perspective of democracy, Amon declared that it 'was not an important element in a constitution for a parliamentary system based on constitutionalism' (Amon 1994a: 76). It was more important, Amon believed, to stamp out corruption rather than to establish a system of political power based on the will of the people. In this sense, progressing democracy was not an objective of Amon's 'constitutionalism'.[7] We must keep this crucial fact in mind when trying to understand the systems established by the 1997 and 2007 constitutions.

---

7   Amon was not the only commentator with such a cool stance towards democracy. Khien also argued against the necessity for haste in the democratic election of the prime minister. In addition, while some advocated for the insertion of stipulations forbidding a coup d'état at the time of the drafting of the 1991 Constitution, Khien argued that this was unnecessary (Khien 1997).

Chapter 1 noted how, as the political role of the courts became more prominent, there were debates concerning the nature of constitutionalism. Constitutionalism can take a legalistic form which, in contrast to democratic majority decision-making, emphasizes enforcing limitations, or it can emphasize democratic political processes. Amon appeared to favor legalistic constitutionalism, while nevertheless critiquing as 'parliamentary dictatorship' the same entity holding both administrative governance and legislative powers. He also accorded greater value to a one-party system of government than to government by a parliamentary assembly. His negative view of a constitution calling for a member of the lower house to be prime minister differed from the usual critiques of constitutionalism and can be seen as an example of Amon's unique train of thought.

Debate in Thailand concerning a new constitution occurred against the background of Amon's thought. In 1995, the Democracy Development Committee published a draft constitution after which a consultative process was held through the 1997 Constitution Drafting Assembly and Drafting Committee. As a result, the 1997 Constitution came into being. Eventually, the 1997 Constitution was repealed with the staging of the 2006 coup d'état. After deliberation by the 2007 Constitution Drafting Assembly and Drafting Committee, a revised 2007 document came into operation. In the sections that follow, I consider the nature of the debate and consultative processes that occurred during these assembly and committee meetings with a view to clearly establishing the aims of both constitutions.

The conception of the Democracy Development Committee

With Prawase Wasi playing a central role, the Democracy Development Committee (*khanakammakan phattana prachathipatai*) released its proposals in the form of a booklet entitled 'Proposal for a Conceptual Framework for Political Reform in Thailand'. In addition to this central document, which brought together the overall elements of political reform, there were an additional fifteen booklets organized by themes. In this section, I will discuss selected elements of the proposal with a focus also on those booklets that addressed key concepts for democratization.

General argument

We will first consider the booklet mentioned above. While the political reform movement in 1990s Thailand sought comprehensive and far-reaching reforms to the national system, we might consider which were regarded as most important. Chapter 1 of the booklet enumerated the strong and weak points of Thai democracy in comparison to other countries and stated the group's commitment to maintaining strong points while eliminating the weak. Included as favorable elements of the Thai political, economic and social system were the presence of the monarchy, the uniformity of the Thai people, Buddhism as a foundation for democracy, and a classless society. Weak points encompassed a failure to monitor and control corruption, vote-buying at election time, the influence of capital on political parties, a distrust among the middle classes of political parties, the concentration of an excess of power in the hands of civil servants and inadequate participation by the people in lawmaking. It was pointed out that these weaknesses compromised the legitimacy and efficiency of the political system and resulted, for example, in non-democratic political parties being controlled by small groups of people, inadequate checks and balances operating between the administrative and legislative powers of government, and weak prime ministerial leadership.

Given the above, we might articulate the meaning and objectives of the political reform movement as: 1. revising the entire political system; 2. monitoring and controlling corruption to ensure politicians act in an honest and upright manner in order to have real impact when problem-solving, for example, the need to guarantee the people's human rights; 3. drafting a new constitution and organic laws (laws deriving from the provisions of the constitution); and 4. steadfastly maintaining the democratic regime of government with the king as head of state. Achieving these objectives was intended to ensure the implementation of political reform through a rationalized parliamentary system.

Summarizing the contents of the book's first chapter reveals the objectives of political reform as eliminating political corruption and furthering the protection of the human rights of the people by enacting a new constitution and reforming the national system. While no policy mechanism to convert these abstract notions into concrete action was provided in this section, Chapter 2 clearly articulated explicit policy reform. The chapter's opening section emphasized the importance of the consonance of all members of society in order to progress political reform (Khanakammakan phattana prachathipatai 1995: 30). The term 'consonance' (*samakkisamachan*) was a keyword that permeated the entire political reform proposal.

According to the booklet, analysis of the constitution should focus on three themes. These were 1. matters concerning the monarchy, 2. matters concerning rights, freedom and agencies investigating state power in accordance with the constitution, and 3. matters concerning the cabinet and the parliament. The first point – maintaining the democratic regime of government with the king as head of state – should be maintained and constitutional articles related to the monarchy should be difficult to be changed in order to bring stability to the monarchy. The second point related to the establishment of institutions such as independent agencies designed to ensure that individuals involved in politics were honest and upright. This section also proposed the introduction of a system of impeachment in cases of corruption, together with the suggestion that limits be placed on the civil liberties based on the constitution of those engaging in anti-religious, anti-monarchy or anti-constitutional acts. It was recommended that cases against those so accused be lodged with the Constitutional Court.

The most concrete recommendations, however, appeared in the third point in which specific issues related to the cabinet and the parliament were detailed. The matters canvassed very closely resembled the problems raised by Amon concerning 'constitutionalism' in that they related to the sense of impending crisis that a system, which lacked the mutual check function between the cabinet and the parliament, could facilitate the degeneration of politics into a dictatorship by majority. The example provided in the booklet of such governance was Nazi Germany under the Weimar Constitution or the Constitution of the German Reich. And, as a measure to guard against autocracy, reference was made to provisions in postwar Germany's Fundamental Law which prohibited the implementation of constitutional freedom and rights in a way that undermined democracy, and which provided for the dissolution of a political party engaging in activities that were contrary to democratic processes. Reference was also made to the fact that, in France, members of the National Assembly who accept a ministerial appointment forfeit their right to assembly membership (Khanakammakan phattana prachathipatai 1995: 45–51).

Regarding the parliament, facilitating participation of various interest groups across the whole of society was proposed to ensure the effective operation of parliamentary processes. Both tricameral and bicameral systems were discussed, however the committee highly recommended the tricameral option. The first of these three houses was to be a lower house comprised of members chosen by the people through an electoral process. Its duty would be to comply with the desires of the people. The main functions of this lower house were to be enacting legislation, overseeing the operation of the government by arguing no-confidence motions, and making appointments to independent agencies created according to the provisions of the constitution (such as the Constitutional Judges Committee, the Anti-Corruption Agency and the Ombudsman). House members had a duty to affiliate with a political party. The second would be similar to an upper house and referred to as the House of the Sages. Its main duties were to be law-making in addition to approving important matters such as the succession of the monarchy and constitutional reform. Members of this house could not accept ministerial positions and were largely to concentrate on law-making. Members required university graduation or higher to qualify, and while they were to be elected through a proportional representation system across the country, they were prohibited from political party membership. The third was to be an advisory house. Its role was to be advising the government and its main duties were to be approving important matters such as the succession of the king and constitutional reform. An important role of this house was its capacity to block any decision of the government or the other two houses that attacked either the monarchy or religion with two-thirds or more of the votes. It was assumed that members would be drawn from groups such as previous prime ministers, previous presidents of the parliament, previous supreme court justices, permanent undersecretaries of each department, military commanders and divisional leaders, while the seventy members of each of the other two houses would be drawn from those with, for example, medical, accounting or legal expertise. The objectives of the three houses system were explained as operating harmonious compromises with the entire society in order to proceed with the conduct of state in a way that accorded with the real-life conditions of society (Khanakammakan phattana prachathipatai 1995: 52–57). It is clear from the above that the system of parliament as proposed by the committee that published the booklet did not prioritize political decision-making through majority rule. Rather the parliament was positioned as an institution working for harmonious compromise between the multiple stakeholders in society.

Interesting elements concerning the role of the prime minister were also included in the proposal. As noted above, the key point of contention at the time of the 1992 Bloody May Incident was the demand that the prime minister be chosen from the popularly elected lower house. In proposals published by the committee a mere three years after this tragedy, however, there is a residual suggestion endorsing a prime minister who was not chosen by popular election. The committee accepted the need to prevent the prime ministerial appointment of an outsider (*knon nok*) who was not an elected member of the lower house and whose candidacy was the result of pressure from forces beyond the parliament. Nevertheless, the option remained to invite as necessary an outsider to assume the prime ministerial role. There were nonetheless changes proposed that would see the name of the candidate presented to the king solely by the president of the lower house.

Concrete proposals were also made regarding a vote for prime minister in the parliament. Accordingly, a secret vote was to be held if the prime ministerial candidate was a lower house member, while the vote was to be made public for candidates from outside the house. Noting that the ability to nominate an outside person as prime minister through an open vote met the needs of realpolitik, the committee suggested that the constitutional requirement for the person performing the role to come from the lower house be removed. It was also argued that the participation of members from both houses in any prime ministerial vote, a vote that might feature candidates from the lower house, the House of Sages or indeed outside the parliament, would further enhance the legitimacy of the position (Khanakammakan phattana prachathipatai 1995: 75–77).

Proposals by individual committee members: non-elected PM, dissolution of a political party

There were altogether fifteen booklets that brought together proposals from individual committee members. This section will consider those with proposals by three members who dealt with matters considered especially important. The first was 'A Politically Appropriate System for Investigating Government' (*rabop khuapkhum truatsop ratthaban thangkanmueang thi mosom*) by Suraphol Nitikraipot from Thammasat University's Faculty of Law. According to Suraphol, whose approach was strikingly similar to Amon's, an appropriate system of functioning checks and balances between the legislative and administrative powers of government was an important element of a parliamentary system. Historically, in early parliamentary models generally, a defined political role was assumed for the head of state (the king). This original system was therefore a dualist one in which cabinet needed the support of not only a parliament but also a head of state. However, as the political influence of the head of state waned, governments drifted into monist systems in which a parliament came under majority party control. It was for this reason that various Western countries undertook constitutional reform after World War II to improve the mutual check functions between the administrative and legislative arms of government. This was referred to as a 'rationalized parliamentary system' with such reforms being called for in Thailand also. The purpose of these reforms would be the creation of a stable cabinet led by a prime minister chosen from the majority party as a means of quelling the past instability associated with coalition government. Prime ministerial leadership would furthermore be enhanced. Reference was also made to the parliament, with the suggestion that there should be limits on cabinet decree and more emphasis on the parliament's law-making functions.

These recommendations might initially appear to accord with the trend of system reforms undertaken in countries in the West. Attention to detail, however, suggests that the reforms proposed were quite Thai specific. Suraphol argued that it was absolutely necessary to choose a prime minister from the parliament's majority party in order to form a stable cabinet. Since past votes for prime ministers in the house had required participating members to adhere to a political party line, it was not possible to say that a prime minister had truly been selected in terms of the will of the members. Accordingly, Suraphol asserted that the selection of the prime minister should occur through a secret ballot to prevent party discipline being enforced. Furthermore, it was suggested that, if the name of a person of talent who was not a member of the parliament was offered as a candidate, there could be no violation of the tenets of either democracy or parliamentary government if such a person's candidacy was subject to a public vote. That is, Suraphol did not see any threat to democracy by parliament members rejecting the decision of the political party with which they affiliated and voting for the prime minister of their choice. This accords with his estimation of the prime ministerial role as one in which the incumbent can demonstrate leadership by declining to be swayed by the interests of a ruling coalition. It is interesting that Amon, as a member of the Democracy Development Committee, and Suraphol, as a committee member presenting his own argument, each gave support to the possibility of a non-elected prime minister (Suraphol 1995).

We will now examine 'The Constitutional Court and a Method of Litigation Inquiry' (*san ratthatammanun lae withi phitcarana khadi ratthathammanun*) produced by Kamonchai Rattanasakawawong, also from the Thammsat University's Faculty of Law. This was the work that proposed a constitutional court. Kamonchai asserted that, in order to bestow democratic legitimacy on a constitutional court, it was necessary that the lower house was responsible for appointing its judges. A selection committee, which consisted of representatives from political parties, would select fifteen nominees and submit these to the parliament which would then vote to select nine judges from the list.

Kamonchai presented research on the 1949 Fundamental Law for the Federal Republic of Germany as an example upon which Thailand could draw when determining the powers of a constitutional court. He explained how this German model prohibited the violation of the constitution by a political party. As is widely known internationally, Germany's postwar reflections on the horrors of the Nazi regime led to the principle of 'defensive democracy' (*streitbare Demokratie*) underpinning the Fundamental Law. Accordingly, provisions such as the following were included in the German Fundamental Law:

> Article 18 (Forfeiture of basic rights)
> Whoever abuses the freedom of expression, in particular the freedom of the press (paragraph (1) of Article 5), the freedom of teaching (paragraph (3) of Article 5), the freedom of assembly (Article 8), the freedom of association (Article 9), the privacy of correspondence, posts and telecommunications (Article 10), the rights of property (Article 14) or the right of asylum (Article 16a) in order to combat the free democratic basic order shall forfeit these basic rights. This forfeiture and its extent shall be declared by the Federal Constitutional Court.
>
> Article 21 (Political parties)
> (1) Political parties shall participate in the formation of the political will of the people. They may be freely established. Their internal organisation must conform to democratic principles. They must publicly account for their assets and for the sources and use of their funds.
> (2) Parties that, by reason of their aims or the behaviour of their adherents, seek to undermine or abolish the free democratic basic order or to endanger the existence of the Federal Republic of Germany shall be unconstitutional.
> (3) Parties that, by reason of their aims or the behaviour of their adherents, are oriented towards an undermining or abolition

of the free democratic basic order or an endangerment of the existence of the Federal Republic of Germany shall be excluded from state financing. If such exclusion is determined, any favourable fiscal treatment of these parties and of payments made to those parties shall cease.

(4) The Federal Constitutional Court shall rule on the question of unconstitutionality within the meaning of paragraph (2) of this Article and on exclusion from state financing within the meaning of paragraph (3).[8]

Advising the introduction into the Thai Constitution of provisions similar to those outlined above from the German Fundamental Law, Kamonchai proposed endowing the soon-to-be established Thai Constitutional Court with the power to arbitrate on such matters. Kamonchai proposed that Thailand should bring an end to the exercise of constitutionally-based fundamental rights that could paradoxically see an individual oppose the constitution or constitutional institutions. He further supported lodging cases with the Constitutional Court through a supreme prosecutor with a view to dissolving political parties that opposed a democratic regime of government with the king as head of state, opposed the order of the nation, or opposed the law or the good order and culture of the people (Kamonchai 1995).

The booklet entitled, 'Improving the Political Party System' (*kanprapprung rabop phakkanmueang*), compiled by yet another member of the Thammsat University Faculty of Law, Boonsri Miwong-ukhot, also makes pertinent points on the dissolution of political parties. Boonsri argued that the freedom of establishing a political party should be protected and dissolving a political party should be made more difficult to make political parties' organization stronger. He also recommended strengthening the role of individual party members while diminishing the influence of capitalists because he thought that the presence of capitalists investing in political parties was one of the factors in vote-buying. He further asserted that both the structure and governance of political parties should accord with the principles of

---

8 Source available at: https://www.gesetze-im-internet.de/englisch_gg/englisch_gg.html

democracy. Differing from Amon who was hostile towards political parties, Boonsri took the position that political parties were important entities in advancing democratization. Boonsri nevertheless also referenced the emergence of the Nazi dictatorship under the German Weimar Constitution, acknowledging that the Weimar Constitution had been no guarantee against the rise of a political party that failed to comply with democratic principles. Like Kamonchai, he proposed that the Constitutional Court should have the power to dissolve political parties that violated the principles of the constitution. Boonsri nevertheless advised against using the dissolution of political parties as a key disciplinary measure and argued that any such ruling should be considered with the utmost degree of caution (Boonsri 1995).

There were two interesting aspects to the Democracy Development Committee's proposals, namely the confirmation of the possibility of the appointment of a prime minister who is not a member of the parliament, and the granting of the power to dissolve political parties to the Constitutional Court. We might consider how it became possible for the political reform movement that followed the events of the 1992 Bloody May Incident, a movement that should have progressed democratization, to propose, even conditionally, these kinds of non-democratic measures. In order to shed light on this matter we will examine the intent of the Suraphol proposal made at the time.

According to Suraphol, the political reform movement in Thailand was established for two reasons: first, to ensure that the large-scale conflict of the 1992 Bloody May Incident would never be repeated, and second, to refuse to permit, under the burgeoning influence of international trends, the operation of autocratic power, and to confirm the importance of monitoring and investigation by outside bodies as a preventative measure against the misuse of power by the state. In response to the question regarding examples of autocratic rulers in Thailand, Suraphol replied by giving not only the name of the non-elected military figure, Prime Minister Suchinda, but also the name of the popularly elected Prime Minister Chatchai Choonhavan (1988–1991). While Prime Minister Chatchai was elected to the parliament by popular vote and selected by the lower house, Suraphol argued that his term of office was marred by endless rumors of corruption that stymied effective governance by the parliament. He accordingly explained that Chatchai, too, was an example of an autocratic ruler. In other words, a popularly elected prime minister could also be considered an autocrat and therefore removed from office by the constitution and the Constitutional Court. While there were repeated references to Hitler and the German Nazi Party even in documents related to the draft of the 1997 Constitution, Suraphol argued that these were merely the most famous examples of autocratic power in the context of majority political party rule. It was this context, he asserted during a July 2017 interview, that saw the dominant party assume a winner-takes-all attitude that resulted in an autocratic mode of governance.

From the interview with Suraphol, it became clear that the scholars who proposed the new constitution at the time recognized that a non-elected prime minister was not necessarily bad, nor was a democratically-elected prime minister necessarily good, and to ban a non-elected prime minister was not an absolute necessity. Given the repeated references to Hitler and the Nazi Party during the new constitutional draft deliberative process, it further can be seen that there was an awareness of a need to require a constitution to manage the power of an autocracy arising from majority party rule rather than a military coup d'état in the background to the introduction of provisions protecting the constitution into the 1949 German Fundamental Law.

As referred to later in this chapter, and as will be touched on later in this book, the stipulations protecting the constitution based on the German Fundamental Law appeared as Section 63 of the 1997 Constitution and Section 68 of the 2007 Constitution. It will be useful to consider the specific wording of these two sections given the severe impact each had on democratization during and after 2006 in Thailand.

1997 Constitution: Section 63

> No person shall exercise the rights and liberties prescribed in the Constitution to overthrow the democratic regime of government with the King as Head of the State under this Constitution or to

acquire the power to rule the country by any means which is not in accordance with the modes provided in this Constitution.

In the case where a person or a political party has committed the act under paragraph one, the person knowing of such act shall have the right to request the Prosecutor General to investigate its facts and submit a motion to the Constitutional Court for ordering cessation of such act without, however, prejudice to the institution of a criminal action against such person.

In the case where the Constitutional Court makes a decision compelling the political party to cease to commit the act under paragraph two, the Constitutional Court may order the dissolution of such political party.[9]

2007 Constitution: Section 68

A person is prohibited from using the rights and liberties provided in the Constitution to overthrow the democratic rule with the King as the Head of the State as provided by this Constitution; or to acquire power to rule the country by means other than is provided in the Constitution.

Where a person or political party acts under paragraph one, the witness thereof has the right to report the matter to the Prosecutor General to investigate facts and to submit a request to the Constitutional Court for decision to order cessation of such act without prejudice to criminal proceedings against the doer of the act.

If the Constitutional Court decides to order cessation of the said act under paragraph two, the Constitutional Court may order dissolution of that political party.

---

9   Translation available at: http://www.asianlii.org/th/legis/const/1997/1.html

In case of order dissolution of that political party by the Constitutional Court under paragraph three, the leader of the dissolute Party and the member of the board of the executive committee under paragraph one are prohibited the right of election for five years from the date of order by the Constitutional Court.[10]

Former Thammsat University Political Science Department academic, Nakharin Mektrairat, participated in the 2007 Constitution drafting process. In a 6 October 2013 interview, Nakharin explained that, rather than prohibiting a military coup d'état, these sections were designed to ensure the removal of a bad government whether elected or not. The 1992 Bloody May Incident occurred when people rose up demanding an elected prime minister. However, the political reform movement and the arguments for drafting a new constitution that followed this tragedy did not regard the prime ministerial legitimacy associated with popular election as such an important point. On the contrary, the option clearly remained for the re-emergence of a prime minister who was unelected.

The 1997 Constitution Drafting Committee

In this and the following section, we will consider the arguments presented during the drafting of the 1997 and the 2007 constitutions. In the case of 1997 Constitution, the drafting was a three-stage process involving the Constitution Drafting Committee (twenty-three meetings), the Draft Amendment Committee (thirty-three meetings) and the Constitution Drafting Assembly (thirty-one meetings). The following will largely focus on the meeting notes of the Constitution Drafting Committee which debated the objectives and policy position of the 1997 Constitution.

Drafting Committee meetings were held on twenty-three occasions in 1997 between 20 January and 30 April. Committee membership was comprised of legal and political science academics from various prominent universities and also of those who formerly held, for

---

10 Translation available at: https://www.constituteproject.org/constitution/Thailand_2007.pdf

example, bureaucratic positions. Bowonsak, a public law scholar from the Chulalongkorn University Faculty of Law, played a central role. In 2001, Bowonsak published an explanatory paper entitled 'The Spirit of the Constitution' (*chettanarom rattathammanun*). Here, he listed the issues to be resolved by the 1997 Constitution as: 1. resolving the problems regarding corruption and military coups d'état, 2. enhancing the protections of the rights and freedom of the people in a shift from 'government by politicians' to 'government by the people', and 3. expanding the people's participation in state governance and politics. He further asserted that participative democratic forms, that is politics by the people, be implemented because the current representative democracy has become the arena for power struggles. His key concepts of the 1997 constitutional draft were the dispersal of central political power and the promotion of participative democracy (Bowonsak 2001). We might consider the extent to which these principles featured in discussions that occurred during the drafting of the 1997 Constitution.

At the fourth committee meeting held on 27 January, Kasem Sirisam argued that 'the problem with Thai democracy' was the 'excess power of the state'. He continued by noting that: 'We need to either contain or disperse current state powers and transfer these to the private sector' ('Records of the Fourth Meeting of the Drafting Committee': 34). We might accordingly conclude that this meeting debated the policy and the policy direction presented in the 1997 Constitution explanatory information provided in Bowonsak's paper.

Provisions to protect the constitution

Initial discussion on the day of the fifth committee meeting involved debate on matters such as legal procedures in the case of a human rights violations, the rights of an accused, the right to access public documents, freedom of information and the right to assembly. After these points were considered, the right to uphold the constitution of the people was raised. The chair of the meeting explained that the provision protecting the constitution would also protect the state, religion, the king and democracy. Referring to the rescinding of the constitution by the military at the time of a coup d'état, Khien Thirawet mused, half-jokingly, that 'While a clause prohibiting a coup d'état would probably contradictorily encourage the military to rescind the constitution, authorizing a coup might see things end with only a coup and the constitution intact'. Phonthep Thepkanchana declared that: 'While the people have duties, upholding the constitution is not among them. If protecting the constitution was listed as a duty of the people, there would be nothing to stop them taking up arms and shooting the members of the military who might initiate a coup. This is against the law. Criminal law forbids members of the public shooting military personnel involved in a coup d'état'. Sawat Saprakuap also opposed including a provision upholding the constitution in the new document. He argued, 'Surely, no matter what, we can never prevent the military abolishing the constitution'.

With various committee members expressing concern, Bowonsak stated that such a provision, which he pointed out was included in postwar Germany's Fundamental Law, would ensure the right to contest and resist those seeking to have the constitution destroyed. Seri Suwannaphanon, however, put forward a different view. Seri observed, 'That sort of provision will merely endorse the right of the people to kill each other now and again. Although there is merit in educating the people to protect the constitution, we should certainly not invite any repeat of the events of the 1992 Bloody May Incident'. Thian Thirawet also opposed including a clause protecting the constitution. He concluded that: 'In reality, that sort of provision is meaningless'.

Once the various views had been expressed, the chair of the meeting summed up and declared: 'The provision will be included'. Bowonsak immediately asked: 'Is the following acceptable to everyone: "The people have the power to protest any rescinding of the democratic regime of government with the king as head of state [*prachachon mi sitti thi cha totan kanlomlang kanpokkhrong rabop prachathipatai an mi phramahakasat song pen pramuk tam ratthathammanu*n]?"' When committee members looked perplexed, he repeated the words, 'the democratic regime of government with the king as head of state'. Seri, however, remained unconvinced, saying: 'I still have concerns. If the military stages a coup d'état and abolishes the constitution, those involved will merely claim that there is no threat to Thailand's democratic regime of government with the king as head of state'. In other words, although there was no agreement on introducing a provision to uphold the constitution or inserting the words 'a democratic regime of government with the king as head of state', the meeting chair brought the argument to a close ('Records of the Fifth Meeting of the Drafting Committee': 66–76).

The popularly elected prime minister

Further interesting discussion relating to the appointment of a prime minister took place during the committee's thirteenth meeting. The initiative was taken by Likhit Thirawekhin who questioned the documentation distributed for the day's meeting: 'On the appointment of a prime minister or ministers, I read that these can come from names on a political party roll, from lower house members representing an electorate, and also from people who are neither of these. Can I confirm that this last point includes the prime minister?' The meeting chair replied: 'We can read the document as including the prime minister, although this is not something that interests me'. Phant Thatniyanon raised several additional matters, pointing out that: 'Committee Member Likhit's question reminds us that if the proposal proceeds in its present form, it is likely to draw strong criticism. The current Thai political environment supports the political legitimacy of a prime minister who has participated in the electoral process'.

As debate continued on the crucial questions of whether a prime minister should be a member of the lower house or whether a prime minister should be legitimized by the election process, Likhit reminded the gathering that it was the authorization by the 1991 Constitution of a prime minister who was not an elected member of the lower house that led to the 1992 Bloody May Incident. He further explained along the lines as follows: Because it was possible that the leader of a party holding government might lose their seat in an election and there also could be cases in which political parties cannot reach a consensus on who should be prime minister, the 1991 Constitution left room for an outsider who was not a member of the house to be invited as prime minister. Constitutional amendment after Bloody May removed that possibility, ensuring instead selection of the prime minister from lower house members. This, however, led to the rise of a politics of numbers resulting in the political party that held the most seats producing the prime minister of the day. Even people who lacked accomplishment could be appointed to the post. It may be that I myself believe in ensuring a path for a prime minister from the outside. The events of Bloody May, however, are still fairly recent and there is no guarantee of the value of that option.

In other words, in spite of he himself understanding the value of allowing a prime minister to take office from outside, in the aftermath of the Bloody May Incident, Likhit called for candidates for the role to be confined to the popularly elected members of the lower house.

Somkit Lertpaithoon took a similar position by declaring: 'Many people lost their lives over the problem of whether the prime minister should be elected by the people, and we should avoid a return to the past'. He continued: 'Theoretically, there is no actual need for a prime minister to be an elected member of the house. Nevertheless, we should adopt this policy in conjunction with the newly designed single and proportional representation system to ensure that people of ability register on the political party roll'. Suchit Bunbongkan mentioned that the working group's proposal, following the French system, stipulates that members of the lower house of parliament lose their parliamentary status if they become ministers. The point is that members of the house of representatives cannot be prime ministers or ministers. Ultimately, it is the same as allowing an outsider to become prime minister. Any selection of an outside person, however, would require a lengthy explanation of the reasons for the choice.

It is apparent that a majority of members felt that appointing a member from outside the lower house was not necessarily a negative for Thailand's politics. Nevertheless, as Likhit cautioned: 'As for ministers, we should open the door wide so that politicians can be appointed regardless of whether they are elected in proportional representation or electoral districts. However, a prime ministerial appointment should be carefully considered to be consistent with the current political climate'. Cognizant that Thai society was still reeling from the shock of the 1992 Bloody May Incident, the final direction of the debate favored a provision requiring a prime minister to be selected from the members of the lower house ('Records of the Thirteenth Meeting of the Drafting Committee': 3–13).

The parliament

There were a range of views presented regarding the parliament. The 1997 Constitution shifted upper house membership from an appointment to election by the people. The constitution was therefore often praised as supportive of democracy. Consideration of the arguments conducted by the Drafting Committee, however, cast doubt on this assessment.

At the outset of the eleventh committee meeting, Bowonsak focused on two main points relating to the parliament: 1. the failure of the lower house to reflect the diversity of Thai society, and 2. the problem regarding the upper house was its appointment of membership by a single person, the prime minister. Bowonsak proposed the means to address these matters. The first was to diminish the influence of money over the system of lower house election while to resolve the second problem, senators should be elected by mutual vote among the people, given that one purpose of this house was to counter the power of political parties in the other chamber. This selection committee would comprise those who had been local parliament representatives, prime ministers, leaders of the opposition in the lower house, and presidents of the lower and upper houses. That is to say, in Bowonsak's initial proposal, the upper house was not chosen by popular vote but by appointment following adjustments to the system in place at the time. He further pointed out that, in accordance with a new proposal requiring a lower house member to resign when accepting a ministerial appointment, the need for a prime minister to come from the lower house could be no longer necessary.

In dissenting, Decho Sawananon declared along the following lines: I feel unhappy with this sort of argument about politicians fighting for their interests, and how many politicians are you talking about anyway? We need to be very cautious about generalizing such an argument.

I can in no way agree that it is fine for ministers to not have lower house membership status or for prime ministers not to be members of the lower house. The prime minister should be a member of the lower house. That is what legitimizes the role. Why criticize lower house members only?

Khien, however, took a different position, replying, it is flawed reasoning to strictly apply the principle, as Decho does, that it is undemocratic for a prime minister not to be an elected member. For example, Prime Minster Banharn (1995) captured the greatest number of votes in his home province, Suphan Buri. Yet there would surely have been a different outcome if a nation-wide vote had been held. Judging something as democratic or otherwise merely by the number of election votes can thus be misleading.

Decho, however, rebuffed this suggestion, pointing out, it is a mistake to believe that the current parliament fails to reflect the diversity of Thai society and that this causes problems in terms of ensuring the approval of the people. Members of the lower house are actually drawn from a wide cross-section of people that includes farmers and former village and ward heads. Any charge of lack of diversity must be accompanied by an analysis of the various cohorts in the parliament and an account of just which groups are absent.

At this point in the discussion, Amon Raksasat spoke out sharply: 'The current constitution and law give too much power to politicians. I'll present documentation on this at tomorrow's meeting'. He then continued: 'The majority of members of Thailand's original parliament were members of the People's Party who initiated the 1932 Siamese Revolution. They were talented and upright men. However, once the group formalized as a political party, the leader became an autocrat [...]. We must therefore remove people lacking merit from both the upper and lower houses' ('Records of the Eleventh Meeting of the Drafting Committee': 19–70).

Debate around political parties and the election system continued into the committee's twelfth meeting. Considerable time was spent on proportional representation and political party membership rolls. Komet Khwanmuang raised the fundamental significance of the proportional representation system, cautioning that 'proportional representation will not prevent vote-buying'. Citing his own research on the issue, he pointed out that the proportional representation system was introduced in Denmark in 1855. There, it was used for the next fifty years as a means of dissolving the political party that monopolized parliament seats. For a long time in Denmark, members of this party were representatives of the working classes. Proportional representation, in fact, was used to break up the power monopoly held by these representatives. There is no guarantee that this system will ensure an inherently anti-vote buying ethos.

There was also debate over whether or not an upper house was in fact necessary. Given that, historically, most other countries operated with a bicameral system, many among the members, including the committee chair, supported its establishment. The powers of an upper house would include considering draft legislation, impeachment and the selection of members for the various new agencies being planned. The problem, however, was how to determine who should be an upper house member. With no recommendation from the Drafting Committee for direct elections, it was assumed, as noted previously, that there would either be an appointment system based on new procedures or an indirect election. Committee member Decho, who had previously spoken, noted that 'Direct election would involve a selection method similar to that of the lower house and surely render an upper house superfluous'. Prachum Thongmi, however, argued that, 'Since the capacity to impeach has strengthened the powers of the upper house, members should submit themselves to the scrutiny of the people through an election'. The committee chair then commented, 'It is important to preserve the social ratio and no specific group should dominate' ('Records of the Twelfth Meeting of the Drafting Committee': 17–105).

It became clear during the eleventh and twelve committee meetings that more than half the members of the Drafting Committee placed greater importance on reflecting the diversity of society in the assembly, in either the Senate or the House of Representatives, than on popular election through elections. Throughout the discussion at the drafting committee, the idea that it was not good for one group to dominate all politics permeated. In addition, it is interesting that the intention of changing the system of appointing senators was not to give legitimacy to the Senate through an election, but to improve the concentration of power in which senators are appointed by the prime minister alone. It is possible that reforms to upper house member appointments were closely related to the constitutional reforms that followed the 1992 Bloody May Incident and which resulted in the prime minister being selected from members of the lower house.

The separation of the three powers

The 1997 Constitution also strengthened judicial power by establishing the Constitutional Court and other independent agencies. Debate linking these innovations to the separation of the three powers occurred during the deliberations of the seventh Drafting Committee meeting.

It was established policy in Thailand to facilitate checks on the implementation of state authority by strengthening the organizations that administered the courts and judicial authority. On this matter, committee member Khien asserted that any expansion of judicial authority must come with a system of checks and balances between the three powers. Khien stated, 'It is my view that the legislature, the executive and the judiciary should each be mutually free and independent and, in terms of checks on the operation of state power, I would like to make sure that there is a balance between these three [...]. What I want to know is how we can best monitor and check the court system, the judicial system and judicial authority'. Kasem had concerns that this was a topic for another occasion. 'Right now', he insisted, 'we should only concern ourselves with the role of the court in monitoring the implementation of state power'. Committee member Anek pointed out that 'The post-war Japanese Constitution clearly indicates that: "The people have the power to dismiss the Justices of the Supreme Court". Although this has never occurred, we should at the least consider that provision from the constitution of post-war Japan'.

Somkhit Sisangkhom articulated the dangers of expanded judicial authority and the related entry of the judiciary into the political sphere. He explained along the following lines: In the current system, we divide the relevant duties into executive or administrative powers, legislative powers and judicial powers. Those with legislative powers enact legislation, while judicial powers have a responsibility to apply the law and to operate according to legal processes. Currently, however, Justices move outside their authority to operate in the political field. Since this causes confusion among the people, these two powers need to be divided. It is unclear why they move outside their domain and conduct politics themselves, making it difficult for us to know what to do. If this remains unresolved, there will be further confusion. Imagine if a judge went off and held a protest. Would this be right? Legal processes should be confined to their own domain. What happens to justice when a justice of the court goes beyond that domain to act politically? What hope can the people have for justice then?

Responding to this contrary opinion, Bowonsak stated to the following effect: There will be a system of impeachment for justices, making it possible to impeach both politicians and justices for matters such as corruption or the accumulation of unusual wealth. In the Japanese system, there are fifteen justices on the Supreme Court bench, and we might question whether or not to trust to the people a system that couples the distribution of a roll of Justice candidates with a roll of candidates for the lower house (house of representatives) at the time of a general election (an election for the lower house). Ultimately, such a system is not used because the people of Japan do not know the justices of the supreme court. We should certainly contemplate overseas systems when considering possibilities. Nevertheless, I feel it would be problematic to introduce something that doesn't fit the Thai context. For example, submitting a roster of judges for approval from the Diet when appointing judges means that our country's political institutions are not stable, so judges have to be heavily involved in politics.

Committee member Suchit pointed out that 'The court will have contradictory roles. It will need to monitor the power of the state while being itself a power of the state. That is to say that the court, too, should be monitored. We must therefore devise a system of checks and balances. There will also be problems with the structure of the personnel administration arm of the court. Without monitoring, this will become a closed system'. He accordingly proposed that: 'We include a representative of each of the three powers into the Justice Selection Committee and ensure that these have connections to the people' ('Records of the Seventh Meeting of the Drafting Committee': 7–19).

It is clear from these discussions that there was a sense during the seventh Drafting Committee meeting that any strengthening of judicial authority as a means of monitoring state power needed to be exercised with caution to prevent a collapse of the balance between the three powers. There was also concern that the people would be confused by judicial incursions into the political sphere. The majority of committee members were of the view that, since the selection of neither the prime minister nor the upper house adhered to the tenets of popular election, Thai democracy differed from the European model. Many, interestingly, nevertheless supported Thailand in consistently maintaining the principle of the separation of the three powers. This may reflect Thai value systems that prioritize 'harmony' and 'balance' over the dominance of any specific authority or force. Although a sector of the committee supported the Japanese system that permitted the impeachment of supreme court justices, this option was not included in any proposal following Bowonsak's critique. As a result, no adequate system was ever really proposed to monitor the court or the justices.

Drafting Committee deliberations were followed by meetings of the Draft Amendment Committee and Constitution Drafting Assembly. Once revisions were made in line with the public support for democratization, a draft constitution was released. As noted, both the political reform movement and the 1997 Constitution aligned with the growing social trend towards democratic processes. However, a detailed examination of the pronouncements made by Bowonsak and his committee member colleagues reveals that the threat of a repeat of the 1992 Bloody May Incident also operated as a backdrop to the reform movement and subsequent enactment of the new constitution. As Suraphol noted during the interview referred to above: 'The origins of the political reform movement lay in a desire to prevent a repeat of discord such as the 1992 Bloody May Incident'. This desire was nonetheless accompanied by a deep-seated anxiety that, with the future prime minister selected from members of the lower house, control of the legislature would continue through a majority political party.

There is no doubt that the 1997 Constitution introduced a range of progressive, democratic provisions absent from the previous document. Examining the reforms through a wide-angled lens, however, suggests that there was simultaneously an adroit return to the pre-1991 Constitution landscape and the revisions introduced at that time. In the final instance, oversight by the mass media and the people prevented a provision authorizing a prime minister not chosen by popular election. However, the establishment of the various courts and independent agencies, and the inclusion of Section 63 protecting the constitution – as ardently urged by Bowonsak – were also features of the 1997 document.

2007 Constitution Drafting Committee

The 2007 Constitution was drafted and enacted after the 2006 coup d'état led to the dissolution of the 1997 document. In the interview cited above, Suraphol explained that: 'Although the 1997 and 2007 constitutions had the same objectives, the 2007 enactment made revisions to loopholes and deficiencies in the 1997 document'. It is important to consider the problematic elements of the 1997 document, the adjustments that were made in 2007 and the elements that remained unchanged. To do this, the chapter will scrutinize arguments presented at the 2007 Constitution Drafting Committee and the Constitution Drafting Assembly. This begins with an examination of the material presented by Somkit Lertpaithoon, a scholar from Thammsat University's Faculty of Law who played a central role in the drafting of the 2007 Constitution, and Vicha Mahakun, a former Supreme Court justice who was also a member of the National Anti-Corruption Commission.

The ethos and origin of the 2007 Constitution

This section will discuss the contents of two papers, namely Somkit's 'The Origin and Ethos of the 2007 Constitution' (*khwampenma lae chettanarom khong rattathammanun haeng ratchaanachakthai phuttasakarat* 2550) and Vicha's 'Judicial Power: A New Factor in the Maintenance of Justice in Society' (*amnat tulakan: ongprakop mai puea kandamrong kwamyutitham nai sangkhom*). Somkit's paper explained that 'While the 1997 document – known as "The People's Constitution" – was abolished by a coup d'état, this has occurred any number of times in Thailand. Each of the new constitutions enacted after a coup have differed'. He nevertheless pointed out that 'Since the 2007 Constitution was enacted following the 2006 coup, the 2007 Constitution has special characteristics. These result from attempts to revise flaws in the 1997 Constitution and continue the inherited spirit and ethos of political reform'. Somkit argued that 'Although some criticize the drafting of the 2007 document as lacking legitimacy, these people completely fail to familiarize themselves with the contents of the document'. According to Somkit, the 2007 Constitution, no less than the 1997 document, was sensitive to the thoughts, opinions and participation of the people. Explaining that the broad framework of the 1997 iteration remained unchanged, he concluded that 'The key spirit of the 2007 Constitution sought to rectify the country's political crisis'.

To Somkit, there were two main problems with the 1997 Constitution, namely, issues inherent in the document itself, and the parliamentary dictatorship that was invoked when the majority political party of the parliament abolished mutual checks between the legislative and executive branches of government. While, with regard to the second point, the problem arose from the character and illegal use of power by party leader Prime Minister Thaksin, he nonetheless saw contributing issues inherent in the 1997 Constitution itself. Somkit stated, 'Immediately before the 2006 coup d'état, Thai politics featured a single individual or a single group that had a total stranglehold on state power'. He further declared, 'Political intervention into constitutional entities such as the independent agencies resulted in the collapse of any system of monitoring power' (Somkit 2007).

It is obvious from Somkit's analysis that the 2007 Constitution agenda accorded exactly with the 1997 document's 'prevention of the monopoly of power by a majority government'. Nevertheless, there were differences between the two in draft policies and procedures. While the 1997 document draft strengthened judicial powers, there was also an emphasis on the need to ensure a balance with the other two powers. When drafting the 2007 Constitution, however, the focus was on how to prevent political intervention in the courts and independent agencies, and how to prevent a power monopoly by the majority political party. Thus, the most significant focal point during the 2007 Constitution drafting process was preventing political intervention in the appointment of members of the Constitutional Court and independent agencies.

Vicha's discussion centered on the courts and independent agencies. He explained that: 'Justices act independently, regardless of the circumstances, when handing down a ruling in the name of the king. The court thus has the confidence of society. Accordingly, not only should the institution of the current court resolve disputes among members of society, it should also provide solutions to social problems' (Vicha 2007). Concerning problems that arose under the 1997 Constitution, Vicha argued, 'Because the Constitutional Court failed to dismiss Prime Minister Thaksin in 2006 on the grounds of corruption following his suspicious stock sell-off, the court lost trust'. He declared that: 'In addition to faithfully interpreting the letter of the law, justices of the court should hand down "correct" decisions that "uphold justice"'. Vicha further asserted that representatives of political parties and institutions of higher education should be removed from the appointment procedures of the Constitutional Court (Vicha 2007).

Vicha's analysis provides insights into how the emphasis in the 1997 constitutional draft on a need for a body to ensure checks and balances between the three arms of power was discarded in 2007 in favor of policies that entrenched judicial authority as a means of controlling the other two. This was in spite of the fact that, with former Supreme Court Justice Vicha playing a key role in compiling the section of the 2007 draft related to the Constitutional Court and independent agencies, there was slight wariness towards the court intervening in politics or playing a political role. Below, we will consider arguments during meetings of the Drafting Committee and several meetings of the Drafting Assembly.

The Drafting Committee and Drafting Assembly

The 2007 Constitution draft process involved three stages: a drafting sub-committee which held thirty-seven meetings, a drafting committee which held sixty-two meetings and a drafting assembly which held forty-three meetings. The sub-committee was broken into three groups: 1. a group discussing the right to free participation by the people and decentralization of authority (eighteen meetings), 2. a group discussing governmental institutions (thirteen meetings), and 3. a group discussing independent agencies and courts (six meetings). In terms of the objectives and policy directions of the 2007 Constitution, we will mainly consider records of the meetings of groups two and three of the Drafting Sub-Committee which debated government agencies and a system of monitoring power. We will also examine the records of the Drafting Assembly which considered the opinion of the people as heard during public hearings held in each region.

The parliament

The organizational design of the upper house was one issue that occupied considerable debate time. While the majority of 1997 Drafting Committee members actually favored appointment, their sensitivity to the support for democracy in the society ensured that a system of popular vote prevailed. Members of the 2007 Drafting Committee, however, again proposed an appointment system as an effective option. As in 1997, debate began with fundamental issues that included: 'Is an upper house necessary? Why a bicameral system? Who do upper house members represent?' At the first meeting of group two, Khomsan Phokhong explained that: 'In England, upper house representation was based on land ownership, and discussions revolved around the monarch and taxes. In other words, upper house members in that country represent a class. In the United States, senators are state representatives, with two elected from each state'. Questions of who the upper house represented and how this differed from the lower house nevertheless remained unresolved, with argument continuing at length on these points. Committee member Khomsan suggested that, in the event of no agreement, a parliament with a single house be considered. Committee chair for the day, Charan Phakdithanakun, declared, 'The upper house represents each and every occupation and all sections of society'. He further observed, 'Since Thailand is not a federation, these people do not represent regions or provinces'. Khomsan, however, took a different approach, pointing out that 'No matter what the occupational group, the extent of its coverage is unclear. Furthermore, we still end up ultimately with the problem of vote-buying'. Argument continued on the role and jurisdiction of the upper house. While there was general agreement that this chamber should validate legislation proposed by the lower house, opinion was divided on granting impeachment powers.

As debate also continued over various selection possibilities for the upper house – election, appointment or a mixture of both – Somkit expressed concern about popular elections along the following lines: It is an error to say that elections are democratic and that we should therefore choose popular election. Elections are merely one of a number of methods. Does democracy necessarily follow on from an election? Hitler was elected to power. Although under the previous constitution the government in Thailand came to power by popular election, this didn't guarantee the democracy desired. While the 1997 Constitution gave many powers to an upper house that was chosen by popular election, ultimately both upper and lower house members were chosen by the same voting bloc.

As a compromise, it was suggested that a selection committee put forward twice the number of nominees as seats, with the final choice being made by the people. Praphan Naikowit, however, declared that this would merely make fools of members of the public. He argued, 'It is best that upper house members are also chosen by direct election [...]. If the upper house is granted the power to impeach, a section of the members, at the least, should be chosen by popular vote' ('Records of the First Meeting of the Drafting Sub-Committee': 2).

At the second meeting, Nakharin Mektrairat introduced the Upper House electoral system of Japan, where a prefecture is an electorate using a national ward directory. Referencing the French and United States systems, he raised the possibility of an indirect election whereby the people select an electoral college and the electoral college elects a representative. He insisted that the legitimacy of senators based on popular elections should not be easily abandoned. Kroekkiat Phiphatseritham suggested that a selection committee present a nominee list five times the number of seats and that an expert panel draw on the list to make the choice. There was, nevertheless, considerable support among Drafting Sub-Committee members for either selection by appointment or a mixed system. Phairoj Phromsan asserted that upper house members had previously been appointed and that 'Appointed members did a better job that those selected by popular vote'. In response to the indirect election proposal, Chayaphon Thawonthon also stated that 'As long as the upper house is not granted the power to impeach, an appointment system is best. It is not necessary to have a system of indirect election' ('Records of the Second Meeting of the Drafting Sub-Committee': 2).

The strong Drafting Committee support for an appointment system related to the overlapping problems of nepotism and voting blocs among members of both the lower and upper houses. At the third meeting, Thanawat Sangthong opposed popular election as the method of selecting upper house members on the following grounds: 'An upper house election system will result in members of no different quality to those of the lower house'. Thanawat was not the only member to hold this view. Many on the committee saw the upper house as 'baby-sitting' the lower house and believed that those appointed to the former should be of higher caliber than lower house members ('Records of the Third Meeting of the Drafting Sub-Committee Group': 2). At the fifth meeting, Phisit Liatham declared that: 'While the upper and lower houses might in theory be independent entities, society is skeptical of that claim. Popular election of upper house members would require candidates to campaign. The mutual independence of the upper and lower houses relates to people's likes and dislikes rather than having anything to do with legitimacy'. In other words, he asserted a need for the independence of each house based not on academic principles but on the demands of society ('Records of the Fifth Meeting of the Drafting Sub-Committee Group': 2).

Later meetings also featured strong calls for an appointment system with the discussion moving to selection committee structure. Roles proposed as committee nominees included previous prime ministers, previous presidents of the parliament, the chief justice of the Supreme Court, the chief justice of the Supreme Administrative Court, the chief justice of the Constitutional Court and the heads of independent agency panels. At the tenth meeting, Yotsak Kosaiyakanon expressed an opposing point of view, voicing concern that the committee might be limited to three justices and four members of independent agencies. 'As a matter of state', he declared, 'this issue should be progressed with the utmost caution. [...] A representative of the people must be included. This should be someone whose ideas are connected to those of the people'. This, however, was a minority position ('Records of the Tenth Meeting of the Drafting Sub-Committee Group': 2).

Once discussion entered the Drafting Assembly phase, a shift of opinion did by degrees occur. At the eighth meeting of this body, Pradit Lueang-aram announced that 'The majority of people from Phetchaburi Province prefer an appointment system' ('Records of the Eighth Meeting of the Drafting Assembly'). At the twelfth meeting, Montri Phetcharakhum observed that some believed that upper house appointments should be the purview of 'a privy council' ('Records of the Twelfth Meeting of the Drafting Assembly'). At the thirteenth meeting, however, Pakon Priyakon responded by making the point that: 'Many people want to see the popular election of the upper house' ('Records of the Thirteenth Meeting of the Drafting Assembly'). At the seventeenth meeting, Montri restated his position: 'The people do not understand why upper house members should be appointed [...]. Many hold the view that representatives of the people should be elected by those people'. At the same meeting, Seri asserted, 'I am opposed to an appointment system for members of the upper house. Democracy is the voice of the people and should be of the people, by the people and for the people' ('Records of the Seventeenth Meeting of the Drafting Assembly'). At the thirty-seventh and final meeting of the assembly, Wutisan Tanchai proposed as follows: 'If we wish to legitimate an upper house with the power to impeach a popularly elected politician, the majority of members should be chosen by the people through popular election' ('Records of the Thirty-Seventh Meeting of the Drafting Assembly').

By the close of argument concerning the selection of upper house members, Drafting Sub-Committee members took a definite position favoring diversity. In other words, they supported the principle that members of parliament should represent the various groups of which society is comprised. This accorded also with the argument at the time of the 1997 draft when diversity, rather than popular election, was prioritized. Since the voices of the people expressed at regional public meetings demanded popular election, however, it was inevitable that the opinions of committee members would also be subject to change.

Discussion regarding the lower house focused on two main points: 1. reforming the election system in the light of the excessive power exercised by the Thaksin administration to prevent the rise of a system of single party dictatorship, and 2. investigating a reduction of the number of seats in the lower house. With respect to the second point, some argued that it was probably not necessary for lower house members to duplicate the role of provincial representatives who attended to regional populations. This assertion arguably expressed the Drafting Committee's understanding of the relationship between the people and the lower house.

The popularly elected prime minister

During the draft of the 2007 Constitution, less attention was given to the prime minister being chosen from members of the lower house than at the time of the 1997 process. At the eleventh Drafting Assembly, assembly member Phairoj stated, 'This assembly agrees that the prime minister should come from members of the lower house. However, this should only be for two terms or eight years' ('Records of the Eleventh Meeting of the Drafting Assembly'). That position was modified, however, during the thirty-second meeting when Siracha Charuenphanit proposed as follows: 'To prevent the chaos that arose in the final stages of the operation of the 1997 Constitution, and to prevent a coup d'état, we might also leave room for the appointment of a prime minister who is not a lower house member [...]. The lower house is granted legitimacy by the people. They therefore should have the discretionary power to decide who will be prime minister' ('Records of the Thirty-Second Meeting of the Drafting Assembly').

Emergency meetings in a crisis

The relative absence of debate at the time of the drafting of the 2007 Constitution on whether or not to authorize a prime minister who was not popularly elected does not mean that Thai intellectuals rejected that notion. During the drafting process, there were moves to request the installation of special emergency meetings at times of crisis. Sections relating to this matter were Section 63 of the 1997 Constitution and Section 68 of the 2007 Constitution, both of which were introduced as articles to protect the constitution. In addition, Section 7 in both the 1997 and 2007 constitutions also related to this issue.

Section 7 of the 2007 Constitution went as follows: 'Whenever no provision under this Constitution is applicable to any case, it shall be decided in accordance with the constitutional practice in the democratic regime of government with the king as head of the state'.[11]

Reference was firstly made to Section 63 of the 1997 Constitution. At the third meeting of the Drafting Sub-Committee, member Praphan sounded a warning regarding the ambivalence of the wording of this section: 'In fact, this provision also has been used to address vote-buying during elections. If that is the case, this should be clearly stated somewhere in either the constitution or the organic laws that derive from the constitution' ('Records of the Third Meeting of the Drafting Sub-Committee Group': 2). At the sixth meeting, committee member Kroekkiat raised the notion of convening a special emergency meeting based on Section 7 in the event of a political crisis. While declaring that

---

11 Translation available at: https://www.constituteproject.org/constitution/Thailand_2007.pdf

those who take part should be representatives of the people, he also proposed including the military. This he justified on the grounds that 'Decisions of these meetings will be binding, and the military will be needed to ensure enforcement' ('Records of the Sixth Meeting of the Drafting Sub-Committee Group': 2).

Kroekkiat repeated this position during the ninth meeting, asserting that 'Regarding Section 7, we should prepare an emergency exit in a crisis'. During the eleventh meeting, Chair Charan stated, 'Because there was no agency to adjudicate and no procedures to follow, Section 7 was, in fact, unworkable. I would like a second paragraph added clearly stating which body or person hands down the relevant ruling'. In response, committee member Yotsak pointed out that 'Past experience suggests that the Constitutional Court lacks the courage to rule in this way. Problematically, the parliament system is designed for normal conditions. So, a ruling based on this section is actually impossible'. Ruchira Techangkun then declared, referencing the fact that both France and Germany confer emergency powers on the president or prime minister, that 'There are many people who, in the context of emergency powers, recall Section 17 of the Interim Constitution (which gave strong authority to the military prime minister during the military dictatorship of the past). But this time, unlike the dictatorships of the past, power is exercised not by individuals but by a council of representatives of legislative, political and judicial powers'. Committee member Pisit recalled 9.11. He argued, 'Thailand also needs to prepare for such an event' ('Records of the Ninth and Eleventh Meetings of the Drafting Sub-Committee Group': 2).

This debate continued throughout the Drafting Assembly. At the fifth meeting, Witthaya Khotkhuean suggested revising Section 7 to ensure its practical use ('Records of the Fifth Meeting of the Drafting Assembly'). At the seventh meeting, however, Soemkiat Woradit expressed opposition to using this section given that the stipulations were so ambivalent and wide-ranging ('Records of the Seventh Meeting of the Drafting Assembly'). At the sixteenth meeting, committee member Vicha observed that, with respect to responding to emergency situations: 'Section 68 determined that the Constitutional Court deal with crisis conditions' ('Records of the Sixteenth Meeting of the Drafting

Assembly'). At the seventeenth meeting, however, a second member contradicted this by declaring, 'What is Section 68? If the people were given a vote, they would surely oppose such a provision. Solutions offered by this section do not conform with democratic principles' ('Records of the Seventeenth Meeting of the Drafting Assembly'). During the eighteenth meeting, Winat Mammungsin further pointed out that 'The definition of crisis is ambivalent' ('Records of the Eighteenth Meeting of the Drafting Assembly').

The arguments outlined above confirm that, despite limited discussion on the actual desirability of a non-elected prime minister during the drafting of the 2007 Constitution, there was a push to use sections 7 and 68 to cede state governance to a joint convention, including the military, at a time of 'crisis' – regardless of the fact that this notion was poorly defined. With no second paragraph ultimately added to Section 7 as requested by Chair Charan, we might conclude that in this respect also inadequate caution was exercised concerning the need for the entity with responsibility for the country's governance to have popular support.

The division of the three powers

The 2007 Constitution gave considerably more political power to the courts (particularly the Supreme Court) than the 1997 Constitution. The 1997 Constitution drew on a Montesquieu-like balance between the three powers, with various voices cautioning against the judiciary having an excess of power in relation to the other two. We will examine arguments conducted by groups two and three of the Drafting Sub-Committee and also by the Drafting Assembly to consider whether similar opinions were expressed during the 2007 drafting process.

Three main points were raised during discussions by group two of the sub-committee: 1. regulating the use of independent agency power, 2. preventing political interference in independent agency membership appointment processes, and 3. strengthening the powers of the ombudsman and the National Human Rights Commission. During the second meeting of group two, the meeting chair asked if there was not, in fact, 'a need for a separate independent agency or special court to investigate activities of independent bodies'.

The most pressing problem concerned whether to continue granting absolute power to the Election Commission to issue rulings – known respectively as 'yellow cards' and 'red cards' – concerning loss of election rights and the conduct of follow-up elections against those suspected of violating election regulations. Committee members Somkit and Phairoj both stated that the Election Commission's powers should be monitored through the court. Nakharin pointed out that 'With the absolute powers of the Election Commission, there are problems concerning its authority to approve and announce the final election result. There is no time framework stating within how many days this should happen. Absolute power needs time limits'. He accordingly suggested, 'We need to spell out in writing – and not merely regarding the Election Commission's yellow cards and red cards – that the exercise of power by independent agencies needs to be monitored through the courts'.

The need to eliminate political interference into the membership appointment process of independent agencies was also raised as a problem. Most Drafting Committee members understood that such intervention compromised agency neutrality. The committee chair introduced a proposal by Montri Phetcharakhum suggesting that the Selection Committee 'be comprised of former prime ministers, former presidents of the parliament, former chief justices of the Supreme Court and the current chief justice of the Supreme Administrative Court' ('Records of the Second Meeting of Group Two of the Drafting Committee').

During group two meetings, discussions of the appointment system of independent agency members continued. In the fifth meeting, Phairoj suggested that: '[The Selection Committee] should comprise the chief justice of the Constitutional Court, the chief justice of the Supreme Administrative Court, the chief justice of the Supreme Court, the head of the National Anti-Corruption Commission and the head of the National Ombudsman's Office'. Committee member Thanawat observed that 'If the Selection Committee is to have five members, then two should be from the Supreme Court, two from the Supreme

Administrative Court and one from the Constitutional Court'. Phisit, on the other hand, suggested that there be 'three Supreme Court representatives, one from the Constitutional Court and one from the Supreme Administrative Court', while Phairoj referenced a suggestion calling for 'one from each of the three courts, one government and one opposition member'. The direction of the discussion thus moved to hand the courts the lead in independent agency Selection Committee appointments. Although there were proposals that such a direction be balanced by the inclusion of political representation from both the government and the opposition, this was a minority point of view ('Records of the Fifth Meeting of Group Two of the Drafting Committee').

We will now consider group three discussions. A central figure in these was Vicha who, as noted, was a former justice of the Supreme Court. Udom Rattha-amarit referred in the first meeting to the confusion caused by the creation of a large number of independent agencies under the 1997 Constitution. He explained along the following lines: The relationship between the many independent agencies created under the 1997 Constitution was never clarified. Some had the same powers, and some had no less authority than the court. This caused problems. There will be difficulties if we retain independent agencies without ensuring that these have less power than the court. We also need to decide who can arbitrate or make these decisions. Other countries have a head of state. In Thailand, however, this is the king who is unable to intervene. So, we must decide who will provide a solution ('Records of the First Meeting of Group Three of the Drafting Committee').

In the fourth meeting, Vicha, who was also the chair, argued along the following lines: I checked the constitutions of other countries and found that courts and independent bodies are included in the judicial powers. In this way, independent institutions should also be positioned within the jurisdiction. Both judicial and quasi-judicial bodies should follow the same procedures. This is unity and, in my opinion, an independent body needs a central integration committee.

Giving an example of the need to coordinate agency activities, committee member Siracha noted, 'The power of the agencies overlaps. A member of the public lodged the same case with the National Ombudsman's Office, the National Human Rights Commission and the

Administrative Court' ('Records of the Fourth Meeting of Group 3 of the Drafting Committee'). Vicha revisited the issue during the fifth meeting, proposing that the power of the Supreme Court be strengthened to give it top ranking in the agency hierarchy: 'We need to decide that the rulings of the Constitutional Court are only binding for the matter in question. They should not be the final hearing. Indictments concerning elections are the responsibility of the Supreme Court's Election Indictment Department. The decisions of the Criminal Division for Persons Holding Political Positions of the Supreme Court can be challenged through an appeal to a plenary session of the Supreme Court. We should ensure that the people can lodge a case directly with the Criminal Division for Persons Holding Political Positions' ('Records of the Fifth Meeting of Group 3 of the Drafting Committee').

A further point of contention was whether or not the courts and the independent agencies that were charged with administering justice should intervene in political matters. At the first meeting, Udom was opposed to burdening the courts with a political role. He explained along the following lines: While independent agencies were created to address distrust in political institutions, they cannot use judicial authority to solve political problems. The court is fundamentally a passive entity that must wait for cases to be lodged by third parties. The losing side in any lawsuit, moreover, is unlikely to agree with the outcome. Problems emerge when we endow various other agencies with all of the three powers of state authority. This is especially the case when we hand these three powers over to the courts who then themselves enter the political sphere. This matter needs very careful consideration.

Committee member Kanchanarat Liwirot expressed the following view: 'Some independent agencies have been given the three powers. How should we maintain a balance when implementing the powers of these agencies? It's all very well to give this authority but there must be a power to monitor and counter those actions. Depending on the circumstances, it would be better to cede [agencies] just one or two powers' ('Records of the First Meeting of Group Three of the Drafting Sub-Committee').

Notwithstanding these criticisms of the powers of the court and independent agencies, Vicha proposed during the third meeting that

'We give the court and independent agencies the power to enact these regulations themselves and regard them as an element of law'. Udom gave an opinion that 'if courts are to issue their own rules, a central principle will be needed'. Committee member Paiboon also mentioned the problem as to whether or not the parliament should rule on free trade agreements, posing the question: 'Can the Constitutional Court judge such an issue?' Vicha responded that 'The people are able to lodge cases with the Constitutional Court'. With some on the Sub-Committee still concerned about the court having a political role, Khomsan warned at the sixth meeting, along the following lines: In drafting the new constitution, we have expanded all aspects of the role of the court. I find this frightening. Surely the court entering politics and politics coming into play has a huge influence on the court's independence. I myself want to limit the court to activities that lead to the confidence and trust of the people. We should fully negotiate on matters related to politics. I think it is a problem to leave everything to the Supreme Court'.

Vicha also acknowledged the dangers inherent in the Constitutional Court dealing with political matters arguing along the following lines: The Constitutional Court is in truth a political court. Chaos will accordingly result if it does not observe the law when handing down a ruling. While it is hidden, there are politics. Furthermore, the people can appeal to the court in matters of freedom of rights. In the United States, rulings on political matters are hugely problematic. This point alone very much raises the possibility of undermining the court. Accordingly, it would be best not to add further to court tasks over and above its current responsibilities ('Records of the Sixth Meeting of Group 3 of the Drafting Sub-Committee').

It emerged during discussions of the draft of the 2007 Constitution that a number of Sub-Committee members clearly had concerns about strengthening the political role of the court. Nevertheless, we cannot say that these fears were shared by Vicha, a central figure in compiling the draft. At the sixteenth meeting of the Drafting Assembly, he firstly declared that 'We have compiled this draft without pressure from any interest group and represent no other group than the people'. Vicha then moved to enumerate various discussion points. He explained,

I firstly want to talk about judicial activism, especially Section 68 and appointing members to each of the independent agencies. There is actually a misunderstanding. Judicial activism involves the court being just and right by handing down decisions that uphold the rights of the people. In this way, the institution of the court acts as a true proxy for the people and cannot function if divorced from the people. Judicial activism emerged in Europe in the 1980s. When political forces could no longer themselves control or revise the system, they had no option but to turn to the courts. They required the Supreme Court and the Constitutional Court to settle matters. We have strengthened the courts to conduct criminal procedures against politicians. We have the Criminal Division for Persons Holding Political Positions of the Supreme Court and the Constitutional Court. However, the Constitutional Court was subject to political intervention, and the public did not tolerate the Constitutional Court, as they perceived it to be a terrible court. We must restore pride to the Constitutional Court. [...] The Constitutional Court has handed down rulings on a range of matters. However, we do not think of this ourselves. The people themselves made proposals based on research into various cases. This included they themselves acknowledging the court as an organization that handed down final decisions. This is an agency that wields each of the three powers – administrative, legislative and judicial. We committee members do not want the courts to get involved in politics. However, there were voices of hope from the public, and the majority of the people were of the opinion that decisions on these issues, whether it be elections or the appointment of members of independent bodies, should go through the grand assembly of the Supreme Court. [...] The court has the confidence of the people. Article 68 provides for the resolution of political crises through the involvement of the court. Intellectuals fear that the court is too involved in politics. However, ceding these matters to the court is an expression of desperation towards political institutions. Some believe that members of independent agency selection committees should be drawn only from justices of the courts. That is because there was political intervention into the process of appointing members of the independent body in the Senate. My own experience was a good example. Although I was recommended as a member of the Election Commission, my appointment was blocked during upper house deliberations. It seems at the least that intervention occurred. Regardless, we need to investigate this point. ('Records of the Sixteenth Meeting of Group Three of the Drafting Sub-Committee')[12]

Although this statement by Vicha emphasized the connection between the courts and the people, he in fact gave much less attention to this point during discussions on the structure of the Selection Committee for the Constitutional Court and independent agencies held by group three of the Sub-Committee. In the first meeting, he presented three elements as a way to explain the direction of draft policy related to independent agencies: 1. altering institutional powers more appropriately, 2. changing the appointment system to ensure truly independent and neutral agencies, and 3. introducing an oversight system for independent agency appointments. As is apparent from group two discussions, there was strong agreement that, in order to achieve the second goal of 'ensuring independent and neutral agencies', politicians should not be involved in the appointment processes.

At the same meeting, however, Thanabun Chirawan was critical of direction as above, arguing that any decision to retain the independent agencies should bring them under the umbrella of assembly control. He asserted, 'It is undemocratic for these bodies to wield all the state powers: administrative, legislative and judicial powers. We currently have an autocratic system dressed up as democracy'. At the second meeting,

---

[12] The author interviewed former Supreme Court Justice, Vicha Mahakun, twice in October 2015. Vicha was pro-Japanese, intelligent and energetic. He remained quite bitter that, in spite of being nominated as a candidate for Election Commission membership by a plenary session of the Supreme Court, his nomination was not confirmed by the Upper House. He believed that then Prime Minister Thaksin had undoubtedly intervened. According to Vicha: 'Being recommended by the Supreme Court, whose members were "people of quality," was without question a written guarantee for the person involved'. He declared it an outrage that a nominee could nonetheless be rejected (interview conducted 5 October 2015).

Anurak Saga-arikun proposed five titles for the Selection Committee for the National Anti-Corruption Commission – the chief justice of the Supreme Court, the chief justice of the Constitutional Court, the chief justice of the Supreme Administrative Court, the president of the parliament and the leader of the opposition. Committee member Khomsan, however, argued that 'The president of the parliament and opposition leader might come under investigation by the National Anti-Corruption Commission. They should therefore be replaced with representatives from other agencies'. At the third meeting, committee member Anurak proposed that 'three Supreme Court justices, two Supreme Administrative Court justices, one Military Court justice and other competent people be appointed as justices of the Constitutional Court'. Vicha replied that the composition of the Constitutional Court, which many members were in favor of, consists of three judges from the Supreme Court, three from the Supreme Administrative Court, and three from qualified individuals. Also, regarding the composition of the committee for appointing qualified persons, the proposal of the chief justice of the Supreme Court, the chief justice of the Constitutional Court, the chief justice of the Supreme Administrative Court, the speaker of the House of Representatives, and the leader of the opposition party was supported.

Regarding the appointment of judges of the Constitutional Court and members of independent bodies, what clearly explained the Drafting Committee's thoughts was the remarks made by member Karun Saingam at the eighth session of the Drafting Assembly. Karun insisted along the following lines: Imagine the legislative branch is blue, the executive branch brown and the judicial branch white. Independent agencies are the entities that assist these three agencies. If the executive branch is involved in the process of appointing the members of the independent agency, the independent agency will also be polluted. Again, these institutions may be intervened in by the executive government. The brown color does not change, it remains dirty. If the legislature fails, so does its child, the executive government. Also, if the parents die, the children die too. Only the judiciary remains. Temporary care of the public should be entrusted to the chief justice of the Supreme Court, the chief justice of the

Supreme Administrative Court and the heads of government ministries and agencies. The process of appointing members of independent bodies can also be subject to political interference if those appointed by the executive government participate. It would be better to leave everything to the judicial branch ('Records of the Eighth Meeting of the Drafting Assembly').

While this was the majority thinking, Choemsak Pinthong expressed concern at the eighteenth meeting that, without an effective outside monitoring system, the upper house, the courts and the independent agencies would form a never-ending closed circle. Choemsak noted along the following lines: In group two, there was talk of members of the upper house appointing justices. In group three there was also talk of making justices appoint members of the independent agencies. Yes, there is agreement. Is this coincidence? I praise the justices. The people speak well of them also. I am however worried. Nor have the people yet conducted an investigation into this whole situation. Looking at the situation overall as a Drafting Committee member, I worry ('Records of the Eighth Meeting of the Drafting Assembly').

It became clear during discussions of the 2007 Constitution draft that there was limited interest in the value of popular elections. A system of appointment was endorsed for upper house members, while a section of the committee advocated for a non-elected appointment for the prime minister also. The most pressing point was the move to cede the country's governance to an emergency meeting at a time of political crisis. Rather than seeking to justify parliament membership through an election process, committee members involved in the drafting of the 1997 Constitution prioritized the value of diversity among parliament members (in both houses).

During the drafting of the 1997 Constitution, in the context of the court and the independent agencies, there were attempts to ensure the maintenance of the clear separation of and balance between the three powers. Yet, while some acknowledged the risk associated with the court's involvement in political matters, the 2007 draft process proceeded without any in-depth discussion on that critical point. As a result, the court, and the independent agencies especially, lost the democratic legitimization of connection to the people. Furthermore, even when the issue of checks and balances arose, this did not refer, as it did during the drafting of the 1997 Constitution, to mutually functioning checks between the three powers. Rather, it concerned checks of this nature between the courts, as the center of judicial power, and the independent agencies. We might say that, under the influence of former Supreme Court Justice and now committee member Vicha, a hierarchy emerged between the various agencies administering judicial and semi-judicial powers that ranked the Supreme Court at the head. Thus, a structure came to operate in Thailand by means of which the legal system dominated the political world. We might coin the term 'judicification' to refer to this phenomenon.

Fear of the masses and provisions to protect the constitution

During the drafting of both the 1997 and 2007 constitutions, a range of opinions were expressed particularly on legitimization through elections, diversity and the separation of powers. This chapter has nevertheless made clear that there has always been an intention to return to the situation 'before' the 1991 constitutional amendments that took place after the 1992 Bloody May Incident. At a seminar entitled 'Political Reform: Have Legal Scholars Lost the Way?' held on 22 May 2002 at Thammsat University Faculty of Law, Amon, the scholar who authored the text *Constitutionalism* that become the theoretical foundation of the 1990s political reform movement, was critical of the 1997 Constitution. He declared the failures of the document to be '1. Strengthening the power of the prime minister too much, and 2. producing parliamentary dictatorship'. He also noted with disappointment that: 'Reading the news makes us aware that we are in an autocracy of business politicians. [...] We can't escape dictatorship. We previously set out to prevent a military dictatorship. We are now captured instead by a dictatorship of the parliament through a political party run by a group of business politicians. [...] Political reform through the 1997 Constitution was a mirage'. Amon's words confirm that the aim of his 'constitutionalism' was to diversify the representative mix of parliament members who had carriage of administrative and legislative government. He had no intention to create strong prime ministers or large-scale political parties.

The reforms undertaken in post-1992 Thailand can appear contradictory at first glance. Politics became the realm of the people resulting in a large-scale mass democracy movement and demanded that the prime minister be legitimized by an election process. It was accordingly decided that the prime minister be chosen from the lower house. The 1997 Constitution was a product of the political reform movement that extolled the advancement of democratic values. Nevertheless, provisions protecting the constitution (Section 63 in 1997 and 68 in 2007) were introduced which gave the court the power to eradicate dictatorial powers stemming from the 'bad political power' that could come with majority rule, such as Adolph Hitler's Nazi Germany. While ostensibly championing political reform, the prominent legal scholars who celebrated constitutionalism were averse to the popular will of the ordinary people permeating the parliament as far as the position of prime minister. Furthermore, depending on the circumstances, they were even prepared to tolerate, as previously, a military coup d'état. As we try to reconcile these apparent contradictions in Thai political reform, we might question the degree to which Amon's line of reasoning was rational.

Let us momentarily step away from Thailand to consider a general history of democracy. Even in advanced overseas nations, including Japan, there can be distrust toward the national assembly and a parliamentary system of democracy. Comparative political studies scholars argue that contemporary representative democracy encompasses two competing strands. There is a liberalist strand embracing a pluralistic political viewpoint that historically assumes competition between elites and mutual checks and balances. There is also a democratic strand that seeks to have politics reflect the political will of the people. Friction arises between these two sets of values particularly since the former aims to suppress 'the tyranny of the majority' through the separation of powers. According to Machidori (2015), both communism and fascism set out to deny the liberalist element inherent in representative democracy. Even if we eliminate the elite who promote liberalism, however, we would be unable to unify the interests of the 'we' of the remaining people (Machidori 2015).

During the drafting of the 1997 Constitution, there was much discussion on the need to avoid the emergence of a German-style Nazi Party or Hitler-like figure in Thailand. Suraphol's statement cited above was but one example. Then, as now, Hitler was the defining symbol of a dictator who came to power through majority party rule. The priority for Amon and the members of both drafting committees was a system designed to guarantee diversity within the parliament, the upper and lower house membership of which should mutually represent the different peoples and groups in Thailand. This was his reason for advocating an appointment system for the upper house. Even his insistence that there was no necessity for a prime minister to be a member of the lower house can be interpreted as a call to guarantee diversity. Considering these points together, we realize that, as in various Western countries in the past, constitutionalism was introduced as a measure in Thailand that would guarantee the diversity of power holders and representatives charged with implementing state authority. While such developments were late in Thailand, democratization followed a similar path to that of Western nations with this mode of governance gradually becoming popularized in a way that profiled the contradictions inherent in parliamentary democracy. Did such a situation create a sense of impending crisis about the future among Thai intellectuals?

Both Amon and Suraphol are public law scholars who received their doctorates in France. Each is familiar with the theories of democracy and constitutionalism in advanced countries. As already noted, in the immediate postwar era, various Western countries conducted reforms that effectively strengthened judicial control over the political realm. Even France, a strongly parliament-centric state with a traditional distrust of the judiciary, introduced reforms that reduced the authority of the country's parliament. The assertions of Amon and Suraphol largely conform with theories of democracy and constitutionalism as argued in advanced countries.

Notwithstanding the understanding as outlined above of political reform and constitutionalism in Thailand, a question remains. We noted how the system of parliamentary democracy encompasses two contradictory and antagonistic strands, one liberalist and one democratic. As suffrage became truly universal in many places after the end of World War II, the will of the people demanded more diverse policy decisions in a way that did not necessarily correspond to the system of parliamentary democracy at the time. As a result, each country experienced a heightening of political distrust which led also to distrust of the parliament (Machidori 2015: 69–76). Now in the twenty-first century, although change is occurring on several fronts, democracy maintains its viability in advanced nations. In Thailand, on the other hand, the 2006 coup d'état had the 1997 Constitution rescinded while a cabinet and parliament appointed by the coup group conducted affairs of state for approximately a year. The newly enacted 2007 Constitution was repeatedly used to overthrow political administrations through the court, while dissatisfaction by the people of Thailand with the court's rulings resulted in the eruption of large-scale demonstrations. A renaissance of the political influence of the military, furthermore, saw yet another coup staged in 2014. We might consider why political reform failed to establish a stable system of parliamentary democracy in Thailand and why the military was able to return to power.

Worachet denounced Thai constitutionalism as unlike that of any other country. The courts continually undermined elected governments; many people in Thailand were opposed to the rulings of the court and related matters. This led to repeated large-scale demonstrations in which citizens voiced their objections to what they saw as the 'double standards' involved. Since there was no such phenomenon in either Germany or France, we need to consider how these sites differed from Thailand. This difference could have derived from different points of origin prompting political reform. We noted the understanding in Western countries of the tension between democracy and constitutionalism that led to a corresponding caution towards the judiciary entering the political realm. Cognizant of the enormity of the brutal and historically exceptional human rights violations committed by the Nazis, the postwar German Fundamental Law included a provision protecting the constitution. That provision granted the Constitutional Court in that country the power to dissolve a political party. All Western countries, moreover, were appalled at Nazi policies with the result that there was a strengthening of the power of the judiciary even in France. In contrast, the trigger for political reform in Thailand was the sense of crisis experienced by intellectuals and conservative groups following the demise of the option of a non-elected prime minister after the constitutional reforms that followed the 1992 Bloody May Incident.[13]

Khien, who was involved in drafting the 1997 Constitution, raised three points concerning Bloody May. The first related to a non-elected prime minister, the second to the military coup d'état and the third to mass demonstrations. Khien asserted that although a non-elected prime minister was vetoed following the1992 Bloody May Incident, the dearth of competent people in Thai politics meant that retaining the option of a non-elected prime minister in the event of a coalition government being unable to agree on a candidate for the role was not necessarily a bad option. He argued that flexibility in this matter would ensure political and economic stability (Khien 1997: 17–18, 65–67). According to Khien, demands to insert prohibitions on coups d'état into the 1997 Constitution draft were not acted upon because these demands came from people lacking knowledge of law or political science. He claimed that including such a statement had no real value and that efforts should be made to eliminate the cause and conditions that led to a coup d'état. These causes and conditions were parliamentary dictatorship and political corruption. In terms of

---

13 According to Prinya Thaewanarumitkul, from the Thammasat University Faculty of Law, while the government count of those who died during the Bloody May Incident at that university was forty-four, this was confined to those who died in hospital. It is currently estimated that an additional 200 people, probably shot by the military during the incident, failed to return to their homes.

Prinya noted that when a representative of bereaving families spoke directly to Suchinda, the former general whose appointment as prime minister provoked the May 1992 bloodshed, Suchinda replied that the dead bodies had been disposed of in the sea off the Rayong coast along the northeast of the Gulf of Thailand. That the bereaved families group continues to present at political seminars and similar events is evidence that the impact of the incident has not been extinguished even today (Interview conducted by author on 13 June 2017).

government intervention in military personnel matters as a means of preventing a coup, he opposed it and expressed concern that such an intervention could undermine the military's defense capabilities (Khien 1997: 74–79).

Rather than an unelected prime minister or a coup d'état, however, the most pressing issue for Khien was the outbreak of mass demonstrations. Khien emphasized that Suchida's selection as prime minister had accorded with the requirements of the 1991 Constitution (prior to the post-Bloody May reforms), and that, even if powerbrokers had enacted the constitution, a revision process should have occurred through peaceful means. He deplored the illegal measures (violent mass demonstrations) taken, measures that had given rise to barbaric acts (Khien 1997: 132). He further asserted the necessity of a system that checked undesirable behaviors to prevent social collapse. Political issues inevitably involve tense competition and should never be adjudicated by either the military or politicians. Rather, a neutral system was needed with, for example, an anti-corruption committee being convened to manage high level bureaucratic personnel matters. If the constitution failed to offer a system of assessing whether or not the actions of the government violated the law, he asserted, people would have no option but to turn to 'the law of the jungle', that is, to mass demonstrations (Khien 1997: 79).

It can be said that Thailand's independent organizations were expected to play a role as a crisis management system amidst the trend of banning non-elected prime ministers and democratizing the Senate. In other words, the aim of establishing independent agencies in Thailand differed from the priority of the West, which was to protect human rights. As we saw in the previous chapter, it was becoming increasingly difficult for King Bhumibol to intervene as the demonstrations became larger, longer-lasting, and more violent. It was Thai independent agencies that were expected to assume the important task of managing any subsequent political crisis. The background to this seems to have been a lack of trust in the organizing capabilities of a government with both a parliament *and* a prime minister chosen by popular vote. As will be discussed in detail in the following chapters, this resulted in Thai constitutionalism ceding an excess of power to the judiciary. Thus, difficult political decisions, the resolution of which required time and ongoing negotiation, were now made by the Supreme Court and the Constitutional Court. Vicha predicted that, no matter the ruling handed down by the Constitutional Court, the side that lost would never consent.

According to the record of the very significant fifth meeting of the 1997 Constitution Drafting Committee, referred to above, many committee members understood that a key objective of their deliberations was to break the 'vicious cycle' of a constitution being overthrown by a military coup. The debate direction included a realization that achieving such an end required the introduction of a provision to protect the constitution, modelled on the German Fundamental Law, into the constitution itself. After all arguments were exhausted, however, committee member Bowonsak suddenly proposed a change of wording which meant that the entity to be protected by such a provision was now 'the democratic regime of government with the king as head of state'. Meeting records confirm how this proposed change left other committee members perplexed. That was because, as discussed, a coup that did not eliminate 'the democratic regime of government with the king as head of state' would not have violated the provision protecting the constitution (Section 63 of the 1997 Constitution). On the other hand, as pointed out at the third meeting of the 2007 Constitution Drafting Sub-Committee, the real-life application of that same provision also targeted election law violations leading to suggestions from Drafting Committee members that this secondary effect should be clearly stated in both the constitution and the organic laws that derived from it. That is to say, depending on the interpretation, the extreme ambivalence of the wording of the provision to protect the Constitution of Thailand was dangerously open to arbitrary use.

Not all documentation relating to drafting either the 1997 or 2007 constitutions is accessible to the public. While most meeting records of the Drafting Assembly, Drafting Committee and Drafting Sub-Committee of both constitutions are in the public domain, the very first 1997 draft, compiled by the staff of the Council of State to become the springboard for future discussion, remains unavailable. It is apparent that, over many years, Thailand had a bureaucratic system of government centered on the military, the bureaucracy and the king. Repeated military coups d'état resulted in both interim constitutions and most substantive constitutions being drafted under the influence of the military. While opposing voices were heard from political party politicians, even the 1997 Constitution, which was drafted under the influence of the political reform movement, was supported by the military and the king. Drafting of the 2007 Constitution, too, occurred under the military administration installed following the 2006 coup d'état. In other words, when discussing constitutional drafts in Thailand we must always be cognizant of the extent of the influence of the military.

This chapter has clearly established that motives for adopting constitutionalism in Thailand. The circumstances in which this occurred were quite different from those that saw the provision protecting the constitution included into the postwar German Fundamental Law, legislation that became a model for Thailand. It is apparent that some Drafting Committee members felt strong mistrust towards a popularly elected prime minister, while, in addition to the conventional role of protecting human rights, expectations were placed on independent agencies to mediate future political crises that might be similar to the 1992 Bloody May Incident. Although the 1997 Constitution was enacted extolling democracy, the people realized that embedded within the document was an anti-popular election intent. This undoubtedly resulted in a range of tensions and inconsistencies within the system blueprint promoted by the document. Counting from the first 1932 Constitution, the 1997 document was the sixteenth iteration. In this sixteenth constitution, very significant changes were made relating to the separation of powers. Some changes were retained and others discarded in the 2007 document. The chapters that follow will provide a detailed investigation into the provisions of the 1997 and 2007 constitutions and the organic laws that derived from these. In doing so, we will consider the system designed for each of the three powers and the influence of both constitutions on democratization in Thailand.

PART II

Constitutional Reform and Power Elected by the People

3

Constitutional Reform and Administrative Power: The Political Implications of 'Directive Principles of Fundamental State Policies'

As discussed in detail in previous chapters, the democratization movement in Thailand gathered pace throughout the 1990s. At this time, both the urban middle-class and traditional elites profiled issues such as corrupt politicians and electoral fraud to express strong discontent with government by popular election. It was in the context of the constitutional reform movement in the 1990s aimed at addressing these matters (Connors 2002: 37–44; Chumphon 2002: 106–111; Thitinan 2009; Harding and Leyland 2011: 22–26) that 'constitutionalism' became the key word of the time (Amon 1994a, 1994b, 1994c). As noted above, the drafting process of the 1997 Constitution reflected strong distrust of popularly elected prime ministers. What sort of controls, then, were implemented to stem government executive powers and what significant changes were made in the 1997 document regarding the separation of powers?

The first point is the creation of independent agencies. The 1997 Constitution was divided into five main sections: the king,[1] human rights, 'Directive Principles of Fundamental State Policies', government administration and independent agencies. Independent agencies, first introduced into the 1997 Constitution as a means of regulating or managing state powers, include a Constitutional Court, an Election Commission, a National Parliamentary Ombudsman and a National Counter-Corruption Commission. While bodies such as constitutional courts and national human rights commissions operate in Western countries also, particular features of these in Thailand include both

---

1 Since 'king' and 'kingship', rather than monarch or monarchy, are used consistently throughout the Constitution of the Kingdom of Thailand, those words are retained here.

the large number of them and their breadth of powers (Worachet 2009: 87–109).

The second point is the changes in the nature and contents of the 'Directive Principles of Fundamental State Policies'. While this element has remained a feature of the Thai constitutions since this section was first introduced in the 1949 Constitution,[2] significant revisions were made in the 1997 Constitution with respect to both content and the legal standing of this section. Until 1997, 'Directive Principles of Fundamental State Policies' merely promoted long-term objectives and the vision of an ideal state. Since the 1997 Constitution, however, the provisions have changed into legally enforceable provisions that can bind the cabinet and the parliament through the judiciary. This change is very important in the sense of the constitutional control of state power. Similar properties carried over into the 2007 Constitution and the current constitution.

Wide-ranging scholarship exists on independent agencies in Thailand (Imaizumi 2003; Ōtomo 2003). However, while several scholars note the importance of the 'Directive Principles of Fundamental State Policies', little objective research into or analysis of these has been conducted. Some papers favorably assess this section of the Thai constitutions as human rights guarantees, however, Chapter 2 demonstrated how both the opportunity and motive for the introduction of the these into the 1997 Constitution largely differ from frameworks that operate in the West. It will therefore be useful to examine a number of specific differences between Western constitutional models and the Constitution of the Kingdom of Thailand.

Focusing on the 'Directive Principles of Fundamental State Policies', this chapter will conduct a comparative review of selected constitutions of both Western and other Asian nations with a view to undertaking a close analysis of the political intent that drove the wide-ranging changes introduced in Thailand at the time of both the 1997 and 2007 constitutional revisions. In addition to examining changes to

---

2   These did not appear in interim constitutions (1959, 1972, 1977, 1991, 2006). 'Interim constitution' refers to a temporary constitution established by military authorities following a stay of the constitution after a coup-d'état and that determined the governance structures of a junta.

the nature and actual content of the section, the discussion will profile the cabinet administrative policy speech as a means of understanding how the articles of the section exert influence on government administrative powers. Drawing on the constitutions of other nations in order to gain insight into the political significance of Thailand's 'Directive Principles of Fundamental State Policies', the chapter highlights both the main characteristics and problematic aspects of the form of constitutionalism that operates in that country. With its advocacy of majority decision-making and esteem for democratic processes, Western constitutionalism seeks to protect human rights through the operation of both the constitution and rule of law to prevent the arbitrary exercise of state power. In contrast, Thai constitutionalism has developed in a way that positions the constitution as a set of all-encompassing 'directive' principles vis-a-vis the power of the state and especially the cabinet. This chapter will clarify that the structure is such that it is possible for an outsider to exercise arbitrary control over the administration through appeals to the Constitutional Court and highlight that one of the underlying features of the 1997 and 2007 constitutions is the restriction on public opinion expressed through elections.[3]

Discussions on 'Directive Principles of Fundamental State Policies' in Thailand

Over the past ten years, one of the key expressions that came to be circulated by the mass media and others who criticized cabinet policies was 'Directive Principles of Fundamental State Policies' (hereafter the 'Directive Principles'). In this section, I will clarify how this notion, which is the title of Paragraph 5 of the Thai Constitution, has been articulated in political critique.

---

3   This chapter will examine the systematic design of the Thai Constitution and clarify the political intent of those who drafted the document. It will not analyze the influence that court rulings have exerted on the political process. With regard to the 1997 and 2007 constitutions, the legal analysis undertaken by Imaizumi (2012) focuses on legislative processes. The purpose of this chapter is to provide a political analysis of both documents through the lens of the democratization of Thai politics.

Pointing out that the 'Directive Principles' section impinges upon all policies of all governments, Kriengsak Charoenwongsak (2003) has observed the term 'Directive Principles of Fundamental State Policies' means the 'policy of the nation state' and thus differs from the 'government policy' of an administration, regardless of political stripe. While 'government policy' will change according to the administration or cabinet in power, Directive Principles of Fundamental State Policies do not change to fit the platform of a particular party or administration. They are in this sense the basis that underpins the policies of a country that all governments must adhere to and seek to implement (Kriengsak 2003).

In terms of government policy and planning, the critical nature of the 'Directive Principles' is apparent from the words of former deputy prime minister and public law scholar, Wissanu Krea-ngam, who argued along the following lines: Populist policies will not solve long-term problems or lead to national reform. Good policy must be grounded in the following five principles. These are: the 'Directive Principles of Fundamental State Policies', monetary and fiscal regulation, rule of law, good governance and accurate assessment of the situation at home and abroad (ASTV Phucatkan, 22 May 2012).

Wissanu's assertions assume that, rather than the will of the people, it is the 'Directive Principles' articulated in Chapter 5 of the Thai Constitution that offer a cabinet prudent policy direction. Accordingly, in terms of policy decision-making, government discretionary power can only be applied through that framework.

Even in terms of the political reform that has preoccupied Thai politics since the 1990s, Royal Academy member, Wichitwong Na Pomphet, similarly asserted along the following lines: The fundamental principles of the constitution cover a broad set of domains. This is particularly the case regarding chapter 5, the 'Directive Principles of Fundamental State Policies', which encompasses almost all aspects of state governance. It is not possible to 'reform' the fundamental principles of the constitution. Calls to reform the Thai nation seek to make the government that administers our nation overhaul everything that is stated in law in relation to the constitution, the National Economic and Social Development Plan and also in relation to administrative authority. Yet, the elements available for consideration in any reform process are limited to matters that are not stipulated by law in relation to the basic principles of the constitution, or the key points of national, economic and social development, or the administrative authority of governance organizations. The Directive Principles of Fundamental State Policies of the 2007 Constitution are extremely well-developed and offer almost no scope for revision (Wichitwong 2010).

While critics of the 'Directive Principles' are in the minority, prominent public law scholar Kanin Bunsuwan (2008), for example, argued along the following lines: The Directive Principles of Fundamental State Policies of the 2007 Constitution are unusual in that they can be read as a significant challenge against the form and manner of writing of the constitution that conform to international principles. In other words, that which is stated as Directive Principles of Fundamental State Policies in the supreme law of the land becomes, in fact, the "policy of the state" and must be strictly adhered to by all governments. The Directive Principles of Fundamental State Policies, in fact, appear to be documented in a way that positions them above policies articulated by [a cabinet] to the parliament (Kanin 2008).

Public law scholar Worachet Pakeerut made a clear statement of opposition to the constitution determining the direction of policy in this way by observing that 'Policy should [be something] that political parties which contest elections articulate to voters' (Worachet 2009).

It is apparent from the above that Chapter 5 of the Constitution outlining the 'Directive Principles' has been interpreted as carrying greater weight than policy options drawn up by a cabinet. We will firstly consider whether such an understanding is evident in the constitutions of other countries that also subscribe to constitutionalism. Secondly, because groups that either promote or oppose the 'Directive Principles' commonly emphasize how the stipulations in question constrain government policy, we must examine the concrete substance of the ongoing ideological dispute in which these groups are engaged and its impact on the operation of Thai cabinets. In other words, we will examine the special features of Thai constitutionalism.

Changes in the 'Directive Principles' of Thai constitutions

The Irish Constitution, which came into effect in 1937, was the first attempt to include a clause indicating 'fundamental national policy' in a constitution, and it was later introduced in the constitutions of countries such as India, Pakistan, Bangladesh, Sri Lanka, Nepal and the Philippines (Kobayashi 1999: 273). The fundamental national policy of these constitutions could not be contested in court, nor did they have the status of rule of law (pursued in further detail in Chapter 4).[4] This item aims at guaranteeing human rights, especially social rights, by the state by articulating the state's long-term goals or ideals. How does this compare to the situation in Thailand? I will examine this question through the frameworks of wording changes to the Thai document and the nature of precedents set by the courts.

History and wording

As mentioned above, Thailand's constitutions have been repeatedly revoked and enacted, but 'the fundamental national policy' was included for the first time in the 1949 Constitution, the fifth constitution. Since then, the item has been included in all constitutions, with the exception of the interim constitutions. In terms of the title, between 1949 and 1991, this item was referred to as 'Directive Principles of State Policy' (*naeo nayobai haeng rat*). By both the 1997 and 2007 constitutions, however, the title had become 'Directive Principles of Fundamental State Policies' (*naeo nayobai phuenthan haeng rat*). Significantly, the chapter featuring this item is located between those of the Thai Constitution that concern 'The Duty of the Thai People' and 'The Parliament'. In other words, it appears prior to the chapter related to the operation of government.

---

4 By the nature of legal standards, I mean the character of the legal system. The nature of court standards refers to rulings in a court of law. In the case of court standards operating, the court is able to use these as standards for making decisions when giving a concrete ruling in a dispute. Furthermore, these can be used as direct grounds when appealing to the court.

The number of articles in the item has seesawed across the decades with nineteen in 1949, seven in 1952, eighteen in 1968, thirty-three in 1974, twenty-one in 1978, twenty-six in 1991, nineteen in 1997 and thirteen in 2007. While the 2007 Constitution features a reduced number of articles, the extremely detailed content makes that document, in terms of word count, the longest of all versions.[5]

As outlined in Table 3.1, comparative examination of the content written in the items of each constitution indicates that there are two types of articles: those common to successive constitutions and those that have been revised or added between 1949 and 2007.

Let us firstly consider common regulations across the constitutions. These include national independence and territorial maintenance, harmonious relations with other countries, maintenance and deployment of military force, promotion of education, support for academic research, preservation of ethnic culture/s, preservation of historical, artistic and cultural heritage, prevention of economic monopoly, promotion of agriculture and industry, protection of farmers regarding issues such as land ownership rights, promotion of agricultural co-operatives, promotion of social welfare, worker safeguards, and facilitation of public health services. Each concerns either state security, the promotion of social and economic development, or the facilitation of human rights protections, and each articulates a long-term national objective.

We should secondly consider revised or appended regulations. There are clear points of difference in the types of constitutional revisions made until 1991, and those made in 1997 and 2007. Major points revised up until 1991 related to efficiencies in national governance, tightening the management of public corruption regulations, ensuring impartiality and timeliness of judicial procedures, promoting the understanding of a democratic regime with the king as head of state, application of science and the arts, environmental protections, protection and development of natural resources, promotion of gender equality, reduction of economic and social disparity, employment support for

---

5 Although the 1973 Constitution had the greatest number of sections at thirty-three, because so many elements were added to specific sections of the 2007 document, the word count increased exponentially.

Table 3.1 Changes in 'Directive Principles of State Policies' or 'Directive Principles of Fundamental State Policies' of Thai constitutions

Constitution	1949 to 1991	1997
Title of Chapter	'Directive Principles of State Policies'	'Directive Principles of Fundamental State Policies'
Legal and judicial enforceability	The provisions in this chapter are to be directive principles for legislating and determining state policies in the administration of the country, and <u>shall not create the right to take legal action against the state.</u>	The provisions of this chapter are intended to serve as directive principles for legislating and determining policies for the administration of state affairs.
Common content	• Maintenance of independence and territory • Harmonious relations with other countries • Maintenance and deployment of military force • Promotion of education • Support for research in the arts and natural sciences	• Preservation of ethnic arts, culture and traditions • Preservation of historical, cultural and artistic heritage • Prevention of economic monopolies • Promotion of agriculture and industry • Protection of the interests of farmers relating to production and marketing
Additional or revised content	• National governance system efficiency • Suppression of corruption in the public sphere • Ensuring fair and impartial justice administration procedures • Promoting the understanding of Thai values, disciplines, concerns for public interests and adherence to the democratic regime of government with the king as head of state • Deploying the sciences and arts in the interests of national development • Promotion and support for decentralization • Environmental protection • Protection and development of natural resources • Promotion of gender equality • Reduction of economic and social disparity • Employment support for people with disabilities • Promotion of and support for sports	• Advocacy for and protection of Buddhism and other religions • Sufficient budget allocation to various independent institutions and courts • Support for popular participation in the scrutiny of the exercise of state powers at all levels and the determination of policies • Establishment and maintenance of a political development plan • Preparation of a moral and ethical standard of holders of political positions, government officials, officials and other employees of the state • Formulating family unity and stronger regions • Establishing laws related to national education • Formulation of an agricultural plan • Promotion of the repeal of laws and regulations and the deletion of statutes controlling commercial affairs that do not correspond with economic necessity • Establishment of the National Economic and Social Advisory Council with the duty to advise and make recommendations to the cabinet

2007
'Directive Principles of Fundamental State Policies'
The provisions in this chapter indicate the will of the state in enacting legislation and determining policies for the administration of state affairs.
• Protection of farmers' rights to land ownership • Promoting the association of farmers • Protection of laborers • Promoting social welfare system • Promotion of public health services
• Promotion and support for the implementation of national administration based on the self-sufficiency economy philosophy • Promotion of local government organizations' participation in the implementation of 'Directive Principles of Fundamental State Policies' • Enabling judicial agencies, which have legal duties to give opinions on the operation of the state and scrutinize the law-making of the state, to perform their duties independently to ensure that the administration of state affairs shall be in compliance with the rule of law principle • Putting in place a political development plan and establishing an independent political development council for monitoring strict compliance with such plan • Formulation of national education plan • Establishment of systems to improve/provide people and academic agency participation in judicial procedures and to improve/provide legal support for people • Formulation of laws to establish an independent law reform agency • Formulation of laws related to the establishment of a judicial reform agency • Improving the taxation systems • Formulation of urban development plans • Provision of budget support for scientific research, investigation and analysis • Establishment of research development agency • Promotion and support of people's participation in the formulation of socioeconomic development policy, government decision-making and inspection of the exercise of state power • Introduction of laws to establish a National Sector of Political Development Fund for the Community • Support for citizen groups that address the need for community

Source: Compiled by the author.

people with disabilities, and promotion of and support for sports. Many of these points were firstly appended to the 1974 Constitution, which came into being as Thailand cast off long-term military rule and evolved into a democratic state. These political conditions supported the emergence of constitutional wording concerning governance and judicial reform, with appended statements relating to environmental protections and the protection of human rights particularly noticeable. Until 1991, however, all of the provisions in this item were limited to descriptions of abstract ideals only.

On the other hand, revisions undertaken in relation to the 1997 and 2007 constitutions have special characteristics that distinguish them markedly from changes made in the past. Particularly apparent is the fact that many additional articles relate to political and governance reform. In relation to political reform, statutes were created regarding the formulation of political development plans, the establishment of ethical standards for those in politics or other holders of public office, the establishment of an independent political development consultancy council to oversee the drawing up and implementation of political development plans, and the establishment of a National Sector of Political Development Fund for the Community. In terms of governance reforms, articles were added concerning improvement to oversights monitoring the implementation of efficiency in matters such as governance systems in a manner that responded to the needs of the electorate. There were also calls for the development of a transparent taxation system that responded to economic and social conditions. The 2007 Constitution furthermore included several articles specifically related to judicial reforms. Under the constitution, the articles regarding the enactment of laws concerning the establishment of legal reform bodies, the enactment of laws concerning the establishment of judicial reform bodies, and the support and assistance of public participation in the examination of the exercise of state power were stipulated in the section. The key point here is that, rather than being confined abstract objectives, these reforms documented concrete stipulations concerning legal processes, the creation of organizational structures, budget dividends and various planned developments.[6] These detailed directives encompass broad fields that even include those such as education, academic research, economics and urban planning. Previously, this section described the state's long-term goals for the protection of human rights, with a focus on social rights, however, the content of this section was changed to stipulate the responsibility of the state or administration to reform the system, focusing on political reform since the 1997 Constitution. This was because the drafting of that constitution occurred in response to the 1990s political reform movement that was characterized by deep distrust of the political class.[7]

The discussion above demonstrates how, apart from matters relating to public order, the 1949 to 1991 constitutions particularly promoted universal values such as social welfare and human rights. In that sense, these documents largely outlined abstract ideals and long-term national goals. Major shifts after that time, however, resulted in the 1997 and 2007 constitutions coming to act as concrete constraints on political policy and law-making.

Legal and judicial status

Particularly significant were changes to the wording of the constitution that related to the document's judicial legal status. As noted above,

---

6 The influence of Amon (1994a), who argued that Thai constitutional revision should occur as part of a package that included reforms of the entire political system, was central in terms of providing a theoretical perspective to political reform in Thailand during the 1990s.

7 The background to the political reform movement was a strong distrust of popularly elected politicians, many of whom came from conservative ranks. The electorate thought that, since the majority of politicians had entered the political domain for self-profit and self-interest, they were concerned with benefitting only themselves and were therefore incapable of engaging in systematic or appropriate law-making. A viewpoint emerged in response to this that legislative matters should be conducted in accordance with the 'Directive Principles' as stipulated by the constitution (Siracha and Somchat 2002: 275–288). The decision that the 2007 Constitution (Section 81, Clause 3) would: 'provide a law establishing an independent law reform organization for the purpose of reforming and developing laws of the nation [...]', reflected a lack of trust in the parliament's legislative abilities.

'national policy' statements in constitutions of other countries have no legal standing. From 1949 to 1991, legal stipulations were also absent from the section of the Thai Constitution, with either the beginning or end of the chapter merely stating: 'The provisions in this chapter are to be directive principles for legislating and determining state policies in the administration of the country, and shall not create the right to take legal action against the state'.

Not only, however, did the 1997 Constitution state that 'The provisions of this chapter are intended to serve as directive principles for legislating and determining policies for the administration of state affairs' (Section 88), the phrase, '[...] and shall not create the right to take legal action against the state' was deleted. The 2007 Constitution also determined that: 'The provisions of this chapter are intended to serve as directive principles for legislating and determining policies for the administration of state affairs' (Section 75), while, predictably, there was no reference to 'not creating the right to take legal action'. This can be interpreted as the 'Directive Principles' of the constitution having the potential, at least, to have legal standing. It is furthermore important to note that, while the 1997 document was couched in a discourse of matters being 'determined as policy', this shifted by 2007 to the much stronger expression, 'have the purpose of'.[8] Thus, while there may be some remnant ambiguity regarding the constitution's legal status, the changes discussed strengthen constraints on the administrative policy-making executive powers of cabinets for whom these fundamental national principles are intended. The changes can therefore be interpreted as definitely giving rise to scope for the relevant sections to be recognized as legal norms or requirements.

In relation to the functioning of the judicial branch of government, furthermore, the 2007 Constitution determined that '[The state is] to undertake that a legal agency providing legal opinions relating to state activities and examining draft laws based on the 'Directive Principles of Fundamental State Policies' shall perform its duties independently so as to ensure that the administration of state affairs is in accordance with the rule of law' (Section 78, Paragraph 6). Through

---

8   The Thai expression is '*chettachamnong*' which can mean 'purpose', 'intention', 'plan' or 'objective'.

this new definition of its functions, the judiciary was now positioned as the institution with oversight of all aspects of national government and administration activity.[9] Thus, revisions to the 1997 and 2007 constitutions ensured that the 'Directive Principles' changed in both substantive content and legal character to emerge as entities with the capacity to be upheld by the Constitutional Court.

What sort of decisions, then, has the Constitutional Court in Thailand made regarding the legal status of these 'Directive Principles'? Since 1998, the provisions of the 'Directive Principles' cited in grounds for prosecution were articles 76, 78, 80, 83, 84, 86 and 87 of the 1997 Constitution and articles 76, 81, 84, 85 and 87 of the Constitution of 2007.[10] While the Constitutional Court did not overtly repudiate the legal status of these clauses, the first clear ruling affirming this was in a decision handed down in 2002. This matter related to whether or not Section 87 of the 1997 Constitution – which dealt with government obligation in matters such as encouraging a free economic system through market forces, guaranteeing and supervising fair competition, and the prevention of monopoly – complied with Section 6, which read: 'The constitution is the supreme law of the state. The provisions of any law, rule or regulation, which are contrary to or inconsistent with this constitution, shall be unenforceable'. Eleven of fifteen justices found that Section 87 complied, while four found against. This clear majority judgment effectively acknowledged the legal status of Section 87 (Constitutional Court Decision 13/2545). While the various wording of 'Directive Principles' implies various differences in the degree of concrete application, this judgment suggests that all sections in Chapter 5, which stipulates these 'Directive Principles' and which previously had been little more than an abstract statement of national

---

9 Concerning the role of the judiciary, the 'Directive Principles' of the 1997 Constitution merely stipulated in Paragraph 1 of Section 75 that: 'The state shall ensure the compliance with the law, protect the rights and liberties of a person, provide efficient administration of justice and serve justice to the people expediently and equally and organize an efficient system of public administration and other State affairs to meet people's demand'. Section 65 of the 1991 Constitution relating to the 'Directive Principles' merely stipulated that 'The state should organize the system of judicial process to ensure justice to the people and to meet the requirement of expediency'.

10 In the 1997 Constitution, Article 75.

objectives, have the strong potential to be recognized as having actual legal force.

The relationship to the executive and legislative powers

What influence, then, did the changes outlined above exercise over the activities of Thai governments? I will discuss this question with particular emphasis on how revisions to the Thai Constitution since 1997 constrain both executive and legislative powers.

In the period between the 1949 and 1991 constitutions, constraints operating on both executive and legislative powers were very clearly stated and merely referred to the maintenance and independence of territory, the deployment and maintenance of the armed forces, and education. Regarding other state duties, the discourse of the document was limited to verbs such as 'encourage', 'advocate' and 'promote'. Since it was, moreover, specified that these provided no basis for legal action against the state, they did not impinge directly on the operation of either executive or legislative powers.

While the 1997 and 2007 constitutions endowed the 'Directive Principles' with the ability to exert legal restraints on both executive and legislative powers, this was not the only pressure exerted upon these. In order to ensure the precise implementation of policy in accordance with the newly reinforced 'Directive Principles', further strict regulations were introduced, particularly vis-à-vis the cabinet.

The 1991 Constitution provided no special regulations pertaining to administrative policy speeches. Only two points concerning the cabinet were stipulated in that constitution. These were only the requirement for the cabinet to deliver an administrative policy speech to the Thai Parliament at the time that a government was formed and the need to implement affairs of state according to the constitution, existing laws and administrative policy. The 1997 Constitution, however, stipulated as follows:

> In stating its policies to the Parliament under Section 211, the Council of Ministers which will assume the administration of the State affairs shall clearly state to the Parliament the activities

intended to be carried out for the administration of the State affairs in implementation of the Directive Principles of Fundamental State Policies provided in Chapter 5 and shall prepare and submit to the Parliament an annual report on the result of the implementation, including problems and obstacles encountered. (Section 88, Paragraph 2)

In other words, the administrative policy speech delivered by a cabinet needed to accord with the 'Directive Principles' which were now positioned as constraints on cabinet policy. The 2007 Constitution further emphasized the need to comply with the policy position stated in that document by listing ten sections relating to specific policy areas, each of which was headed with the words: 'The state shall act in compliance with the following [...] policies'.

In this way, the 1997 Constitution triggered a transformation of the 'Directive Principles' into entities that directly constrained cabinet policy and law-making, a trend that became even more pronounced in the 2007 Constitution. Thus, the constitution itself came to exercise strict and detailed curbs on the implementation power of both the cabinet and the parliament. We might therefore consider the concrete impact of these changes on the cabinet administrative policy speech.

The influence on cabinet (executive power): changes in the administrative policy speech

Changes to cabinet administrative policy speech

Before examining the nature of the changes that constitutional revisions imposed on cabinet administrative policy speeches, it is useful to be aware that there are three sections to these speeches: introduction with a statement of declaration, statement of the various policies and conclusion. This chapter will pay particular attention to the discursive structure of the introductions and conclusions to the policy speeches delivered by selected prime ministers with a view to examining the influence of constitutional reform on these speeches.

We will firstly consider the policy speeches of the Banharn and Chavalit cabinets (formed in 1995 and 1996 respectively), both of which operated under the 1991 Constitution. This constitution stipulated no particular regulations relating to cabinet policy speeches. Prime Minister Banharn began by declaring: 'In this address, cabinet will settle upon the policy measures of the state. I will announce the intent, policies and objectives of this cabinet's administration [...]'. His speech concluded: 'In order to ensure the maximum benefit for the nation and its people in the aforementioned affairs of the state, I faithfully promise that the government resolves to conduct its business conscientiously and honestly in strict accordance with the policies outlined above [...]'. Prime Minister Chavalit's introductory statement similarly declared: 'The cabinet shall respect and uphold a democratic regime of government with the king as head of state, while building harmony and unity and also creating political, economic and social trust and confidence so that the people of the nation can live fulfilling lives [...]'. He concluded: 'Each of the aforementioned are fundamental policies that provide a framework for administration by the government. Those responsible will establish both planning and implementation schedules and must determine in detail the method and specifics [of their actions]. [...] In addition, even though not stated here, if there is something of benefit to the nation and its people, the government will implement this without hesitation'. These extracts confirm that administrative policies actively determined by their own cabinets were the focus of the address delivered by both prime ministers, and that affairs of state would be conducted according to these policies.

Formed in 1997, however, the Chuan Cabinet was the first to assume power under the auspices of the 1997 Constitution. Prime Minister Chuan began his address as follows:

> In this address, cabinet will settle upon the policy measures of the state. Cabinet will uphold the system of parliamentary democracy that acknowledges the king as head of state, *giving consideration to the stipulations of Chapter 5 of the Constitution concerning the Directive Principles of Fundamental State Policies.* In addition, *in order to accord with the stipulations of the constitution,*

we aim to accelerate policy development in the areas of political and administrative reform, devolution of power to the regions, and electoral participation [...] and implement these within the parameters of the law.

The speech concluded:

> The cabinet and I, in responding to the needs of the people and *following the stipulations of the constitution*, understand very well the government's important mission to implement all measures honestly, sincerely and transparently so that review and criticism is possible. The government will establish foundations based on legal and other mechanisms and, *hastening to consolidate and streamline measures ancillary to the constitution, create a completely united system that ensures the thorough implementation of constitutional matters* [...].

It thus becomes clear that revisions to the 1997 Constitution saw a shift in the nature of cabinet administrative policies so that, rather than expressing the will of the cabinet itself, these were now characterized by an insistence on implementing the stipulations of the constitution, particularly those of the 'Directive Principles'.

With the Samak Cabinet (formed in 2008) the first to be inaugurated under the 2007 Constitution, the discursive tendency of the administrative policy address delivered on behalf of that group was similar to that of the Chuan Cabinet. The introductory section of the Samak Cabinet's administrative policy speech read: 'Here, the cabinet will uphold a system of parliamentary democracy that acknowledges the king as head of state and formulates national policies *cognizant of the Directive Principles of Fundamental State Policies that are based on the stipulations of Chapter 5 of the Constitution* [...]'.

The conclusion declared:

> The government resolves to implement policy *according to the Directive Principles of Fundamental State Policies*. The government policy program announced here presents policies that will be

implemented in the years that follow based on an urgent need for problem-solving and also *on the Directive Principles of Fundamental State Policies of Chapter 5 of the Constitution*. As a means of conducting administration *according to the stipulations of the constitution*, and of implementing policies that achieve anticipated objectives, the government will review and decide upon the course of action for government agencies, while also developing administrative systems and introducing bills [...].[11]

It is thus evident that under the 2007 Constitution also, cabinet administrative policy was positioned to ensure the consistent implementation of the stipulations of the constitution with particular emphasis on the 'Directive Principles'. There is no doubt that, from the time of the introduction of the 1997 Constitution Law, rather than comprising a set of long-term national objectives, the 'Directive Principles' operated to constrain the direction of cabinet policy. However, it was not only executive government that was constrained by these 'Directive Principles', and neither was the degree of constraint in other areas confined to the abstract.

Attachment of appendix

There is an additional matter to consider in the context of changes to the cabinet administrative policy speech arising from the 1997 Constitution Law. This is the existence of material appended to that text. Previously, the official government gazette merely published a written version of the cabinet speech. With the implementation of the 1997 Constitution Law, however, two types of tables were also appended to the document.

---

11 For the first time in Thai history, the 2007 Constitution was subject to a national referendum prior to its promulgation – 56.69% of the electorate were in favor, with 41.37% opposed. Significant regional differences were apparent with only 36.53% approval in the northeast. As a result, Prime Minister Samak's cabinet policy speech alluded to revisions to the constitution, and on this point differed from the policy speech delivered by Prime Minister Chuan who sought to faithfully implement the constitution.

The first was a schedule listing of important laws to be enacted in terms of the administrative policies of a particular cabinet. It was decided that, in the event of rejection by the lower house, the stipulations of the constitution enabled a cabinet to call for a second vote through a joint meeting of both houses on laws published in this schedule. In the case of lower house opposition, the relevant stipulation offered a means of certain implementation of administrative policy that accorded with the constitution by enabling the enlistment of upper house support. Such a stipulation acted as a counter to any lower house predominance in legislative debate.

The second appended element was a table comparing and contrasting the 'Directive Principles' from Chapter 5 of the Constitution with cabinet administrative policy. As the extract provided in Table 3.2 demonstrates, this table profiles how specific elements of cabinet administrative policy correspond to the 'Directive Principles'. In other words, rather than being confined to abstract or theoretical form, the 'Directive Principles' of the constitution here have concrete application to the various elements of cabinet policy. From 1997, the 'Directive Principles' text set out highly detailed and concrete instructions related, for example, to the enactment of law and the establishment of organizations. These 'Directive Principles' thereby exercised strong actual restraint on policy. While it is not unusual for the constitution law of other countries to also impose a duty to abide by the constitution on the holders of political power, this usually functions in an abstract sense only. That is, the specific provisions of the constitution do not work as constraints on the substance of cabinet administrative policy.[12] As long as there is no violation of important principles of fundamental human rights, all discretionary power is given to those holding political

---

12 Most countries require compliance with their constitutions. For example, Article 56 of the Fundamental Law for the Federal Republic of Germany, Article 5 of the Fifth Constitution of the French Republic, and Article 2 Clause 1.8 of the Constitution of the United States of America each require a declaration protecting the constitution on the occasion of a president taking the inaugural vow. In the past, it was the practice for Thai ministers of state also to vow to protect the constitution at the time of their swearing in. This requirement expanded, however, with the 1997 Constitution, and we now face the problem of the Thai Constitution being distinguished by its operation as a concrete constraint on the administrative policies of a cabinet.

Table 3.2 Abhisit Cabinet Policy Speech Appendix (partial excerpt)

Constitution	Cabinet Policy
Article 77 The state shall protect and uphold the institution of kingship and the independence, sovereignty and integrity of its jurisdictions and shall arrange for the maintenance of necessary and adequate armed forces and ordnances as well as up-to-date technology for the protection and upholding of its independence, sovereignty, security of state, institution of kingship, national interests and the democratic regime of government with the king as head of state, and for national development.	1. Emergency policies that were undertaken in the first year (1.1., 1.1.1–1.1.3) 2. Polices to guarantee national security (2.1–2.5)
Article 78 The state shall act in compliance with the following state administration policies: (1) to carry out the administration of state affairs with a view to establishing the sustainable development of society, the economy and national security by promoting the implementation of the sufficiency economy philosophy with significant regard to overall benefits of the nation;	1. Emergency policies that were undertaken in the first year (1.1, 1.1.1–1.1.3) 4. Economic policy 4.2 Policies related to economic structural reform (4.2.1, 4.2.1.3) 8. Policies related to good national governance and administration 8.1 Government efficiency (8.1.1–8.1.8)
(2) to organize a system for the central administration, provincial administration and local administration with clear limits, powers, duties and responsibilities suitable for national development, and to support the Changwat's formulation of a development plan and provincial development budget for the benefit of the public within that area;	8. Policies related to good national governance and administration 8.1 Government efficiency (8.1.3–8.1.4)
(3) to decentralize powers to local government organizations in order to promote self-dependency and self-determination of local affairs, to promote local government organization participation in the implementation of directive principles of fundamental state policies, to develop local economies, public utilities and assistances as well as a comprehensive and nationally uniform information infrastructure in the localities, including to develop a competent Changwat into a large-sized local government organization after having due regard to the will of the people in that Changwat; […].	8. Policies related to good national governance and administration 8.1 Government efficiency (8.1.1–8.1.2, 8.1.5)

Source: Compiled by author based on administrative policy speech delivered on behalf of the Abhisit Cabinet.

Note: This table compares cabinet policies of affairs of state with the 'Directive Principles of Fundamental State Policies' of Chapter 5 of the 2007 Thai Constitution.

power. In contrast, the 1997 Constitution diminished the scope in Thailand of cabinet political decision-making. This, undoubtedly, has been a special characteristic since that time of the Thai Constitution.

Other amendments to the 2007 Constitution further strengthen constitutional restrictions on legislative power. Articles 303 and 304 listed laws that were stipulated for either legislation or revision within one or two years of delivery of the administrative policy speech by the first cabinet to assume power after the election that followed the promulgation of the 2007 Constitution. As evident from tables 3.3 and 3.4, the laws obligating either legislation or revision covered a wide range of fields and drew on wording that often fell outside that of the 'Directive Principles'. These included individual rights matters such as access to judiciary procedures, worker safety and social welfare entitlements, freedom of speech for individuals and the mass media, rights and freedoms in education and access to public health and social services. Also listed were laws relating to political reforms such as the establishment of political development and agricultural councils, the creation of the peoples' sector political development fund for the community, and laws relating to key political issues including foreign affairs, devolution of power to the regions and budgetary matters. Although many elements featured in these stipulated laws already had been referred to in the constitution itself, the section now operated in a way that actively constrained the government's administrative and legislative capacity. Put another way, by spelling out detailed restraints on executive power through stipulations deriving principally from the 'Directive Principles', the Thai Constitution ingeniously constrained legislative power also by ensuring that implementation occurred through the medium of executive power.

The notion of constitutionalism is grounded in the checks and balances inherent in the separation of powers between the parliament, the executive (or cabinet) and the judiciary.[13] There is, however, no

---

13 While in theories of the separation of powers, the central plank is usually the parliament (the legislative power), a particular feature in Thailand is the extraordinarily low level of trust among conservative Thai commentators and intellectuals in the parliament and its members (Nidhi 2010: 116–117). Royalists have declared from the time of the 1949 Constitution that 'the will of the people cannot be trusted' (Hewison and Kengkij 2010). Even today,

Table 3.3 List of laws to be enacted or amended according to Article 303 of the 2007 Thai Constitution

Chapter	Section	Content Detail
Chapter 3 'Rights and Freedoms of the People'	Section 40	Individual rights in law
	Section 44	Right to the guarantee of personal safety and security at work, right to a guarantee of a secure living
	Part 7	Freedom of expression for individuals and the press
	Part 8	Rights and liberties in education
	Part 9	Right to public health services and welfare
	Part 10	Rights to information and complaints
	Section 56	Right to be informed and have access to public information
	Part 12	Community rights
	Section 61 (Paragraph 2)	Enactment by law of the creation of an independent consumer protection agency
Chapter 5 'Directive Principles of Fundamental State Policies'	Section 78 (7)	Establishment of Political Development Council
	Section 81 (4)	Establishment of an independent organ for judicial reform
	Section 84 (8)	Establishment of a farmer advisory council
	Section 87 (4)	Establishment of a National Sector of Political Development Fund for the Community
	Section 80	Revision of those laws that promote learning in outside-school settings, autonomous learning, life-long learning, community school learning and education in systems various to these, and that aim to develop the nation's education in accordance with Section 80, and revision also of laws that determine the organizations that have carriage for providing appropriate education and ensuring system compliance at all standard education levels
Chapter 9 'Cabinet'	Section 190 (Paragraph 5)	Law based on section 190, paragraph five, at least with the details on the procedure of the conclusion of treaty, which ensures the checks and balances between the cabinet and the parliament, transparency, efficiency, and popular participation, and also with the details on independent study and research carried out before the negotiation of the treaty without a conflict of interest between the State and the researcher at any time during the enforcement of the treaty
Chapter 11 'Constitutional Organs'	Section 256	The establishment of a National Human Rights Commission

(2) Based on Section 176, due within two years from the day on which the cabinet administrative policy speech is delivered

Chapter	Section	Content Detail
Chapter 5 'Directive Principles of Fundamental State Policies'	Section 86 (1)	Scientific and technological development, the promotion of development in various fields, budget distribution and the establishment of research development organizations
Chapter 8 'Money, Finance and Budget'	Section 167 (Paragraph 3)	Enacting laws related to state monies and finance as a means of determining a monetary and public finance regulatory framework
Chapter 14 'Local Government'		The enactment of laws relating to staged plans for the decentralization of power to local government agencies, laws relating to regional annual income, laws relating to the establishment of local government organizations, laws relating to regional public servants, and other laws based on Chapter 14 stipulations relating to local government

Source: Created by the author.
Note: Based on Section 176, due within one year from the day on which the cabinet administrative policy speech is delivered.

Table 3.4 Laws made compulsory under Section 304 of the 2007 Constitution

Chapter	Section	Content Detail
Chapter 13 'Ethics of Holders of Political Office and National or State Public Office Holders'	Section 279	The enactment of ethics laws and ordinances

Source: Created by the author.
Note: To be drafted from the day of the promulgation of the 2007 Constitution and enacted within one year.

mechanism within the system outlined above designed to control power through judicial review. Furthermore, the legislative fields targeted for constraint are far-reaching, encompassing issues that range from human rights guarantees to political matters. To understand better how the Thai Constitution stipulations that apply to both executive power and legislative power appear from the standpoint of sound democratic principles, we might compare and contrast constitutions of selected countries, including Thailand, whose documents are based on a Western model.

The particular characteristics of the 'Directive Principles' of the Thai Constitution

The legal status of 'basic national policy' – comparisons with other countries

In terms of why a section on basic national or state policy appears in a constitution, this section will consider the particular characteristics of the 'Directive Principles' of the Constitution of the Kingdom of Thailand by comparing it with those of other countries. We will begin

---

lack of confidence in voter decision-making results in a tendency to interpret majority parliament government as mob rule or despotism (Suraphon 2006: 25–239; Khien 2011: 11–15). Furthermore, even as they recognized the national government, many gave voice to the importance of the element of direct democracy, as reflected in the institutional arrangements of the 1997 and 2007 constitutions.

by reviewing the general legal character of the 'basic national policy' provisions of various constitutions.

As noted previously, the first constitution to include a section or chapter on basic national policy was the 1937 Constitution of Ireland. Article 45, which aimed to protect socially based human rights through the Assembly of Ireland (Dáil Éireann), stipulated things such as protection from economic exploitation, voter right to paid work, protection of the socially weak such as the elderly, and prohibitions against work-based discrimination. Since this section merely offered general advice that could not be subject to court proceedings, it clearly had no formal standing in law.

In Asia, the 1949 Constitution of India was the first one to follow the Irish model. Article 37 of the fourth chapter of the Indian Constitution also stated clearly that the 'National Policy Guidance Principles' could not be subject to challenge in a court of law. A new distinguishing feature, however, was the obligation on the state to take a legislative role. The constitution included several articles aimed at protecting human rights centered on social rights, with particular emphasis on facilitating education, the right to work and environmental protection.[14] Article 2, entitled 'Declaration of Principles and State Policies', of the 1987 Constitution of the Republic of the Philippines also laid out state policies divided into twenty-two sections. The drafting of this document confirmed the overthrow of the Marcos regime and the country's democratization. In this sense, it was an expression of the political situation of the time. The 1987 Philippines Constitution accordingly intermingled objectives such as the impartiality of the public service and the abolition of corruption with the intention to establish a new state with human rights protections. These stipulations were

---

14 For example, Article 38: Securing social order for the promotion of the welfare of the people; Article 39A: Equal justice and free legal aid; Article 41: Right to work, education, and in certain cases to public support; Article 43: A living wage for workers; Article 45: Provision of free compulsory education for children; Article 46: Promotion of educational and economic interests of Scheduled Castes, Scheduled Tribes and other weaker members of society; Article 48: Organization of agriculture and animal husbandry; Article 48A: Environmental protection and improvement and safeguarding forests and wildlife; Article 50: Separation of the powers of the judiciary and the executive; and Article 51: Promotion of international peace and security.

nevertheless presented in abstract terms and had no direct impact on either governance or law-making. Neither could they be grounds for any challenge in a court of law.

Examining the 'national policy' statements of selected other constitutions in this way confirms how the legal status attributed to the 'Directive Principles' in Thailand distinguishes the Thai Constitution as a particular case.

Constraints on the administrative policy speech

When considering the specific constraints that the Thai Constitution exercises over government administrative policy choices, there are two pertinent points for comparison with the constitutions of other countries. The first is whether or not and in what way other constitutions directly constrain either executive power and/or legislative power. The second point is the wording of the articles relating a cabinet's administrative policy. This chapter accordingly compares the types of constraints that operate on executive and legislative powers in the principal Western constitutions that were the subject of research at the times at which revisions occurred to the Thai constitutions.

The Fundamental Law for the Federal Republic of Germany – 1949

Germany, like Thailand, has a parliamentary system of government. There is no statement in the German Constitution that corresponds to Thailand's 'Directive Principles of Fundamental State Policies'. Rather, the sections that operate directly on executive and legislative powers appear in the basic rights section covered in articles 1 to 19. Clause 1 of Article 1 stipulates, 'Human dignity shall be inviolable. To respect and protect it shall be the duty of all state authority',[15] while Clause 3 declares, 'The following basic rights shall bind the legislature, the executive and the judiciary as directly applicable law'. This clearly confirms the legal status of this section of the German Constitution. What are the basic rights so protected? In general terms, the relevant

---

15 See the official German government English translation of the Constitution of the Federal Republic of Germany. Available at: https://www.gesetze-im-internet.de/englisch_gg/englisch_gg.html#p0019

articles largely concern human rights that emphasize individual freedoms.[16] Furthermore, according to Article 65, the role of the federal chancellor is only to 'determine and be responsible for the general guidelines of policy [...]'. Unlike Thailand, there is no systematic framework requiring the German Chancellor to comply closely with matters stipulated in the constitution.

Constitution of the French Fifth Republic – 1958

While France also has a parliamentary government, the considerable limits operating on the power of the president make this a 'semi-presidential' system.[17] Firstly, no section of the French Constitution corresponds to the Thai 'Directive Principles', and while there is no comprehensive statement addressing human rights in the French document, that country's French Constitutional Council (Conseil Constitutionnel) has established precedent that recognizes the legal status of the preamble to the 1946 Constitution, the 1789 Declaration of the Rights of Man [sic] and of the Citizen, and 'various fundamental principles inherent in the various laws of the Republic' (Tsujimura 2010: 231).

The two means given in the French Constitution of conveying administrative policy are the presidential message and the statements of government program or general policy by the prime minister. Nothing stated in the Constitution of the Fifth French Republic, however, particularly constrains the content of a presidential message. The sole

---

16 These include Article 2, the right to free development of personality and the right to life and physical integrity; Article 3, equality of all before the law, equality of women and men, and the prohibition of discrimination; Article 4, freedom of faith and conscience; Article 5, freedom of expression, freedom of access to knowledge, and freedom to learn; Article 7, the school system and religious instruction; Article 8, freedom of assembly; Article 9, freedom of association; Article 12, freedom to choose one's work, prohibition on forced labor; Article 12a, compulsory military or alternate civilian service; Article 14, right to ownership and inheritance, state expropriation; and Article 17, right to petition.

17 Noting that France saw value during World War II in installing a president as a means of curbing the powers of the French National Assembly, Amon (1994a: 26–28) explains how the 1990s Thai political reform movement also gave as one of its objectives the formation of a cabinet with strong leadership that would be able to resist the parliament.

reference concerns Article 5, Paragraph 1, which reads: 'The President of the Republic shall endure due respect for the Constitution. He [sic] shall endure, by his arbitration, the proper functioning of the public authorities and the continuity of the state'.[18] There is clearly no reference to any detailed restraint on administrative powers at the policy level. Concerning the prime ministerial declaration of the government platform and/or general policy, Article 49, Paragraph 1, stipulates that this is subject to deliberation by the parliament (Assemblée Nationale).[19] The document gives no specific direction concerning government policy, with Article 20, Paragraph 1, merely stipulating, 'The Government shall determine and conduct the policy of the Nation'. In terms of monitoring this policy, Article 24, Paragraph 1, stipulates, 'Parliament shall pass statutes. It shall monitor the action of the Government. It shall assess public policies'. The document consistently assigns policy decisions to the country's executive, i.e., to the Council of Ministers, while giving the power to monitor these to law-makers (i.e., the parliament).

Constitution of the United States of America (1788)

Nothing in the United States Constitution corresponds to Thai 'Directive Principles'. The only legal restraints on either executive power or legislative power relate to the infringement of human rights as outlined in the First Amendment.[20]

---

18 See the official French government authorized translation of the Constitution of the Fifth Republic, available at: https://www.elysee.fr/en/french-presidency/constitution-of-4-october-1958

19 Article 49, Paragraph 1, reads: 'The Prime Minister, after deliberation by the Council of Ministers, may make the Government's programme or possible [sic] a general policy statement an issue of a vote of confidence before the Parliament'. If, however, the government 'programme' or general policy statement is rejected, the prime minister must tender the government's resignation to the president.

20 The First Amendment reads: 'Congress shall make no law respecting an establishment of religion, or prohibiting the free exercise thereof; or abridging the freedom of speech, or of the press; or the right of the people peaceably to assemble, and to petition the Government for a redress of grievances'.

Is there any article in the United States Constitution relating to administrative policy? With regard to the presidential address, Article 2, Section 1, Paragraph 8, merely stipulates the duty of a president to defend the constitution.[21] Furthermore, regarding the president's power, Article 2, Section 3 stipulates only that: 'He [sic] shall from time to time give to the Congress Information of the State of the Union, and recommend to their Consideration such Measures as he shall judge necessary and expedient [...]'. In other words, presidents in the United States will rely on their own judgment when making policy decisions rather than being constrained by constitutional parameters or operating under a general impost to defend the constitution.

The above review of major Western constitutions confirms that these are based on the separation of powers. In this division, the executive administrative power of a cabinet determines policy, a parliament representing the legislative power monitors policy and a judiciary has the legal power to investigate policy or constitutional violations. Direct constitutional restraints on any of these three powers involve human rights guarantees only. In contrast, the structure itself of the Thai constitution constrains the policy direction of cabinet administrative powers across a range of fields and even directs the activities of legislative powers. Furthermore, the 'Directive Principles' encompass a wide range of policy fields. Since these can be attributed with legal status in a court of law, it means that the judiciary, the body to which an appeal is lodged based on the items, broadly constrains both executive and legislative powers. We might therefore conclude that a special characteristic of the Thai system is the operation of constitutional support for an institutional arrangement that enhances the power of an extremely forceful judicial mechanism while diminishing respect for the representatives of the people who comprise both the parliament and the cabinet.

---

21 Article 2, Section 1, Paragraph 8 reads: 'Before he enters on the Execution of his Office, he shall take the following Oath or Affirmation:– "I do solemnly swear (or affirm) that I will faithfully execute the Office of President of the United States, and will to the best of my Ability, preserve, protect and defend the Constitution of the United States"'.

The 1997 and 2007 constitutions of Thailand could be situated as a 'primary entity' or 'primary will', the stipulations of which transcend the general policy making powers of a popularly elected government. This is in fundamental contrast to those forms of constitutionalism designed not merely to respect, but to protect democratic processes based on a voting majority while also guaranteeing fundamental human rights.

Concrete constraints on executive and legislative powers

What is the actual extent of the concrete restraints exercised by the 'Directive Principles' over executive power and legislative power? Currently (2021), a cabinet that represents the executive power devises a 'National Policy Plan' based on the 'Directive Principles'. This is accompanied by a 'Law-making Plan' outlining implementation details. Governments are required to table an annual progress report on these plans in the parliament. In that the constitution provides broad guidelines concerning administrative and legislative directions, it in fact manages the operation of the parliament. Penalties, on the other hand, are not stipulated.

When determining whether the items operate merely as abstract restraints on executive and legislative powers, it is useful to be aware that wording from Chapter 5 of the Constitution, the 'Directive Principles of Fundamental State Policies', has already been the basis of appeals to the Constitutional Court. These have concerned matters ranging from laws and edicts on states of emergency to decisions regarding the constitutionality of budget disbursement. Although as of 2021 there has been no legal ruling of unconstitutionality directly based on the wording of the 'Directive Principles', neither has the court rejected the legal status of the Constitution's Chapter 5. This leaves open the possibility of some later decision having strong influence on future policy.

Among the list of laws obligated to be implemented according to Section 303 of the 2007 Constitution, we might pay attention to the Section 12, Article 67, 'Community Rights', which is the article of Chapter 3, 'The Rights and Freedoms of the Thai People'. While this is not an article of the Chapter 5 'Directive Principles', it stipulates in detail the procedures that must be adhered to in terms of convening a meeting of public officials when the implementation of legislation has the potential to impact on a community in terms of issues such as health or the environment. In 2009, the Thai Central Administrative Court drew on Section 67 to issue a suspension order to seventy-six enterprises, including chemical and iron and steel entities, planned for inclusion in the Map Ta Phut Industrial Estate. This ruling is noteworthy as an example of constitutional stipulations demanding direct change in matters of state enterprise. Included in the Section 303 list of laws obligated to be enacted are five provisions of the 'Directive Principles', four of which are laws regarding agencies to be newly established. These are a law on a council of political development under Section 78 (7), an independent law reform body under Section 81 (4), a council of farmers under Section 84 (8), and the establishment of a people's political development fund under Section 87 (4). These organizations were established between 2008 and 2010. Section 89 of the 1997 Constitution, included in Chapter 5 outlining the 'Directive Principles', also required the creation of a national economic and social council, which was established in 2000.

It is clear from the above that any claims that restraints exerted by the 'Directive Principles' on either executive or legislative power are purely abstract is problematic. On the contrary, the stipulations discussed function unequivocally in concrete form. While the provisions of the constitution do not stipulate in detail anything that actually deprives the cabinet of discretionary powers, given that policy direction must accord with the constitution, and that constitutional provisions have already been accepted as the basis for an appeal before the courts, the possibility of future Constitutional Court rulings against the government cannot be discounted.

The constitutionalism of Thailand: repressing democracy

Forms of constitutionalism that regulate state power through the operation of a constitution focus on the protection of human rights through the checks and balances inherent in the separation of powers and a system of judicial review. These assume the creation and effective functioning of a constitution, a legislative framework and a political system that will prevent, limit and/or deter government autocratization or arbitrary government decision-making. Such systems are supported also by notions of the inviolability of human rights through the political power of the majority and by the judicial review processes that guarantee these (Sakaguchi 2001). Constitutionalism, which originated in Europe and the United States, is based on the premise of respect for democracy (majority rule) and is combined with the protection of human rights by courts as the judgment of minorities and has now been adopted in countries around the world.

There is little doubt that the Thai constitutions of both 1997 and 2007 present huge problems in relation to these points. 'Constitutionalism' may well have been a keyword of the political reform movement of the 1990s. Yet, because there was relatively little respect for any sense of democracy as majority rule, both the 1997 and 2007 constitutions – which grew out of the 1990s reform movement – established systems that invested courts with the ability to exercise undue controls over both the administrative and legislative powers of a government.

In order to conduct national politics according to the 'Directive Principles', the cabinet administrative policy speech delivered to the parliament must comply with the stipulations of those principles. In addition to this restricting legislative power regarding what is possible in terms of cabinet administrative powers, the 'Directive Principles' themselves have been written into the constitution drawing on a discourse that is detached from the will of the people. The possibility that future court rulings might exert excessive constitutional restraints over executive and/or legislative power surely contravenes democratic principles. Furthermore, the attribution of legal status to the detailed stipulations of the 'Directive Principles' creates the potential for violations of democratic processes that extend beyond constraints on executive and legislative powers. In other words, the restrictions on state powers that operate through the Constitution of Thailand result in a form of constitutionalism that differs from that Western-style constitutionalism that protects minorities while respecting majority rule in terms of decision-making. It is no exaggeration to say that this creates a systematic arrangement whereby the courts, which are totally free from review or oversight by electors, restrict both the legislative and administration powers for which the people's direct and indirect representatives carry responsibility.

The restraints on state powers that operate through the Thai Constitution demonstrate some features that might superficially be regarded as similar to the constitutions of Western nations.[22] In Thailand, however, the stipulations of the constitution are positioned comprehensively as of a 'higher order' than the cabinet, thus creating a nuance that is largely in opposition to Western constitutionalism which aims to prevent the tyranny of the majority. The idea of the Thai Constitution as of a 'higher order' perhaps derives from perceptions that the document has been handed down from the king. While that point exceeds the parameters of the current chapter, we can justifiably speculate that this is the case given that a number of the 'Directive Principles' of the 2007 Constitution relate to the king and kingship. These include a Section 77 reference to 'the democratic regime of government with the king as head of state', a Section 78 stipulation concerning 'the implementation of the sufficiency economy philosophy with significant regard to overall benefits of the nation',[23] a Section 80 (3) stipulation regarding education for 'awareness [and] devotion to the democratic regime of government with the king as head of the state', a Section 83 stipulation to implement a 'sufficient economic policy', and a Section 87 (5a) stipulation to 'to support and provide education to the people in relation to the development of politics [...]

---

22 This tendency can be seen in how, with the deliberate intention of emphasizing their compliance with global standards, the Constitutional Court and the National Committee for Enforcing the Prevention of Public Corruption make extensive posts on their public homepages referring to the websites of other countries' constitutional courts and to their constitutions. Those Thai entities also highlight information about their participation in international conferences and their interaction with other (international) public corruption regulation bodies.

23 The economic philosophy advocated by the previous King Bhumibol was known in Thai as *'setthak it phophiang'*. In 2009, then Democratic Party Prime Minister Abhisit drew on this concept in an address to the United Nations General Assembly.

under the democratic regime of government with the king as head of state'. It is this emphasis on the role of the king in the constitution that perhaps best demonstrates the true significance of the putatively abstract restraining power inherent in the 'Directive Principles'.

The following two points must further be considered in any discussion of concrete restraints exercised by the Thai Constitution on administrative and legislative powers. Firstly, the institutional arrangement operating in Thailand is an attempt to use the constitution as a means of denying power to the people's representatives who are chosen by election. In other words, the document has the special character of diminishing opportunities for review by the people of the electorate who express their will through the ballot-box. This accordingly gives weight to review that occurs through the constitution and the court. By successfully concealing the potential for the judiciary – one of the key arms in the theory of the separation of powers – to restrain both executive and legislative powers, the mechanism created by the Thai Constitution differs from the original essence of constitutionalism. Following on from this is the danger of the court assuming autocratic control. Scholars working in the field of comparative constitutional studies have warned for some time of the danger of courts affiliating with vested interests, noting a global trend towards 'judicial states' (Higuchi 1994: 506c–508). While according to the separation of powers, other power entities have the capacity to exercise influence over a judiciary that might be tending to dominate, Thai constitutionalism has in fact developed a system in which there is an inherent danger of the court becoming an instrument of autocratic control.

One of the most important principles of democracy is that of a parliamentary process based on majority rule. With the will of the people expressed through the ballot box, the parliamentary majority forms a cabinet that implements election promises as government policy. In constitutionalism, this process acts as a curb on the exercise of state power. Based on its interpretation of constitutionalism, however, Thailand has instituted a system whereby the Constitutional Court can in effect exercise power over policy formed by agencies comprised of elected representatives of the people. This has resulted in a rejection of majority rule and an accompanying denial of the will of the people. In other words, although conducted under the guise of political reform, ongoing system revisions in Thailand, including the constitutional revisions of the 1990s, have limited the operation of Thai democracy.

4 | Constitutional Reform and Legislative Power: An Analysis of Electoral System Reforms

Since the 1990s, there has been ongoing reform of the electoral system in Thailand. The 1991 Constitution was revised on five occasions, mainly in relation to legislative authority (the Senate and House of Representatives). These revisions included electoral system reform. The conduct of large-scale electoral system reforms were also new features of both the 1997 and 2007 constitutions.

Even before the 1990s, Thailand's electoral system had undergone repeated change. Until the 1980s, the main points of contention were: the ratio of elected to government appointed parliament members, whether or not bureaucrats and senior public servants (including members of the military) could take a ministerial position in the cabinet, and whether or not the Senate should be granted the right to conduct a vote of no-confidence in the cabinet.[1] From the middle of the 1970s, priority was given to the growth of political parties with the 1978 Constitution introducing provisions that stimulated the enlargement of political parties. For the military, these constitutional issues were issues related to the institutional basis for preserving influence in parliamentary politics (Murashima 1987). In 1983, when the period of validity of the 1978 Constitution's transitional provisions concluded, changes occurred preventing the appointment of serving bureaucrats to ministerial positions,[2] while revisions to the 1991

---

1 In addition, there were repeated revisions of the method of calculating the number of seats in the lower house and the voter eligibility for Thai nationals whose father is a foreigner. Nevertheless, changes were minimal in terms of the Ministry of the Interior consistently taking carriage of electoral administration, the regulation of electoral corruption, and the introduction of counter fraud strategies relating to vote-counting procedures at polling booths.

2 The provisions of the 1978 Constitution, which operated until 21 April 1983, permitted serving bureaucrats to hold concurrent ministerial positions. At this time, the stipulations of that document relating to political parties and election were also determined not to be applied (Murashima 1987: 163).

Constitution made in 1992 ensured a non-member of the House of Representatives was prohibited from becoming prime minister. In this sense, democratization in Thailand progressed to a large degree at the system level by the early 1990s. Then, what were the characteristics of the electoral system reforms under the two constitutions enacted after that – the 1997 Constitution and the 2007 Constitution – and what kind of changes did they bring about in Thai politics?

Scholarly discussion of the drafting of both the 1997 and 2007 constitutions indicates that priority issues for the 1997 document were the elimination of vote-buying (*khai sitthi sue siang*) as electoral corruption, the need for policy to be the centerpiece of electoral campaigns, the strengthening of political parties and the creation of stable government (Bowonsak 1999). Enacted following the coup d'état that brought down the Thaksin administration (2001–2006), however, the 2007 Constitution redirected focus to excess political power. That is, the objective in that instance was to reform the system in a way that would diminish the power of a political administration (Somkit 2008: 29).[3] In this sense, the 1997 and 2007 constitutions focused on issues that were diametrically opposed.

When considering political system reforms arising from either constitution, existing scholarship tends draw on the example of the Thaksin administration to profile the relationship between the electoral system, the scale and structure of political parties and the workings of government power. A typical claim is that, while the 1997 Constitution instituted large-scale electoral reforms in order to create stable government and strengthen political parties, the greater-than-expected power of the Thaksin administration created an effective dictatorship (Hicken 2006; Freedman 2007; Reilly 2007). Reforms instituted by the 2007 Constitution thus aimed to reduce government power (Ockey 2008; Kuhonta 2008; Hicken 2009: 141; Croissant 2011). The electoral systems advocated in the two documents thereby stood in a 'pendulum' relationship to each other (Thitinan 2009).

One might consider whether the changes brought about by electoral system reforms after the 1997 Constitution were only the

---

3   This was referred to as 'suppressing state authoritarianism'.

establishment of a stable government and the strengthening of political parties. One might also consider points of commonality between the electoral system reforms advocated in the 1997 and 2007 constitutions. Valuable though it is, current scholarship focuses on the differences between these documents. Changing the angle of analysis to include similarities has the potential to provide new insights into the workings of Thai electoral system reform. Through a detailed discussion of the provisions of the so-called 'Organic Act on Political Parties' (hereafter Political Party Law) and 'Organic Act on Elections' (hereafter Election Law), each of which had a version that derived from the 1997 and 2007 constitutions, this chapter will provide an innovative investigation of the changes that accompanied the series of electoral system reforms referred to above.

Revising the 1991 Constitution: beginning of electoral reform

Amendments in 1992

The 1991 Constitution was enacted by the leaders of the 1991 military coup that ousted the popularly elected Chatchai Choonhavan administration (1988–1991). While the content of the document largely followed that of the previous 1978 Constitution, issues addressed during drafting related to the 1978 provision permitting the appointment of a prime minister from unelected members of the military in addition to elected members of the House of Representatives.[4] The bloody incident noted in Chapter 2 that occurred in response to the appointment of the non-elected Suchinda Kraprayoon to the position of prime minister triggered constitutional reform on the matter of prime ministerial appointments. Other reforms included restrictions on the power of the Senate (the upper house) and provisions concerning the speaker of the parliament.

---

4   Since the 1978 Constitution permitted the appointment of a non-elected prime minister, a system emerged that was referred to as 'semi-democracy' (*prachathipatai khrueng bai*), or 'managed democracy', comprised of a House of Representatives (lower house) of elected members and a non-elected prime minister.

In June 1992, revisions occurred on three occasions. The first handed the role of speaker of the parliament to the leader of the House of Representatives, rather than – as had been the case – leader of the then government-appointed Senate. The second required House of Representatives rather than – as had been the case – Senate provisions to apply during a joint sitting of both houses when no joint sitting provision existed. The third involved the scrapping of the power of a third of the members of the Senate to table a motion before the cabinet demanding general debate on a matter of national governance. September 1992 revisions required that the position of prime minster come from the members of the House of Representatives,[5] and that the countersignature on a prime ministerial appointment document be the leader of the lower house rather than – as had been the case – of the Senate. The wide-ranging additions made during the 1992 revisions enhanced the status of the House of Representatives in the Thai parliamentary system by seeking to ensure that the country's lower house very much reflected the will of the people.

Amendments in 1995

Constitutional revisions undertaken until 1992 saw Thailand make noticeable progress towards democratization. From that time, however, intellectual commentators began to profile the problem of electoral corruption and fraud, so that calls to reform the House of Representatives electoral system also gathered momentum.[6] The final constitutional revisions of February 1995 indeed included electoral system reform. Although the long-used system permitting the multiple seat electoral constituency system remained largely intact, there were changes to provisions relating to voting rights, election eligibility and political parties. The voting age, for example, was lowered from twenty

---

5   Constitutions that limited the prime ministerial appointment to the House of Representatives were those of 1974, the 1992 revisions of the 1991 document, 1997 and 2007 only.

6   Following the September 1992 election, there were claims of regional vote-buying and the exercise of influence by regional power brokers (Murray 1996: 254).

to eighteen, while pre-conditions for eligibility to stand as a candidate also changed.[7]

Electoral reforms in the 1997 and 2007 constitutions

The 1997 Constitution

Intellectual leaders of the political reform movement found the 1995 electoral system revisions insufficient (Amon 1994a). Noting that there had been no real improvement, they demanded radical change as the only means of eliminating electoral corruption and fraud. The 1997 Constitution therefore involved large-scale reforms that completely changed the previous electoral system. The long-in-place multiple seat electoral constituency system was replaced with a combination of single-seat representation (400 seats) and proportional representation (100 seats).[8] With the exception of those with experience in either the House of Representatives or the Senate, candidates now needed to hold a bachelor's degree or equivalent qualification.[9]

---

7 Prior to revision, candidates needed to comply with one of the following four stipulations: 1. to have had their name recorded as a resident in the prefecture (*changwat*) in which they were standing for 180 consecutive days prior to the day of nomination; 2. to have been previously either a member of the House of Representatives for a seat in the prefecture for which they were standing, or a member of that prefecture's legislature, or the head of a provincial governance organization in that prefecture; 3. to have been born in the prefecture; or 4. to have been educated for two consecutive years at an educational institution in the prefecture for which they were standing.

8 While some argue (Ferrara, Herron and Nishikawa 2005: 29) that the mixed system facilitates compromise between various stakeholders, the system in Thailand, where it was stipulated that a minimum of 5% of the vote was required in order to secure a seat in the proportional representation system, promotes the emergence of large-scale political parties and strengthens government power.

9 If we examine the academic record of candidates in the two general elections (1995 and 1996) held prior to the promulgation of the 1997 Constitution, we see that 42% in 1995 and 50.5% in 1996 did not have tertiary qualifications. The 2000 Thai census indicated considerable regional difference in retention rates from schooling to university, with 17.8% for Bangkok, 6% for the Central Region, 3.8% for the Northern Region, 3.3% for the North-Eastern Region, and 3.9% for the South.

Membership of the upper house was changed from appointment to popular election.[10]

I previously noted that the central focus of the political reform movement was the regulation of political corruption and the creation of stable government. Law scholar Bowonsak Uwanno, who made a major contribution to the drafting of the 1997 Constitution, explained that the constitution introduced two methods of conducting lower house elections as a means of discouraging vote-buying. The proportional representation system (100 seats) introduced in the 1997 Constitution was the election system that would select the political party to assume the task of governing the nation, he reasoned, and if voters felt they wanted a certain party head to be their prime minister, then they would elect the party concerned.[11] To Bowonsak, furthermore, while voters elected an actual candidate, a member of the house could do nothing as a mere individual representing an electorate. He thus emphasized the importance of political parties in the governance of the nation (Bowonsak 1999: 281–282). Bowonsak futher stressed the need when electing a member of the House of Representatives to be cognizant of the policy platform of a candidate's party (Bowonsak 1999: 289–292). The party, he argued, was crucial to the creation of stable government and at a time when there was no obligation on a House of Representatives member to belong to a political party, having a block of members who only supported argument, or voted during debate, in a way that benefited either their own electorates or their own selves was a recipe for government instability. Accordingly, Bowonsak (1999:

---

10 For the 200 senators, a multi-seat constituency system was adopted, with each prefecture as one constituency. A member of a political party, a person who holds an official position in another political party, or a member of the House of Representatives, or a person who has been a member of the House of Representatives in the past and whose resignation as a member of the House of Representatives has not passed one year as of the date of acceptance of the candidacy, was stipulated to have no rights to be elected as a senator.

11 According to data collected in a survey conducted by the Election Commission concerning voting activity at the time of the 2001 general election, in response to the question, 'Do you vote for the candidate or the party at election time?' 41% of voters in single seat constituencies and 59% of voters in proportional representation constituencies answered that they voted for a political party (Sathaban Phrapokklao 2001: 49–50).

120–121) declared the creation of stable government through a political party system to be the primary role of a constitution.

In prescribing electoral system reform, the 1997 Constitution thus focused on the role of political parties as a means of managing political corruption and creating stable government. Was it really possible, however, for the political party to become a universal panacea for the many problems associated with elections in Thailand?

The main revisions intended to influence the activity of political parties were as follows.

a. Introducing a system of election on both a single-seat constituency system (400 members) and party-list proportional representation (100 members) (Section 98).
b. Having the whole territory of Thailand as the party-list proportional representation electorate. Preventing a candidate simultaneously running for a seat in a single-seat constituency and a seat in a proportional representation constituency (Section 99).
c. Having a system of proportional representation in which a political party whose vote does not exceed 5% of the total of the national vote is unable to take a seat (Section 100).
d. Giving voters the right to cast a total of two votes, one from the candidate roll for the proportional representation system and one for a candidate in the constituency system (Section 104).
e. Making a condition of eligibility for election to the lower house that a candidate be a member of any but only one political party for ninety consecutive days at least before candidature is lodged (Section 107 [4]).
f. Ensuring the conduct of fair and equitable House of Representatives elections through the state allocating time for political party radio and television broadcasts (Section 113, Paragraph 4).
g. Requiring an election to be held within forty-five days of expiration of the term of the lower house (Section 115).

h. Requiring an election to be held within sixty days of the dissolution of the lower house (Article 116).
i. Having a lower house member who leaves the party to which they are affiliated, or voted by more than three quarters of the members to be excluded from the party, lose their right to sit in the house (Section 118, Paragraph 8).
j. Permitting the submission of bills or bills of organic acts by a member of the lower house only when the political party of which they are a member passes a resolution agreeing to the submission of the bill and with the support of not less than twenty members of the house (Section 169).

With the introduction of the proportional representation system, the role of political parties during election campaigns became more prominent. Furthermore, with a proportional representation system candidate's chance of election depending on their position in the order of names on a ballot roll, the party held a strong position vis-à-vis the candidate. Because an election had to be held within forty-five days of a lower house term expiring, or within sixty-five days of the house being dissolved, and because a candidate needed to be a party member for a period of ninety days or more before the day of nomination as a candidate, it became extremely difficult for a House of Representatives member to change parties. Since a house member who lost the right to belong to a party for failing to comply with the conditions of party membership also lost their job, the individual member was largely subordinated to the party machine.

In addition to these provisions, the 1997 Constitution provided that if a member of the House of Representatives was appointed prime minister or minister of state, they would be disqualified from being a member of the House of Representatives. As a result, while adopting a parliamentary cabinet system, the executive power and the legislative power were strictly separated. With the amendment of the Organic Act on Elections in 2000 stipulating that the costs of a by-election held following an elected member being appointed to the cabinet were to be borne by the relevant member and the party to which they belonged, the likelihood of an elected member being appointed to a cabinet became almost non-existent, leaving ministers unable to move against the will of the prime minister.

When considering the outcomes that eventuated from the newly introduced provisions, we might recall Bowonsak's insistence that political parties were the key to regulating election fraud and creating stable government.[12] Closer examination of the 1997 Constitution provisions related to political parties, however, reveals greater management and supervision of house members by the party to which they belonged, and greater party executive influence on a party's internal workings. Since it was those elected through proportional representation who had the greatest likelihood of being appointed to cabinet, there was absolutely no doubt that the party executive machine that created the proportional roll ballot paper had a huge influence over those candidates and members who sought cabinet appointment. When a cabinet was formed, those first appointed were generally the central party members whose names were listed at the top of the proportional representation ballot. Since the cabinet – the administrative power of a government – was made up of those who were close to their party executive committee, the task of law-making – of exercising legislative power – was left to members of the House of Representatives who were not part of that clique.

This power relationship between a party executive and ordinary members derived from the overwhelming precedence of the administrative wing – the cabinet – vis-à-vis the legislative powers. In this sense, by strengthening the electoral role of political parties, the 1997

---

12 It is doubtful that those who drafted the 1997 Constitution were aware that they were creating a system environment that could lead to the birth of a party of the very large dimensions of the Thai Rak Thai Party (Thailand Patriotic Party/Thais Love Thailand Party). A series entitled 'Reports Presented to the Democracy Development Committee with Recommendations for Political Reform' compiled for the drafting of the 1997 Constitution argued in favor of a single representative per constituency system on the grounds that 'minority groups too would be given the chance to have their own representatives', and 'young people would have opportunities to stand as new candidates'. The report suggested that a proportional party-list system gave 'small parties the same chance as large parties to be elected' and put 'the role of controlling the country in the hands of a number of parties'. This suggests that both systems were regarded as offering benefit to 'minority groups' (Phaithun 1995).

Table 4.1 Comparison of provisions related to political parties (1)

1991 Constitution	1997 Constitution
Section 99: Multiple-seat constituency system (360 seats)	Section 98: The introduction of a single seat constituency system (400 seats), and party-list proportional representation system (100 seats).
	Section 99: The electoral district for the party-list proportional representation system shall be all of Thailand. A candidate is not permitted multiple nominations across the two electoral systems. The candidates from each party are elected based on an ordered list available to the public.
	Section 100: A political party whose proportional representation list does not receive more than 5% of the total national vote is unable to take a seat in the house.
	Section 104: A voter has the right to cast two votes, one for a candidate on the proportional representation list and one for a constituency candidate.
Section 105: In order to qualify as a candidate for a House of Representatives election, it is necessary to be a member of any but only one political party.	Section 104, Paragraph 7: In order to be nominated for a House of Representatives election, a candidate must have been a member of one only of any political party for at least ninety consecutive days prior to nominating.
	Section 113: To ensure the conduct of fair and honest elections, the state shall provide the following support. Paragraph 4: Allocation of television and radio broadcast time to political parties.
Section 111: When a term of the House of Representatives expires, an election must be held within sixty days.	Section 115: When a term of the House of Representatives expires, an election must be held within forty-five days.
Section 112: When the House of Representatives is dissolved, an election must be held within ninety days.	Section 116: When the House of Representatives is dissolved, an election must be held within sixty days.
Section 114, Paragraph 7: When a member of the House of Representatives resigns from the party to which they belong, or has their membership terminated by a vote of the party to which they belong, the individual is disqualified from being a member of the house.	Section 118, Paragraph 8: If a member of the House of Representatives resigns from the party to which they belong or has their membership terminated by the political party to which they belong through a resolution voted upon by not less than three-fourths of a joint meeting of the party's executive committee and party members of the House of Representatives, the individual is disqualified from being a member of the house.
Section 137: A member of the House of Representatives may only submit a bill when the party of which they are a member votes in favor of the submitting of that bill and with the support of not less than twenty members of the house.	Section 169: A member of the House of Representatives may only submit a bill or an organic law bill (deriving from the constitution) when the party of which they are a member votes in favor of the submitting of the bill and with the support of not less than twenty members of the house.

Source: Compiled by the author.

Constitution election system reforms created a structure that made it easy for the administrative powers of the cabinet to control and regulate the legislative powers of the House of Representatives.[13]

The 2007 Constitution

In 2006, claiming corruption in the Thaksin Shinawatra administration, the military held a coup d'état and revoked the 1997 Constitution. The 2007 Constitution was drafted and enacted largely by those with connections to the judiciary under an interim civilian government established by the military.

Yet again, the electoral system became the subject of huge reform. The single-seat electoral constituency system reverted to a multiple-seat electoral constituency system, with 400 seats chosen by this system and eighty by a party-list proportional representation system. The period of prime ministerial appointment was limited to not more than eight consecutive years. The 1997 Constitution stipulation regarding candidate educational qualifications was abolished for members of the House of Representatives but retained for cabinet appointments and the Senate. Senate membership revisions resulted in approximately half the 150 upper house seats being chosen by popular election with the remainder[14] by appointment.[15]

When considering the significance of the electoral system reforms implemented by the 2007 Constitution, comparison with the relevant

---

13 As if to confirm this interpretation, the 1997 Constitution raised the bar by stipulating that the support of two-fifths of current lower house members was necessary to propose a general discussion preceding a no-confidence censure vote against the prime minister. This figure had been one-fifth in the 1991 Constitution.

14 The Upper House Appointment Committee was made up of a total of seven members: the chief justice of the Constitutional Court, the chair of the Election Commission, the chair of the National Ombudsman Committee, the chair of the National Anti-Corruption Commission, the chair of the National Audit Board, one justice of the Supreme Court who was appointed by the full bench of the Supreme Court, and one justice of the Supreme Administrative Court. Appointments were made from recommendations given by various organizations in the science, government, private, specialized professional and other sectors.

15 The 2007 Constitution was criticized as 'undemocratic' especially since there was a return to the non-election of half the Senate members. Protests

1997 Constitution stipulations that impacted on political parties reveals the major points as follows:

1. Parallel systems of multiple representation constituencies (400 seats) and proportional representation party-list constituencies (eighty seats) (sections 93 and 94);
2. Right of a political party to submit a list of candidates for election on a proportional basis for some or all constituencies (Section 95);
3. Eight *changwat* (province) proportional representation party-list clusters with each *changwat* cluster regarded as one constituency having ten members of the House of Representatives (Section 96);
4. A candidate being a member of any and only one political party for a consecutive period of not less than ninety days up to the date of applying for candidacy in an election, or being a member of any and only one political party for a consecutive period of not less than thirty days up to the date of applying for candidacy in an election in the case where the general election is conducted following the dissolution of the House of Representatives (Section 101, Paragraph 3);
5. No mergers of political parties having members sitting in the House of Representatives during a term of the house (Section 104);
6. The date for new general elections to be fixed at not less than forty-five days but not more than sixty days as from the date of dissolution of the House of Representatives (Section 108).

In addition, the 5% minimum vote required in the 1997 Constitution for a party to gain a seat in the house in the proportional representation system was eliminated, with the country moving in 2007 from one single country-wide to eight *changwat* (provincial) proportional repre-

---

occurred in April 2007 when, in the first version of the document, the Constitution Drafting Committee appointed 160 members to the Senate (Chambers 2009: 24–25).

sentation constituencies. Since reversion to a multiple-seat electoral constituency system reduced the number of dead or wasted votes (votes that ultimately did not impact on the outcome of the election), a break was applied to the emergence of huge political parties that had resulted from the 1997 Constitution. Furthermore, because it became easier for members to change political party, the party no longer stood, as it had under the 1997 Constitution, in an overwhelming position of strength vis-à-vis its members.[16] By abolishing the stipulation of a member losing their position in the House of Representatives when appointed to the cabinet, moreover, it was no longer the case that those elected through the proportional party-list representation had the greatest chance of becoming cabinet members. The sum result of such revisions, however, was effectively to make null and void the 1997 Constitution's attempt to create a strict division between the country's administrative powers and legislative powers. We might even say that the 2007 Constitution created a template in which administrative power – the cabinet – controlled the legislative powers – the House of Representatives.[17]

While the above appears to cast doubt on the claim that the 1997 Constitution created a system that strengthened the role of political parties, can we say that the 2007 Constitution merely weakened the 1997 system?

Common points of the two constitutions

One element common to the two constitutions was the introduction of strict provisions, not included in previous documents, concerning the dissolution of political parties.

Section 63, Paragraph 1, of the 1997 Constitution stated that: 'No person shall exercise the rights and liberties prescribed in the consti-

---

16 Although the 1997 Constitution required that any proposal to attach laws or draft laws to the constitution be voted upon by affiliated political parties, this condition was removed from the 2007 Constitution.

17 Conditions to propose a general debate leading to a vote of no confidence in a prime minister were eased, in that it became sufficient to have the names of one-fifth of the current lower house members in the case of the prime minister and one-sixth for a minister of state.

Table 4.2 Comparison of provisions related to political parties (2)

1997 Constitution	2007 Constitution
Section 98: Introduction of election on a single-seat constituency system (400 seats) and party-list proportional representation system (100 seats).	Sections 93 and 94: Members elected through a multiple-seat constituency election system (400 seats) and party-list proportional representation system (eighty seats).
	Section 95: A political party has the right to nominate candidates in all or some party-list proportional representation constituencies.
Section 99: The electoral district for the proportional representation party-list system shall be all of Thailand. A candidate is not permitted multiple nominations across the two electoral systems. The candidates from each party are elected based on an ordered list available to the public.	Section 97: A candidate is not permitted multiple nominations across the two electoral systems. Section 96: The division of the country into eight *changwat* (provincial) constituencies with each having ten seats. Section 97: There shall be no multiple nominations across the two election systems.
Section 100: A political party whose proportional representation list does not receive more than 5% of the total national vote is unable to take a seat in the house.	
Section 104: A voter has the right to cast two votes, one for a candidate on the proportional representation list and one for a constituency candidate.	Section 93: A voter has the right to cast two votes, one for a candidate on the proportional representation list and one for a constituency candidate.
Section 107: Paragraph 4: In order to nominate for a House of Representatives election, a candidate must have been a member of one only of any political party for at least ninety consecutive days prior to nominating.	Section 101, Paragraph 3: A candidate must be a member of any but only one political party for a consecutive period of not less than ninety days up to the date of applying for candidacy in an election, or be a member of any but only one political party for a consecutive period of not less than thirty days up to the date of applying for candidacy in an election in the case where the general election is conducted following the dissolution of the House of Representatives.
	Section 104: No mergers of political parties having members sitting in the House of Representatives during that term of the house.

tution to overthrow the democratic regime of government with the king as head of the state under this constitution or to acquire the power to rule the country by any means which is not in accordance with the modes provided in this constitution', while Paragraph 3 of the same section declared: 'In the case where the Constitutional Court makes a decision compelling the political party to cease to commit [the acts stipulated], the Constitutional Court may order the dissolution of such political party'.

1997 Constitution	2007 Constitution
Section 113: To ensure the conduct of fair and honest elections, the state shall provide the following support. Paragraph 4: Allocation of television and radio broadcast time to political parties.	
Section 115: When a term of the House of Representatives expires, an election must be held within forty-five days.	Section 107: When a term of the House of Representatives expires, an election must be held within forty-five days.
Section 116: When the House of Representatives is dissolved, an election must be held within sixty days.	Section 108: When the House of Representatives is dissolved, an election must be held within forty-five days.
Section 118, Paragraph 8: If a member of the House of Representatives resigns from the party to which they belong or has their membership terminated by the political party to which they belong through a resolution voted upon by not less than three-fourths of a joint meeting of the party's executive committee and party members of the House of Representatives, the individual is disqualified from being a member of the house.	Section 106, Paragraph 7: If a member of the House of Representatives resigns from the party to which they belong or has their membership terminated by the political party to which they belong through a resolution voted upon by not less than three-fourths of a joint meeting of the party's executive committee and party members of the House of Representatives, the individual is disqualified from being a member of the house.
Section 169: A member of the House of Representatives may only submit a bill or an organic law bill (appended to the constitution) when the political party of which they are a member passes a resolution agreeing to the submitting of the bill and with the support of not less than twenty members of the house.	Section 139: An organic law bill may be introduced only by the following: [...] 2. members of the House of Representatives of not less than one-tenth of the total number of the existing members of the House of Representatives or members of the House of Representatives and senators of not less than one-tenth of members of both houses. Section 142: A bill may be introduced by the following: [...] 2. At least twenty members of the House of Representatives.

Source: Compiled by the author.

The 2007 Constitution strengthened these provisions with the addition of a fourth paragraph to Section 68 and also by newly adding Section 237. The additional Section 68 paragraph read as follows: 'In the case where the Constitutional Court issues a dissolution order under paragraph three, the right to vote in an election of the president and the executive committee of the dissolved political party at the time the act under paragraph one has been committed shall be suspended for a period of five years as from the date of such Constitutional Court order'. Paragraph 1 of the new section, Section 237, read: 'A candidate in an election who commits an act or causes or supports another person to act in violation of the Organic Act on Election of Members of the House of Representatives and Obtaining Senators or regulations or notifications of the Election Commission that results in an election not being carried out in an honest and fair manner, shall have their right to vote suspended under the Organic Act on Election of Members of the House of Representatives and Obtaining Senators'.

Concerning the 'act of the person' referred to in Paragraph 1, Paragraph 2 of Section 237 continued as follows:

> If there appears evidence to reasonably believe [...] that the chairman of the executive committee of a political party conspired with or neglects at such commission, or such commission is known to him but he fails to restrain or amend such act for the maintenance of honest and fair election, it shall be deemed that such political party has committed an act to acquire powers to rule the country by a means which is not in accordance with the provisions of this Constitution under Section 68. In such case, if the Constitutional Court orders to dissolve such political party, the right to vote of the chairman of the executive committee of a political party shall be suspended for the period of five years as from the date such order is made.

The 1998 and 2007 Organic Act on Political Parties

Shifts in political party laws

Each revision to the so-called Organic Act on Political Parties (*phraratchabanyat phakkanmueang*), or Political Party Law, led to an expansion in the number of sections. These grew from forty-seven in 1968 and fifty-four in 1974, to become sixty-six in 1981. From the time of the 1997 Constitution, it was decided that the importance of the Political Party Law and 'Organic Act on Elections' (Election Law) justified these being designated as special laws derived from the constitution (*phraratchabanyat phakkanmueang*). Those holding political power were obligated to implement these laws within one or two years of the promulgation of the constitution, a condition that strengthened their status in relation to other laws. With ninety-five sections, the 1998 Political Party Law (*phraratchabanyat prakop ratthathammanun waduai phakkanmueang* Pho. So. 2541) corresponded to the provisions of the 1997 Constitution. The 140 Sections in total of the 2007 law (*phraratchabanyat prakop ratthathammanun waduai phakkanmueang* Pho. So. 2550) were enacted in line with the Constitution of 2007.

Given the marked increase in the number of sections in the 2007 Political Party Law compared with that of 1998, the following section will consider the types of provisions that were expanded while also noting the specific characteristics of each law. Comparison with the 1991 law, in use until 1998, will assist in clarifying these special characteristics. Table 4.3 compares the chapter division of the 1981, 1998 and 2007 laws.

1998 Political Party Law

Paragraphs added to the 1998 Political Party Law related to funds used by a party, state subsidies and the dissolution and amalgamation of parties. Categories emerged that appeared to strengthen political parties, including the donation of party support funds.

Since the detailed stipulations on the management of political party funds have been dealt with elsewhere, this chapter discusses the changes to the respective laws with a focus on three elements that have the potential to exert a strong influence on election outcomes. These are: the establishment of political parties, the dissolution of parties and the duties of the leader and executive of a party.

The establishment of political parties

The actual stages in the process of establishing a political party have remained unchanged since the 1970s. The person or entity who wishes to form a party first forms a Political Party Establishment Committee (*khana phuroem chattang phakkanmueang*) and then lodges notice with

Table 4.3 Chapter divisions of the 1981, 1998 and 2007 political party laws

1981	1998	2007
Chapter 1: 'Formation and Registration of Political Parties' (Sections 7–29)	Chapter 1: 'Formation of Political Parties' (Sections 8–19)	Chapter 1: 'Formation of Political Parties' (Sections 8–16)
Chapter 2: 'The Operation of Political Parties' (Sections 30–45)	Chapter 2: 'The Operation of Political Parties' Part 1: The Operation of Political Activities (Sections 20–36) Part 2: Political Funds (Sections 37–44)	Section 2: The Operation of Political Parties (Sections 17–43)
Chapter 3: 'The Cessation of Political Parties' (Sections 46–49)	Chapter 3: 'Support for Political Parties' Part 1: Political Party Donations (Sections 45–55) Part 2: State Support for Political Parties (Sections 56–64)	Chapter 3: 'Finance and Support for Political Parties' Part 1: Political Party Finances (Sections 44–52) Part 2: Political Party Revenue (Sections 53–54) Part 3: Political Party Donations (Sections 55–72) Part 4: State Subsidy to Political Parties (Sections 73–86) Part 5: Political Party Expenditure (Sections 87–90)
Chapter 4: 'Penalties' (Sections 50–66)	Chapter 4: 'Cessation and Dissolution of Political Parties' (Sections 65–69)	Chapter 4: 'Loss of Status, Cessation of Dissolution of Political Parties' Part 1: Loss of Status of Political Parties (Section 91) Part 2: Cessation of Political Parties (Section 92) Part 3: Dissolution of Political Parties (Sections 93–98)
	Chapter 5: 'Amalgamation of Political Parties' (Sections 70–73)	Chapter 5: 'Amalgamation of Political Parties' (Sections 99–103)
	Chapter 6: 'Penalties' (Sections 74–91) 'Transitory Provisions' (Sections 92–95)	Chapter 6: 'Penalties' (Section 104) Part 1: Criminal Penalties (Sections 105–121) Part 2: Administrative Penalties (Sections 122–132) Transitory Provisions (Sections 133–140)

Source: Compiled by the author.

a supervisory authority such as the Election Commission.[18] If they fulfil the set conditions within the timeframe determined by the Political Party Law, they are able to register formally as a political party.

According to Section 7 of the 1981 law, a political party establishment committee required the membership of at least fifteen people who were Thai nationals by birth over twenty years of age. Once the party name, party emblem, party policies and the names, addresses and occupations of establishment committee members had been lodged with the registrar's office (Section 8), and an investigation by the political party registrar identified no issues of concern, permission was given to make a call for members. If, within a year, party membership exceeded 5,000 (more than five states in each area and more than fifty names in each state), a party establishment conference was convened at which policies, rules and the executive body were determined (Section 9). The party leader then made an application to the political party registrar and, if permission was granted, arrangements were made to establish the party.

In the 1998 law, the time limit for establishing a party tightened considerably with the need to register more than 5,000 party members within 180 days and also to have at least one branch established in each region (Section 29). Furthermore, there was a marked increase in the number of matters to be covered by party rules. According to Section 22 of the 1991 law, party rules covered the following matters: party name, party emblem, party headquarters, the election, duration of office and loss of office of the party leader and the responsibilities of the executive, party branches, the party conference, the powers and duties of party members, responsibilities towards party members, members joining and being expelled from the party, party member rules and regulations, method of candidate selection, and management of finances. Section 11 of the 1998 law added matters relating to the election, term of office, removal from office and powers and duties of

---

18 Although elections had long been administered in Thailand by the Ministry of the Interior, this became the task of the Election Commission, an independent agency constituted under the 1997 Constitution. Accordingly, the role of the political party registrar was given to the chair of the Election Commission.

branch committee members, branch conferences, political awareness education for party members and the public, and the dissolution of either the party or a branch, while sections 37–44 set out very detailed stipulations regarding party and branch finances, assets and the preparation of account records. Furthermore, Section 13 stipulated that at the time of party registration, minutes of meetings of the party establishment committee should also be lodged.

Duties of the party leader and party executive

While according to the 1981 law the party leader was the external party representative (Section 33), stipulations regarding the duties of the leader and chair of the party executive were confined to management of the register that recorded financial matters such as income and expenditure and management of the party assets register (Section 35).

Changes to the 1998 law, however, required the party leader to now maintain correct information related to party membership, to be kept at a party's headquarters. This information was subject to scrutiny by the political party registrar. Furthermore, according to Section 34, the party leader, who had to lodge a report on changes in party membership numbers to the political party registrar at the end of January each year, was also required by section 35 to submit an annual information report on party activities to the political party registrar at the end of March. Section 42 required the executive to lodge with the political party registrar within thirty days of their appointment a statement of their financial assets, including those of wives and children below the age of majority. Section 43 also required the executive to ensure that election funds expended on candidates did not exceed the limit stipulated by law. Section 48 required the party leader to issue a receipt listing all matters required by law when accepting political donations, while there was also a duty according to Section 49 to have these transferred to an account in the name of the party leader and report the matter to the political party registrar within seven days.[19] Clearly, the 1998 law considerably expanded the responsibilities of both a party leader and party executive.

---

19 Conventionally, reference to a 'political party' specified the party leader or party executive.

The dissolution of political parties

In the 1981 law, party dissolution was included in the chapter heading that previously related only to party cessation. I will discuss what this dissolution involved.

Section 46 of the 1981 law stipulated five instances leading to party dissolution. These were as follows: 1. when this occurred according to party rules; 2. when the number of party members falls below 5,000, or when the number of members in each prefecture falls below fifty for at least half a year; 3. when the party was unable to nominate candidates for more than half the seats of the lower house; 4. when a dissolution ruling was handed down by the courts, and 5. when there was non-compliance with party conference regulations in the law. Section 47 gave three points according to which the courts might give a ruling of party dissolution. These were 1. opposition to the democratic regime of government with the king as head of state, 2. violation of national security, the law, public order or the morals of the nation, and 3. committing an illegal act such as accepting donations from a foreign interest.

Section 65 of the 1998 law expanded the reasons for dissolution to seven cases, as follows: 1. based on party regulations; 2. when the number of party members falls below 5,000; 3. amalgamation with another party; 4. dissolution by the Constitutional Court's judgment: 5. non-compliance with party conference regulations in law; 6. failure to lodge the annual report of party activities; and 7. failure to lodge a statement of expenditure three times a year. Section 66 determined five matters that might result in a dissolution ruling being handed down by the Constitutional Court, as follows: 1. an overthrow of the democratic regime of government with the king as the head of state or attempting to seize political power through a process that did not comply with the constitution; 2. opposition to the democratic regime of government with the king as head of state; 3. violation of national security, the law, public order or the morals of the nation; 4. giving political party membership to a person who did not hold Thai nationality from birth; and 5. committing an illegal act relating to the acceptance of political donations. Section 53 forbade the acceptance of political donations from organizations as advised by the Electoral Committee. Section 69, furthermore, determined that, in the case of a political party being dissolved on the grounds of a violation in relation to the lodgment of either the report of political party activity or the income statement report, or on the grounds of one of the five matters that resulted in a ruling of dissolution by the Constitutional Court, executive members were unable to establish a party, become executive members of a party, or be on the establishment committee of a new party for the following five years. In addition, as stated previously, where a party's conduct of constitutional amendment violated the notion of democratic regime of government with the king as head of state, the 1997 Constitution introduced the stipulation that the party concerned could be dissolved. This led to a situation in which it was possible for party dissolution to be based on grounds other than corruption. Attempts at constitutional amendment could conceivably also have this outcome.

It is clear from the above that the three points that characterized the 1998 law were stricter conditions for the establishment of political parties, expansion of the responsibilities of the party leader and executive, and additional justifications for party dissolution.

The 2007 law

With 140 sections that made it one and half times as long as the 1998 document, the 2007 law featured a large number of additions and changes. As with the 1998 law, many of the expanded 2007 stipulations related to the management of party funds and party dissolution. In addition, penalties were now classified into criminal penalties and administrative penalties. The following will outline the 2007 revisions by comparing this law with its 1998 iteration.

The establishment of political parties

Additions to the 2007 law saw further changes to the establishment of political party rules. Section 8 lowered the membership age restriction of the party establishment committee from twenty to eighteen, while the bar for new party membership was lowered a little to more than 5,000 members within a year and the creation of a minimum of one branch in each region. Party regulations, however, were specified in much greater detail. Section 9 stipulated that the name, initials and emblem proposed by a party establishment committee could not be similar to those of an another party establishment committee, party already registered, or party that had previously been dissolved in terms of the Political Party Law.

In terms of party rules, while the previous law had merely stipulated that there could be no opposition to the fundamental principle of democratic regime of government with the king as head of state, this wording was modified in 2007 to read that a party/government must 'be consistent with' democratic regime of government with the king as head of state. In addition, Section 10 of the law forbade opposition to any matter determined by the Election Commission to be 'in conformity with fundamental principles of the democratic regime of government with the king as head of state'. Section 11 stipulated that the term of office of members of a party executive committee would be stipulated by law and, while re-election was possible, would not exceed four years. Section 12 required that, when an 'application for the formation of a political party' was lodged with the Political Party Registrar, it should be accompanied by a 'letter of consent' regarding the 'use of a venue within the Kingdom [of Thailand] as the political party's office'.

The duties of the party leader and party executive

Through Section 17, the 2007 law determined that the executive committee of a political party 'shall have the powers and duty to carry out political activities in conformity with the constitution, the laws, the political party's policy, regulations and the resolutions of its general meeting with prudence, caution and honesty, in the interests of the country and its people'. The executive was also required to 'promote democracy within the political party'.

Other additional stipulations were the Section 17 requirements that 'Members of the executive committee must share responsibility for the executive committee's resolutions and performance as per the rules prescribed in the political party's regulations and this organic act'. It was nonetheless noted that executive committee members 'shall not be liable for responsibility [...] if able to prove that they were not involved in these actions and declared their opposition [by submitting] a written letter declaring their opposition to the chairman of the meeting within seven days of the meeting'. Section 18 added the stipulation that 'The executive committee of a political party must control and ensure that its members do not conduct themselves in any way contrary to the constitution, laws or the Election Commission's regulations or notifications'. Section 38 of the 2007 law newly stipulated that: 'A political party's consideration of the nomination of candidates for the election of the House of Representatives under both the constituency and party-list systems shall be the shared responsibility of its executive committee and its candidate selection committee'. Regional branches, furthermore, were now responsible for the recommendation of election candidates, with Section 39 stating, 'When a lower house election is held, a branch committee meeting will be held to approve the recommendation of candidates for both the single-representative constituency or party-list constituency positions'.

The dissolution of a political party

Three new political party dissolution stipulations related to elections, as follows: 1. in the case of a violation of election law or of the rules or advice issued by the Election Commission, an election would be declared unjust and dishonest; 2. when the party, the party executive or a person employed by the party gave either direct or indirect support to a person standing in a Senate election; and 3. when a party plotted, supported or gave tacit approval to the deception of another person or other political party or to another person who committed an election irregularity. Furthermore, Section 98 stipulated that when rules related to donations were violated, or when a party was dissolved as a result of the order of the Constitutional Court, then 'the leader of the political party or any member of the executive committee [who] has participated in, been an accomplice to, ignored or known of the offense without curbing or rectifying it', shall have their 'right to stand for election for a period of five years from the date of the dissolution order' revoked by the Constitutional Court.

It becomes apparent by considering the changes that occurred to political party laws between 1981 and 2007 that the processes related to new party establishment became much more complex and that more and more matters generally were stipulated by law. In particular, the 2007 law introduced a number of vague criteria for regulation and judgment, increasing the number of matters that could be regulated or judged at the discretion of the Election Commission. These provisions allowed the Election Commission to deny party registration for a variety of reasons. Furthermore, while the provisions of previous laws focused largely on individual candidate responsibility for irregularities, the 1998 law placed much greater responsibility on the party leader and party executive for the management and guidance of party members and candidates. However, each political party has thousands of members on its roster, with as many as 500 candidates. Judging from this situation, it can be said that political parties are now more likely to be dissolved than in the past due to amendments of the constitution and the Political Party Law.

The 1998 and 2007 Organic Act on Elections

Shifts in election laws

Like the Political Party Law, the Organic Act on Elections (the Election Law (*phraratchabanyat kanlueaktang samachik sapha phuthaen ratsadon*) expanded with each revision, growing from eighty-seven to 102 sections between 1968 and 1979. This expansion became even more pronounced when the Election Law became associated with the constitution, resulting in 115 sections to the 1998 law (*phraratchabanyat prakop ratthathammanun waduai kanlueaktang samachik sapha phuthaen ratsadon lae samachik uthisapha* Pho. So. 2541) and 161 to the 2007 law (*phraratchabanyat prakop ratthathammanun waduai kanlueaktang samachik sapha phuthaen ratsadon lae kandaimasueng samachik uthisapha* Pho. So. 2550). Additional chapters and parts of the 2007 law concerned dishonest and unfair election procedures, the case of an election, and the appointment of members to the Senate. The latter was added following stipulations in the 2007 Constitution that moved Senate membership from full popular election to appointment for approximately half the seats in the upper house. The number of sections stipulating penalties rose from eighteen in the 1998 law to twenty-six in the 2007 iteration.

It will be useful to examine the special characteristics of the 1998 and 2007 laws by comparing these to the 1979 law discussed above. Table 4.4 compares the chapter divisions of the three pieces of legislation.

The 1998 law

In comparison to its 1979 predecessor, additions to the 1998 law involved election expenditure, election activity methods (campaigns) and the casting of ballots by eligible voters outside an electoral district. Elements concerning election expenditure and campaign activity appear to derive from the attempt to manage and regulate election corruption and fraud that was a stated objective of the 1997 Constitution. The discussion below will accordingly focus on stipulations related to those matters.

Holding re-elections

Instituted by the 1997 Constitution to take carriage of the conduct of election administration, the Election Commission had the power to order a re-election if it suspected that electoral wrongdoing had occurred. We will consider the conditions according to which re-elections could be ordered.

It will be useful to begin by examining the provisions for repeat elections under the 1979 law which was administered at the time by the Ministry of the Interior.

There were two instances stipulated in the law relating to re-election. The first was Section 71 which provided for either voting or vote aggregation not proceeding because of natural disaster, and which required the relevant provincial governor to declare the election null and void and to announce a new election date at the relevant polling place within three days. The second was Section 78 which concerned the right of a voter, candidate or a party that nominated a candidate, to judge an election unfair after a provincial governor announced an election result and to file an application with either the Provincial Court or the Bangkok Civil Court within thirty to 120 days, depending on the violation concerned, for the election to be declared null and void. In the latter case, the court was to forward the application to the Supreme Court. If the Supreme Court ruled the election unfair, it could either call for a re-election or merely cancel the election of the successful candidate who committed election fraud. Where it was ruled that an election irregularity occurred but that a re-election was not necessary, the court could cancel an appeal. The court ruling was to be explained by the Minister for Justice to either the Leader of the House of Representatives or the Minister of the Interior. Five matters were stipulated as bases for an appeal in the second instance, as follows: nomination of a person who did not have the right to nominate as outlined in Section 26; a violation of the upper limit of election campaign expenditure as outlined in Section 32; failure to lodge an election campaign expenditure report within three months of the election result being announced as outlined in Section 34; irregularities in the gathering of votes by the official responsible for conducting the election as outlined in Section 51; or an illegal act by the official responsible for conducting the election as outlined in Section 52.

According to the 1998 law, circumstances giving rise to the right to lodge an appeal requesting a repeat election with the Election Commission were as follows: 1. where natural disaster resulted in the polling place not able to be used, the vote would be stopped, and a new polling date would be determined within thirty days and made public at least seven days prior to the date determined (Section 64); 2. where vote counting took place at a polling place but the arrival of a ballot box was more than twelve hours late, the vote would be regarded as irregular and the Election Commission would order a repeat election to be held at the relevant polling place (Section 68); 3. in the case where an inconsistency existed between the result of the vote count and the information report made by the Polling Place Committee (Section 69); 4. where there is only one candidate and that candidate fails to poll more than 20% of the vote (Section 74); 5. where there are clear irregularities committed by a candidate prior to the announcement of an election result and that candidate gained the maximum number of

Table 4.4 Chapter divisions of the 1979, 1998 and 2007 election laws

1981	1998	2007
Chapter 1: 'General Provisions' (Sections 6–16)	Chapter 1: 'Election of Members of the House of Representatives' Part 1: General Provisions (Sections 6–7) Part 2: Constituencies, Polling Groups* and Polling Places (Sections 8–11) Part 3: Election Officials (Sections 12–19) Part 4: Voters and Voter Rolls (Sections 20–28) Part 5: Candidates and Candidacy (Sections 29–39) Part 6: Election Expenditure and Means of Election Campaigns (Sections 40–50) Part 7: Polling (Sections 51–67) Part 8: Counting Votes and Announcing Election Results (Sections 68–78) Part 9: Polling of a Voter Residing Outside a Constituency (Sections 79–85)	Chapter 1: 'Election of Members of the House of Representatives' Part 1: General Provisions (Sections 6–7) Part 2: Constituencies, Polling Groups*, Polling Places (Sections 10–14) Part 3: Election Officials (Sections 15–22) Part 4: Voters and Voter Rolls (Sections 23–33) Part 5: Candidates and Candidacy (Sections 34–48) Part 6: Election Expenditure and Means of Election Campaigns (Sections 49–60) Part 7: Polling (Sections 61–80) Part 8: Counting Votes and Announcing Election Results (Sections 91–93) Part 9: Polling of a Voter Residing Outside a Constituency. (Sections 94–102) Part 10: Proceedings for an Election Not Conducted in a Fair or Honest Manner (Sections 103–113) Part 11: Election Petition – Lodging an Objection to an Election (Sections 114–116)
Chapter 2: 'Suffrage/ The Right to Vote and Candidacy' (Sections 17–26)	Chapter 2: 'Election of Senators' (Sections 86–93)	Chapter 2: 'Election and Appointment of Senators' Part 1: Senate Elections (Sections 117–125) Part 2: Senate Appointments (Sections 126–135)

votes in the constituency (the Election Commission shall also revoke that candidate's right to vote for one year) (Section 85, Part 1);[20] 6. where irregularities on the part of someone involved in the conduct of the election are discovered prior to the day of polling (voting at that polling place or in that constituency shall be stopped and a new polling day determined) (Section 86, Part 6); 7. where evidence exists,

---

20 Sections 85, Parts 1, 6 and 7 were added at the time of revisions to the law in 2000.

1981	1998	2007
Chapter 3: 'Voter Rolls' (Sections 27–31)	Chapter 3: 'Election Petitions' (Sections 94–97)	Chapter 3: 'Penalties' (Sections 136–161) Transitory Provisions (Sections 162–165)
Chapter 4: 'Election Expenditure and Means of Election Campaigns' (Sections 32–37)	Chapter 4: 'Penalties' (Sections 98–115)	
Chapter 5: 'Voting Stations and Voting Places' (Sections 38–41)		
Chapter 6: 'Election Officials, Voting Investigation Committees and Aggregating Officers' (Sections 42–52)		
Chapter 7: 'Voting' (Sections 53–70)		
Chapter 8: 'Voting Audits and Aggregate' (Sections 71–77)		
Chapter 9: 'Election Petitions' (Sections 78–80)		
Chapter 10: 'Penalties' (Sections 81–93) 'Transitory Provisions' (Sections 94–102)		

Source: Compiled by the author Note: *nuai lueaktang.

after vote-counting has concluded, of irregularities in the conduct of the election in a relevant constituency, it is possible for the Election Commission to stop the declaration of the result and to conduct a repeat election (Section 85, Part 7); 8. within thirty days of the declaration of an election result, a voter, candidate, or political party that nominated a candidate had the right to lodge an appeal to the Election Commission to request a repeat election on the grounds of irregularities at the polling place or in the constituency, although in the case of a violation of the stipulation related to a candidate lodging an expenditure report, the appeal period was within 180 days (Section 94). Section 95 stipulated that where an investigation by the Election Commission led to a decision to have a vote recount of a repeat election, such a direction would be handed down, as determined in the eight cases outlined above.

Disenfranchisement – revocation of the right to vote

In the 1979 law, twenty-one cases, set out over seven sections, stipulated circumstances leading to revocation of the right to vote. The following led to the revocation of voting rights for a period of ten years: 1. a public official applying pressure to a candidate or a political party (Section 84); 2. nomination of a person who did not meet the conditions for candidature (Section 84); 3. seeking to influence or induce the vote of a voter through means prohibited by law after the date of an election is called (Section 84); 4. voting at a polling station at which one's name was not registered on the voting roll (Section 84); 5. voting by a person who did not have the right to vote (Section 84); 6. voting other than on the official ballot paper, holding an unused ballot paper (Section 84); 7. placing a ballot paper in a ballot box or making a modification to the voter roll without the legal power to do so (Section 84); 8. causing a voter to misunderstand something about a candidate or the party with which a candidate was affiliated (Section 84); 9. opening a ballot box while voting is taking place (Section 84); 10. destroying or altering or removing a ballot box or ballot papers (Section 84); 11. tampering with ballot papers, making a valid vote invalid, making an invalid vote valid (Section 84); and 12. an election official deliberately miscalculating the vote count or illegally disposing of votes (Section 91).

Offences that led to a five-year revocation of voting rights were as follows: 1. violation of the prohibition of duplicate candidacy (Section 85); 2. violation of prescribed duties or of the law by election officials (Section 85); 3. a candidate exceeding the upper limits of funds designated for election expenditure (Section 86); 4. a candidate failing to report within the designated time or making a false report on election expenditure (Section 87); 5. a candidate transporting a voter to a polling station for free or at a reduced price (Section 89); 6. making a mark on a ballot paper (Section 89); 7. a person without authority obstructing the entry of a voter to a ballot place (Section 89); 8. a voter requesting or receiving a benefit for casting a vote (Section 89); and 9. a voter failing to return a ballot paper (Section 91). Many stipulations, as demonstrated by the above, related to the administration of polling booth places and stations.

It is apparent from consideration of changes that occurred through the 1998 law that stipulations relating to the administration of polling stations remained fundamentally the same. Newly added was the revocation of voting rights for ten years for violating restrictions related to election activities in a Senate election (Section 101). Furthermore, the responsibilities of the party leader came under closer scrutiny and the right to vote was revoked for five years in the case of either a candidate or a party leader who violated expenditure limits during an election campaign (Section 102) or failed to submit an expenditure report within the time limit or with the necessary accompanying evidence (Section 104).

Other stipulations included falsely claiming to others that a candidate had committed an illegal act. If the false claim of that act had the voting rights of the candidate in question revoked, or interfered with the election result, then the person concerned had their own voting rights revoked for ten years. If the Election Commission was notified of the false act, the perpetrator could have their voting rights revoked for twenty years. When such an act was either undertaken by, supported or tacitly overlooked by the head of a political party, then that party could be subject to dissolution according to the Organic Act on Political Parties (Section 101, Part 1).[21] Furthermore, it was determined that the person whose act caused a repeat election would be required to fund the new ballot (Section 113, Part 1). This expansion in the scope of cases which led to repeated Election Commission election rulings confirms a marked development in the parameters of election regulation violation.

---

21 Section 101, Part 1, and Section 113, Part 1, were added at the time of the 2000 revisions of the law.

The 2007 law

The 2007 Election Law had approximately one and a half times the number of sections compared to the 1998 law. Additions to chapters were Part 10 of Chapter 1 which covered cases of elections not being conducted fairly and honestly and Part 2, related to Senate appointments, which was added to Chapter 2 on elections and appointments to the upper house. The latter followed changes that saw approximately half the upper house selected by appointment rather than chosen through popular election. In addition, the number of sections on penalties in Chapter 3 grew from eighteen in 1998 to twenty-six in 2007. We will accordingly examine the characteristics of the 2007 law with a focus on the stipulations related to election violations.

Encouragement of reports about election fraud

One of the features of the 2007 law was the encouragement of reports about election fraud by people. Where a ruling of guilt was handed down regarding the infringement of election campaign activity regulations, it was stipulated that an amount of money that was up to half the amount of the fine paid by the offender be paid to the informant. Furthermore, while a voter was forbidden at the time of a vote to request or receive some benefit, Section 137 determined that no penalty would apply to that voter if before, during or within seven days of the vote, information regarding this act was provided to the Election Commission.

Disenfranchisement – revocation of the right to vote

There was one further important stipulation in the 2007 law. The 1997 Constitution stipulated that a constituency with only one candidate had to receive at least 20% of the vote to win. In the 2 April 2006 House of Representatives election that followed the dissolution of the lower house, however, there was huge confusion when opposition parties, led by the Democratic Party, which believed that the rival Thai Rak Thai Party would win office, boycotted the election. As a result of candidates avoiding the one-name constituencies, the qualifications of hastily improvised candidates became problematic. There were repeated infringements of conditions such as no multiple party membership and the need to have been registered with a party for ninety days. Although the chair of the Election Commission had misgivings about proceeding with the election, an extension would have violated the constitutional stipulation that a ballot must be held within sixty days of the dissolution of the lower house. When the election went ahead (as scheduled), the stipulations outlined above resulted in no member being elected in thirty-eight constituencies. Accordingly, a repeat election was held. Even then, however, ten candidates from governmental parties failed to receive 20% of the vote. While there was talk of a third election, the Election Commission came under considerable pressure from various quarters with a view to preventing this. This included a ruling by the Central Administrative Court against a third election.[22] In May of the same year, the Constitutional Court handed down a ruling that the election was invalid. In order to prevent the recurrence of such cases, the 2007 law stipulates that any individual or political party is prohibited from standing for election in order to avoid constituencies with only one candidate. An individual who violated this stipulation could have their voting rights revoked for ten years, while violation by a political party could have the voting rights of both the party leader and executive revoked for ten years with the additional threat of the party being dissolved (Section 141).

Two points are clear from the above examination of Thai election laws. Firstly, stipulations related to election corruption accelerated the tendency to broaden the responsibilities of party leaders and executives which accordingly facilitated the dissolution of a political party through a ruling of the Election Commission and the Constitutional Court. At the time of revision of the Political Party Law and the Election Law in line with the 1997 Constitution, there was a sharp rise in the chance of political parties and candidates being the subject of a ruling by the court or the Election Commission. In the following section we will confirm how revisions to the constitution and to the various laws impacted on political practice.

---

22 The order was based on petitions to the Central Administrative Court made by the three opposition parties as follows: 1. conducting the election thirty-seven days after the dissolution of the lower house was to the advantage of the government party; 2. the meeting of the Election Commission that determined the election day did not have a quorum.

The political impact of election system reform

Election results

Lower house elections conducted under the 1997 Constitution occurred in 2001, 2005 and 2006. In the first two of these, Thaksin's Thai Rak Thai Party achieved historic victories. After nominating candidates in the 2001 House of Representatives election, the new Thai Rak Thai Party won 248 (49.6%) of the available 500 seats. The party had an even more overwhelming victory in the 2005 election at which time it captured 377 (75.4%) of the seats in the lower house chamber.[23] However, following the 2007 coup d'état, the Constitutional Tribunal handed down a ruling that saw the dissolution of three political parties, including Thai Rak Thai.[24]

Two House of Representatives elections were conducted under the 2007 Constitution – in 2007 and 2011. Parties associated with the Thaksin faction triumphed in both. In the 2007 election, the People Power Party took 233 (48.5%) of the available 480 seats. In the election that followed the 2011 constitutional revisions, the Pheu Thai Party (For Thais Party) was successful in 265 (53%) of the chamber's 500 seats. However, in 2008, when no election was held, political power shifted to the Democrat Party. The People Power Party, which had held government, was dissolved.

The above discussion provides insights into the role that both the courts and the Election Commission came to play in denying election results following the promulgation of the 1997 Constitution. The discussion now turns to an examination of the circumstances surrounding party dissolution and the regulation of election corruption and fraud.

---

23 The ratio of seats taken by the leading party in previous elections was 26.7% in 1979, 28.3% in 1983, 28.8% in 1986, 24.3% in 1988, 21.9% in March 1992, 21.9% in September 1992, 23.5% in 1995, and 31.8% in 1996 (Siripan 2006: 63). It was usual for more than ten political parties to take seats in any given election.

24 The Constitutional Tribunal was the organization established following the coup d'état group forcing the dissolution of the Constitutional Court.

The dissolution of political parties

Under the transitional constitutions of 2006 and 2007, promulgated following the 2006 coup d'état, the respective dissolution of one-term government political parties occurred. What crimes were cited to justify these events?

Constitutional Tribunal ruling 3-5/2550, 30 May 2007

During the lower house election of April 2006, the Thai Rak Thai Party was indicted for giving money to two other political parties and illegally falsifying party membership records in order to induce candidates from these other parties to nominate in constituencies in which only one candidate was standing. While only two Thai Rak Thai executive members were named as having handed over funds, the party was unable to hold executive meetings during the course of the indictment and the Constitutional Tribunal connected the activities of the two named members to the entire Thai Rak Thai Party. Ultimately, the activities of the two members of other parties who received the funds were also regarded as actions by the party to which they belonged. Although coup leaders had abolished the 1997 Constitution, the 1998 Political Party Law was judged as remaining valid. The Thai Rak Thai Party and the other two parties were accordingly dissolved under that law, while the voting rights of executive members were revoked for five years under Decree No. 27 of the coup group (the Council for Democratic Reform under Constitutional Monarchy (CDRM)). Section 66 of the 1998 Political Party Law, which was the basis for the dissolution of the Thai Rak Thai Party, read:

The Constitutional Court may issue an order dissolving a political party that has carried out any of the following: 1. an act which shall overthrow the democratic regime of government with the king as head of state or shall gain the power in administration of the state by unconstitutional means, [or] 3. an act which may endanger the security of the state or may be contrary to law or public order or good morals.

The first of these had been newly introduced following the promulgation of the 1997 Constitution.

Constitutional Tribunal ruling 20/2551, 2 December 2008

The Supreme Court ruled that People Power Party Deputy Leader Yongyuth had violated Section 53 of the 2007 Political Party Law by being unfairly involved in his own elder sister's election campaign.[25] This had a domino effect at the time of the December 2007 House of Representatives election – held under the 2007 Constitution – that left no doubt as to the responsibilities of political parties. Following the Supreme Court decision, the Constitutional Court argued that as a political power broker within the party, Yongyuth should have acted to prevent unjust elections. Drawing on Section 68 and Section 237, Paragraph 2, of the 2007 Constitution, the court then ordered that the People Power Party be dissolved while also revoking the voting rights of the party leader and executives for five years.

This court ruling, which, in fact, ordered the dissolution of the party holding government, broadened the scope of the responsibilities of political party executives regarding election fraud and corruption, and interpreted an act committed by an individual member of an executive as an act of the party itself. We might regard these outcomes as the result of revisions to the law and the constitution that gave both those documents greater powers with respect to party dissolution.

Dissolution rulings, moreover, were applied incessantly to small-scale parties that lay outside the sphere of government activity. Between 1999 and the first half of 2012, with the exception of dissolution related to political party amalgamation, a total of ninety-three parties received a dissolution ruling from the Constitutional Court. Petitions in these cases were largely lodged by the Political Party Registrar (the head of the Election Commission). In 2001, the year in which most petitions were lodged, sixteen parties received resolution notices. Many were dissolved under the 1997 Constitution, the stipulations of which led to a total of seventy parties being dissolved.

The most-often cited reason for dissolution was the failure to fulfill the necessary conditions of party establishment as determined by the Political Party Law. One impediment to party establishment was the need to 'establish a branch according to the stipulated condition of

---

25 This was a stipulation to regulate election irregularities generally, including vote-buying.

gathering more than 5,000 party members within 180 days'.²⁶ Other often cited reasons included failure to fulfil requirements for a quorum as determined by law at a party conference, failure to lodge a report of party activities within the required number of days and non-lodgment of a necessary report of party subsidy expenditure. With the Political Party Law imposing so many responsibilities onto party executive committees, some even lodged dissolution petitions themselves, citing the difficulty of discharging all necessary tasks. Without doubt, the obligations imposed on party executives through both the 1998 and 2007 political party laws created an extraordinarily large burden for those who assumed these roles.²⁷

The crackdown on election corruption

The promulgation of the 1997 Constitution set the scene for court rulings that disallowed the qualifications of prospective candidates. As a result, the revocation of voting rights through charges of unfair elections and the consequent conduct of repeat elections became commonplace. In 2001, repeat elections for the House of Representatives were conducted in sixty-two wards, while fourteen candidates had their voting rights revoked. In the 2005 general election, the voting rights of only one candidate were revoked, leading to claims that the Election Commission was being influenced by the government party. After the 2007 general election, re-elections were conducted in fourteen constituencies on four separate dates. Two persons had voting rights revoked. At the time of the 2001 general election, two constituencies had repeat elections while a recount was ordered in one other. These circumstances led to claims of voter 'poll fatigue' (Ji 2002).

Notwithstanding the large number of re-elections, the workings of the system resulted in a considerable lapse of time before the

---

26 There were also examples in which activities relating to the establishment of party branches and member recruitment seemed not to comply with the law, including cases of parties dissolved because, while branches were established and members recruited in five places, a member in one place was less than the required twenty years of age.

27 This certainly appears to have also prevented a flood of political parties claiming political subsidies.

confirmation of an election result. For example, ten days after the 2007 election, the Election Commission had finalized only 397 of 480 seats. In another case, with results for only 350 of the 500 available seats finalized ten days after the 2011 election, it was impossible to say whether the Pheu Thai Party's Yingluck Shinawatra or the Democrat Party's (Mark) Abhisit Vejjajiva would become prime minister. Even after the declaration of election results, moreover, some House of Representatives members lost the right to sit in the house and had their voting rights revoked. In fact, an election result could sometimes drag out interminably. In the month following the 2011 election, for example, a ruling was handed down revoking the voting rights of an elected member while a similar ruling was made almost a year later in June of the following year.[28]

With many appeals lodged with the Election Commission on the grounds of election corruption or fraud by an elected member, members in such constituencies were declared unsuccessful candidates. While candidates who were not elected also had the potential to engage in irregular vote-gathering activities, appeals were generally lodged against successful candidates. Analysis of the circumstances related to the 2011 general election indicates that the Election Commission heard 122 appeals related to that event.[29] Of these, sixty-four were between candidates. Forty matters concerned unsuccessful candidates lodging appeals against the winner of the election. In twenty-one other cases, voters appealed the result of an election. These included instances of candidates and voters coming together to appeal against another candidate. Few appeals seemed to be based on serious offences. There were, for example, claims of promising benefits to a region during a newspaper interview, taking pride in one's own success in a project implemented in the regions, violating laws related to the format or size

---

28 In June 2012, the Election Commission ruled to revoke the voting rights of a lower house member of the Pheu Thai Party for defaming a lower house member of the Democrat Party during the conduct of the general election in July of the previous year. Accordingly, a re-election was conducted in that constituency (*Bangkok Post*, 20 June 2012).

29 Among the resolutions that are posted to the Election Commission homepage, there are aggregates/totals for matters investigated only. See http://www.ect.go.th/newweb/th/writ/index1.php?GroupID=32

of election signs, and defaming other candidates.[30] There were many cases in which appellants made claims without clear evidence of vote-buying by area, village and constituency leaders.[31] A large number of claims were therefore dismissed. The broad definition of 'election corruption or fraud' created a tendency for appeals to be lodged with the Election Commission on trivial grounds that nevertheless arose from the wording of the sections of the law that dealt with those matters.

Law amendments destroying political parties and elections

The above has provided a detailed analysis of the political party laws and the election laws that derived from the respective 1997 and 2007 constitutions. It accordingly became clear that, while there were points of difference between the two constitutions, there were also similarities. Points of difference related to both the administrative and the legislative powers (of the lower house). While revisions to the 1997 Constitution framework strengthened the influence of the administrative branch within parties and thereby facilitated administrative powers controlling legislative powers, the 2007 Constitution reduced the influence of the administrative power over those of the legislative. In contrast, common points in both constitutions strengthened the power of management and control through the courts and independent agencies towards both law-making and administrative powers.

With both constitutions giving greater powers to the courts and independent agencies, lawmakers remained the target of rulings handed down by these entities. While the 1997 Constitution appeared to raise the profile of political parties, it nevertheless provided a

---

30 One example of defamation involved a campaigning candidate saying to an audience '[Then] Prime Minister Abihisit is a terrible person so please vote for the [opposing] Pheu Thai Party'.

31 One voter appeal, for example, claimed that money had been handed over by unknown persons who indicated that the funds came from 'such-and-such' a party.

means for the country's administrative power to exert control over the legislative power. Electoral system revisions that followed on from the 1997 Constitution resulted in repeated dissolutions of political parties and orders for repeat elections. Close consideration of the Political Parties Law and the Election Law, both of which provide the foundation for regulating political activities in Thailand, reveals that the insistence in these on an extraordinarily broad definition of the sphere of responsibility of the party leader and party executive resulted in ongoing Election Commission rulings for repeat elections and the revocation of voting rights. This occurred even in cases in which evidence of election corruption or fraud was opaque.[32] We can only conclude that the outcomes of the sequence of electoral reforms implemented in Thailand ultimately exceeded the primary objectives of ensuring stable government and controlling and regulating electoral corruption and fraud. There was, instead, an excessive denial of election outcomes.

We must ultimately interpret the political events discussed above as the suppression of the legislative power of the Thai House of Representatives, the role of which was enhanced by the country's 1992 constitutional reforms. This also resulted in the imposition of restraints on the power of the voters who choose the lawmakers of the lower house through the ballot box. While, on the one hand, the primary objective of regulating election corruption and fraud assisted the expression of the will of the people through fair and honest elections, dissolving entire political parties because of an individual executive member's misdeed or ordering repeat elections on the basis of flimsy or non-existent 'evidence' contradictorily denied that same popular will expressed through elections and accordingly

---

32 As a representative example of doubt arising towards a judgment of electoral fraud or corruption, we might cite the ruling against Deputy Leader Yongyuth that led to the dissolution of the People Power Party. The ruling arose on the grounds that Yongyuth had given gifts to constituency leaders at the time of his sister's campaign. While it was a fact that he met these leaders at a Bangkok hotel, the decision was made in spite of no firm evidence that gifts exchanged hands. His voting rights were revoked, and the election was conducted again. The decisions of the Election Commission were given before the case went to the Supreme Court, and the guilty verdict was handed down by a slim three-two margin.

bequeathed to the members of the House of Representatives that make the country's laws. In the final analysis, the so-called reform processes weakened voter confidence and their expectations of parliamentary democracy, threatening ultimately to inflict irreparable damage on the 'representation of the will of the people' that is the function of a democratic system.

PART III

Constitutional Reform and Power Not Elected by the People

5 | Constitutional Reform and Anti-Corruption – The Creation of Corruption: Legal Provisions and Criticism of Politicians

On 19 September 2006, a military coup d'état brought down the popularly elected Thaksin administration which had enjoyed a historic high in terms of seats won at the previous election. Following the coup, a May 2007 Constitutional Tribunal ruling dissolved Thaksin's governing Thai Rak Thai Party, while the Supreme Court found former Prime Minister Thaksin – and his administration – guilty of corruption in 2008 and again in 2010. Claims of corruption were also used to justify the coup. Although Thaksin supporters gained power again in December 2007, Prime Minister Samak Sundaravej lost his job after being found guilty of corruption by the Supreme Court in September 2008. In fact, beginning with former Minster of the Interior Sanan, jailed after a 2000 guilty verdict, many serving cabinet members or individuals with experience of either the cabinet or House of Representatives were forced to step down from powerful political positions after corruption convictions.

As Thailand democratized throughout the 1990s, the power of popularly elected politicians gradually replaced that of the military figures who had dominated Thai politics in the preceding decades. Notwithstanding never-ending revelations of wrong-doing and the accompanying control efforts outlined above, however, corruption appeared to grow all the more prevalent.[1] While fierce criticism of

---

1 Corruption first became a political issue under former military dictator Prime Minister Sarit Sarit (in office from 1959 to 1963). In the 1960s, corruption was prevalent due to collusion between the military and bureaucrats and Chinese businessmen (Riggs 1966). Some studies view corruption in Thailand as a tradition dating back to the Sakdinah era and point out the cultural aspects of corruption (van Roy 1970). With the dawn of democracy in the mid-1970s, party politicians from the business world began to enter politics, but the basic social structure remained unchanged (Neher 1977). Under the democratic system, the patron-client relationship in Thai society was linked to vote-buying in elections, and it became

corruption has been an ongoing feature of the Thai political world, there is no existing in-depth analysis of this situation or of how or why charges of corruption continue to be the most consistent justification for the 2006 coup d'état. It will therefore be useful to probe the perception that a growth in corruption accompanied the emergence of democracy in Thailand.

Since it is not an offence that occurs in the public eye, it is difficult to accurately grasp the extent to which political corruption in Thailand has in fact become more prevalent or serious. Many Thai scholars regard the semi-democratic administration of Prime Minister Prem Tinsulanonda (1980–1988) as the least corrupt government, arguing that corruption levels that emerged during democratization were similar to those seen during the military dictatorship (see, for example, Nualnoi 2005: 248). Reports suggest a perception among members of the general public, also, that corruption, particularly among politicians, has become more widespread (Nualnoi 2005: 248). Having conducted a comparative estimate of corrupt monies associated with military and democratic governments as a means of analyzing the complexities behind these surface impressions, however, Pasuk and Sungsidh (1994) point out that the problem was much more acute under military regimes. Thus, before hastily concluding that corruption grew worse with democratization, we might take into account the fact that the abilities and powers of corruption regulatory agencies expanded markedly during that time and consider how this might have resulted in an expansion of corruption charges. There is no doubt that the 1997 Constitution strengthened both the reach and organization of the National Counter-Corruption Commission (*khanakammakan pongkan lae prappram kanthutcharit haeng chat*)[2] in ways that create

---

widely recognized that corruption among politicians had worsened (Niyom 2006a). It has been pointed out that corruption is often carried out through the collusion of politicians, bureaucrats and businessmen (Juree, 2011: 81–82; Suchit, 2002: 188–190): Only the corruption of politicians began to be recognized as having gotten much worse. The military strongly denounced corruption among politicians and criticized the parliamentary government centered on businessmen as not truly politics for the majority (Tamada 1988).

2   The National Counter-Corruption Commission was first established in 1973 as the Corruption Prevention and Management Commission and

the impression that this became a more efficient agency than its previous iterations (Ōtomo 2003: 151–152). Nevertheless, one might also question whether or not it was principally this heightening of the powers of regulatory bodies that led to a growth in cases of corruption during the democratization era. Instead, one might seek to understand changes to the nature of the acts with which politicians were charged. In other words, it is important to consider the possibility that the democratization process was accompanied by a marked expansion of activities that came to be defined as 'corrupt'.

Previous research often demonstrates how definitions of corrupt acts have changed in terms of both legality and public perception. Gardiner (1993), for example, argues for three elements in any corruption definition – legal, public interest and popular opinion. This scholar further notes the difficulties in measuring the relative value judgments operating in each. Leading corruption scholar, Arnold J. Heidenheimer (1970), points out that corruption norms differ not merely between countries and societies, but also between eras and times. In classic research conducted several decades ago on third world corruption, moreover, James C. Scott noted the potential for claims of corruption to be deployed as political weapons.[3] In the absence of firm legal definitions, meanings of corruption remain particularly fluid and thus heighten the proclivity of a politician to denounce an opponent as corrupt. This is one reason that it is insufficient merely to consider changes to prevention and regulatory agency powers when judging the prevalence or otherwise of corrupt practice. An aspect that must be

---

came under the auspices of the Office of the Prime Minister in 1975. Then, however, financial statement reports were confidential and only made public following a two-thirds majority ruling by the commission that there was evidence of 'unusually wealthy' (Manit 2008: 196). With the ability to conduct financial statement audits of politicians and political employees, conduct criminal prosecutions, and petition for the dismissal of politicians, the National Counter-Corruption Commission, established under the 1997 Constitution, had strengthened powers and heightened independence when compared to its earlier form (Ōtomo 2003: 143–144).

3 Discussing the problem of corruption in the 1950s, James C. Scott (1972: 9–10) points out that, without exception, the many military governments that took power in Africa and Asia in the 1950s gave corruption as the central reason for seizing power.

closely examined when considering what constitutes corruption is the body of legal stipulations that form the basis of such acts. Regulation of corruption among politicians has been a particular objective of the constitutional reforms conducted by Thai politico-legal authorities since the 1990s, with various laws also implemented to that end. This often resulted in actions not previously regarded as corrupt being condemned as corruption. We might even say that various legal revisions themselves created forms of corruption. Drawing on the hypothesis that the definition shifts that followed revisions to the constitution and associated laws became a factor in the growing numbers of Thai politicians charged with corruption, the discussion that follows will consider how these shifts shaped the direction of politics in Thailand.

Shifts in the legal definition of corruption

Regulation of corruption among politicians is currently based on legislation such as the Penal Code (*pramuan kotmai aya*),[4] the Constitution (*ratthathammanun*) the Counter Corruption Law implemented in 1999 (*phraratchabanyat prakop ratthathammanun waduai kanpongkan lae prappram kanthutcharit* Pho. So. 2542),[5] the Criminalizing [Political]

---

[4] Among these, the Criminal Code is the oldest, having been first introduced in 1908. While the current law was implemented in 1956, its fundamental structure remained unchanged from the 1908 iteration (Iida 1999). There are twenty sections, largely concerning corruption by officials (*cao phanakgan*), relating to the 'crime of public corruption'. These include prohibitions on the dishonest use of power by officials with responsibility for the procurement and management of assets, tax matters and accounting, and the falsification of documentation.

[5] Following its implementation in 1975, this law was revised in 1978, significantly revised in 1999 and extensively revised once more in 2011. Its status from 1999 was that of 'organic law' (*phraratchabanyat prakop ratthathammanun*), that is, a law that derived from and was subject to the provisions of the Thai Constitution and that thereby ensured the implementation of important provisions in the Constitution. In the 2007 Constitution it was determined that 'organic law' procedure would differ from that of regular laws with respect to submission to and deliberation before the parliament. The Organic Law on the Election of Members, the Organic Law on Political Parties, and laws pertaining to various independent agencies also fall into this category.

Constitutional Reform and Anti-Corruption

Table 5.1 Chronology of the implementation of major laws regulating corruption and relevant political incidents

Democratization: Businesspeople Enter the Political Sphere	1973	Student Revolution
	1975	Counter Corruption Law
	1976	Coup d'état
Semi-democracy	1978	**1978 Constitution**
	1987	Revisions to the 1975 Counter Corruption Law
Political Reform Movement	1991	Coup d'état and 1991 Constitution
	1992	Bloody May Incident; Revisions to 1991 Constitution
	1996	Assets and Liabilities Statement by Members of the Senate and House of Representatives Law
	1997	**1997 Constitution**
Shift of Political Power Through Elections	1999	Criminalizing [Political] Tendering for State Agencies Law
		Organic Act on Counter Corruption
	2000	Anti-Money Laundering Law
		Regulation of Ministerial Equities and Shareholdings Law
Shift of Political Power Through the Judiciary	2006	Coup d'état
	2007	Court dissolution of Thai Rak Thai Party; 2007 Constitution
	2008	Court dissolution of the Samak and Soomchai administrations

Tendering for State Agencies Law (*phraratchabanyat waduai khwamphit kiaokap kansanoe rakha to nuaingan khong rat* Pho. So. 2542), the Anti-Money Laundering Law (*phraratchabanyat pongkan lae prappram kanfokngoen* Pho. So. 2542), and the Regulating Ministerial Equities and Shareholdings Law, implemented by the Minister for the Interior in 2000 (*phraratchabanyat kanchatkan hunsuan lae hun khong ratthamontri* Pho. So. 2543). As set out in Table 5.1, laws relating to the regulation and control of corruption were largely enacted from the mid-1990s. Among these, the Constitution and the National Counter Corruption Law play the major roles. The discussion therefore focuses on those documents when examining the nature of changes to the legal definition of corruption in Thailand.

Restrictions introduced in the 1991, 1997 and 2007 constitutions

This section will consider changes to definitions of corruption in those sections of each of the constitutions of 1991, 1997 and 2007 that were drafted with the aim of regulating corrupt acts.[6] Since all three documents regard corruption as justification for limiting candidature rights, the discussion will profile sections related to restrictions on the right to nominate as a candidate for the House of Representatives and restrictions placed on members of the House of Representatives and the cabinet.

Restrictions on the eligibility to be elected for the House of Representatives

Table 5.2 sets out information on the sections in each of the three constitutions related to restrictions on the eligibility to be elected for the House of Representatives. Particular attention is given to 'unusually wealthy or unusual asset increase' and 'false assets and liabilities statement'.

The first flagging of concerns related to 'unusually wealthy' or 'unusually accumulative assets' (hereafter 'unusual assets increase') came with specific wording in the 1991 Constitution (Section 107, Paragraph 8) stipulating the withdrawal of the eligibility to be elected for the House of Representatives from 'a person who has been sentenced or ordered by the court to forfeit assets to the state owing to unusual wealth or unusual assets increase'.[7] It was not, however, until

---

6 The 1997 Constitution was enacted with the backing of the political reform movement comprised largely of Bangkok intellectuals. The 2007 Constitution was enacted under an assembly that was appointed by the leaders if the 2006 coup d'état. In both cases, however, politicians were excluded from the drafting process. In order to ensure the implementation of their provisions, furthermore, both constitutions required the enactment of 'organic laws' that had to be brought into practice within set periods of time as determined in the respective documents.

7 Leaders of the 1991 coup d'état used the words 'unusually wealthy' in Section 26 of their Revolutionary Group Decree and established an Assets Examination Committee with the objective of auditing corrupt acts by the cabinet of the previous government. In 1993, however, the Supreme Court denied compatibility with the Constitution of Section 26 of the Revolutionary Group Decree, and the proposed forfeiture of the assets of

the 1999 Counter Corruption Law was implemented that a concrete definition of what actually constituted 'unusually wealthy' became available. With only an amorphous definition of this concept operating, it was at that time more effective to restrict an individual's nomination rights on the grounds of 'unusual assets increase'. While the Assets and Liabilities Statement by Members of the Senate and House of Representatives Law (*phraratchabanyat kansadaeng sapsin lae nisin khong samachikwuthisapha lae samachiksapha phuthaen ratsadon* Pho. So. 2539), implemented in 1996, placed a legal obligation on parliament members to provide information of this nature to the leaders of their respective chambers,[8] these provisions remained weak and ineffective in the absence of an audit report provided by a specialist agency or any mechanism to make the information public.

The 1997 Constitution implemented a significant corruption regulation reform that was also adopted during 2007 revisions. This was the stipulation that political office holders (*phu damrongtamnaeng thang kanmueang*) lodge an assets and liabilities statement with the National Counter-Corruption Commission. Those so obligated were the prime minister, ministers of state, members of the House of Representatives, members of the Senate, other political office holders and members of assemblies and leaders of regional political bodies as stipulated by law (Section 291, 1997 Constitution; Section 259, 2007 Constitution). Lodg-

---

ten members of the former cabinet was aborted. Powerbrokers such as Field Marshall Thanom Kittikachorn and Field Marshall Sarit Thanarat, who were prime ministers in the era of military administrations that stretched from the end of the 1950s to the beginning of the 1970s, did, however, have assets forfeited. After Sarit's death, Prime Minister Thanom issued a prime ministerial order (*khamsang nayokratthamontori*), based on Section 17 of the Interim Constitution of 1959, which permitted a prime minister to hand down orders as necessary, to have Sarit's assets seized. After the 1973 student uprising, based on Section 17 of the 1959 Interim Constitution, Prime Minister Sanya Dharmasakti in turn confiscated former Prime Minister Thanom's assets. While neither of these two prime ministerial orders cited the words 'unusually wealthy', it was apparent that each had an element of asset forfeiture as a tactic against a political rival.

8   There was a stipulation in the 1974 Constitution, also, requiring members of the Senate and the House of Representatives to make information on their own financial circumstances available to the leader of the parliament. That constitution, however, was abolished two years later following the 1976 coup d'état.

Table 5.2 Restrictions on the eligibility to be elected for the House of Representatives (partial extract – summary)

1991 Constitution	1997 Constitution	2007 Constitution
Section 107	Section 109	Section 102
A person under any of the following prohibitions shall have no eligibility to be elected in an election of members of the House of Representatives:	A person under any of the following prohibitions shall have no eligibility to be elected in an election of members of the House of Representatives:	A person under any of the following prohibitions shall have no eligibility to be elected in an election of members of the House of Representatives:
(7) having been expelled, dismissed or removed from official service, a state agency or a state enterprise on the grounds of dishonest performance of duties or corruption;	(6) having been expelled, dismissed or removed from the official service, a state agency or a state enterprise on the grounds of dishonest performance of duties or corruption;	(6) having been expelled, dismissed or removed from the official service, a state agency or a state enterprise on the grounds of dishonest performance of duties or corruption;
(8) having been ordered by a judgment or an order of the court that his or her assets devolve on the state on the grounds of unusual wealth or an unusual increase in his/her assets;	(7) having been ordered by a judgment or an order of the court that his or her assets devolve on the state on the grounds of unusual wealth or an unusual increase in his/her assets;	(7) having been ordered by a judgment or an order of the court that his or her assets devolve on the state on the grounds of unusual wealth or an unusual increase in his/her assets;
(11) having been removed from office by the resolution of the Senate or the House of Representatives under Section 92; (12) having been removed from office by the judgment of the constitutional tribunal committee under Section 9.	(13) being under prohibition from holding a political position under Section 295 (being prohibited from holding any political position or holding any position in a political party for five years because of false statements of assets and liabilities);	(13) being under prohibition from holding a political position under Section 263 (being prohibited from holding any political position or holding any position in a political party for five years because of false statements of assets and liabilities);
	(14) having been removed from office by the resolution of the Senate under Section 307 (A resolution for the removal of any person from office by votes of members of the Senate); provided that, from the date of the resolution to the election day, five years has not elapsed.	(14) having been removed from office by the resolution of the Senate under Section 274 (A resolution for the removal of any person from office by votes of members of the Senate).

Source: Compiled by the author.
Note: Summaries of sections in brackets above appended by the author.

ment was to occur within thirty days of the date of both appointment and retirement, with members also obligated to provide information relating to the assets and liabilities of spouse/partner and children under the age of majority. Evidentiary documentation with each page signed by the member was stipulated to ensure the truthfulness of material lodged, while the provisions called for a retired member to repeat the process within thirty days of the first anniversary of their departure from political office. Section 259 of the 2007 Constitution required those lodging statements to also include assets or liabilities administered by a third party in addition to those under the direct control of the individual.

The 1997 Constitution gave the National Counter-Corruption Commission the power to audit the statements lodged and to require forfeiture to the National Treasury of 'unusually wealthy or unusual assets increase' (Section 294, 1997 Constitution; Section 262, 2007 Constitution). If an individual intentionally failed to lodge either the schedule or necessary evidentiary documents, or deliberately lodged a falsified schedule or concealed information that should have been lodged, the commission could forward the matter to either the Constitutional Court as determined in Section 295 of the 1997 Constitution, or to the Political Litigation Bureau of the Supreme Court of Thailand as determined by Section 263 of the 2007 Constitution. Section 295 of the 1997 document prevented an individual holding political office for five years once the court handed down a ruling of false statement lodgment. However, this penalty became even more severe in Section 263 of the 2007 Constitution which prevented a perpetrator from holding any political party position whatsoever over that period of time.

Matters forbidden to members of the House of Representatives and cabinet

As is clear from tables 5.3 and 5.4 below, the relationship between politicians and business was regarded as particularly serious in terms of what was off-limits for those in the political world. Stipulations targeting these relationships consistently expanded upon each round of constitutional revision. Prohibitions to becoming 'a party to any concession from the state, government agency, or government enterprise or a party to a contract with the nature of an economic monopoly' appeared in each constitutional iteration from 1991 to 2007 (Section 108, Paragraph 2, 1991 Constitution; Section 110, Paragraph 2, 1997 Constitution; Section 265, Paragraph 2, 2007 Constitution). In the 1991 document, this was merely a proviso appended to the Section 108 stipulation: 'Any special privilege or contractual arrangement conceded to a candidate prior to elections was not applicable'. The 1997 Constitution, however, deleted this proviso, adding instead a much broader second paragraph to Section 110 which stated that no member 'shall receive any concession from the state, a state agency or state enterprise, or become a party to a contract of the nature of economic monopoly with the state, a state agency or state enterprise, or a become partner or shareholder in a partnership or company receiving such concession or become a party to the contract of that nature'. Thus, the scope of the provision now covered not merely direct contractual relationships, but also indirect matters such as financial investment and stock or share deals. Section 48 of the 2007 Constitution stipulated, 'No person holding a political position shall be the owner of or hold shares in a newspaper, radio or television broadcasting or telecommunication business', whether or not this be 'in one's own name, or through the business ownership or shareholding of others on one's behalf, or by other direct or indirect means that enable the administration of such business in the same manner as an owner or shareholder of such business'. This, in effect, prevented politicians from holding an interest in mass media operations. It is obvious from the circumstances in which many businessmen and industrialists entered the political world[9] that this stipulation was almost certain to be contravened. This is particularly the case when we consider that, while outlining what an individual could not own or have a financial interest in, the provision made no concrete statement regarding the parameters within which they *could* control or administer an operation in a way that did not amount to actual ownership or financial investment. The likelihood of contravention was also heightened by the fact that Section 265 of the 2007 Constitution extended these restrictions to the spouse/partner and children under the age of majority of the member involved.

---

9   There was a consistent stream of businesspeople entering politics from the 1970s in Thailand. Although financial support to political parties came from those involved in large-scale Bangkok businesses, provincial businesspeople came to occupy the majority of lower house seats (Tamada 2006).

If the 1997 Constitution was a watershed in terms of rigorously restricting politicians' share investment activity, an even stricter set of regulations was imposed on cabinet members. In stipulating that 'A minister shall not be a partner or shareholder of a partnership or a company or retain his or her being a partner or shareholder of a partnership or a company up to the limit as provided by law', the 1997 Constitution established an upper limit for shareholding and investment activity. Section 4 of the Regulation of Ministerial Equities and Shareholdings Law (*phraratchabanyat kanchatkan hunsuan lae hun khong ratthamontri* Pho. So. 2543), implemented in 2000, determined this maximum limit at '5% of the total capital or total number of shares listed'.[10] Section 269 of the 2007 Constitution ensured that largely the same provisions were applied to partners and children under the age of majority also.

The above strongly suggests that corruption by politicians as stipulated in various Thai Constitutions largely referred to 'unusual wealth accumulation or reduction in liabilities', 'failing to lodge an assets statement as required by law within the time stipulated', 'becoming an investor or shareholder in a company in a relationship of privilege to the government', and the prime minister or ministers of state holding equities or shares that exceeded the level stipulated by law (currently 5%). Following the promulgation of the 1997 Constitution, however, provisions relating to asset statements and shareholdings expanded noticeably.

The Organic Act on Counter Corruption (1999) – What was regulated?

Let us now closely examine the kinds of corruption that were not merely covered by constitutional definitions. In order to understand shifts in other corruption provisions, we might compare the Organic Act on Counter Corruption that was promulgated in 1999 (the 1999

---

10 If assets or shares held by a minister exceeded this 5% limit during their time in office, Section 15, Paragraph 2, of the law required them to report this to the chair of the National Counter-Corruption Commission and then transfer the administration of the financial entity involved to a third party.

Table 5.3 Matters forbidden to members of the House of Representatives

1991 Constitution	1997 Constitution	2007 Constitution
Section 108 A member of the House of Representatives shall not: (1) hold any position or assume any duty in any government agency, state enterprise, or hold a position of member of a local assembly, a local administrator or a local government official except minister or other political official; (2) receive any concession from the state, a state agency or a state enterprise, or become a party to a contract of the nature of economic monopoly with the state, a state agency or a state enterprise whether directly or indirectly; (3) receive any special money or benefit from any state agency or state enterprise except that given by the state agency or a state enterprise to other persons in the ordinary course of business. The provision of (2) shall not apply in the case that the member of the House of Representatives already received a concession or became a party to a contract of such nature before he or she is elected.	Section 110 A member of the House of Representatives shall not: (1) hold any position or assume any duty in any government agency, state enterprise, or hold a position of member of a local assembly, a local administrator or a local government official except other political official other than minister; (2) receive any concession from the state, a state agency or a state enterprise, or become a party to a contract of the nature of economic monopoly with the state, a state agency or a state enterprise, or become a partner or a shareholder in a partnership or a company receiving such concession or becoming a party to the contract of that nature; (3) receive any special money or benefit from any state agency or state enterprise except that given by the state agency or a state enterprise to other persons in the ordinary course of business. Section 111 Through the status or position of member of the House of Representatives, interfere or intervene in the recruitment, appointment, reshuffle, transfer, promotion and elevation of the salary scale of a government official holding a permanent position or receiving salary and not being a political official, an official or employee of a state agency, state enterprise or local government organization, or cause such persons to be removed from office.	Section 265 A member of the House of Representatives and a senator shall not: (1) hold any position or assume any duty in any government agency, state enterprise, or hold a position of member of a local assembly, a local administrator or a local government official; (2) receive, interfere with or intervene in any concession from the state, government agency, a state agency or a state enterprise, or become a partner or a shareholder in a partnership or a company receiving such concession or becoming a party to the contract of that nature, whether directly or indirectly; (3) receive any special money or benefit from any government agency, state agency or state enterprise except that given by the government agency, the state agency or a state enterprise to other persons in the ordinary course of business; (4) perform any act prohibited under Section 48. The provisions of (2), (3) and (4) shall also apply to spouses and children of members of the House of Representatives or senators and to other persons who have acted as instructed, as accomplices or as entrusted in relation to the acts under this section. Section 266: Through the status or position of member of the House of Representatives or senator, interfere or intervene with the following matters, directly or indirectly, for the benefit of him or other persons or of a political party: (1) the performance of official duties or routine works of a government official, official or employee of a government agency, state agency, state enterprise, an enterprise in which the state is a major shareholder or a local government organization; (2) the recruitment, appointment, reshuffle, transfer, promotion and elevation of the salary scale of a government official holding a permanent position or receiving salary and not being a political official, an official or employee of a government agency, state agency, state enterprise, an enterprise in which the state is a major shareholder or local government organization; or, (3) the removal from office of a government official holding a permanent position or receiving salary and not being a political official, an official or employee of a government agency, state agency, state enterprise, an enterprise in which the state is a major shareholder or local government organization.

Source: Compiled by the author.

Table 5.4 Matters prohibited to members of cabinet

1991 Constitution	1997 Constitution	2007 Constitution
Section 163 A minister shall not hold a position or perform any act provided in Section 108 or which is contrary to the duties of the minister, except the position required to be held by law, and shall not be a manager or an officer or an advisor or a representative or employee in a partnership, company or any organization that engages in a business with a view to sharing profits or incomes.	Section 208 A minister shall not hold a position or perform any act provided in Section 110, except the position required to be held by law, and shall not hold any other position in a partnership, a company or any organization that engages in a business with a view to sharing profits or incomes or be an employee of any person. Section 209 A minister shall not be a partner or a shareholder of a partnership or a company or retain his or her being a partner or shareholder of a partnership or a company more than the limit provided by law. In the case that any minister intends to continue to receive benefits in such cases, such minister shall inform the president of the National Counter-Corruption Commission within thirty days of the date of the appointment and shall transfer his or her shares in the partnership or company to a juristic person who manages assets for the benefit of other persons. The minister shall not commit any act that, by nature, amounts to the administration or management of shares or affairs of such partnership or company.	Section 267 The provisions of Section 265 shall also apply to the prime minister and ministers, except the case of holding office or taking action by law, and such persons shall not hold any position in a partnership, a company or an organization carrying out business with a view to sharing profits or incomes or be an employee of any person. Section 268 The prime minister and a minister shall not perform any act provided in Section 266 (no intervention in government agencies by members of the Senate or House of Representatives), except for the performance of powers and duties pursuant to the administration of state affairs as stated to the parliament or as provided by law. Section 269 The prime minister and a minister shall not be a partner or a shareholder of a partnership or a company more than the limit provided by law. In the case that the prime minister or any minister intends to continue to receive benefits in such cases, the prime minister or minister shall inform the president of the National Anti-Corruption Commission within thirty days from the date of the appointment and shall transfer his or her shares in the partnership or company to a juristic person who manages assets for the benefit of other persons. The prime minister and minister shall not commit any act that, by nature, amounts to the administration or management of shares or affairs of such partnership or company under paragraph one. The provisions of this section shall also apply to the spouse and children who are not sui juris of the prime minister and ministers, and the provisions of Section 259, Paragraph 3, shall apply mutatis mutandis.

Source: Compiled by the author.
Note: Summaries of sections in brackets above appended by the author.

Counter Corruption Law), implemented under the 1997 Constitution, with the previous Counter Corruption Law of 1975 (revised in 1987).

Changes in targets

The 1975 Counter Corruption Law featured a mere twenty-six sections. In spite of several additions at the time of the 1987 revisions, there was no noticeable change in the length. The 1999 iteration, however, expanded exponentially to 113 sections which greatly increased the number of provisions as well as extending the length. For the first time, the law was also divided into chapters, as follows: 1. 'National Counter-Corruption Commission', 2. 'Powers and Duties of the National Counter -Corruption Commission', 3. 'Asset Audits' (Part 1: Political Assets and Liabilities Report of Political Office Holders; Part 2: National Employees), 4. 'Fact-finding', 5. 'Dismissal', 6. 'Criminal Proceedings Against Political Office Holders as Stipulated in Section 308 of the Constitution', 7. 'Petition for Transfer of Funds to the National Treasury', 8. 'Criminal Proceedings Against Political Office Holders as Stipulated in Section 308 of the Constitution', 9. 'Conflict of Interest,' 10. 'Office of the National Counter-Corruption Commission', and 11. 'Penalties'. The introduction of many sections that honed-in on individuals in the political world is immediately clear from this chapter structure.

Greater precision in the definition of those being targeted was also apparent in the preamble of the law. According to Section 3, the 1975 law focused on 'employees of the state' (*caonathi khong rat*) who were stipulated as 'public servants holding a permanent position or in receipt of a salary, provincial employees, or employees of the state or state owned business organizations'. This group remained the focus of the 1987 revisions also and, apart from the fact that the sphere of 'employees of the state' expanded to include 'heads of organizations, provincial assembly members, ward heads and village heads who conduct local government matters as required by law', there was fundamentally no change in content from the 1975 document. While it seemed that the term 'employees of the state' was broadly defined as referring to all political employees and permanent civil servants, the corresponding procedures concerning employment dishonesty interestingly assumed the permanent public servant as largely a nonpolitical employee. The 1999 Counter Corruption Law provided greater category precision regarding individuals being targeted, with the Section 4 list including the following:

> [T]he prime minister, ministers of state, members of the House of Representatives, members of the Senate, other political officials as based on the Political Civil Servant Law,[11] political parliamentary officials as based on the National Civil Servant Regulation Law, the governor/mayor of Bangkok, members of the Bangkok Municipal Assembly, special municipal staff or assembly members, and leaders and members of provincial local government in receipt of a salary in excess of an amount stipulated by the National Counter-Corruption Commission.

It is clear that the targets of regulation here were politicians.

Changes to definitions and categories of corruption

When considering the definitions and categories of corruption stipulated in the various laws, it is useful to be aware that the 1975 Counter Corruption Law did not actually specify the nature of the corruption being countered. However, a key element of the irregularities targeted was 'unusually wealthy'. This is apparent from the Section 20 provisions which declare as follows:

> [I]n the case of it being evident that any employee of the state has unusual wealth, the commission has the power to conduct an audit, and force the individual involved to provide details of their own assets and liabilities in a manner and within the time determined by the commission. When the audit confirms that the relevant individual has unusual wealth and that this has not been acquired in a lawful manner, the individual involved shall be deemed to have used their powers unlawfully and when the

---

11 Although political civil servants as stipulated in this 1991 law included roles such as the prime minister, deputy prime minister, minsters, deputy ministers, ministerial advisors and secretaries, and press officers, senators and members of the House of Representatives were not included.

commission considers a dismissal order, it shall convey this position to the prime minster.

Without a concrete definition of the term 'unusually wealthy', however, even this lengthy stipulation lacked legal clarity.

Revisions in 1987 to the law divided corruption into two distinct categories: corrupt government business (*kanthutcharit nai wongratchakan*) and illegal acts related to government business (*kanprapruettimichop nai wongratchakan*). Section 3 of the law stipulated 'corrupt government business' to be 'doing or not doing any act that exceeded one's role or duties, or exercising power that exceeded that of one's role or powers in order to gain a benefit that could not be gained lawfully for oneself or another party'. 'Illegal acts of government business' were stipulated as follows:

> [When] a government performed or did not perform any act that exceeded their role or power, or exercised power over and above the duties of their role, and whether or not doing or not doing these acts constituted "corrupt government business", it will be considered a violation of either a law, regulation, rule, order or cabinet decision concerning the receipt, protection of, or use of state funds or assets. This includes dereliction of public duty.

While 'unusually wealthy' remained the target of Counter-Corruption Commission regulation, in the absence of a legal definition of that term, we might question the efficacy of the law.

The 1999 Counter Corruption Law revised the definitions of actions targeted for regulation. These were now divided into three distinct categories, namely: 'corruption in duties of employment' (*thutcharit to nathi*), 'unusual asset increase' (*sappasin phuemkhuen phitpakati*) and 'unusually wealthy' (*ram ruai phitpakati*). Section 4 stipulated 'corruption in duties of employment' as performing an action in order 'to gain a benefit that is unable to be gained legally for oneself or another party, conducting or not conducting an act related to one's role or responsibility, or in spite of not essentially having the role or the responsibility oneself, making a third party believe that one did hold that role or responsibility and performing or not performing an act arising from either that role or responsibility, or making use of such powers'. 'Unusual asset increase' was stipulated in the same section as indicating 'at the time of departure from office, an unusual growth in assets or unusual reduction of liabilities in comparison to the assets and liabilities listed in the statements lodged during the individual's time in office'. Section 4 also provided clarity for the first time in terms of stipulating what constituted 'unusually wealthy', which until that time had lacked a concrete definition. The law determined this to be 'the execution of a duty or exercise of power in one's role that led to receiving unusually large assets, assets expanding unusually, liabilities reducing unusually, or the illegal acquisition of assets'.[12] It is evident that, in comparison to the two previous iterations, the 1999 Counter Corruption Law set out concrete standards and regulatory procedures.

The addition of conflict of interest

The most important single change to the 1999 Counter Corruption Law, however, was the introduction in Section 9 of 'conflict of interest' (*kankhatkan rawang prayotsuanbukkhon lae prayotsuanruam*).[13] Since various provisions relating to 'conflict of interest' had operated even

---

12 The 2003 case against former Minister for Public Health Rakiat was argued on the definition of 'unusually wealthy'. The defendant pointed out the content of four different sections of the law in terms of a definition of 'unusually wealthy', and how the individual presenting on behalf of the Audit Committee of the National Counter-Corruption Commission failed to clarify how the assets owned by himself constituted 'unusually wealthy'. He emphasized that there was a responsibility for the Audit Committee to firstly explain how a defendant's assets related to notions of 'unusually wealthy', and, that in the absence of this being done, the court had no option but to dismiss the case. Arguing that the defendant had provided insufficient evidence, the court gave a guilty ruling. This ruling resulted in 'unusually wealthy' being interpreted as meaning 'not able to offer proof of acquiring an asset legally'.

13 Heavy revisions in 2011 to the Counter Corruption Law included a new stipulation that an individual who violated Section 9, Paragraph 1 on conflict of interest would be charged with a criminal act. In addition, a statement on 'The Promotion of Corruption Prevention and Regulation' was added to Section 9, Paragraph 1, while 'Membership of the Committee to Prevent and Regulate Provincial Corruption' was added to Paragraph 2 of the same section.

prior to the 1991 Constitution, this was not an entirely new concept in Thailand. Previous constitutions, however, merely determined two prohibitions on politicians in this context, namely: 1. not receiving special privilege or entering into a monopoly contract with the state, a public agency, a state agency or a state owned business, and 2. not receiving special monies or benefits in any shape or form that exceeded that of one's usual work from a public agency, a state agency or a state owned business. In the 1990s, however, stipulations related to conflict of interest expanded markedly in conjunction with attempts to regulate the relationship between politicians and businesspeople.

Perhaps the most important addition was Section 100 of the Counter Corruption Law. Here, prohibitions against 'conflict of interest' were set out as follows:

> An employee of the state shall not: 1. enter into or become an interested party in a contract with a government agency that holds the power of supervision, control, audit or legal proceedings on behalf of said state; 2. become a holder of equity in shares in a unlimited company or company that concludes a contract with a government agency that carries out tasks while holding the power of supervision, control, audit or legal proceedings on behalf of said state; 3. take over or receive a privilege from the state, a government agency, a government organization, a government owned business, or a provincial government, or from the holder of a contract that has direct or indirect monopoly characteristics with the state, a government agency, a government organization, a government owned business or a provincial government, or from a holder of equity or shares in a unlimited company or company that is a privileged recipient of or the holder of such a contract; 4. in the case of the character of the benefit of a private business either contradicting or not being consistent with the public good or public interest, or in the case of influencing the independence of the work accomplishments of a state employee, hold an interested party relationship as an official, advisor, representative, employee or employed person of a private business that is under the supervision, control or financial audit of a government agency to which the state employee in question is attached or works for [...].

That which fell within the sphere of conflict of interest was thus regarded as broadly encompassing contract relationships, holding equity or shares and employment relationships, with a focus on the control and supervision powers exercised in the course of one's own work duties. The term 'state employee' often featured in the wording of the Counter Corruption Law and we might ask to whom, precisely, did this refer. According to a National Counter-Corruption Commission communique, Section 100 of the law applied to the prime minister and ministers of state.[14] In other words, the notion of 'conflict of interest' that was newly stipulated in the 1999 Counter Corruption Law was a crime designed to target the political class.[15]

Broadening the definition of corruption

Analysis of the wording of the relevant constitutions and laws very much confirms that the 1997 Constitution was a watershed document in terms of speedily broadening the legal definition of political corruption. We can divide this broadened sphere into two categories, namely provisions related directly or indirectly to actual conflict of interest and those related directly or indirectly to 'unusual wealth accumulation'. As demonstrated in figures 5.1 and 5.2, this broadened corruption definition was the result of a shift from more classic interpretations to new understandings of what corruption entailed. Figure 5.1 points out how the transformation of earlier corruption notions, such as receipt of bribes or the equivalent, led to an emphasis on 'conflict of interest'. While ethics, a notion well outside the usual sphere of political discourse, was also put in the spotlight,[16] most attention focused on 'conflict of interest'. In this way, corruption morphed from

---

14 National Counter-Corruption Commission communique, 28 February 1999.
15 The Criminal Code also has a provision that stipulates against a conflict of interest relationship in a work task in which the person in charge is supervising themselves. While in the Criminal Code this is an ordinary citizen, the Counter Corruption Law mainly targets politicians and high-ranking bureaucrats and government officials.
16 The 2007 Constitution was the first to include a chapter (Chapter 13) related to the ethics of government employees and state officials. The document also gave the ombudsman the power to propose or advise upon provisions relating to ethics (Manit 2010: 181).

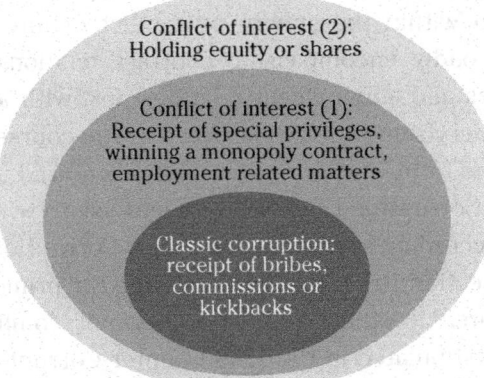

Figure 5.1 The structure of a legal definition of corruption (1)
Source: Compiled by the author.

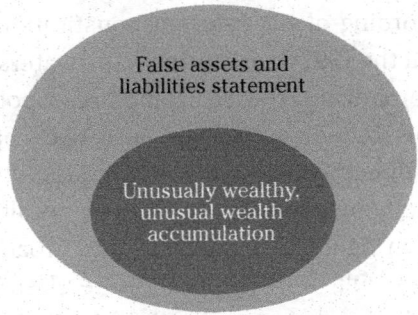

Figure 5.2 The structure of a legal definition of corruption (2)
Source: Compiled by the author.

the older meaning of blatant acts, such as 'receiving special privileges' or 'being granted a monopoly contract', to the regulation of potential misdemeanors such as having excess shareholdings. Figure 5.2 deals with the duty to lodge 'an assets and liabilities statement' as a means of regulating 'unusually wealthy' or 'unusual wealth accumulation', with the manner and timeframe of lodgment also incorporated into the definitions operating.

Given the amorphous nature of 'conflict of interest', however, these new forms of 'corruption' created definitional 'grey areas' that presented new regulatory challenges (Thiraphat 2010: 158–161;

Bertok 2008: 85–86). Even a violation in strict legal terms when lodging an assets and liabilities statement, for example, was impossible to determine necessarily as corruption. In other words, the definition of corruption moved from 'black' through 'dark grey' to 'light grey', becoming during the process a frustratingly ambiguous notion.

Policing corruption and its problems: false statement of assets and liabilities

Anti-corruption situation regarding submission of statement of assets and liabilities

Following the establishment of the Constitutional Court and National Counter-Corruption Commission in 2000, there was a systemization of the audit process of the statement of assets and liabilities that politicians were required to lodge by law. This led to indictments of politicians on charges of lodging false statements. Table 5.5 demonstrates how, through the introduction of criminal penalties for assets and liabilities statement infringements, many politicians were brought before the courts. The enormity of the changes that occurred once the Constitutional Court and National Corruption Commission processes began to operate is evident from the fact that, prior to the 1997 Constitution, the former National Counter-Corruption Commission made only a single successful prosecution of a politician. After that time, the sole not-guilty verdict came during the 2001 Thaksin trial. The high rate of convictions leaves no doubt that lodgment of a false assets and liabilities statement by a politician was considered a serious crime. The outset of the chapter referred to a heightened perception among the general public of political corruption becoming more acute as Thailand democratized. The regulatory circumstances pertaining to the lodgment of false assets and liabilities statements has contributed to that perception.

We might closely consider both the response to the criminalization of the lodgment of a false assets and liabilities statement and how this impacted, if at all, on the regulation of corruption.

Table 5.5 List of cases related to false statement of assets and liabilities and violation of the upper limit of shareholdings

Charge	Previous Positon/s	Ruling
2000 (7 cases)		
False statement of assets and liabilities	Minister for the interior, deputy prime minister	Guilty
False statement of assets and liabilities	Prime ministerial secretariat	Guilty
False statement of assets and liabilities	Advisor to minister for education	Guilty
False statement of assets and liabilities	Advisor to under minister for public health	Guilty
False statement of assets and liabilities	Senator	Guilty
False statement of assets and liabilities	Advisor to office of the prime minister	Guilty
False statement of assets and liabilities	Cabinet secretariat	Guilty
2001 (3 cases)		
False statement of assets and liabilities (Thaksin)	Deputy prime minister; prime minister when charged	Not guilty
False statement of assets and liabilities	Senator	Guilty
False statement of assets and liabilities	Member of municipal assembly	Guilty
2002 (8 cases)		
False statement of assets and liabilities	Member of municipal assembly	Guilty
False statement of assets and liabilities	Advisor to under minister for business and commerce	Guilty
False statement of assets and liabilities	Advisor to office of the prime minister	Guilty
False statement of assets and liabilities	Advisor to under minister for foreign affairs	Guilty
False statement of assets and liabilities	Secretary to office of the prime minister	Guilty
False statement of assets and liabilities	Assistant secretary to minister for communications	Guilty
False statement of assets and liabilities	Advisor to under minister for agriculture and cooperative unions	Guilty
False statement of assets and liabilities	Advisor to under minister for agriculture and cooperative unions	Guilty
2003 (5 cases)		
False statement of assets and liabilities	Advisor to minister for foreign affairs, advisor to deputy prime minister	Guilty
False statement of assets and liabilities	Prime ministerial secretariat	Guilty
False statement of assets and liabilities	Office of the prime minister; minister for public health	Guilty
False statement of assets and liabilities	Deputy minister of industry	Guilty
False statement of assets and liabilities	Member of the House of Representatives	Guilty
2004 (4 cases)		
False statement of assets and liabilities	Member of municipal assembly	Guilty
False statement of assets and liabilities	Member of the House of Representatives	Guilty
False statement of assets and liabilities	Member of provincial assembly	Guilty
False statement of assets and liabilities	Member of provincial assembly	Guilty

The crime of false assets and liabilities statement – problematic aspects in Thailand

There are many countries throughout the world that require politicians and high-ranking bureaucrats to submit an assets and liabilities statement. However, since the chief focus is enhancing credibility with voters, there is generally no penalty involved (Messick 2008: 38–43). Rather than a means of regulating corruption that has already

Charge	Previous Position/s	Ruling
2005 (0 case)		
2005 (0 cases): The National Counter-Corruption Commission was dysfunctional.		
2006 (0 cases): The coup occurred.		
2007 (10 cases)		
False statement of assets and liabilities (5 cases)	Members of provincial assemblies	Guilty
False statement of assets and liabilities (4 cases)	Members of municipal assemblies	Guilty
False statement of assets and liabilities (1 case)	Member of sub-district (*tambon*) Assembly	Guilty
2008 (1 case)		
Violation of the upper limit of shareholding Exceeding 5% shareholding limit (partner's assets)	Minister for public health	Guilty
2009 (3 cases)		
False statement of assets and liabilities	Deputy minister of the interior, advisor to minister for information, communication and technology	Guilty
False statement of assets and liabilities	Minister of natural resources and environment, speaker of the House of Representatives	Guilty
False statement of assets and liabilities	Senator	Guilty
2010 (2 cases)		
Violation of the upper limit of shareholding (44 members of both the House of Representatives and Senate – members or partners)	Members of the House of Representatives and Senate	6 Convicted
False statement of assets and liabilities	Advisor to deputy minister of agriculture	Guilty
2011 (2 cases)		
Violation of the upper limit of shareholding Exceeding 5% shareholding limit (partner's assets)	Minister of science and technology	Dismissed
False statement of assets and liabilities	Member of the House of Representatives	Guilty
2012 (1 case)		
False statement of assets and liabilities	Minister of education, minister of agriculture and cooperative unions	Guilty

Source: Compiled by the author from rulings of the Constitutional Court and Supreme Court.
Note: Data until July 2012. While the 1997 Constitution designated the Constitutional Court as the presiding authority for the lodgment of false statements, in the 2007 Constitution this became the purview of the Supreme Court.

occurred, the worth of such an approach is its preventative potential. In this context, it is useful to examine the situation in Thailand.

What has been regulated

Matters to be listed on an assets and liabilities statement were income (regular, from assets and property, and from capital gains), expenses, assets (cash, bank deposits, investments, credit, land, houses, vehicles and privileges etc.), and liabilities (withdrawals in excess of bank deposits, debts with financial institutions, debts related to promissory notes) of the person in question, their spouse/partner and children under the age of majority including children born to married parents, children born to parents who were not married and adopted children. This was an extraordinarily large body of information and was accompanied by a large number of evidentiary documents.[17] Cabinet members were required to submit an updated form each time they were appointed to a new post, which sometimes meant submitting a statement annually. The detailed comparison by the National Counter-Corruption Commission of selected forms previously submitted could detect inconsistencies and identify omissions in earlier documents. Some forms in which an audit found irregularities had been submitted more than twenty years previously.

Beginning with previous Minister for the Interior Sanan's conviction in 2000, many cabinet level politicians lost their position as a result of assets and liabilities statement irregularities. In addition to cabinet members, there were many other parliament members and advisors to deputy ministers found guilty of statement irregularities. Infringements that led to charges included omissions in statements of assets (bank accounts, land holdings) or liabilities, failure to attach the necessary documents, inconsistencies between information provided on the current form and statements previously lodged and exceeding the stipulated limits for assets and shareholdings. However, it has not been linked to serious corruption prosecutions (Wichitwong 2010: 66). A further development occurred when Section 35 of the 1999 Counter Corruption Law required the assets and liabilities statements of the cabinet and members of the parliament generally to be made public within thirty days of being submitted.[18] There has accordingly been

---

17 The format used appeared on the assets and liabilities statement submission document of the National Counter-Corruption Commission. Accessed 1 March 2012 at: http://www.nacc.go.th/images/article/freetemp/article_20110727090041.pdf

18 Although only cabinet documents were initially made public, 2011 revisions resulted in the material lodged by all members of the parliament being released.

a tendency in recent years for senators and civil society groups to conduct detailed checks of assets and liabilities statements with the specific aim of detecting errors.[19] Following the implementation of the 2007 Constitution, the focus of assets and liabilities statement audits became the violation of the maximum limit on shares held by members of the Thai Cabinet.

Section 4 of the Regulation of Ministerial Equities and Shareholdings Law (*phraratchabanyat kanchatkan hunsuan lae hun khong ratthamontri Pho. So.* 2543) stipulated that an individual performing a ministerial role should not hold investments or own shares that exceeded 5% of the total value, or total number, of shares in a concern. Section 5 stipulated that an individual wishing to continue receiving benefit from such a source was required to give notice to the chair of the National Counter-Corruption Commission within thirty days of appointment and, within ninety days of giving that notice, transfer administration of the relevant assets or shares to a legal entity that managed such matters on behalf of third parties. The 2007 Constitution revised this stipulation to apply also to a spouse/partner and to children below the age of majority. As a result, some ministers were dismissed when their wives infringed the share-holding limit. While in power, former Prime Minister Thaksin was taken before the Constitutional Court by twenty-eight members of the House of Representatives for holding shares in excess of 5% in Shin Corporation (ShinCorp), a company in which his family had held long-standing interests. That case was dismissed in a close eight-six ruling through lack of evidence. Under the 2007 Constitution, Chaiya, the minster for public health in the Samak administration, exceeded the share limit in terms of holdings by his wife and resigned upon losing the right to be a minister of the state once convicted of failing to give notice of that fact within thirty days of

---

19 A well-known case involves that of Ruangkrai who challenged the Thaksin administrations and was appointed to the Senate in 2007. His party conducted detailed checks of many politicians' assets and liabilities statements, regardless of the political party involved, identifying so many problematic aspects that newspaper journalists raised questions about interference in the political process. Even in terms of work undertaken by the National Counter-Corruption Commission, there were an extraordinarily high number of audits conducted of assets and liabilities statements (Khanakammakan Po. Po. Cho. 2010).

his ministerial appointment. Although Deputy Minister of Commerce Wirun was also indicted for exceeding the share-holdings limit, his dismissal on the grounds of a previous judgment occurred prior to that investigation concluding. A senator tried to sue Finance Minister Surapong in the Constitutional Court, accusing him of exceeding the limit on the shares held by his wife. We might note that, even under the provisional Surayud administration formed by the military following the 2006 coup d'état, five cabinet members infringed the shareholdings limit and subsequently resigned.[20]

Current stipulations relating to shareholdings impose limits on both House of Representatives and Senate members. Section 265, Paragraph 2, of the 2007 Constitution prohibits any such member from becoming the holder of equities or shares in a company that is the principle of a contract acquiring the right to work or conduct a project with the state or a state-owned enterprise or that holds the character of such a contract. In 2012, the Election Administration Commission audited parliament members and referred forty-four members of the Senate and the House of Representatives to the Constitutional Court for investigation on suspicion of violating that stipulation. The shares held by many of those members were in large corporations that were widely known by name. After investigating the nature of the contracts of the companies involved and how these related to state and government organizations, the court handed down a guilty verdict for six members who then lost their right to sit in the assembly.

It is apparent from the regulatory environment discussed above that stipulations relating to shareholding in Thailand are easily infringed and do not constitute corruption in the true sense of the word. During assets and liabilities statements audits, moreover, these stipulations are used as ammunition to find fault and then gener-

---

20 Five members of the main cabinet from the Surayud administration, formed after the 2006 coup, resigned after criticism that their shareholdings exceeded 5%. However, the Council of National Security (CNS) declined to apply the limits related to shareholdings to its own political administration. It was, however, clearly understood that this was a stipulation that many people contravened.

ate meaningless charges that contribute little to truly combatting corrupt acts.

Penalty stipulations

Penalties for submission of false assets and liabilities statements in Thailand are extraordinarily heavy. Not only does Section 263 of the 2007 Constitution prevent a convicted individual from holding a paid political position for five years, that individual, in fact, is unable to take any role in a political party during that time. In other words, they are unable to stand for office at a forthcoming election. While penalties in other countries can incur fines and/or even a prison sentence of less than a year, there are no prohibitions on holding political office or other political party positions. This severity is a special characteristic of the Thai political world.[21] There are, furthermore, few instances of other countries imposing upper limits on equity and shareholdings.[22]

Information that is not factual in a statement of assets and liabilities does not necessarily constitute proof of corruption or illegal activity. Politicians, moreover, have expressed their dissatisfaction with the complex and difficult to understand format of the form on which the statement must be lodged.[23] Although the presence of incor-

---

21 Some developed countries have no prescribed penalties. There is no penalty for falsification in Japan. Germany has a maximum fine of half the individual's annual salary, while the United States also fines offenders. South Korea and the Philippines both have a jail sentence of less than one year and a fine.

22 To give examples from other countries, Germany requires reporting to the leader of the parliament in the case of holding in excess of 25% of shares that also come with voting rights, while Australia and South Korea require a politician to declare holdings in, for example, a company whose activities are in some way the subject of parliamentary debate. There is, however, no other place with a provision as strict as restricting the shareholdings of a member of the cabinet to 5%.

23 In an eight-five vote of the bench, Under Minister for Transport (and former deputy minister for industry) Pichet was found guilty of failing to declare liabilities in an assets and liabilities statement and was accordingly prevented from holding political office for five years. Following the decision, Pichet declared: 'This decision makes me a technical victim of the assets statement procedure and thus prevents me from working for the upright and honest people of Thailand'. Then Prime Minister Thaksin stated, 'Although both Under Minister Pichet and the government need to take heed of the court's decision, I must make clear to everyone that he has

rect information in a statement could not definitively be assessed as corruption, such an infringement could result in exclusion from political life for five years. Given the career damage incurred by the individual in receipt of this penalty for a comparatively trivial misdemeanor, we might question whether any sort of rational balance exists in Thailand between support for democratic processes and the corruption regulatory environment.

Confusion around a point at issue – intentionality

There is an additional element that comes into play in legal definitions associated with the submission of false assets and liabilities statements. We might expect decisions relating to whether or not corruption has occurred in the context of 'unusual asset increase or liability reduction' to depend on whether an act is legal or illegal. However, both the 1997 and 2007 constitutions, and also the 1990 Counter Corruption Law, sharply profiled 'intentionality' in 'instances in which an assets and liabilities report is not lodged by the stated time or in which there is incorrect information in the material lodged'. Although 'intentionality' must of course be considered, the existence or otherwise of intentionality and the existence or otherwise of corruption are not the same thing. We might accordingly ask whether in some instances too much weight was given to this point. Even in the famous 2001 Thaksin case, intentionality was the point argued most vociferously. Leaving aside arguments around whether or not omissions, or providing information that does not accord with the facts, really constitutes corruption, perspectives related to points of law could take on lives of their own. Given that most cases resulted in guilty verdicts, however, it appears that consideration of 'intentionality' failed to act as any sort of preventative measure against meaninglessly excessive regulation.

---

no connection to corruption' (*The Nation*, 6 August 2003).

Policing corruption and its problems: conflict of interest

The fall of the Thaksin and Samak administrations

Accusations of corruption levelled against the two previous Thai prime ministers, Thaksin and Samak, were ultimately argued in terms of the criminality of 'conflict of interest'. While there was a focus on whether or not conflict of interest could encompass government policy matters and what the parameters were to prime ministerial powers, at the end of the day the case was conducted in spite of imprecision on these matters in the wording of the law.[24] Because notions of conflict of interest were so nebulous, the ruling handed down by the court equivocated greatly in its interpretation of the wording of the law. Below, the discussion considers judgments handed down in three cases that demonstrate the enormous damage the criminal act referred to as conflict of interest could have on the political administrations concerned.

Judgment concerning violation of the Counter Corruption Law (Supreme Court Political Criminal Litigation Bureau judgment, 21 October 2008)

After then Prime Minister Thaksin's wife, Potjaman, successfully bid for Ratchadaphisek Road land put up for auction at the end of 2003 by the Financial Institutions Development Foundation (*kongthun phuea kanphuenfu lae phatthana rabop sathabankann-goen*),[25] it was ruled that Thaksin himself had been involved in a conflict of interest. The basis of the charges were sections 4, 100 and 122 of the Counter Corruption Law coupled with wording from the Criminal Code. In the judgment, conflict of interest was confirmed through Section 100 of the Counter

---

24 When determining whether or not conflict of interest has occurred, the range of powers held by an individual being accused is important. This is because Section 100 of the Counter Corruption Law makes it clear that the balance of public and private interest operating in terms of the administrative and supervisory powers exercised by the accused government official in the course of their work is the basis upon which conflict of interest is decided.

25 This organization was established under the auspices of the Bank of Thailand in November 1985 according to the Emergency Decree Regulation on the Affairs of the Bank of Thailand Act.

Corruption Law while the guilty verdict carrying a jail sentence of two years was determined by Section 122. The court confirmed a conflict of interest on the grounds that the operations of the Financial Institutions Development Foundation, which administered the land being auctioned, fell within the state's supervisory sphere. Based on the stipulations of Section 11 of the 1991 National Governance Provisions Law (*phraratchabanyat rabiap borihanratchakan phaendin* Pho. So. 2534), Thaksin as prime minister was seen as having supervisory powers over the entire country – and therefore over the agency in question – through the Constitution, the law and government policy.[26]

Assets forfeiture ruling (Supreme Court Political Criminal Litigation Bureau judgment, 26 February 2010)

Five policies implemented under the Thaksin administration resulted in legal action for infringements of conflict of interest. It was ruled that shares owned by Thaksin's relations were in fact owned by Thaksin himself and that he had therefore violated the share ownership limit and Section 100 of the 1999 Counter Corruption Law. The former prime minister was thus determined to have a conflict of interest, found guilty in four of the five cases before the court and accordingly required to forfeit a portion of the relevant assets to the state. This was an extremely important ruling in that argument centered around the relationship between political policy and conflict of interest. The four key points of the guilty ruling were as follows: 1. changing the telecommunications license fee to an excise tax; 2. altering a contract by lowering the tax rate for the private mobile phone enterprise

---

26 In this case, Thaksin's legal team requested a ruling by the Constitutional Court on the constitutionality of sections 26 to 27, Section 39 and Section 43 of the Counter Corruption Law, based on sections 4, 100 and 122 of the 2007 Constitution. Handing down a ruling of constitutionality, the Constitutional Court pointed out that while there was no stipulation on the relevant legal wording that a presumption of guilt was necessary when a defendant provided evidence of their own innocence, it was necessary, as in a criminal case, for a prosecutor to provide evidence of criminal activity as intent on the part of all accused (Constitutional Court Ruling, 5 August 2008). However, in the Supreme Court judgment that followed there was no definite clarity concerning the corrupt nature of the activities undertaken by Thaksin and his associates.

agreement concluded between mobile phone company AIS and the publicly-owned Telecommunications of Thailand (TOT); 3. approving a broadcast satellite business; and 4. raising the amount being lent to Myanmar by the Export-Import Bank of Thailand.[27] In each case, investigations were commenced by the Assets Examination Committee (*khana kammakan truatsop kankratham thi ko hai koet khwamsiahai kae rat*) established by coup leaders on the grounds that Prime Minister Thaksin had profited personally through policies benefiting Shin Corporation (Telecommunications) and Shin Satellite Corporation, companies operated by his relatives. Investigations were continued by the National Anti-Corruption Commission.

The key factor at the time determining the existence or otherwise of conflict of interest in terms of government policies was the sphere encompassed by prime ministerial powers. Were the series of policies the result of Thaksin's exploitation of his authority and position or not? Although Thaksin himself did not, in fact, make decisions about or operate the companies involved, the ruling was made from the standpoint that, through appointing each of the finance, transport, and information technology and communications ministers, the prime minister has supervisory control of organizations operated under the auspices of those ministries. Since the 1991 National Governance Regulation Law gave comprehensive supervisory powers to Thaksin as prime minister, it was ruled that he not only held the power to direct, but also carried the ultimate responsibility for the implementation of all

---

27 Space limitations permit only a brief introduction of this incident involving the raising of the level of funds being lent to Myanmar by the Export-Import Bank of Thailand. The incident was initiated by October 2003 correspondence from the Myanmar Minister of Foreign Affairs to his Thai counterpart requesting monetary support in relation to matters such as equipment purchases for infrastructure projects. In February 2004, Myanmar requested that the loan amount be raised and the interest lowered. The Thai Minister for Foreign Affairs sent correspondence to the bank's governance department indicating that Prime Minister Thaksin was not opposed to this. The governance department of the bank ultimately voted to approve the request in May. This sequence of events suggests that Prime Minister Thaksin was neither strongly opposed to nor supportive of the transaction and that, although the Ministry for Foreign Affairs had carriage of the matter, it was actually the bank itself that progressed matters by conducting a vote.

government matters related to the ministries and ministers involved. As in the previous ruling, the prime minister was here determined to have extremely broad powers related to the entire state including matters arising generally from policy and policy implementation in which he was not directly involved.

Ruling on termination of qualification as prime minister (Constitutional Court ruling, 9 September 2008)

Following his appearance while in office as host of a television cooking show, former Prime Minister Samak was indicted for having infringed constitutional provisions forbidding other employment. The penalty was loss of eligibility to hold the position of prime minister. The case centered on claims of violations of sections 91, 182 and 267 of the Constitution. The court ruled that Samak violated his eligibility conditions in terms of Section 267 and was thus disqualified from holding the role of prime minister in terms of Section 182.

Section 267 determined that 'The prime minister and ministers shall neither hold any position in a partnership, a company or an organization carrying out business with a view to sharing profits or incomes nor be an employee of any person'. The point at issue was the definition of 'employee'. Both precedent and prevailing opinion in Thailand confirmed that acting as the host of a television program did not constitute becoming an 'employee' of the company involved. However, it was ruled that, because the intent of Section 267 was to prevent dishonest acts by cabinet members and to avoid conflicts in which private and public interests clashed, it was necessary to interpret the relevant wording – here the term 'employee' as it operated in Section 267 – more broadly than had been the case in established precedent. It was particularly necessary to broaden the sphere of applicability of the term 'employee' in a case involving the prime minister.

It is apparent from the wording of the rulings in the Thaksin and Samak 'conflict of interest' cases that guilty verdicts were given in both instances because the parameters of the duties of the individual heading the government – the prime minster – were determined to be extremely broad. It is unlikely that either Thaksin or Samak would have been judged in the past to have committed corruption at least in the legal sense. Not only might we question whether or not the pair were guilty of these newly constructed 'corrupt acts', we might also ask what impact the verdicts had on democratization in Thailand.

Problematic aspects of 'conflict of interest' definitions
General definition

The situation in Thailand reflects a broader international concern with regulating 'conflict of interest'[28] violations by politicians, high-ranking bureaucrats and others in the public domain. Organization for Economic Co-operation and Development (OECD) guidelines define such a conflict as one between the public duty and private interests of a public official, in which the public official has private-capacity interests that could improperly influence the performance of their official duties and responsibilities (Bertok 2008: 85). It is nevertheless acknowledged that conflict of interest is extremely difficult to regulate. That is because rapid changes to the environment in which conflict of interest arises, in conjunction with the emergence of new forms and pathways that deliver and control public goods and services, has blurred the dividing line between public and private and thereby created new 'conflict of interest' grey zones (Bertok 2008: 86). At the very least, there are two general contrasting categories of co-existing interest – public and private (Guzzetta 2008: 24). Yet, not only are there diverse ways in which public and private interests differ, we must acknowledge that the tight and complex economic interconnection between business and politics

---

28 There are largely four Thai language expressions covering this concept. These are: 1. *khwamkhatyaengkan rawang phonprayotsuanton lae phonprayotsuanruam* (conflict of public and private interest), 2. *phonprayotkhatkan* (opposing interests), 3. *khwamkhatyaeng nai prayot* (clash of interests), and 4. *phonprayotthapson* (overlapping interests). The notion of 'public interest' that is critical to judgments of conflict of interest is interpreted very widely in Thailand and seen to include political, cultural, religious, social, family, legal, emotional and ideological dimensions (Medhi 2008: 96). Entering the political world through election success can lead to excessive pursuit of 'private interests' (Suchit 2002: 188–190), while there are some scholars (Suraphon 2006) who regard the King of Thailand as representing the 'public interest'.

that characterizes contemporary society makes it extremely difficult to draw a rigorous distinction between these two. Furthermore, while public servants represent and act for the public, they themselves are not necessarily that public. Approaches and frameworks devised to control conflict of interest matters very much reflect the social, political and governance context in which these matters are located and a reasonable point of equilibrium must be sought between the public interest and the private interest of those working in the public domain (Bertok 2008: 91). The difficulty of settling on a legal definition reveals the limits of regulating corruption through the law alone. While conflict of interest can constitute serious corruption, the difficulties associated with imposing restrictions at the legal level present a clear social threat of over-regulation. This is precisely why other countries are placing more emphasis on preventing corruption.

Thailand as a special case

As Thailand entered the twenty-first century, three keywords characterized the country's politics: populism (*prachaniyom*), policy corruption (*kankhorapchan choeng nayobai*) and conflict of interest. Each was used to critique the Thaksin administration.[29] In present-day Thailand, the term 'conflict of interest' is often used when denouncing Thaksin. This was the term also often notably used in the past when

---

29 The Thaksin administration enjoyed the strongest electoral support in Thai history. One reason for this was the policy platform proposed and quickly implemented by the prime minister. When presenting this policy sequence, Thaksin furthermore ensured the broad circulation of information on each project (Kowit 2010: 114–116). Anti-Thaksin factions, however, attacked this as 'populism' (Tamada 2009), with frequent use of the term 'policy corruption'. According to a 12 June 2007 report in *The Nation*, 'policy corruption' referred to Prime Minister Thaksin pork-barralling by devising policies favorable to corporations and business concerns operated by his family members (*The Nation*, 12 June 2007). However, even those intellectuals who were critical of Thaksin tacitly conceded that no illegality was involved, claiming instead that this so-called 'policy corruption' was 'a new, skillful corrupt practice' (*The Nation*, 1 October 2007). Yet policy by nature encompasses a broad sphere, and any benefits were not confined to corporations run by Thaksin's relatives. Although there was no essential corruption related to Thaksin's policies in a legal sense, the mass media and intellectuals who wanted to criticize these by making that claim repeatedly used the expression 'policy corruption'.

attacking the then prime minister's policies. In Thailand, therefore, serious debate occurred over whether or not to make policy an actual target of conflict of interest regulation (Nithi 2009). The inclusion of policy in matters pertaining to conflict of interest make it important to recognize the boundaries of the powers of the cabinet involved. The balance of policy and power, particularly in stipulations referring to employment relations, contractual relations, equity or shareholdings, becomes an important boundary line when determining if corruption has occurred. Yet the conceptually abstract nature of conflict of interest meant that the meaning of this term was never determined with any clarity in the wording of Section 100 of the Counter Corruption Law. Thus, whether or not conflict of interest in policy terms encompassed the sphere of cabinet powers also remained unclear. The key to understanding a Thai definition is to be aware that there is a preference to being initially with two points, each of which leaves a margin for interpretation, and that settling on a final definition can only occur after various precedents become available to consider.

It was only after the 2006 coup that the regime was actually legally overthrown for conflicts of interest. After the coup, a push to broaden the definition of 'conflict of interest' in law was evident in two facts. The first was in the actual text of the rulings related to the Thaksin and Samak indictments. These cases, as suggested by the discussion above, gave rise to the contradictory possibility of an administration authorized as having far-reaching – we might say almost limitless – powers infringing conflict of interest regulation through the very powers that it was authorized to hold. Comparisons with international definitions of conflict of interest confirm how reckless or even dangerous such a definition might be. The second push to broaden the conflict of interest definition came in the form of a draft law on the matter compiled after the 2006 coup and then presented to the parliament. This very important draft became a harbinger of how regulating conflict of interest would exercise influence on Thai political activities. This chapter closes with a discussion of that bill.

Concerns about the future – Conflict of Interest Bill

Following the 2006 coup d'état, efforts were made by the interim Surayud administration to legislate a 'conflict of interest law'.[30] Largely drafted by scholars, the law was adopted by the government-appointed assembly in September 2009.[31] However, following a fifty-one-member appeal, the Constitutional Court in November 2008 cited an absence of quorum numbers at the third reading to declare the bill unconstitutional (Thiraphat 2010: 183–185). Although the proposed legal framework never eventuated, the bill had nonetheless proceeded to voting stage in a plenary session of the assembly. The fact that members of the National Counter-Corruption Commission referred to the proposed law's contents when attending international conferences, moreover, suggests the generally high level of expectation that this 'conflict of interest' regulation draft would be implemented (Medhi 2008: 103–104). Although it never came into effect, we might closely examine the proposed law's contents as indicative of the kinds of corrupt practices that coup leaders set out to regulate. The importance of this draft lies in the fact that it provides insights into how later corruption regulation mechanisms would impact on government in Thailand.

Firstly, we might clarify the definition of what the proposed law sought to regulate. Section 3 designated 'employees of the state' as follows:

> [A] public servant or provincial worker who holds a permanent position with or in receipt of a salary from the state, a worker of a state-owned business or a state organization or a person who is involved in such a task, and regardless of whether a worker who works under provincial self-government law, or a state owned business or another state enterprise, an employee of a committee, a minor committee, a public department, a state owned enterprise or state owned organization, or an individual or a body that used

---

30 In Thai, the draft Conflict of Interest Law is known as *rang phraratchabanyat waduai khwamphit kiaokap kankhatkan rawang prayotsuanbukkhon lae prayotsuanruam*.

31 This was the assembly by appointment inaugurated following the 2006 coup.

or was delegated to use the political power of the state in order to carry out some task according to the law.

This section further designated 'political workers' – as distinct from 'employees of the state' – as 'the prime minister, members of the House of Representatives, senators, political civil servants with the exception of the prime minister and minister of state who were designated according to the political civil servant regulations, provincial leaders and provincial assembly members, and in addition state workers who held other positions as the National Counter-Corruption Commission determined'. Concerning the families of these individuals, Section 3 designated a 'spouse or partner' as 'a person who, even if not legally married, included any man or woman living in a husband or wife relationship with the individual concerned', while the same section defined a relative as 'whether or not arising from a legal relationship, an individual's parents, an individual's birth children or children of their spouse/partner, siblings or those who have either the same mother or father, or both, of the individual or individual's partner/spouse, the uncle or aunt of the individual or individual's partner/spouse, the grandparents of the individual or individual's partner/spouse, and the children and/or grandchildren of siblings or those who have either the same mother or father, or both, of the individual or individual's partner/spouse'.

In terms of a definition of conflict of interest, Section 5 of the bill stated as follows:

1. An act [...] as determined by the Counter-Corruption Commission, 2. The illegal use of state funds that an individual received or received, knew about or kept secret in relation to the execution of public employment, work responsibility or role, 3. The dishonest use of assets of the state or a state organizations for the benefit of oneself or another party without the right to receive this interest, 4. Whether direct or indirect, repealing, proposing, organizing or approving a state plan in a way that gives dishonest benefit to oneself or a particular individual, or 5. Whether direct or indirect, dishonestly using the right or exerting the influence held

by oneself towards the free determination of intent in the use of power grounded in one's duties as an employee of the state.

These stipulations furthermore applied also to the spouse/partner and children of a state employee whose acts were considered to be the acts of the individuals involved themselves. In addition, in the case of the state employee knowing or being aware, the stipulations applied also to acts by relatives other than partners/spouses and their children, and such acts were also stipulated as those of the employee themselves.

A point that is clear from these definitions is that an extraordinarily broad range of applicability was envisaged for the proposed law in that regulatory areas included both individuals and their use of state powers. Not only was the definition of 'relative' remarkably extensive, the fact that conflict of interest parameters encompassed even state projects in the preparatory stage implied the possibility of a prime minister and ministers of state being legally convicted of conflict of interest for what were essentially matters of policy with no concrete element. In order that politicians not be vilified as corrupt, furthermore, detailed audits of their stakeholder relationships with their own policies – and the relationships of a wide-range of relatives also – became necessary. The term, 'policy corruption', became a stock phrase used in attacks on the Thaksin administration. We might regard the legal classification of this as a crime as an important objective of the proposed law. Was it actually possible, however, to include policy matters in concrete legal definitions relating to conflict of interest? The grey area involved in conflict of interest, in addition to the extreme difficulty involved in obtaining successful convictions of those grounds, were both noted above. This problem does not merely relate to the Thaksin case. Even if one of the many businessmen turned politicians withdraws from their previous activities, family members continue to be involved in these concerns.

Given that policy often involves economic issues affecting the whole country, to understand conflict of interest as the receipt of indirect as well as direct benefit presents the danger ultimately of disrupting the structure of parliamentary democracy in Thailand. This is because those entering the political world who also engage in some sort of work or own even a small asset holding run the risk of being accused of conflict of interest. Such a risk effectively discourages the individuals concerned from becoming politicians. While the proposed law never became a formal legal document, it presented a serious challenge to democratization in Thailand by heightening the likelihood of using allegations of corruption to justify a future coup d'état.

Regulating 'potential' corruption

This chapter has examined the assumption that broadening the legal definition of corruption through revisions to Thailand's constitution and laws as the country has democratized has led to perceptions that corruption among politicians is now more blatant and widespread. In addition to a marked refining of the legal definition of corruption following constitutional revisions conducted over the previous two decades, there has also been an ongoing and ultimately unhelpful broadening of 'grey areas' designated as corrupt. We might, in fact, conclude that constitutional reform has resulted in more and more behaviors being classified in this way.

As constitutional revisions and the associated response of the courts expanded definitions of corruption to encompass a wider sphere of activities, criticisms of corruption among politicians became increasingly trenchant. In the 1990s, in fact, many intellectuals argued that Thailand was hostage to money politics. The growth in activities encompassed in the legal definition of corruption that followed revisions to the constitution and associated laws produced a kind of vicious circle that led to greater criticism of corrupt behavior. In the twenty-first century, particularly, there has effectively been a gradual systemization of how cases of corruption against politicians are argued before the courts. Since courts are held in relatively high esteem among the various administrative mechanisms of the state, the handing down of guilty verdicts clearly ferments distrust among voters against politicians and also against the parliamentary democracy that politicians represent. This surely partially explains why the citizens of Bangkok, who violently resisted the military during the 1992 Bloody

May uprising, gave enthusiastic support to troops involved in the 2006 coup d'état.³²

We must question, however, whether the types of corruption created through these legal revisions can actually be regulated. Rather than indicating the commission of corrupt acts, the various guilty rulings handed down to cabinet level politicians might be seen instead as a function of the broad parameters of and ambivalence associated with definitions of 'conflict of interest'. While it has generated judgments merely of possible rather than actual corruption, the provision of incorrect information in assets and liabilities statements has had an enormous influence on politician's fates. Put another way, rather than achieving integrity in the political sphere, excessive regulation of corruption can actually destabilize the basis of parliamentary democracy. Ultimately, we must conclude that the sequence of Thai constitutional and legal revisions discussed above has very much failed to establish any meaningful balance between democratic development in Thailand and the regulation of corruption in the political sphere.

---

32 The 1991 Constitution firstly did not limit the prime minister to members of the House of Representatives. As a result, Bloody May broke out when Suchinda, who was a member of the military, broke a public pledge, assumed the position of prime minister and was violently resisted by Bangkok citizens. In September 1992, the constitution was revised with Section 159 stipulating that 'The prime minister must be a member of the House of Representatives'. So strong were feelings of opposition to the uprising in which many died that members of the military were unable to walk the streets in their uniforms. After the 2006 coup d'état, however, images were broadcast around the world of Bangkok people having photographs taken with soldiers and providing them with food. While interviewing local people, the author also heard many anecdotes of members of the middle class who had participated in the Bloody May events of 1992 and resisted the Suchinda administration but who offered food to soldiers after the 2006 coup. Their reason for this later support was corruption among politicians.

6 | Constitutional Reform and the Judiciary: Institutional Problems of the Constitutional Court and Independent Agencies

In 2012, there was a fierce political dispute in Thailand over constitutional amendments. The battle unfolded between the ruling Pheu Thai Party, which promoted constitutional amendments, and judges, members of independent organizations, senators and conservative intellectuals who resisted the movement. One point at issue was the independent agencies established to bring electoral violations and corruption under control. Independent agencies emerged under the 1997 Constitution which itself was a product of the political reform movement. Fierce debate raged over whether these bodies, which included the Election Commission and the National Anti-Corruption Commission, should be abolished or defended at all costs.

Advocates of independent institutions sanctify the judgments of courts and independent agencies, arguing that citizens and politicians should obey the rule of law. On the other hand, Tida Tawornseth, chairwoman of the Red Shirts, the movement generally regarded as supporting former Prime Minister Thaksin (2001–2006), criticized the system as follows: 'Yingluck might well have been elected prime minister, but Thai democracy is still 20%. That's because there are senators by appointment and independent agencies' (*The Nation*, 6 May 2012). Recent years have seen a growing emphasis on the need for 'rule of law' (*lak niti tham*),[1] a term that first appeared in the text of the 2007 Constitution. The independent agency debate can also be interpreted as conflict over the application of 'rule of law'.

As noted in the introductory chapter, research on democratization also focuses on the rule of law as a means of ensuring the quality of

---

1 There are two Thai terms that can be rendered as the English 'rule of law'. These are '*nithi rat*' and '*lak niti tham*'. According to Worachet (2012), the first derives from the German legal system and the second from the British. While the term '*nithi rat*' was used in the draft of the 2007 Constitution, this eventually became '*lak niti tham*'. Worachet argues that those compiling the constitution were unaware of the difference (Worachet 2012).

democracy (O'Donnell 2005). While definitions are many and varied, scholars generally agree that a minimum condition of democracy is the conduct of 'free and fair elections' (Dahl 1971; Diamond 1999: 7–15). In addition to those conditions, aspects such as whether the election is truly fair and whether the exercise of state power is being inspected are being questioned. Several studies also emphasize the importance of the existence of various regulatory agencies to ensure the quality of democracy, and have shown that the higher the independence of the Board of Audit and anti-corruption agencies and the stronger their authority, the higher the quality of democracy (Kubo 2012: 29–30).

While independent agencies in Thailand were established in accordance with global norms, a range of operational problems emerged. Existing scholarship focuses on two aspects, particularly political influence applied to the Constitutional Court and other agencies, and also the nature of the authority that these entities hold. Regarding the former, a considerable body of work argues that the independent entities and Constitutional Court established under the 1997 Constitution failed to function effectively following interference by influential politicians such as former Prime Minister Thaksin (Pasuk and Baker 2004: 173–176; Niyom 2006a: 69; Vitit 2009: 86; Thitinan 2009: 34; Khien 2011: 32; Harding and Leyland 2011: 162–163). Some argued at the time that strengthening the authority of these entities by, for example, conferring administrative, legislative and judicial functions upon the Election Commission, would lead to a toughening of counter-corruption measures (Ōtomo 2003; Harding and Leyland 2011). Recently, however, the authority of the Election Commission, especially following the implementation of the 2007 Constitution, has been criticized as excessive (Worachet 2009).

While the media and intellectuals censured the Constitutional Court and other independent agencies established under the 1997 Constitution as dysfunctional, Thaksin supporters regarded those operating under the 2007 Constitution as undemocratic. With the 2006 coup d'état as a watershed moment, the organizational blueprints for agencies established under the 1997 and then 2007 constitutions were different in some respects. In 2007, it was said that constitutional reforms were introduced to strengthen the independence of the relevant agencies and enhance their powers to ensure their ability to function impartially. We might, however, question whether strengthening the power of independent bodies such as the Constitutional Court produced proactive rulings that were fair and reasonable and whether this strengthening enhanced their capacity to perform the expected role in terms of the rule of law.

A key point to consider is the fact that independent agencies in Thailand, including the Constitutional Court, were established as a 'package'. This permitted the Constitutional Court and other agencies to assume a specific role in terms of judicial mechanisms and to then work in tandem to oversee and control corruption among politicians. In this chapter it is argued that examining Thailand's independent agency problems through the lens of this organizational package, the package that gave each entity the power to work hand-in-hand with the others, results in new understandings of the challenges facing democracy in Thailand. Adopting an approach that is largely absent from previous scholarship, the chapter will foreground the 'package' comprised of the Constitutional Court and other independent agencies in an attempt to unpack the organizational design. Highlighting the dangers inherent to democracy, the discussion ultimately concludes that, by operating under euphemisms such as 'cleaning-up politics' and 'rule of law', the Constitutional Court and independent agency package has actually reined in the powers of the people's representatives, chosen by popular election, and thus curtailed Thailand's democratic system of elected government.

The discussion begins with a general outline of how Thailand's Constitutional Court and other independent agencies were established and their organizational design in terms of the 1997 and, later, 2007 constitutions. It then considers the investigatory systems of these entities before turning to problems associated with the conduct of corruption oversight by the independent agencies and Constitutional Court of Thailand.

Background of the organizational reforms

The concept of independent agencies and the Constitutional Court in Thailand emerged from the political reform movement of the 1990s which arose from growing dissatisfaction with political pork-barreling and money politics among the urban middle class. As noted in chapters 1 and 2, the leader of the political reform movement was legal scholar Amon Chantharasombun (Thiraphat 2010: 217–220), who proposed three reform objectives: reducing the vote-buying considered endemic in regional areas during elections, promoting the entry of candidates of good character into the political world, and investigating the illegal use of power by politicians (Amon 1994b: 48–49). Amon further insisted that political reforms to the constitution and the establishment of statutory agencies under the constitution – the independent agencies – should occur in one move as a package. At the time, Amon proposed four entities designed to combat corruption: an audit commission (*sathaban kiaokap kantruatgoenphendin*), a council of state, a national counter-corruption commission (*khanakammakan po po po*) and a constitutional court (Amon 1994b: 18).

Formulated in response to the political reform movement, the 1997 Constitution, as noted in Chapter 1, was also known as 'The People's Constitution' (*ratthathammanun chabap prachachon*) and lauded as the most outstanding constitution in the history of Thailand (Harding 2012: 119). Its three objectives were to promote and protect the people's right to freedom, to facilitate participation by the people in investigating and overseeing the state's use of power, and to reform political structures in a manner that enhanced stability and efficiency (Manit 2008: 53–54). The three institutions offered as necessary measures to control and investigate the use of power by politicians were an upper house, independent agencies and the people (Wannatham, Seni and Thasothon 2002: 54). Accordingly, seven 'independent agencies determined according to the constitution' (*ongkon-isara tam ratthathammanu*), including new courts, were established. These were the Election Commission (*khana kammakan kanlueaktang*), the Parliamentary Ombudsman (*phu truat kanphendin khong ratthasapa*), the National Human Rights Commission (*khana kammakan sithi manutsayachon haeng chat*), the Constitutional Court (*san ratthathammanun*), the Administrative Court (*san pokkhrong*), the National Counter-Corruption Commission (*khana kammakan pongkan lae prappram kanthucharit heang chat*) and the National Audit Commission (*khana kammakan truat guen phendin*). These agencies were to function with their own secretariats and retained autonomy in terms of personnel and budgets.

Following the proclamation of an interim constitution after the 2006 coup d'état and the discarding of the 1997 document, a new constitution was enacted in 2007. Although drafting occurred under the influence of the coup d'état group, as was the case with the 1997 Constitution, politicians were formally excluded from this process.

The 2007 Constitution instituted major organizational reforms to the Constitutional Court and other independent agencies, with the Constitution Drafting Committee declaring the following five objectives: 1. to strengthen the independent investigatory agencies and the courts by improving their administrative authority and efficiency; 2. to make genuine improvements to the autonomy and neutrality of independent agency membership appointments by not having the upper house as the sole organization with carriage of this task; 3. to introduce an organizational system that monitors the workings of the independent agencies established in accordance with the constitution; 4. to ensure a system that enables the people to participate easily in the judicial proceedings of the court and independent agencies; and 5. to ensure a swift method of investigation into the use of illegal power by the state (Manit 2008: 73–74).

Institutional reforms based on these objectives saw the number of independent agencies, including the Constitutional Court, increase to ten. In addition to the constitutional and administrative courts, there were four existing constitution-based independent agencies, namely the Election Commission, the National Ombudsman (*phu truat kanphendin haeng chat*), the National Anti-Corruption Commission and the National Audit Commission. A further three were added, namely the National Human Rights Commission, the Public Prosecutor and the National Economic and Social Consultative Commission (*sapha thi prueksa setthakit lae sangkhom haeng chat*). In 2010, the Legal Reform Commission (*khana kammakan phatthana kotmai*) was established.

The following section provides specific details of the institutional design regarding the selection of personnel and the nature of the authority exercised by these bodies.

The 1997 Constitution: emergence of the independent agencies 'package'

There were three agencies for whom the appointment of personnel and range of powers was detailed in the 1997 Constitution. These were the Constitutional Court, the Election Commission and the National Counter-Corruption Commission. This chapter will largely focus on provisions related to the appointment of staff and the range of powers of these bodies as a means of understanding the organizational characteristics of both the Constitutional Court and independent agencies.

Selection of committee members

Constitutional Court (fifteen members)

The fifteen-member bench of the Constitutional Court was made up of five Supreme Court justices, two justices from the Supreme Administrative Court, and eight members determined by an upper house ballot of nominees recommended by a selection committee. There was a total of thirteen selection committee members. These were the chief justice of the Supreme Court, four deans of law, or equivalent, from national higher education institutions voted by their peers, four deans of political science, or equivalent, from national higher education institutions chosen by their peers, and four members from all parties with representatives in the lower house chosen by their peers.

The Election Commission (five members)

There were five members of the Election Commission. These were chosen by a vote of the upper house from five candidates nominated by a selection committee and a further five nominated by the full bench of the Supreme Court (ten candidates in all). The members of the ten-person selection committee were the chief justice of the Constitutional

Court, the chief justice of the Supreme Administrative Court, four rectors of all state higher education institutions chosen by their peers, and four members from all political parties represented in the lower house chosen by their peers.

National Counter-Corruption Commission (nine members)

The nine members of the National Counter-Corruption Commission were chosen by upper house ballot from eighteen candidates recommended by the selection committee. The fifteen-member selection committee consisted of the Supreme Court chief justice, the chief justice of the Constitutional Court, the chief justice of the Supreme Administrative Court, seven rectors of national higher education institutions chosen by their peers, and five members from all parties with representatives in the lower house chosen by their peers.

While membership of each agency's selection committee included representatives from political parties, representatives of the judiciary and intellectuals or scholars, those with legal backgrounds dominated. In other words, notwithstanding some diversity in membership representation, the organizational design of each committee entrenched judicial power.

Principal powers

Constitutional Court

The main powers of the Constitutional Court under the 1997 Constitution were: 'determining the constitutionality of political party resolutions and regulations' (Section 47); 'investigating and determining attempts to acquire power in a way that overthrows the democratic regime of government with the king as head of state or does not accord with the constitution' (Section 63);[2] 'determining the validity of the qualifications of upper and lower house members' (Section 96); 'determining the

---

2   The coup d'état in Thailand, on the other hand, was legitimized by the consent of the king. This legitimacy was also confirmed legally in the 2006 Interim Constitution and in Section 309 of the 2007 Constitution. There are three word categories that refer to a coup process. These are *kabot*, meaning to inflict damage on a monarchy, *patiwat*, meaning to change a system, and *ratthaprahan*, meaning to immediately change a government.

Table 6.1 Membership of the Constitutional Court and independent agencies (the 1997 Constitution)

Agency	Member numbers	Requisite Qualifications
Constitutional Court • Appointed by the king on the advice of the upper house • Term of office: 9 years	15	Section 256 (1) Being of Thai nationality by birth; (2) being 45 years of age or more; (3) having been, in the past, a minister, a member of an independent agency other than the Administrative Court, or having served in a position not lower than deputy prosecutor general, director-general or its equivalent, or position not lower than professor; (4) not prohibited under Section 106 or Section 109 (1), (2), (4), (5), (6), (7), (13) or (14); (5) not being a member of the Lower or Upper House, political official, member of a local assembly or local administrator; (6) not being or having been a member or holder of a political party position during the three years before taking office; (7) not being a member or justice of another independent agency.
Election Commission • Appointed by the king on the advice of the upper house • Term of office: 7 years	5	Section 137 (1) Being of Thai nationality by birth; (2) being 40 years of age or more; (3) be a graduate with a bachelor's degree or equivalent; (4) not being prohibited under Section 106 or Section 109 (1), (2), (4), (5), (6), (7), (13) or (14); (5) not being a member of the lower or upper house, political official, member of a local assembly or local administrator; (6) not being or having been a member or holder of a political party position during the five years before taking office; (7) not being a member or justice of another independent agency.
National Counter-Corruption Commission • Appointed by the king on the advice of the upper house • Term of office: 9 years	9	Sections 297 and 256 (1) Being of Thai nationality by birth; (2) being 45 years of age or more; (3) having been a minister or, with the exception of the Administrative Court, member of an independent agency, or at least deputy-prosecutor or director-general or equivalent, or a position not lower than professor; (4) not being prohibited under Section 106 or Section 109 (1), (2), (4), (5), (6), (7), (13) or (14); (5) not being a House of Representatives member, senator, political official, local assembly member or local administrator; (6) not being or having been, in the 3 years before taking office, a member or office holder of a political party; (7) not being a current justice or member of another independent agency.

Source: Compiled by the author.

Notes:
1. Section 106 excluded the following groups from suffrage: those of unsound mind, Buddhist clergy or those undertaking such training, those detained by a warrant of the court or other lawful order, and those whose right to vote had been suspended.
2. According to Section 109, the following groups were disqualified from nominating as candidates for the lower house: drug addicts; bankrupts; those serving prison sentences or detained under a warrant from the court; with the exception of an offence committed through negligence, those

Selection Method
Sections 255 and 257 • 5 Supreme Court justices (holding the position of justice or above) chosen from the full bench of the Supreme Court. • 2 justices of the Supreme Administrative Court chosen by the full bench of the Supreme Administrative Court. • A selection committee consisting of: chief justice of the Supreme Court; 4 deans of the faculty of law, or equivalent, of all state higher education institutions, selected by their peers; 4 deans of the faculty of political science, or equivalent, of all state higher education institutions, selected by their peers; 4 representatives chosen by their peers of all parties represented in the lower house. From a vote of not less than 3/4 of current members, the committee recommended to the president of the upper house 10 legal studies specialist candidates and 6 political science specialist candidates. The upper house then voted and the first 5 legal studies candidates and first 3 political science candidates who received votes equal to more than half the number of all current senators were selected.
Section 138 • A 10 member selection committee consisting of: chief justice of the Constitutional Court, chief justice of the Supreme Administrative Court, 4 rectors/vice-chancellors of all state higher education institutions chosen by their peers, 4 members from all political parties represented in the lower house chosen by their peers. From a vote of not less than 3/4 of the current members, the committee recommended 5 candidates to the president of the upper house. • A general meeting of the Supreme Court recommended 5 candidates to the president of the upper house. An upper house ballot selected the first 5 members to receive more than half the votes of existing members.
Sections 297 and 257 and with Clause 7 of the 1999 Organic Act of Counter-Corruption • A selection committee consisting of the chief justice of the Supreme Court, the chief justice of the Constitutional Court, the chief justice of the Supreme Administrative Court, 7 rectors of national higher education institutions chosen by the peers, 5 members from all parties represented in the lower house chosen by their peers. The committee recommends to the president of the upper house 18 candidates chosen by no less than 3/4 of its current members. An upper house ballot selected the first 9 members to receive more than half the votes of existing members.

released for less than five years after serving a sentence of two years or more; those who had been expelled, dismissed or removed from government service, a state agency or a state enterprise for dishonesty or corruption; those prohibited from holding political office under Section 295 (that is, for lodging a false assets and liabilities statement); those removed from office by the upper house according to the provision of Section 307 unless a period of five years had elapsed between the date of the resolution and election day.

validity of the qualifications of members of the Election Commission' (Section 142); 'investigating and determining matters lodged by the National Ombudsman's Office' (Section 198); and 'investigating and determining the validity of assets and liabilities statements lodged by politicians and senior bureaucrats' (Section 295). Moreover, with the prohibitions of Section 63 regarding attempts 'to acquire power' or 'overthrow the democratic regime of government with king as head of state', the Constitutional Court could decree the dissolution of that political party. The court further heard cases on matters such as the constitutionality of laws proposed by the Ombudsman's Office and the behavior of public servants (Section 198), in addition to the veracity of assets and liabilities statements lodged by political officials forwarded from the National Counter-Corruption Commission (Section 295).[3]

The Election Commission

The Election Commission, whose president was also the Political Party Registrar, had carriage of the conduct of all levels of election procedure and national referenda. According to Section 145, the Election Commission had the authority to investigate disputed decisions and to order the conduct of a second vote in the case of an election or a referendum not being conducted fairly or impartially. In the case of a disputed decision or an unfair/impartial vote, the commission also had the power to request proceedings from courts, prosecutors and investigators for hearings, investigations and adjudications (Section 147).

---

3 Other powers granted to the court included determining the constitutionality of the rulings and regulations of political parties (Section 47); rulings on the qualifications to sit in the assembly in the case of a lower house member purged from a political party (Section 118); rulings concerning the prohibition on submitting a law or organic law with similar content to a deferred or withheld law or organic law (Section 177); rulings concerning the conflict of interest involving a member of the parliament related to budget legislation (Section 180); determining the constitutionality of a declaration of a state of emergency (Section 219); determining the constitutionality of laws or organic laws (Section 262); determining the constitutionality of draft procedural rules for the parliament (Section 263); determining the concrete constitutionality of laws referred by courts (Section 264); and conciliating in disputes related to bureaucratic powers between administrative agencies (Section 266).

National Counter-Corruption Commission

The three main areas of power of the National Counter-Corruption Commission related to 'public disclosure of the assets and liabilities statements of political officials', 'dismissal by the upper house' and 'criminal investigation into political officials'. The commission's investigative powers gave it the authority to refer irregularities in the assets and liabilities statements of political officials or unusual growth in assets to the head of the Supreme Public Prosecutor's Office, while it could also refer a deliberate failure to submit or the deliberate falsification of an assets and liabilities statement to the Constitutional Court (sections 293–295). Furthermore, when a member of the upper house or voter applied for a dismissal vote against a member of the cabinet, a member of the parliament, the chief justice of one of the courts or a member of an independent agency, the president of the upper house requested the National Counter-Corruption Commission to conduct an investigation and submit a report. When a decision was made to legally progress such a matter, the National Counter-Corruption Commission had the authority to prosecute the case itself (Section 305).

Although much existing research pays close attention to the legislative and judicial powers of the independent agencies, it is also useful to adopt a more comprehensive view of the connections between the Constitutional Court and other agencies. Such a viewpoint acknowledges the operations of each as part of a broader 'package' and thereby provides insights into the system as a whole. What emerges is a structure in which the Election Commission, the National Counter-Corruption Commission and the ombudsman play an investigative and indictment role (or at least can request to indict) with the Constitutional Court handing down rulings and the upper house having the final say on key points. In other words, Thailand's independent agency package provides what is effectively a single sequential legal procedure that encompasses investigation, indictment and handing down rulings on cases.

The 2007 Constitution: strengthening and expanding the 'package'

The following outlines the key reforms that followed the enactment of Thailand's 2007 Constitution.

Changes to membership selection

The Constitutional Court (nine members)

Constitutional Court membership was reduced from fifteen to nine comprising three Supreme Court justices, two Supreme Administrative Court justices, two members with judicial expertise and two members with political science or political administration expertise. The judicial and political specialists were chosen by a five-member selection committee comprised of the chief justice of the Supreme Court, the chief justice of the Supreme Administrative Court, the president of the lower house, the leader of the opposition parties in the lower house, and the head of one of the independent agencies chosen by their peers. In addition, the Senate was changed to only be able to vote on whether or not to approve this personnel proposal.

The Election Commission (five members)

Two were chosen from nominees from the Full Bench of the Supreme Court while three came from nominees proposed by the selection committee. The seven-member selection committee was composed of the chief justice of the Supreme Court, the chief justice of the Constitutional Court, the chief justice of the Supreme Administrative Court, the president of the lower house, the leader of the opposition in the lower house, one member selected by the full bench of the Supreme Court and one member selected by the full bench of the Supreme Administrative Court. The Senate had the power only to vote on whether or not to approve this personnel proposal.

The National Anti-Corruption Commission (nine members)

Nine nominees for National Anti-Corruption Commission membership were recommended by the selection committee to the president of the upper house and then approved by a vote of that house. The five-member selection committee was composed of the chief justice of the Supreme Court, the chief justice of the Constitutional Court, the chief justice of the Supreme Administrative Court, the president of the lower house and the leader of the opposition in the lower house.

The adoption of the 2007 Constitution resulted in membership of the three constitutionally determined independent agencies under discussion being overwhelmingly dominated by the judiciary.[4] Changes were also made to how senators are selected. Under the 1997 Constitution, all senators were elected through election, approximately half of whom under the 2007 Constitution assumed their seats by appointment (*kansanha*) rather than popular election. The seven-person selection committee, which oversaw these appointments, comprised the chief justice of the Constitutional Court, the president of the Election Commission, the president of the agency of the National Ombudsman, the president of the National Anti-Corruption Commission, the president of the National Audit Commission, a justice of the Supreme Court and a justice of the Administrative Court. In other words, selection was monopolized by the courts and the independent agencies. It is clear that, through the upper house appointment of members, a close association developed between that body and Thailand's independent agencies which, in turn, led to an expansion of judicial influence.[5] It was true that the courts themselves could not indict. This led some to assert that the judiciary was the safest of the three arms of administrative power. Nevertheless, the 'package' that

---

4 The document entitled, 'The Constitutional Court and Methods of Deliberation on the Procedural Law of the Constitution: A Summary Proposal Presented to the Developing Democracy Committee', produced during the drafting of the 1997 Constitution, assumed that the lower house would regulate Constitutional Court appointments. A second document, 'Supplementary Policies to Constitutional Reform: The Constitutional Court', released in 2006 by the Supplementary Policies to Constitutional Reform Research Committee of the lower house secretariat, recommended a strengthening of parliamentary control of the Constitutional Court.

5 Appointed members of the upper house included many who were closely associated with the coup d'état group. According to the Election Commission list of members, this included twenty of seventy-four in 2008 and ten of seventy-three in 2011.

Table 6.2 Membership of the Constitutional Court and independent agencies (the 2007 Constitution)

Agency	Member numbers	Requisite Qualifications
Constitutional Court • Appointed by the king on the advice of the upper house • Term of office: 9 years	9	Section 205 (1) Being of Thai nationality by birth; (2) being 45 years of age or more; (3) having been, in the past, a minister, a justice of the Supreme Military Court, a member of an independent agency or the National Human Rights Commission, or having served in a position not lower than deputy prosecutor general, director-general or its equivalent, or position not lower than professor; or a lawyer with more than 30 years continuous experience; (4) not prohibited under Section 100 or Section 102 (1), (2), (4), (5), (6), (7), (13) or (14); (5) not being a member of the lower or upper house, political official, member of a local assembly or local administrator; (6) not being or having been a member or holder of a political party position during the 3 years before taking office; (7) not being a member or justice of another independent agency.
Election Commission • Appointed by the king on the advice of the upper house • Term of office: 7 years	5	Section 230 (1) Being 40 years of age or more; (2) being the holder of a bachelor's degree or higher; (3) having the qualifications listed in Section 205 (1, 2, 4 and 6) and not being prohibited under these; (4) not being a justice of the Constitutional Court, a member of the National Ombudsman's office, a member of the National Anti-Corruption Commission, the National Audit Commission or the National Human Rights Commission.
National Counter-Corruption Commission • Appointed by the king on the advice of the upper house • Term of office: 9 years	9	Section 246 (1) Persons free of the prohibitions outlined in Section 205; (2) those with experience as ministers, Election Commission member, member of the National Ombudsman's Office, members of the National Human Rights Commission or the Auditor General's Office, a person employed in the civil service at a position of director-general or higher, a person with the position of professor or higher, a representative of a private organization or legal specialist with not less than 30 years practice, with the organization concerned confirming this experience.

Source: Compiled by the author.
Notes:
1. Section 100 excludes the following groups from suffrage: Buddhist clergy, novice clergy, those undertaking such training or who have retreated to a monastery; those whose right to vote has been suspended; those detained by a warrant of the court or other lawful order; and those of unsound mind or who are cognitively incapacitated.
2. The following groups have their suffrage rights revoked for lower house elections according to Section 102: Drug addicts; bankrupts or those bankrupted by fraud; those serving prison sentences

Selection Method

Sections 204 and 206
- 3 justices of the Supreme Court with at least the status of justice chosen by the full bench of the Supreme Court.
- 2 justices of the Supreme Administrative Court chosen by the full bench of the Supreme Administrative Court.
- A selection committee comprised of: chief justice of the Supreme Court, chief justice of the Supreme Administrative Court, president of the lower house, leader of the opposition, 1 head of an independent agency chosen by their peers.
  By vote of at least 2/3 of all current members, the committee recommends to the president of the upper house 2 legal studies specialist candidates and 2 social science specialist candidates. In the case in which the upper house does not confirm a candidate, the name shall be forwarded with rejection reason to the selection committee for a follow-up choice.
  Where a vote of all members of the selection committee re-elects the same candidate, that election shall stand. If not confirmed by an all-member vote, there will be a follow-up election.

Section 231
- The full bench of the Supreme Court shall recommend the names of 2 candidates to the president of the upper house.
- A selection committee consisting of: chief justice of the Supreme Court, chief justice of the Constitutional Court, chief justice of the Supreme Administrative Court, president of the lower house, leader of the opposition in the lower house, 1 name selected by the full bench of the Supreme Court, 1 name selected by the full bench of the Supreme Administrative Court. These latter 2 nominees should not be a member of a selection commission of justices or another independent agency. Through a vote of 2/3 of existing members, 3 nominees are recommended to the president of the upper house.
  The upper house votes to confirm the nominees.
  Should the upper house not confirm a nominee, the name is sent back to the selection committee or to the full bench of the Supreme Court for a follow-up selection.
  If through a second vote of more than 2/3 of the members of the selection committee or the full bench of the Supreme Court the outcome is the same as the first vote, the nominee is confirmed. In the case of no decision, a further follow-up vote is held.

Section 246, Section 204 (paragraphs 3 and 4), Section 206 and Section 207
- A selection committee consisting of: chief justice of the Supreme Court, chief justice of the Constitutional Court, chief justice of the Supreme Administrative Court, president of the lower house and leader of the opposition.
  From a vote of 2/3 of current members, the committee recommends 9 candidates to the president of the upper house. The upper house conducts a vote confirming these candidates.
  Should the upper house not confirm a nominee, the name is sent back to the selection committee with rejection reason for a follow-up selection.
  Where a vote of all members of the selection committee re-elects the same candidate, that election shall stand. If not confirmed by an all-member vote, there will be a follow-up election.

or detained under a warrant of the court, and, with the exception of convictions for negligence or minor offences due to negligence, those released for less than 5 years after serving a sentence of 2 years or more; those expelled, dismissed or removed from government service, a state agency or a state enterprise for dishonesty or corruption; those receiving a ruling or an order of the court that their assets be forfeited due to unusual wealth; those prohibited from holding political office for 5 years under Section 263 for lodging a false assets and liabilities statement; and those removed from office by the upper house according to Section 274.

combined courts and independent institutions could be regarded as 'a judiciary that can prosecute itself'.

Strengthening powers

Changes to independent agency powers were implemented through a range of stipulations. Additional powers given, for example, to the Constitutional Court included, 'holding hearings against those who overthrew the democratic regime of government with the king as head of state or sought to acquire the power in a manner not in accord with the constitution' (Section 68, addition of Paragraph 4); 'determining the constitutionality of an organic act bill' (Section 141); 'determining voters' requests for the constitutionality of laws' (Section 212); 'determining the constitutionality of a treaty into which the country enters' (Section 190); 'determining whether a political party should be dissolved because of Electoral Law violations or whether the leader or officials of that party should lose the right to vote' (Section 237); and 'determining the constitutionality of human rights legislation tabled by the National Human Rights Commission' (Section 257).[6]

Powers granted to the Election Commission were as follows: 'Lodging a matter related to loss of qualification to hold a seat in either the lower or upper houses with the Constitutional Court' (Section 93, addition of Paragraph 3); 'filing an appeal with the Supreme Court in the case, following the declaration of an election result, of a ruling by the Election Commission of the necessity of either a follow-up election or revocation of voting rights' (Section 236); 'establishing regulations concerning prohibited administrative practices of a caretaker cabinet in the interim between the resignation of one cabinet and the swearing-in of new members' (Section 236); 'promoting and encouraging education practices that inform the people about Thailand's democratic regime of government with the king as head of state' (Section 236); 'the power

---

6   Furthermore, while the 1997 Constitution gave the Constitutional Court the authority to investigate failure by the holder of a political position to lodge a statement of financial assets, to lodge a false report or to conceal assets, this power was transferred to the Supreme Court's Political Criminal Proceedings Division (Section 263).

to make the final decision in the case of a ruling of a follow-up election or revocation of voting rights prior to the declaration of election results' (Section 239); and 'investigating allegations of corruption or wrong-doing regarding the selection of members of the upper house and lodging an appeal with the Supreme Court' (Section 240).

While there was no particular change to the National Anti-Corruption Commission, Section 279 of the new constitution determined that 'in cases of political employees and civil servants committing gross violations of the Code of Ethics, the office of the National Ombudsman shall forward its concerns to the National Anti-Corruption Commission, and this shall be regarded as justification for dismissal by the upper house'.

Especially striking among changes to the three agencies under discussion was the strengthening of Election Commission authority. The enactment of the 2007 Constitution gave the Election Commission the power to lodge a concern with the Constitutional Court regarding a decision related to loss of qualification to hold office on the part of a member of the parliament. Accordingly, in addition to having oversight of politicians while elections were under way, the Election Commission became a body that constantly monitored and surveilled the members of the parliament.

Sections 68 and 237 also demand attention. Section 68, in fact, tightened the provisions of Section 63 of the 1997 Constitution. An additional fourth paragraph meant that, in the case of the Constitutional Court ruling that a political party be dissolved, the voting rights of the party leader and executive members were revoked for five years. Furthermore, Paragraph 2 of Section 237 determined that 'when the violation of a law or regulation by a candidate causes an election to fail to function fairly, that candidate's right to vote will be revoked'. It was further determined that 'it shall be regarded as an infringement of Section 68 when a party leader or party executive member is aware of the relevant violation but fails to stop or resolve it and, when this leads to a ruling of party dissolution by the Constitutional Court, the right to vote of the party leader and party executive members shall be revoked for five years'. Ambivalence, however, in stipulating precisely what constituted a violation of Section 68 resulted in the Constitutional Court itself determining the kinds of behavior that contravened this provision.

Surveillance of the Constitutional Court and independent agencies

Control and oversight of the Constitutional Court and independent agencies

We will now examine the nature of the system established to audit and oversee the Constitutional Court and other independent agencies whose powers were strengthened as outlined above.

1997 Constitution

Under the 1997 Constitution, concerns regarding the absence of qualifications or violation of prohibitions by a member of the Election Commission could be expressed in a petition by one tenth of the members of the lower house, or the upper house, or the total number of current members of both houses. This petition could then be presented to the president of the parliament. It was the president's role to lodge the matter with the Constitutional Court. When a member of the National Counter-Corruption Commission was suspected of committing a fraudulent or dishonest act related to the irregular accumulation of wealth or their employment position, then a petition of one quarter of the members of the lower house, or the upper house, or the total number of members of both houses, could be lodged with the Supreme Court.

In addition to the above provisions, in order to remove a justice of the Constitutional Court, a member of the Election Commission, the Parliamentary Ombudsman's Office, or the National Audit Commission, a petition of one quarter of the total current members of the lower house, the upper house, or 50,000 people with the right to vote, could be lodged with the upper house. A successful dismissal vote required a three-fifths majority of all current upper house members.

2007 Constitution

There were no changes in the 2007 Constitution to the method of lodging complaints concerning members of the Election Commission. Revisions nonetheless enabled concerns relating to National Anti-Corruption Commission members to be lodged with the Supreme Court through a petition comprised of more than one-fifth of lower house members, or upper house members, or the total number of current members of both houses. Other changes enabled a petition by more than 20,000 voters requesting dismissal to be lodged with the upper house.

It is important to now examine these systems of oversight. Carriage of the mechanisms that ultimately decided the appointment of Constitutional Court justices and independent agency members resided with the upper house. The enactment of the 2007 Constitution, we might remember, saw approximately half the members of this body appointed, with the selection committee responsible for these appointments chosen from those associated with the courts and the heads of independent agencies. In other words, it can be said that this surveillance system is actually nothing more than an impeachment by 'relatives'.

System to prevent constitutional amendment

Any discussion of Constitutional Court or independent agency oversight also calls for consideration of constitutional amendment or reform. Both the 1997 and 2007 constitutions introduced provisions that made it extremely difficult for a popularly elected government to implement constitutional amendment. Both Section 63 of the 1997 Constitution and Section 68 of the 2007 document stated, 'It is prohibited to propose a motion concerning constitutional reform that alters the democratic regime of government with the king as head of state or that acquires the power to govern in a manner that does not comply with the constitution'. If an elected government's attempt at constitutional reform was undermined by a questionable Constitutional Court ruling, the political party of the government in question could face dissolution. In other words, any move to revise the constitution came with considerable risk.[7] Furthermore, as noted also in Chapter 7, a decision handed down in July 2012 gave individual citizens themselves the right to lodge a case directly with the Constitutional Court (Constitutional Court ruling 18-22/2555). That ruling resulted from an action lodged by an appointed member of the upper house. Thus, the Constitutional Court was the entity that decided if constitutional reform could proceed. Furthermore, the criteria for judging a matter as unconstitutional were extremely ambiguous. As a result, while both the 1997 and 2007 constitutions ceded extraordinary powers to the court and independent agencies, the independent agency 'package' structurally protected that court and those agencies from reform attempts by popularly elected governments.

Crackdown by the Constitutional Court and independent agencies

The following will consider the influence that independent agencies and the Constitutional Court had on Thailand's popularly elected governments and the types of changes to the oversight of these agencies that emerged following the systematic revision of the 2007 Constitution. The focus will be on cases lodged until 2012 during which time there was increasing criticism of independent agencies and the Constitutional Court.[8]

With independent agencies and the Constitutional Court responsible for the oversight of the behavior of politicians since 2000, opportunities for rulings to occur markedly increased. For instance, politicians charged with and found guilty of lodging a false assets and liabilities statement numbered seven in 2000, two in 2001, eight in 2002, five in 2003 and four in 2004. The operation of these agencies according to the precepts of the 1997 Constitution, however, was

---

7 In addition, the 2007 Constitution stipulated that the National Ombudsman would monitor and make recommendations regarding points of dispute relating to constitutional amendment.

8 Instances from 2013 until immediately prior to the 2014 coup d'état will be discussed in Chapter 7.

criticized as dysfunctional. We might therefore consider the changes that occurred with the 2007 Constitution. One distinct difference was the repeated post-2007 overthrow of a popularly elected government by the court. Of the many cases in which the independent agencies and Constitutional Court were involved until August 2012, seven trials had the potential to bring down a popularly elected government. This section examines those seven.

As set out in Table 6.3, the seven trials in question involved the 2001 charge that Thaksin lodged a false assets and liabilities statement; the April 2006 charge of an invalid election; the 2007 charge calling for the dissolution of the Thai Rak Thai Party; the 2008 charge indicting Samak of conflict of interest; the 2008 charge calling for the dissolution of the People's Power Party; the 2010 charge calling for the dissolution of the Democrat Party; and the 2012 charge regarding reforms to the 2007 Constitution. All convictions were against Thaksin factions and, with the exception of the 2007 dissolution of the Thai Rak Thai Party, all were handed down by the Constitutional Court. The dissolution of the Thai Rak Thai Party occurred under the interim constitution enacted following the 2006 coup d'état and was ordered by what is generally referred to as the 'constitutional tribunal' (*khana tulakan ratthathammanun*).[9]

When considering the information above, it is evident that, with the exception of the ruling related to the reform of the 2007 Constitution, independent agencies were involved as the plaintiff in all cases. Of these six, four involved the Election Commission, one involved the National Counter-Corruption Commission and one the Parliamentary Ombudsman's office. Furthermore, on three occasions, an independent agency actually lodged the indictment directly. Specifically, in 2001 the National Counter-Corruption Commission laid the case against Thaksin, in April 2006 the Parliamentary Ombudsman laid charges of an invalid election, while in 2008 the Election Commission charged Samak with no longer qualifying to hold the office of prime minister. Of the three cases involving the dissolution of political parties, each was

---

9   The coup group dissolved the Constitutional Court to form instead a constitutional tribunal (*khana tulakan ratthathammanun*) with members drawn from the justices of each of the country's courts.

Table 6.3 List of lawsuits related to the overthrow of popularly elected governments

Year of Ruling	Charge	Defendant	Independent Agency Involved	Provision	Ruling
1997 Constitution					
2001	Charge of submission of a false assets and liabilities statement (Constitutional Court ruling 20/2544)	Prime Minister Thaksin	Constitutional Court, National Counter-Corruption Commission	Section 295	Not guilty
2006	Lawsuit regarding nullification of April 2006 general election (Constitution Court ruling 9/2549)	Election Commission	Constitutional Court, Parliamentary Ombudsman	Sections 2, 3, 104 and 144	Guilty
2006 Interim Constitution					
2007	Charge calling for dissolution of Thai Rak Thai Party and 2 other political parties (Constitutional Tribunal ruling 3-5/2550)	Thai Rak Thai Party (and 2 other political parties)	Constitutional Tribunal,[2] Political Party Registrar[3]	Sections 66 (1 and 3)[4] and 67 of the 1998 Organic Act of Political Party, Revolutionary Decree No. 27	Guilty
2007 Constitution					
2008	Charge of loss of qualification to hold office by Prime Minister Samak (Constitutional Court ruling 12/2551)	Prime Minister Samak	Constitutional Court, Election Commission	Section 267 and 182 (7)	Guilty
2008	Charge calling for dissolution of People Power Party (Constitutional Court ruling 20/2551)	People Power Party	Constitutional Court, Political Party Registrar	Sections 68 and 237	Guilty
2010	Charge calling for dissolution of the Democrat Party (Constitutional Court ruling 15/2552)	Democrat Party	Constitutional Court, Political Party Registrar	Sections 62 and 65 of the 1998 Organic Act of Political Party	Not guilty
2012	Charge related to amendment of the 2007 Constitution (Constitutional Court ruling 18-22/2555)	President of the parliament, the cabinet, the Pheu Thai Party, etc.	Constitutional Court	Section 68	Not guilty

Source: Compiled by the author.
Notes:
1. The author has provided a simplified overview of each charge.
2. Following the dissolution by the coup group of the Constitutional Court, an alternate body known in Thai as *khana tulakan ratthathammanun* was established under the 2006 Interim Constitution. Membership comprised the chief justice of the Supreme Court, the chief justice of the Supreme Administrative Court, five Supreme Court justices and two justices of the Supreme Administrative Court.
3. The Political Party Registrar was the president of the Election Commission.
4. Charges against the other two political parties were applied under Sections 66 (2 and 3) and 67.

indicted by the Supreme Public Prosecutor's Office, which received a petition from the Political Party Registration Registrar (the president of the Election Commission). The 2012 case relating to reforms to the 2007 Constitution was directly lodged by an electorate.

When we consider the details of each case, we find that four of the seven defendants were political parties while two were serving prime ministers. The ruling that invalidated the April 2006 election is a special case in which an independent agency became a defendant. In two of the four cases involving political parties, the basis of the indictment was Section 68 of the 2007 Constitution. While Section 66 of the 1998 Political Party Law was used as the grounds for the ruling to dissolve the Thai Rak Thai Party and two other political parties, this was implemented under the 2006 Interim Constitution and echoed the provisions of Section 63 of the 1997 Constitution.

It is thus clear that, taking advantage of the 2006 coup d'état, Section 63 of the 1997 Constitution and Section 68 of the 2007 Constitution were used as justification for rulings that brought down elected governments. In other words, Section 68 of the 2007 Constitution was used not merely in the case of electoral violations but also in rulings that questioned the advisability of constitutional reform. Furthermore, all political parties overthrown by such rulings belonged to the Thaksin political faction. With the Thaksin faction out of office, the Democrat Party administration (2008–2011), which assumed power without facing the electoral process (2008–2011), was ultimately not brought down by a ruling of an independent agency or the Constitutional Court. The important point to keep in mind, however, is how the series of indictments discussed were characterized by the independent agencies working in tandem with – integrating with – the Constitutional Court.

Judgments: neutrality and fairness

The system under the 1997 Constitution: the Thaksin administration (2001–2006)

Claims were made that, under the 1997 Constitution, Thaksin's political intervention led to dysfunction in the workings of the independent agencies and the Constitutional Court. Proof of this claim was said to be the not-guilty ruling in the case of Thaksin's 2001 indictment on the grounds of submitting a false assets and liabilities statement, and the dismissal in February 2006 by the Constitutional Court of the allegation that Thaksin was no longer qualified to hold the post of prime minister as a result of stock sales of ShinCorp (Constitutional Court ruling 4/2549).

Suchit, a justice of the Constitutional Court at the time that the first ruling was handed down, stated that serious thought was given by members of the court bench to the possibility of political influence and that opinion was divided among justices (Suchit 2006: 45–46). Points of contention concerning the sale of ShinCorp were 1. whether Thaksin held more than 5% of the stock sold, and 2. whether he was involved in the stock sale to Temasek Holdings (*The Nation*, 17 February 2006). The Constitutional Court dismissed the case on the grounds of insufficient evidence. In response, the opposition and NGOs vociferously argued that it was the duty of the Constitutional Court to find such evidence and a campaign was mounted to have the court purged (*The Nation*, 16 February 2006). In response, the court argued that 'while this body has the authority to request additional evidence, the decision of whether or not to accept a suit is grounded in the nature of the materials and documents submitted' (*The Nation*, 18 February 2006).

The April 2006 general election

On 24 February 2006, in order to evade criticism of his administration, Prime Minister Thaksin dissolved the lower house to conduct an election and seek a mandate from the people. On 27 February, however, the three majority opposition parties announced a boycott of this election. Although the Election Commission opened general election nominations on 2 March, the majority opposition parties did not lodge candidate names.

Intellectuals, the media and NGOs all voiced extreme opposition to the conduct of a general election. The principal points of objection included claims that 'independent agencies are no longer effective' and 'we need a new government to make amendments to the 1997

Constitution'. There were also accusations that 'the 2 April general election might be manipulated to the advantage of the government. An election is merely one aspect of a democracy. We should revise the constitution before holding an election'. Some further argued that 'in order to defuse a political crisis, any election should be postponed for 120 days. Under Section 7 of the 1997 Constitution, the Election Commission has the authority to postpone an election.[10] The best strategy would be for the Election Commission to appeal to the Administrative Court and the election proclamation to be declared invalid'. Opposition to the Election Commission conducting a general election as scheduled gradually gathered force.

Notwithstanding the boycott by the major opposition parties, the 2 April election proceeded as planned. Around 70% of electorates fielded a Thai Rak Thai Party candidate only and there were large numbers of blank ballots. On 4 April, the Election Commission decided that a follow-up election would be held in electorates without a successful candidate, and this was conducted in mid-April. Even following the general election, however, criticism of the validity of the process was rife and the backlash against the Election Commission continued. Intellectuals and NGOs declared, for example, that 'the 2 April election was invalid' and that 'Section 7 should have been used to postpone a second election for a maximum of 120 days'. There were also claims of an 'abuse of power by the Election Commission'.

Intellectuals, the media and anti-government NGOs all insisted on the 120-day extension for a follow-up to the April 2006 election. This was because, as pointed out in Chapter 4, the provisions of the 1997 Constitution made it difficult for a member of the lower house to change political party affiliation. The 120-day election extension would have facilitated the possibility of such a change by government members.

When a lecturer of the faculty of law at a famous university requested that a case be lodged with the National Ombudsman against the Constitutional Court to the effect that the 2 April general election was

---

10 Section 7 of the 1997 Constitution determined, 'where there is no provision under this constitution applicable to a case, it shall be decided in accordance with the political procedures of democratic regime of government with the king as head of state'.

invalid, the ombudsman agreed. Acknowledging that 'We ourselves merely determine the law and carry out our duty', the Election Commission, which had conducted the election, declared '[we have not] overstepped our authority. We had all power necessary to conduct a follow-up election' (*The Nation*, 27 April 2006). Statements made by King Bhumibol, however, saw the situation swiftly change. Declaring that 'The Supreme Court holds the right to hold dialogue with the Constitutional Court and the Administrative Court', the king requested Supreme Court intervention (*The Nation*, 29 April 2006). As a result, the three courts – Supreme, Supreme Administrative and Constitutional – were convened for discussions together under Supreme Court leadership and a second election was ultimately decreed on the grounds of the invalidity of the April 2006 elections.

Two reasons were given for rejecting the ruling handed down by the Constitutional Court. The first was that the brief time between lower house dissolution and the conduct of the election benefited the ruling government. The second was that inappropriate voting booth layout could not adequately ensure the confidentiality of the vote. There was, however, no constitutional provision related to the first ruling, while the only difference to previous elections in layout was an opposite aspect to a booth. Insufficient evidence made it impossible to determine whether this compromised the confidentiality of the vote.[11] Furthermore, the joint meeting of the three courts issued resignation notices to the members of the Election Commission. Those who refused were detained and found guilty by the Criminal Court with sentences of four years imprisonment and ten years loss of voting rights (Nelson 2008: 12–14).

From the 2006 coup d'état to the 2007 constitutional system

We might consider whether the decisions of the independent agencies and the Constitutional Court become more neutral or fair once Thaksin was deposed. In doing so, it will be useful to examine the rulings in the

---

11 The ruling on constitutional violations by the Election Commission in the conduct of the election was eight-six, while the ruling on the necessity or otherwise of conducting a second election was nine-five.

two cases related to the overthrow of the Thaksin administration, and the 2007 ruling on the dissolution of the Thai Rak Thai and two other political parties.

The 2007 ruling that the Thai Rak Thai Party and two other political parties must be dissolved was handed down by the constitutional tribunal established in 2006 following the coup d'état. In order to avoid having electorates in which only a single Thai Rak Thai Party candidate nominated for the April 2006 general election, there were differences of opinion over whether to solicit other political parties to put forth candidates for nomination also. In addition to the guilty ruling leading to the dissolution of three political parties, party executive members lost voting rights for five years. The basis for the judgment was a revolutionary decree issued by the coup group. The constitutional tribunal that handed down the ruling was comprised of justices from each Thai court, and was assembled under the influence of the coup d'état group. Justices of the courts played a significant role in the drafting of the 2007 Constitution, and clearly enjoyed harmonious relations with those involved in the coup.[12]

Following the enactment of the 2007 Constitution, independent agencies and the Constitutional Court actively undermined popularly elected governments. Although the People Power Party, the successor to the Thai Rak Thai Party, won the lower house election in December 2007, rulings of the Constitutional Court defeated the administration of the party twice in 2008. Debate erupted concerning the impartiality of these decisions.

A representative example, discussed also in Chapter 5, was the 2008 ruling that saw Prime Minister Samak disqualified from holding office. With Samak's hosting of a television program determined as equivalent to his being an 'employee', a guilty ruling was handed down on the grounds of infringing the 'conflict of interest' conditions forbidden under the constitution. Another famous contentious case was the judgment made against Red Shirts executive member Jatupon of expiration of qualifications to be a member of the lower house (Constitutional Court ruling 13/2555). Standing as a candidate for the

---

12 The majority of the thirty-five members of the Constitution Drafting Committee were either justices or lawyers (Vitit 2009: 83).

Pheu Thai Party in a multiple-seat representative electorate, Jatupon was arrested on the day of the July 2011 lower house election. There was debate over whether or not this disqualified him from being an assembly member. With the election results finalized in August, the Election Commission ruled in November that Jatupon lacked the necessary qualifications and requested a determination to that end by the Constitutional Court. While the Constitutional Court issued the ruling as requested, there were clearly problems concerning the court's interpretation of the text of the constitution. Section 102, Paragraph 3 of the 2007 Constitution stipulated that those who did not exercise their right to run for the House of Representatives were those falling under Section 100, paragraphs 1, 2 and 4. Section 100, paragraph 3, on the other hand, which referred to 'those detained by a warrant of the court or other lawful order' was excluded. However, the Constitutional Court forcibly ruled him absent of qualifications to sit in the parliament through an interpretation that amalgamated the constitution with the Political Party Law. The important point to keep in mind is that this problematic ruling emerged from the collusion of the Election Commission and the Constitutional Court.[13]

Independent agencies and the Constitutional Court, by contrast, declined to bring down the Democrat Party government. Although the Election Commission also lodged a claim with the Constitutional Court charging executive members of the Democrat Party with misappropriating funds, the Constitutional Court dismissed the case on the grounds that the commission had exceeded the time limit of fifteen days in its preparation for the case and that these preparations were therefore outside the law. The court appeared unwilling to step into a sphere that might be seen as illegal.[14]

---

13 In 2000, the Election Commission brought into effect a rule that made it possible to revoke autonomously the right of candidates to stand in a second election for the upper house. The parliamentary ombudsman filed an action on the grounds of a suspected violation of the constitution and the Constitutional Court ruled that this was the case (Constitutional Court ruling 24/2543). Here we see the court's surveillance function in action.

14 The court's unjust rulings became a particular topic of discussion from around 2010 (Phopu 2010).

Constitutional Reform and the Judiciary 291

Photo 6.1 Red Shirts

The independent agencies package and 'dictatorship by law'

In order to highlight the operation of rule of law in Thailand, this chapter conducted a thorough analysis of the design of the organizational 'package' that links the country's independent agencies and Constitutional Court. As noted in general scholarship on democratization, countering corruption is an indispensable element in any attempt to enhance democratic processes. It is clear, however, that there are problems in Thailand with both the systematic organization, and the role expected, of independent agencies and the Constitutional Court. From one perspective, this can be explained by the fact that criticisms of these entities as dysfunctional under the 1997 Constitution arose not because they failed to perform their duties in accordance with the constitution and the law, but because they failed to unseat the Thaksin administration. Although independent agencies and the Constitutional Court had themselves at times been subject to violent attack, the enactment of the 2007 Constitution saw these bodies repeatedly undermine and overthrow administrations linked to the Thaksin faction. As outlined in this section, coordination between the agencies and court as a means of removing Thaksin's allies took precedence over handing down rulings that were fair or just.

Independent agency and Constitutional Court organizational design differed under the 1997 and 2007 constitutions in Thailand, particularly in terms of membership. As evident from the chaos that followed the April 2006 general election, these agencies operated according to the strict letter of constitutional provision and the law under the 1997 Constitution and, until the Supreme Court intervened at the request of King Bhumipol, were unable to action the expectations of Bangkok intellectuals that they overthrow the Thaksin regime. For that reason, the 2007 Constitution strengthened the influence of the courts, with the Supreme Court at the summit, in the selection processes of independent agency members. In reality, however, there had been organizational problems right from the inception of Thailand's independent agencies and Constitutional Court. Section 63 of the 1997 Constitution and 68 of the 2007 Constitution ensured the power to easily dissolve political parties, in spite of the fact that there was no necessity for this as a means of containing corruption. In addition, notwithstanding the powers bestowed upon them, the independent agencies ultimately failed to comply adequately with their own accountability obligations, a situation exacerbated by the 2007 Constitution. Awareness of how these entities operate as a 'package' – which includes the upper house – rather than stand-alone bodies gives even greater clarity to this point. Notwithstanding the many legally problematic rulings handed down since May 2006, it has been extremely difficult as discussed in this chapter for a popularly elected government to oppose an independent agency. This was regardless of how unjust a decision against that government might have been. Furthermore, as also noted, the organizational design of the system has even made it difficult to undertake constitutional reform. It is therefore possible to conclude that popularly elected government in Thailand is under siege from the independent agency package.

Amalgamating the powers of the courts and the independent agency system, both of which lack accountability, creates the risk of each becoming a tool of the dictatorship. The 1997 Constitution foregrounded the role of the judiciary in the fight against corruption. Yet it is difficult to say that the judiciary discharged its duties in a fair and neutral manner. Thongchai Winichakul, for example, has expressed alarm at the tendency of the judiciary to form alliances with powerbrokers in Thailand (Thongchai 2008: 32).[15]

The Thaksin administration assumed power in 2001, four years after the 1997 Constitution brought Thailand's independent agencies and Constitutional Court into existence. In other words, these agencies were not initially established in order to target the Thaksin administration. There is nonetheless a strong possibility that the intellectuals who drafted the 1997 Constitution prepared the document as a tool to assist in the overthrow of a popularly elected government that might cause 'problems' in the future.

Independent agencies and the Constitutional Court had a wide range of functions, many of which were extremely valuable.[16] It is therefore not the intention here to flatly deny the significance of either. Nevertheless, inherent within the organizational structure of these entities was the power to dismantle parliamentary democracy.

While, on the one hand, Nitrat and other scholars seeking change loudly condemned the independent agencies, conservative scholars, as they always have, advanced arguments defending these institutions at all costs.[17] Even in recent years, Amon, the progenitor of both the independent agencies and the Constitutional Court, indirectly criticized what he regarded as the deficiencies of contemporary

---

15 Although there was also debate concerning the constitutionality of the coup d'état group's assets investigation committee and the meaning of 'conflict of interest', a ruling favorable to the coup group was handed down.

16 The effective maneuver measures of minorities in the parliament in determining the constitutionality of draft bills by the Constitutional Court has been noted (Imaizumi 2008).

17 Charun Inthachan, a Justice of the Constitutional Court, declared, 'Without an effective monitoring system, power is used to the wrong ends' (*Daily News*, 21 July 2012):
http://www.manager.co.th/Daily/ViewNews.aspx?NewsID=9550000089502 (accessed 19 August 2012).

politicians by declaring: 'What we are looking for are statesmen [*ratthaburut*, politicians seeking to do good]' (*Prachatai*, 23 October 2009). While there is certainly a case in support of a nonpartisan investigation into the relationship between political powerbrokers with the ability to exercise influence and the independent agencies and the Constitutional Court, it seems that as a minimum we need an in-depth review of the organizational design, and a reconsideration of the roles, of the country's independent agencies. In Thailand, the excessive restrictions placed on legal processes by the independent agency package has in effect become 'dictatorship by law'. This results in the paradoxical situation whereby Thailand's independent agencies undermine and subvert the country's parliamentary democracy.

7 Constitutional Reform and 'Non-Elected' Legislative Power: The 2007 Constitution and a New Mission for the Senate

The coup d'état in September 2006 overthrew the 1997 Constitution. This made the 2000 election the first and only popularly elected Senate since the founding of parliament in 1932.[1] Drafted under the 2006 Interim Constitution, the 2007 document created a Senate totaling 150 members. This new configuration amalgamated seventy-six popularly elected members, each representing one Thai province, and seventy-four government appointed seats.

While considerable commentary exists on the Senate chosen by full popular election following the 1997 Constitution, little research has been conducted into the 'half-elected, half-appointed' Senate established following the 2006 coup d'état. There was no doubt that the introduction of a partial senate appointment system would draw strong criticism. It is important, therefore, to question what motivated the 2007 Constitution Drafting Assembly to call for this change. Was there an alternative,[2] and what, furthermore, was the role expected of those given a senate seat by appointment?

Previous research has labelled the senate system changes introduced in the 2007 Constitution as a 'semi-U-turn' (Chambers 2009: 26). Certainly, this term sums-up how the move involved a return to half rather than all seats – as was the previous practice – being filled by appointment. These 2007 revisions were generally justified

---

1 A senator byelection was also held in 2006, but the general election in April of the same year was ruled invalid, and a coup d'état took place in September, so the senator who was elected at that time did not work.
2 The first draft released in April 2007 by the Constitution Drafting Committee proposed 160 senate seats, seventy-six representing provinces and eighty-four representing various elements of the business world, all filled by appointment. After protests by citizen groups, the second draft released in June amended this to seventy-six elected provincial representatives and seventy-four appointments. With Vice-Chairperson Charan declaring, 'Appointed members are selected from candidates who are upright, without blemish and neutral', the draft was accepted (Chambers 2009: 24–25).

as necessary to protect the Senate from political influence. Previous Prime Minister Thaksin was generally offered as the exemplar bad influence in this respect (Pasuk and Baker 2004: 173–176; Ockey 2008: 22; Bidhya 2010: 65; Vitit 2009: 84; Harding and Leyland 2011: 81). If this had been the sole objective, however, it would have been simpler to retain popular elections while strengthening legal provisions on eligibility to nominate for the Senate in the sections of the constitution determining relations between political figures. This would also have greatly reduced the charges of making 'undemocratic revisions' that were levelled against those who drafted the 2007 Constitution. Tamada's analysis of senators popularly elected at the 2000 upper house election demonstrates that the figure of 55.5% with prior civil service backgrounds was little different from the 52.3% of appointed senators in 1996 (Tamada 2003: 239–242). That is to say, whether elected or appointed, many senators had civil service backgrounds, an occupational breakdown that was unlikely to alter regardless of whether a system was or was not based on full popular election.[3] Any explanation that relies merely on removing political influence fails to adequately explain the reasons for the revisions made.

To identify a clear motive for this partial 2007 reversion to a system of senate seats by appointment,[4] we need to clarify the fundamental

---

3   During the era of senate by appointment, the percentage of civil servants gradually fell while that of businesspeople expanded. In the last all-appointed Senate of 1996, 52.3% of seats went to civil servants and 30.1% to businesspeople (Tamada 2003: 241).

4   According to draft documentation relating to the 2007 Constitution, the drafting committee first proposed 160 Senate seats, with seventy-six provincial representatives and eighty-four from various other groups. All seats were to be filled by appointment. However, following opposition from the Constitution Implementation Council, which supported popular election, it was decided that the provincial representatives would be chosen by popular vote. Ten seats were then removed from the seats by appointment block, reducing the total number of senate seats to 150, in order that seats chosen by popular election exceeded the number of appointed seats. However, since the relevant minutes were deleted, the facts surrounding the original choice of 160 seats is unclear. The drafting sub-committee's insistence on a system of appointment was explained as necessary to prevent relatives of House of Representatives members becoming senators, with the decision repeatedly justified in terms of needing to select knowledgeable people of experience as senators (Minutes

points of contrast in how the election and appointment systems legitimate a senator's position in the parliament. Whether or not the member had a civil service background, the legitimacy of a parliament member selected by an election process was popular vote. Appointed members, however, were legitimated by their relationship to the political figure who appointed them. This facilitated a member being controlled by the person or persons responsible for bestowing the position, who might require the individual appointed to take carriage of some sort of task. We must in other words consider the possibility that obligations were imposed on Senate members appointed through the 2007 Constitution. This chapter will accordingly provide insights into the characteristics of the Senate formed under the provisions of the 2007 Constitution. The discussion proceeds on the assumption that the revisions undertaken in 2007 to the method of selecting members for the Thai upper house functioned ultimately to allocate certain tasks to appointed members for implementation by the parliament. Attention will also be given to the election system and the changes to power that followed the 2008 and 2011 Senate elections.

The selection of Senate members

The following will clarify the aim of the revisions to the senate appointment system devised in the 2007 Constitution. We will accordingly examine the system itself and the results of member selection.

Member numbers and length of appointment

The 2007 Constitution stipulated a senate comprised of a total of 150 members – seventy-six elected and seventy-four appointed. This was fifty less than the 1997 Constitution which stipulated 200 members. There was a slight drop also in House of Representatives numbers in the 2007 Constitution, which made provision for 480 members, 400 chosen by individual constituency election and eighty by party-

---

of 2550 [2007] Constitution Implementation Council 22 June; Minutes of 2550 [2007] Constitution Drafting Sub-Committee 13 March).

list proportional representation.[5] This contrasted with 500 House of Representatives members in the 1997 document, 400 also chosen by individual constituency election and 100 by party list proportional vote. The 1991 Constitution stipulated 270 members in an appointed senate, with 360 in the lower house. We can interpret the progressive percentage fall of senate seats in the parliament with each constitutional revision from 42.8% in 1991, through 28.5% in 1997, to 23.8% in 2007 as evidence of the march of democratization in Thailand.

The duration of appointment of a senator is six years. Only one consecutive term is permitted.

Qualifications for recommendation as a senate election candidate and/or subject of appointment

To be recommended as either an election candidate or appointee to the Senate, an individual must meet the following conditions: 1. be born in Thailand; 2. be above forty years of age; 3. have completed education to bachelor level or above; 4. not have a parent, spouse/partner or child who is a member of the House of Representatives or working in a political position; 5. not hold any other position with a political party or be the member of a political party, not nominate or be recommended within five years (until the day of the election or being recommended) of the day of stepping down or resigning as a member of a political party or a position related to politics; 6. not be a member of the House of Representatives, or in the case of having been a member, not nominating within five years (until the day of the election or being recommended) of stepping down or resigning; 7. not have infringed matters stipulated in candidature conditions for the House of Representatives (Section 102 with the exception of Paragraph 10); and 8. not be a minister of the state, a member of a provincial assembly, have control of provincial governance or be a person who holds any other political position, and if one has held one of these positions, not nominating until five years have elapsed. The majority of these stipulations, which were considerably strengthened in 2007 after

---

5 Constitutional revision in 2011 stipulated a change to 375 members by constituency election and 125 by party-list proportional representation.

first appearing in principle in the 1997 Constitution, were intended to eliminate political influence on the Senate. The 2007 strengthening occurred through the addition of a new matter to point four above and lengthening the required time between the end of a previous term of office and subsequent election or appointment in points five, six and eight above from one year to the much more severe five years.

The system of popular election

In addition to meeting the conditions outlined above, a candidate needed to comply with any one of the following in order to run for a senate election: 1. have had one's name recorded on the resident registrar in the province for which one was running for a continuous five years prior to the date of candidacy; 2. be born in the province for which one was running; 3. have been educated for at least five continuous years at a facility in the province for which one was running; or 4. have worked as a civil servant for at least five continuous years in the province for which one was running or have had one's name entered into the resident register of that province. These conditions, which advantaged civil servants who were transferred to various locations across the country, were substantially similar to those of the 1997 Constitution. There were, moreover, election campaigning restraints so that, while candidates could campaign, they were restricted in terms of discussing matters related to senate work. Neither could they make campaign promises to voters.[6] This was in spite of the fact that a candidate elected without providing sufficient information on their policy could not truly be said to represent the will of the people. The

---

6 The following points were given in support of restricting election activities: 1. it would provide opportunities for those who were competent and intelligent but who struggled to find the funds to enter politics; and 2. following the election, Senate members could conduct their matters free from political interference (Samnakgan Lekhathikan Sapha Phuthaenratsadon 2006: 90–91). The perception among Thai intellectuals was that the country's political system operated under the influence of so-called 'political business', meaning that it was difficult for conscientious, capable people to enter the political world (Chumphon 2002: 141). This perception was not confined to the upper house but was also a central theme guiding revisions to the House of Representatives election system.

system furthermore advantaged candidates who were widely known or who had a wide local network.[7] This led to a high likelihood of people such as well-known persons, those with experience in public office, and civil servants being elected. A similar situation had pertained through the 1997 Constitution.

The greatest points of difference between the 1997 and 2007 constitutions concerned the number of senators elected per constituency. While both constitutions designated a province as an election ward, the 1997 Constitution divided the 200 Senate seats among each province according to population ratio.[8] The 2007 Constitution, however, made each province a single seat regardless of population. This revised distribution completely overlooked the principle of one vote one value and (with the exception of Bangkok) gave a per-person seat advantage to areas with large numbers of provinces, such as the southern and central regions, over the more heavily populated northeast.

It is presumed that many civil servants are from the capital and central regions. This is because there are large regional disparities in the number of highly educated people.[9] In spite of the expansion in recent years of tertiary education opportunities for provincial students, those from the capital and central provinces were certainly advantaged as prospective candidates in the past. We can also say that the disregard of regional population ratios in the post-2007 Constitution

---

7   Before the conduct of the 2000 Senate election, some voiced concerns that approximately 70% of those elected would come from the traditional bureaucratic elite while there was also the opinion that a result in which about half of those elected had civil service experience would be a comparatively positive result (Funston 2000: 1010–102). It was further claimed that a total of one third of senators were related to other parliament members (Sombat 2002: 208).

8   The 1997 Constitution stipulated that the Senate have 200 seats according to population as recorded in the previous year's Resident Registration Roll and that the number of voters for whom one senator would be responsible was to be calculated according to the population ratio of each province. The same method of calculation applied to House of Representatives seats.

9   Figures from the 2000 census gave the percentage of university graduates among higher education participants by region as 17.8% for Bangkok, 34.1% for the Central Region (excluding Bangkok), 3.8% for the North, 3.3% for the North-East and 3.9% for the South. This demonstrates the clear higher education dominance of Bangkok and the Central Region. Available at: http://web.nso.go.th/pop2000/pop_e2000.htm (accessed 1 July 2011).

seat distribution formula created a system that further advantaged central province candidates.

Selection by appointment

The selection process for senate appointments introduced in the 2007 Constitution differed from previous government appointment methods. The process began with the formation of a Senate Personnel Selection Committee. This was composed of seven members: the chief justice of the Constitutional Court, the head of the Election Commission, the head of the Office of the National Ombudsman, the head of the Anti-Corruption Commission, the head of the National Audit Board, one justice of the Supreme Court nominated by the full bench of the court, and one justice of the Supreme Administrative Court nominated by the full bench of the court. Clearly, the courts and independent agencies monopolized the Senate Personnel Selection Committee. In reality, even independent agency representatives were largely from the judiciary. Since the role of ultimately voting to approve appointments to these bodies lay with the Senate itself, the selection process created close links between the Senate, the judiciary and independent agencies. Attention was given to the independent agency and court relationship in Chapter 6.

The task of the Personnel Selection Commission was to choose suitable senate appointments from recommendations made by the education sector, the state sector, the private sector and the professional and other sectors. When appointing senators, commission members were required to give consideration to the knowledge, specialties and experiences of a candidate that would be beneficial to senate business, to gender balance, to a balance of individuals from the various sectors of society and to providing opportunities for those in less privileged social positions. According to the organic law (that is, law derived from constitutional provisions) related to the selection of members for both the House of Representatives and Senate, organizations that were able to nominate candidates were legal corporate entities established for three years or more in Thailand, and organizations that did not operate either for profit or political purposes. These organizations were required to register, providing evidence that they fell into one of the two categories given, in accordance with regulations and in a method determined by the Election Commission. When registering, an organization was required to lodge the following documents: a copy of the certificate of proof of being a corporate entity; a copy of a statement confirming the organization's objectives and rules or regulations; a copy of proof of the organization operating for three continuous years to the day of the recommended appointment; a copy of a certificate of residence, citizen identification, or identification papers issued by either a public or national organization verifying the individual representing the organization or their delegate; and documentation authorizing the individual concerned to represent the organization.[10]

The procedures outlined above appeared to provide an opportunity for the inclusive representation of a wide range of groups and organizations. Because it was necessary for recommendations from public interest groups, however, and because various restrictions operated on organizations that were able to register, there was an in-built tendency for those recommended to have social status and positions of prestige. We might ask whether or not, as with the election system, the types of people appointed to the Senate were in fact the former civil servants and people with connections to public officials/workers who might be expected to have a systemic advantage. We might also consider the political significance of the appointments made.

An analysis of senate election and appointment outcomes

This section will scrutinize the backgrounds of elected and appointed Senate members with a view to determining differences between

---

10 The relationship between a candidate and recommending body did not need to be close. For example, Senator Ruangrai, who was selected as an appointed member in 2008, had been a civil servant with the Board of Audit and originally sought nomination by the Certified Public Accountant group. When this did not eventuate, he ran with the backing of Centurion Park Condominium Residents Group and was appointed on behalf of the private sector.

these groups. This should provide insights into the political intent behind the introduction in the 2007 Constitution of a system of partial senate appointments.

2008: popularly elected members

Candidates

Across Thailand, 505 candidates ran for the seventy-six designated Senate seats contested in the 2008 election.[11] This is an average of 6.6 candidate nominations per seat. In the House of Representatives elections conducted the previous year, the average number of candidates per party list seat had been 15.7, with 9.7 for individual candidate seats. These figures confirm a range of systemic barriers operating against candidate participation in Senate elections. Moreover, while there were thirty-five candidates in Bangkok, nineteen provinces had a mere four candidates, eight had only three and five had only two, while in one province there was only a single candidate. This can perhaps be explained by the fact that many more living in metropolitan areas fulfilled the election eligibility criteria. Voters have also reacted sensitively to the undemocratic reform of the senatorial election system, and voter turnout dropped from about 71.8% in the 2000 Senate election to 55.6% in the 2008 Senate election.

According to Election Commission data, the largest occupation group among those running for election was the approximately 31% who were current or former civil servants. Following this was the 26.7% who were self-employed or operating their own business, while the third largest group was legal professionals at 18%. Only 1.9% of candidates were politicians. In terms of educational qualifications, 61.9% held the bachelor's degrees required by the constitution as the minimum level for candidature and 35% held master's degrees, with 2.9% holding doctorates. These figures demonstrate that, significantly, almost 38% held a master's degree or above.

---

11 Thirty-three candidates were disqualified, making the final number 472.

Table 7.1 Occupational classification of candidates and elected senators in the 2008 upper house election

Candidates		Elected Members	
Former civil servants	31.09%	Former civil servants	38.15%
Independent businesspeople and commercial operators	26.73%	Independent businesspeople and commercial operators	36.84%
Lawyers and jurists	18.02%	Lawyers and jurists	2.63%
Employed people	6.73%	Employed people	3.95%
Scholars, teachers and academics	5.35%	Scholars, teachers and academics	5.26%
Agriculture	1.98%	Agriculture	2.63%
Others	10.1%	Others	10.54%
Total	100.00%		100.00%

Source: Compiled by the author from Election Commission records.

Members elected to the Senate

In terms of those elected in 2008, Election Commission data indicate that 38.1% were current or former civil servants, 36.8% were self-employed or operating their own business, 5.2% had academic or teaching backgrounds and a mere 1.3% were politicians. A significant majority, in other words, were current or former civil servants and self-employed or operating their own business. Since Election Commission occupation statistics regarding members elected during the 2000 Senate election indicate that 36.5% were civil servants, 12.5% were lawyers or jurists, 17.5% were self-employed businesspeople and 3% were politicians, it is evident that, while there was almost no change in civil servant representation percentages between the two elections, there was a huge rise in self-employed businesspeople and a concomitant drop in those with legal backgrounds. This data, however, provides limited information on those elected. To gain a more complete picture we must examine the schedule of individual senators compiled by the Election Commission.

The above analysis of individual senator records indicates that thirty-four individuals, or 44.7% of all elected members, had civil service experience. This was the largest group in available Election Commission data. There is a strong probability, however, that the figure is in reality even higher. For example, a senator from Nakhon Sawan Province described his occupation as self-employed before becoming a member, but his career shows that he worked as a teacher (public servant) for thirteen years. Although many elected senators did not provide a detailed work history, it is reasonable to speculate that some were employed as civil servants in the past. Furthermore, within the categories of civil service experience, six were from the Ministry of the Interior, two had army backgrounds, seven were from the police, eight had been teachers, two were medical doctors and nine came from other fields. Since each constituency encompassed a single province, there were limits to the area that could realistically be covered when campaigning. As a result, there was a strong advantage to candidates who had previously been provincial governors, district heads, or Ministry of Interior bureaucrats whose networks included well-known figures who had perhaps been a provincial governor. Teachers and police were also advantaged by the strong regional connections created through their work. Furthermore, of ten senators who reported their occupation as independent businessperson, eight had experience as mayor, constituency head, village head, senator, member of the House of Representatives, member of a provincial self-governing assembly or a similar position. Six of the eleven who reported being in business were former senators.[12] Only two individuals, one a former mayor and one a former provincial assembly member, unequivocally recorded their occupation as a politician. Interestingly, the latter was a senator from Yasothon Province, who was a member of the People's Assembly (*samatcha haeng chat khong prathet thai*) set up in 2006 by leaders of the coup d'état to choose the drafters of the 2007 Constitution. He was the sole popularly elected senator listed in Election Commission records with this background.

This analysis of the 2008 popular Senate election outcomes confirms that there was no huge change to the previous trend of individuals with civil service backgrounds occupying the majority of elected Senate seats.

---

12 The 2007 Constitution stipulated that those elected as senators in the 2006 election could run once more in the election that followed.

2008: appointed members

When determining the types of individuals appointed in 2008 to Senate seats, we might consider whether there were similarities between this group and those elected. We will therefore draw on Election Commission data to examine the occupational background of those appointed and whether or not there was, as with elected members, a majority of individuals with civil service experience.

Nominees

Seventy-four Senate seats were reserved in 2008 for appointed members. A total of 1,087 individuals were nominated across the academic sector, the state sector, the private sector, the specialist professional sector and the sector comprising 'others'. Given the various institutional restrictions impinging on the recommendation process, this very competitive rate of 14.6 nominees for a single seat is exceptionally high. The greatest number of recommendations came from the private sector at 447, while 'others' followed with 253. The state sector recommended the least, with 114.

Election Commission occupation data indicates that the largest percentage group among those recommended was current and former civil servants at 34.3%. This was followed by self-employed businesspeople and those with commercial operations at 22.1%, academics at 9.6%, and lawyers and the judiciary at 7.1%. In terms of educational qualifications, while 0.09% had not completed undergraduate studies, 36% held a bachelor's degree, 48.5% held a master's degrees and 15.2% held doctorates. These percentage figures are considerably higher than for the same attribute among candidates for popular election to the Senate.

Appointed members

In terms of the occupational categories of appointed members, 41.8% were current or former civil servants, 17.5% were independent businesspeople or individuals conducting commercial operations, and 10.8% were academics or teachers. We might note that the percentage with civil service experience is higher than among appointed Senate members, while there is also a larger cohort of those with academic

Table 7.2 Occupational breakdown of 2008 upper house nominees for Senate appointment and for appointed Senate members

Nominees/Recommendees		Appointed Members	
Former civil servants	34.32%	Former civil servants	41.89%
Independent businesspeople and commercial operators	22.17%	Independent businesspeople and commercial operators	17.57%
Scholars, teachers and academics	9.66%	Scholars, teachers and academics	10.81%
Lawyers	7.18%	Lawyers	4.05%
Employed people	5.98%	Employed people	1.35%
Private sector managers and workers	5.24%	Private sector managers and workers	4.05%
Specialist professionals	4.32%	Specialist professionals	6.76%
Consultants	3.22%	Consultants	6.76%
Medical doctors	1.75%	Medical doctors	4.05%
Other	6.16%	Other	2.71%
Total	100.00%		100.00%

Source: Compiled by the author from Election Commission documents.

or teaching experience. The categorization of senators into the five occupational sectors designated above was explained to reflect voices from diverse groups in society. Nevertheless, in addition to this resulting in no change to the numerical dominance of those with civil service experience, representation from the agricultural sector – the majority group in Thai society – was a mere 2.7%. With 32.4% holding bachelor's degrees, 52.7% with master's degrees and 14.8% with doctorates, there is no doubt that the Thai Senate, especially appointed members, was drawn from the cream of the country's educated elite.[13]

Although the percentage of those with civil service experience among appointed members is slightly higher, we cannot claim that there is any decisive difference between elected and appointed members in terms of this occupational category. When seeking to understand why the appointment system was introduced in the face of wide criticism, it is insufficient merely to claim that the objective was to send many senators with civil service backgrounds. Greater clarity might be gained by examining the detailed individual records of those involved.

---

13 One justification for the introduction of appointed seats to the Senate was to permit the selection of members from a range of occupations. It was asserted that such people would not have a chance to become senators in a system of popular election only (Manit 2008: 21).

Between 2008 and 2011, seventy-six members were appointed to the Senate. The occupation sector breakdown of these as listed in their individual records is as follows.

- Academic sector (fourteen in total): seven with civil service experience (four scholars, three others), two politicians, one architect, two university scholars, one teacher, one businessperson.

- State sector (fifteen in total): thirteen former civil servants (three Ministry of the Interior, two army, one navy, one airforce, two police service, four other), one politician, one businessperson.

- Specialist professional sector (fourteen in total): five former civil servants (one navy, one air-force, one police service, one scholar, one other), two scholars, two company employees, one politician, one engineer, one agricultural worker, one businessperson, one mass media.

- Private sector (fourteen in total): six businesspersons, three politicians, two former civil servants (one army, one Board of Audit), two lawyers, one Election Commission member.

- Other sectors (nineteen in total): eight former civil servants (two army, one air-force, two police service, one judge, one scholar, one other), one politician, one teacher (private), one scholar, one dentist, two lawyers, one businessperson, one self-employed businessperson, one constituency head (*kamnan*), one National Socio-Economic Advisory Council member, one educational provider.

The thirty-five former civil servants total given above comprised 46% or close to half of the total number of all appointed member seats. Former civil servants were appointed from all sectors, with a total of 13% having previous military service. This was in contrast to the elected member group in which there were many members with a background of Ministry of the Interior or police. Interestingly, even among appointments from the private sector, which generally invokes a business image, there was an individual from the army. Close examination of the background of Senator Phumisak, who recorded his occupation as 'business' and was appointed on behalf of the private sector, reveals that he, too, formerly held an army post. Obviously, only examining occupational background fails to reveal the true picture of previous senatorial work experience. We still need to turn to individual records to discover the actual facts.

Close scrutiny of the backgrounds of appointed members reveals certain commonalities that cut across the sectors and the occupation categories. Firstly, many appointed members were associated with either the National Legislative Assembly (*sapha nitipanyat haeng chat*),[14] formed by the leaders of the 2006 coup d'état, the People's Assembly or the Constitution Drafting Assembly (*sapha rang ratthathamnanun*), given the task of drafting the 2007 Constitution.[15] Aggregating information recorded in individual member records reveals that a total of twelve previous members of the National Legislative Assembly were spread across all five occupation sectors – two from the academic sector, two from the state sector, four from the specialist professionals sector, one from the private sector and three from the other sectors. These encompassed a broad range of occupations that included one lawyer, one politician, one engineer, one education sector worker, five former civil servants, one scholar, one teacher in the private sector and one mass media worker. Four had been members of the People's Assembly, one was an academic, one was a specialist professional, and two were from the private sector. Six in total had participated in the drafting of the 2007 (2550) Constitution with one from the state sector,

---

14 The National Legislative Assembly was established in 2006 in accordance with the 2006 Interim Constitution. It was comprised of up to 250 members appointed by the king and was stipulated to function as an upper and lower house and parliament.

15 The 2007 Constitution Drafting Assembly was formed from 100 members appointed by the king in order to draft the constitution. The National Security Council chose these from candidates voted for by the People's Assembly.

one specialist professional, and four from the private sector. Adjusting the total for two who had, in fact, been members of both the People's Assembly and 2007 Constitution Drafting Assembly, there was a total of twenty individuals involved in these entities.

The second point to make is that many appointed members had committee, sub-committee or consultancy experience with an independent agency. There was one Board of Audit consultant, one National Counter-Corruption Commission consultant and one sub-committee member, one Election Commission member and one consultant, two members of the Provincial Election Commission, one member from the Office of the Ombudsman, five members of the National Socio-Economic Advisory Committee, and one consultant judge from the Constitutional Court, comprising fourteen in total. A sector breakdown indicates that three were from the state sector, two were specialist professionals, four were from the private sector and five from the 'other' sector.

The third point involves the inclusion of members with experience of participating in law-making at some level. Individual record information confirmed that one appointed member worked for twelve years as a member of the Council of State (*samnakgan khanakammakan krisdika*) that oversaw law-making matters, while seven had participated in researching and drafting various laws related to labor and the environment. Apart from these, in addition to being a former judge of the Appellant Court, Senator Prasopsuk, who was selected as the head of the Senate,[16] had worked with the Council of State and was a legal specialist who had been connected to the judiciary and legislative fields for more than thirty years (*The Nation*, 15 March 2008).

Different individuals entered information into their personal records in different ways. Some provided itemized details while others

---

16 Some had argued that the speaker of the Senate should be a member chosen by popular election rather than appointment (*The Nation*, 2 March 2011). Ultimately, an appointed member emerged as Senate speaker. Manit (2008: 241) argued that there were more popularly elected than appointed senators, so the 2007 Constitution emphasized their importance. Given that the Senate speaker was an appointed member, however, it is difficult to say that due recognition was given to members who became senators by popular election.

gave nothing much at all. The figures above are therefore likely to refer to the least number of individuals concerned. In any event, Senate members first appointed under the 2007 Constitution fell generally into three categories: 1. those with close connections to coup leaders, 2. those who contributed to drafting the 2007 Constitution, and 3. the considerable number with specialty legal backgrounds regardless of stated occupation.

2011: appointed members

In 2011, a second round of Senate appointments was conducted. While Section 297 of the 2007 Constitution firstly determined the term of Senate office be three years, as this term came to an end it was decided a two-consecutive-term limit would not apply to those selected in the first appointment term. In other words, those who were also given a seat in the first round of the 2007 Constitution appointments could, in fact, hold a seat for a period of nine years. On this occasion, seventy-three seats were available for appointment.[17] Of these, approximately one third were reappointments from 2008. Scrutiny of occupations by sector reveals the following.

- Academic sector (fourteen in total): six former civil servants (four scholars, one medical doctor, one air-force personnel), three politicians, two businesspersons, one lawyer, one architect, one employed person.

- State sector (fourteen in total): thirteen former civil servants (four Ministry of Interior personnel, four army personnel, one air-force personnel, one scholar, two others), one businessperson.

- Specialist professional sector (fourteen in total): eight former civil servants (two police officers, two navy personnel, one air-force personnel, two scholars, one teacher), two business-

---

17 The number of appointed members fell by one seat when the number of provinces increased from 76 to 77 in March 2011.

people, one politican, one scholar, one lawyer, one mass media personnel.

- Private sector (sixteen in total): seven businesspeople, four politicians, one former civil servant (police officer), two lawyers, one employed person, one self-employed professional.

- Other sectors (fifteen in total): six former civil servants (three police officers, two army personnel, one other), four businesspeople, two lawyers, one politician, one scholar, one not specified.

The overall percentage of former public servants in the above is 44.7%.

Concerning relationships with the coup leaders, two academics, one from the state sector, three specialist professionals, and two from 'other', eight in all, were members of the National Legislative Assembly, while one from the private sector was a member of the People's Assembly. Two were on the Constitution Drafting Assembly, one of whom was also a People's Assembly member. This made ten in total. Nine appointed members had connections to independent agencies – one as an Election Commission consultant, three as provincial Election Commission members, two with the Office of the Ombudsman and three with the National Socio-Economic Advisory Committee. Considered on a sector basis, two were from the academic sector, one was from the state sector, one from the private sector and five from 'other'. It is furthermore useful to be aware that two had experience with the Department of Special Investigation (DSI), the body with carriage of regulating/investigating corruption by politicians. There were also four individuals with law-making experience – one from academia, one specialist professional, one from the private sector and one from 'other'.

We might note also that Senator Somchet, a former member of the army selected on behalf of the state sector, was the director-general of the National Security Council (*khana montri khwammankhong haeng chat*) formed by the leaders of the coup, while Senator Boonchai, appointed on behalf of the private sector, also had close connections to that council. Senator Sak, a lawyer appointed as a specialist professional representative, had been a member of the Assets Examination Committee (*khana kammakan truatsop kankratham thi ko hai koet khwamsiahai kae rat*) that inquired into allegations of corruption against the Thaksin administration (*The Nation*, 13 April 2011). Like the 2008 appointees, those appointed to 2011 Senate seats had close associations with coup d'état leaders.

To consider the impact on the roles of senators of the appointment patterns outlined above, we will firstly examine changes to the Senate's powers that followed the promulgation of the 2007 Constitution.

Changes to Senate powers

Since the 1997 Constitution, the Senate in Thailand has been given a series of new roles. Importantly, this constitution expanded matters stipulated as Senate powers in the 1991 Constitution – such as deliberating on proposed laws, deliberating on budget proposals, overseeing the constitutionality of cabinet declarations of emergency, and calling upon the cabinet for general debate – to selecting members for the Constitutional Court and Election Commission and determining the dismissal from office of political officials and workers. In understanding the nature of the changes that occurred in the 2007 Constitution, we might recall that the chapter introduction touched upon suspicions that political influence operated on the Senate following the promulgation of the 1997 Constitution, with particular concern about the neutrality of personnel selected for independent agencies (*The Nation*, 24 March 2008). The provisions of the 2007 Constitution removed the actual selection of independent agencies from the Senate itself, largely consigning the process to court justices and independent agency heads. The role of the Senate was confined to final approval of appointments only. This may explain why some scholars argue that the 2007 Constitution slightly curtailed Senate powers (Harding and Leyland 2011). Since, however, approving independent agency appointments is merely one of various Senate responsibilities, we might examine the powers held by Thailand's upper house prior to the 1997 Constitution.

Joint session of both houses

In terms of the various tasks of the parliament, such as deliberating on laws and the budget, the House of Representatives has theoretical precedence over the Senate. When measuring the degree of influence held by the Senate, therefore, we need to consider its relationship to the lower house. Below we will examine the processes that unfold during joint sessions of the parliament when both the House of Representatives and Senate come together to deliberate.

Joint sessions under the 2007 Constitution

Section 136 of the 2007 Constitution stipulated sixteen points in relation to joint sessions as follows: 1. approving the appointment of a regent as per Section 19; 2. accepting the oath of the regent before the parliament as per Section 21; 3. accepting amendments to the Palace Succession Law BE 2467 as per Section 22; 4. accepting and acknowledging the Palace Succession Law BE 2467 as per Section 23; 5. the passing of a resolution for consideration by the parliament of other matters during a legislative ordinary session under section 127; 6. the approval of the prorogation of a session under section 127; 7. proroguing the parliament as per Section 128; 8. enacting the rules of procedure of the parliament as per Section 137; 9. approving deliberations on either organic or general laws as per Section 145; 10. consulting on organic laws or new laws as per Article 151; 11. approving deliberations on constitutional amendments, or organic and general laws as per Section 153, Paragraph 2; 12. administrative policy speech as per Section 176; 13. general debate as per Section 179; 14. approval of a declaration of war as per Section 189; 15. consideration and approval of treaties as per Section 190; and 16. constitutional amendments as per Section 291.

Four of these sixteen matters pertained to the throne, while four concerned the constitution. Points pertaining to the constitution increased from the time of the 1997 Constitution. It was in this document that laws concerning essential elements of the constitution were designated as organic laws. From there was an increase in the number of sessions of both chambers of the parliament related to those laws. As discussed in the previous section, those appointed to Senate positions were characterized by their relationships with coup d'état leaders, their involvement in drafting the 2007 Constitution and their prior law-making experience. If new missions were to be assigned to the Senate, any hint as to what these might have been perhaps lay in those points. To determine if this is the case, the next section examines the particular stipulations relating to the Senate's role in legislating organic laws, that is, laws relating to matters prescribed in the constitution, and to constitutional revisions or amendments.

Procedures for enactment of organic laws

The organic laws stipulated in points nine, ten and eleven relating to joint sessions listed above fall into nine varieties: 1. House of Representatives elections, and Senate elections and appointments; 2. the Election Commission; 3. political parties; 4. national referenda; 5. trial proceedings for the Constitutional Court; 6. trial proceedings in criminal lawsuits against persons holding political positions; 7. the National Ombudsman; 8. counter corruption; and 9. the state audit. These organic laws related to elections, political parties and the country's principal independent agencies. All were determined as essential to the administration of the state and might be regarded as deriving from the fundamental elements of the 2007 Constitution.

Entities determined by the 2007 Constitution as able to submit bills of organic laws were the cabinet, one tenth of current members of the House of Representatives or one tenth of the combined membership of the Senate and the House of Representatives, and the Constitutional Court, the Supreme Court, or independent bodies based on the constitution, under the jurisdiction of the president of the court and the head of an independent body under the organic laws. Clearly, regardless of the gravity of the laws involved, there was a wide range of entities able to submit such bills of legislation.

When we examine these stipulations in detail, however, problems arise in terms of democratic process. Firstly, almost half of the members of the Senate are appointed and thus not chosen by the will of the people. Given that the seventy-four appointed Senate members monopolized 15.5% of the seats in a joint sitting, they could easily command the 'one-tenth' of the combined membership of the Senate and House of Representatives needed to table an organic law.

As noted, furthermore, many of these appointed individuals had close ties to the military. A further concern for democracy was the fact that the courts represent the judicial power in the three elements of state power. This conventionally involves reviewing materials enacted by the legislative body. It was therefore surely a problem in terms of the separation of powers that the Constitutional Court, which should review enacted laws, was itself submitting laws. Neither were independent agency members chosen by a democratic people's vote. Not only did the courts have a strong influence on that selection process, the powers bestowed upon independent agencies resulted in them, in fact, having very close ties to the judiciary. In other words, especially when considered – as noted – from the perspective of the separation of powers, the stipulations regarding the entities with authority to submit organic laws appear highly irregular. Previously, the 1997 Constitution stipulated that only members of the House of Representatives or the cabinet could table both laws or organic laws, while even the 1991 Constitution, which determined all senators as government appointments, stipulated that a law could only be tabled by members of the House of Representatives or the cabinet. The only one among the three most recent constitutions that permitted law-making by an agency not selected by popular vote was the 2007 document.

In addition to the matters discussed above, the 2007 Constitution featured a significant change in the deliberative process of an organic law. The House of Representatives and the Senate conducted these deliberations across three stages as follows: stage one, giving in principle approval; stage two, deliberating further and voting on individual sections; stage three, involving the final vote. In order for an organic law to pass the final vote and be implemented, a joint sitting majority was insufficient. It was, in fact, necessary to have more than half the vote of current sitting members in each house. In contrast to the 1997 Constitution, which made no distinction between the deliberations of general or organic laws, the 2007 Constitution separated these and provided extremely detailed stipulations, as outlined above, regarding organic laws. However, since it is stipulated that the provisions concerning the enactment of bills shall apply mutatis mutandis to the deliberation process, if the Senate does not agree with the house, the bill will be put on hold and sent back to the house. After 180 days have passed, the bill can be debated again in the House of Representatives, and it must be approved by more than half of the total number of members of the House of Representatives.

A further element then came into play. The 2007 Constitution stipulated that, following a parliamentary vote of approval, a law should be forwarded to the Constitutional Court prior to being sent to the palace for ratification by the king. If the Constitutional Court, the role of which was to deliberate on the constitutionalism of the document, determined that the law or a specific section infringed the constitution, the offending element was excised. If the excised section was considered essential to implementation, the organic law in question was cancelled in full.

When the partial wording of a section was excised by a ruling of the Constitutional Court, the document returned to both the House of Representatives and the Senate, and the deliberation process began anew. Any revisions by either the upper or lower house needed to be approved by a majority vote of current members of both the Senate and House of Representatives. Unlike the 1997 Constitution, the 2007 Constitution significantly required a senate majority for an organic law to be accepted.

It is also stipulated that, before the prime minister presents a bill for the king's assent, a member of the House of Representatives, the Senate, or members of both houses, representing at least one-tenth of the total number of existing members of both houses, may submit an opinion to the effect that the constitutionality of the bill is questionable to the speaker of each house or the speaker of the parliament and the speaker will send the matter to the Constitutional Court for ruling. Since, as noted above, appointed members of the Senate constituted 15.4% of joint-sitting seats, with the relatively low level of one-tenth of members required to proceed with such a move, this group was a significant block operating on the passage of both organic and general laws. There is also a way of valuing the change in the system of those who have the right to submit bills and bills of organic law positively as promotion of legislative and judicial control of the legislative process (Imaizumi 2012). However, in the case of the 2007 constitution, considering that the appearance of appointed lawmakers under the influence of the coup d'état group was set, the political nature of the system change should be questioned.

Constitutional amendments

Wide-scale changes regarding constitutional revisions or amendments were introduced into the 1997 Constitution. The 1991 Constitution allowed for either the cabinet, or one-third the total number of current members of the House of Representatives, or one-third the current members of both the upper and lower houses, to propose a motion for constitutional revision or reform. Members of the House of Representatives were allowed to submit motions and participate in motions if the political party to which they belonged passed a resolution. In both the 1997 and 2007 constitutions the previous 'one-third' fell to 'one-fifth', while the 2007 Constitution released individual House of Representatives members from adhering to a party line. The 2007 document also made it possible for a petition signed by more than 50,000 voters to propose a constitutional amendment.

From the time of the implementation of the 1997 Constitution, changes such as those outlined above have been largely explained as lowering the bar and thus facilitating constitutional revision. This certainly seems to be the case from bare statistics alone. Such an approach, however, overlooks a key factor, namely, the ratio of Senate seats to those of the House of Representatives. We have seen how the percentage of seats occupied by Senate members in the parliament gradually reduced from 42.8% in 1991, through 28.5% in 1997, to 23.8% in 2007. As Thailand embraced democratization, this decrease was probably predictable. Nevertheless, upper house influence could be retained by proposing simultaneous reforms involving a parallel reduction in the number of members required to support the deliberation of a law. With 1991 constitutional provisions giving the Senate 48.2% of parliament seats, one-third of all current members needed to vote in favor for a law to pass a joint sitting. Although in the 1997 document, the senate seat percentage was reduced to 28.5%, the fraction of members required for a successful vote was reduced at the same time to a mere one-fifth. And while the senate member percentage fell even further in 2007, the release of House of Representatives members from voting along party lines made it easier for individual members to come together in independent blocks. However, unlike the deliberation process of bills of organic law, the House of Representatives still has the upper hand in the process of constitutional amendment. This is because a constitutional amendment can be approved by a majority vote of the total number of existing members of both houses. While this suggests House of Representatives ascendency, it would be a mistake to regard this as heralding an end to Senate influence in that process.

As for the amendment of the constitution, the 1997 Constitution initiated a series of major changes. This is evident in wording from the 1997 Constitution, carried over to 2007, disallowing any constitutional amendment 'which has the effect of changing the democratic regime of government with the king as head of state or changing the form of [the] state'. Since it was unclear precisely what was meant by 'the democratic regime of government with the king as head of state' or changing 'the form of [the] state', interpreting this very abstract stipulation became the task of the Constitutional Court. The ambiguity of the passage was compounded by the fact that there was no clear stipulation determining the individual or entity that might lodge a case claiming that an infringement had occurred. Although it was obvious that the court itself could not raise such a matter, there was no clarity concerning who actually could. Furthermore, there was a second element that complemented this extremely ambiguous stipulation. This was the stipulation, given in both Section 63 of the 1997 Constitution and Section 68 of the 2007 Constitution, that the Constitutional Court could intervene when control of the state was gained through a means determined as intended to overthrow Thailand's democratic regime of government with the king as head of state. When conducting such an intervention, the Constitutional Court could not only rule against an individual or their political party and thereby halt such a process, it could furthermore dissolve the party involved. In other words, it became possible – depending on the position adopted by the Constitutional Court – for a political party to face dissolution after tabling a motion for constitutional revision. It is thus no exaggeration to say that constitutional revision could only proceed with the approval of the Constitutional Court. The body with carriage of the crucial matter of approving judicial appointments to the Constitutional Court was the Senate. Clearly, the sequence of constitutional revisions that led to this situation also undermined the legislative power.

We can conclude from the above that the 2007 Constitution handed the Senate the new role of 'guardian of the constitution'. This role was set in motion through the introduction of a system of partial senate appointment. It became the role of appointed members to 'guard' the constitution and thereby ensure that there be no destabilization of the intentions of the 2006 coup d'état leaders who were, in fact, the real drafters of the 2007 document. Thus, while senate powers may superficially have been curtailed, by now approving Constitutional Court appointments and also appointments to independent agencies, the Senate developed close relationships with these bodies which, in turn, strengthened its role all the more.

Conflict around constitutional amendments

To understand why the Thai Senate assumed the role of 'guardian of the constitution', we might examine the enactment processes of the 2007 Constitution and associated organic laws. Both came into being without review by the popularly elected lower house. Coup d'état leaders effectively enacted the 2007 Constitution to ensure the constitutionality of the coup. Once the Thaksin faction was returned to power at the December 2007 elections, therefore, conflict over constitutional revisions was soon evident between appointed senators and the pro-Thaksin government.

Enactment of the 2007 Constitution

The 2007 Constitution was drafted by a Constitution Drafting Assembly and Constitution Drafting Committee that was selected by members of the People's Assembly. The People's Assembly was appointed by the National Security Council formed by the leaders of the coup d'état

(Endō 2008). In the effective absence of a parliament – in the sense of a popularly elected body – the new constitution was put to a referendum for the first time in Thai history. Given that voter turnout for the poll was a mere 57.6%, 56.6% of whom agreed while 41.3% opposed and 1.9% voted informal, it is difficult to claim that the document had popular support. In fact, strong opposition arose because of the close relationship between the coup leaders and various members of the Constitution Drafting Assembly and Constitution Drafting Committee (*The Nation*, 17 August 2007). Moreover, since the referendum was conducted with a sense of urgency to have the constitution ratified, there was never any in-depth discussion or serious debate of the content (Worachet 2009: 156–158). As a result, the referendum failed to legitimate the new constitution in any democratic sense.[18] The Constitution Drafting Committee also had carriage of three organic laws relating to elections, political parties and the Election Commission. Although a detailed investigation of these laws was carried out by a thirty-three-person committee, membership of this committee included ten from the National Legislative Assembly, twelve appointed through that assembly, and the remainder from the Constitution Drafting Committee (*The Nation*, 23 August 2007). The organic laws were then hastily approved by the National Legislative Assembly and brought into force in October 2007.

These efforts to retain a coup-friendly constitution made moves for constitutional reform a certainty once a government that reflected the

---

18 Although coup leaders claimed that being subject to the decision of a referendum made the 2007 Constitution the first in Thai history to have democratic legitimacy, many perceived problems in the conduct of the vote. For example, in order to legitimate their own actions that had purged the country of a popularly elected government, coup leaders mobilized constituency leaders (*kamnan*), village leaders, teacher groups, regional division military leaders and even the National Internal Security Operations Command (Chairat 2009: 66). Furthermore, had the draft 2007 Constitution been rejected at the referendum, it had been decided that the National Security Council would choose one of the documents from the past and, after revisions, present this to the king (Harding and Leyland 2011: 24). However, there was to be no option for the people to choose. It has been suggested that, rather than expressing the coup leaders' anti-Thaksin position, many people ultimately voted for the constitution in order to ensure a swift return to parliamentary democracy (Suchit 2009: 90).

will of the people was returned to office in the 23 December election. Several key sections of the 2007 Constitution articulated the viewpoint of the coup leaders, most importantly Section 209 which confirmed the constitutionality of the coup. Had this section been removed, it would have been possible to have declared null and void the purging of the previous political administration that had occurred through various court rulings following the 2006 coup, and a range of system changes that even included the constitution itself. Other sections that coup leaders regarded as non-negotiable were 68 and 237, which determined the dissolution of political parties, and any section that strengthened the power of independent agencies and heightened the powers of the judiciary. Defending the constitution at all costs was an absolute coup leader priority. It was in this context that the role of constitutional defenders or guardians fell to members of the Senate, particularly those whose seats had been bestowed by appointment.

The Senate vs the People's Power Party government (2008)

The advent of the Samak administration following the December 2007 election confirmed the Thaksin faction's ongoing power. In his administrative policy speech, delivered immediately after his appointment, Prime Minister Samak declared a review of the constitution a necessity,[19] and by late March 2008 had set the wheels of constitutional revision in motion. Not surprisingly, the sections targeted were 237 and 309 (*The Nation*, 26 March 2008). Senate members who had been appointed to their seats in March 2008 quickly raised their voices in opposition. In a counterattack on the Samak administration that profiled his own 'vocation' as a loyal upper house member, Senate Leader Prasopsook declared, 'Fragmentary constitutional reform will damage rather than benefit the political system' (*The Nation*, 27 March

---

19 Prime Minister Samak gave clear notice that he intended to implement a constitutional review by stating in his speech as follows: 'Although the current constitution is the first to be recognized by a referendum, it has become clear that there are many differences of opinion with respect to the document. In order to undertake revisions that ensure true alignment with democratic principles, the government will progress a re-evaluation of the constitution'.

2008). Within six months, a ruling of the Constitutional Court led to the fall of the Samak administration, while the prime minister himself was disqualified from holding office. According to the court, Samak had violated the constitution with a conflict of interest by acting as host of a television program. The complainants in the case were the Election Commission and thirty Senate members (Constitutional Court ruling 12-13/2551). In December the same year, on the grounds of election irregularities by Deputy Leader Yongyoot, Samak's People's Power Party was dissolved according to sections 68 and 237 of the Constitution (Constitutional Court ruling 20/2551).

The Senate vs the Pheu Thai Party (2012)

In July 2011, the Yingluck administration (the Pheu Thai Party government), which was the government of the Thaksin factional line again, was established. From there, the battle over the revision of the constitution resumed. Concrete movements began in February 2012, and in order to establish a constitution drafting committee, discussions began at a joint session of both houses of parliament to revise Article 291 of the 2007 Constitution. Opposition, however, was immediately voiced by members of the 2007 Constitution Drafting Assembly and appointed members of the Senate. Senate appointee, Surachai, and others held a press conference to declare their conviction that any revision of Section 291 would be in violation of the Constitution and that a new constitution could present a threat to the power of the king. Senator Surachai also declared that members of a parliament usually do not draft constitutions because they would have a 'conflict of interest' (*The Nation*, 5 March 2012).

At the end of February, following debate during a joint sitting, the proposed revisions passed the first stage of deliberations with more than 60% of the vote that included support from some opposition and also some Senate members. Although appointed senators cast opposing votes, the resolution received the support of a majority of the current total members of both houses. It was therefore impossible, in pure numerical terms, to prevent the revision proceeding. The second stage of deliberations concluded at the end of April. With deliberations entering the third stage, however, forty senators petitioned the Constitutional Court. The court thereupon ordered a temporary stay in order to examine the constitutionality of the revisions proposed. Regarding this matter, the Constitutional Court was criticized for violating the legislative power, so it had to explain the situation at a press conference (*The Nation*, 6 June 2012). In a 13 July ruling, the court determined that, because the content of the revision was imprecise, there was no violation of the constitution (Constitutional Court ruling 18-22/2555). Rather than the ruling itself, however, the critical aspect of this case was the precedent set for citizens to appeal directly to the Constitutional Court – without the mediation of a body such as a prosecution office – to question the constitutionality of proposed constitutional revisions. In this case, in fact, the prosecutor had been opposed to the indictment going ahead (*The Nation*, 8 June 2021). It was for this precise reason that the appointed senator petitioned the court directly. As noted above, the wording of the relevant section was completely opaque regarding just who could petition the Constitutional Court to prevent constitutional revisions. This case, however, set a critical precedent by giving senators appointed to the upper house, with the support of the Constitutional Court, a future pathway to prevent the implementation of important constitutional revisions.

The Constitutional Court and the 2014 coup d'état[20]

With the ruling of the Constitutional Court putting arguments around revisions to the 2007 Constitution on hold, the Yingluck administration set out to implement an amnesty law, known as the 'People's Reconciliation Law'. The government originally proposed this law to offer an amnesty to all citizen participants in the demonstrations that broke out following the 2006 coup and thereby mitigate the political ruptures that had been present since that time in Thailand. During the second reading, however, the bill was amended to give amnesty also to

---

20 The following is a revision with additions of an article published by the author in the academic journal *Synodos*, entitled 'The Thai General Election and the Constitutional Court: What is Currently Happening in Thailand?' (30 January 2014). Available at: http://synodos.jp/international/6865

those involved in riots that broke out in central Bangkok in 2010 leaving more than ninety people dead. When further amendments broadened the legislation still more to give amnesty even to figures such as former prime ministers Thaksin and Abhisit – many held the latter responsible for the violent suppression of the 2010 Red Shirt Movement in central Bangkok – there was huge opposition from the media, from sections of Thaksin's faction and also from anti-Thaksin groups. In spite of anti-Amnesty Law protests, the legislation was passed in the House of Representatives. The law nevertheless met its demise following the Senate voting it down on 11 November 2013.

Arrangements for revisions to the 2007 Constitution nonetheless proceeded. The two main focus points were: 1. reversing the 2007 Constitution stipulation that half the members of the Senate be appointed and half selected by popular vote to a system of popular vote for all Senate seats; and 2. revising the 2007 Constitution Section 190 provision that the parliament approve all agreements with foreign countries so that such ratification be required for certain agreements only. Once the Constitutional Court handed down a ruling on 20 November 2013 that the first proposal violated the constitution, with a similar ruling on the second given on 8 January 2014,[21] these revisions came to nothing. The appeal against each revision cited a violation of Section 68 of the 2007 Constitution as grounds for the case. In ruling that each revision violated Paragraph 1 of that section, the Constitutional Court determined that both proposals were attempts to restrain the governance power of the state through methods that were outside the provisions of the constitution. However, the appeal to dissolve the governing party and to strip its members of the board of the executive committee of the right of election was dismissed as not applying under the current circumstances (Constitutional Court ruling 15-18/2556; 1/2557).

---

21 Point one involved Wirat Kanyasiri, legal advisor to the opposition Democrat Party and also member of the House of Representatives making a case to indict the leader and deputy leader of the parliament and 381 members of the House of Representatives and Senate, while two involved appointed Senator Somchet and others, who even touched on Section 7, making a case also to indict the leader and deputy leader of the parliament, in addition to 312 members of the upper and lower houses.

Yet again, provisions designed to preserve the constitution were activated against the Thaksin faction, and the Constitutional Court handed down a ruling that this group was acting in violation of the constitution. Debate was also once more generated by the fact that a Constitutional Court ruling intervened in attempts at constitutional revision by an elected government and the parliament. Concerns were particularly expressed at the fact that the government and the parliament – the very bodies that ultimately represented the people – seemed to lack any power to amend the constitution. If this was the case, what did the 'Democratic regime of government with the king as head of state' refer to? Questions were furthermore asked about the validity and meaning of the 'guardians of the constitution' provisions that had been introduced in 1997 and then carried over and strengthened in 2007. Three days after the ruling of unconstitutionality relating to revisions to Senate appointments was handed down, the Nitirat group issued a statement at Thammasat University in Bangkok. Nitirat leader, Worachet Pakeerut, pointed out that the constitution made no reference to the Constitutional Court having the power to investigate either the proceedings or content of constitutional revision or amendment. It was Nitirat's opinion, he declared, that both rulings were unconstitutional. Worachet further questioned the court's broad interpretation of Section 68, arguing that this went against the democratic principle of 'checks and balances' and against the very principles upon which the structure of the state was based. Worachet further expressed concern that an expansion of the Constitutional Court's suite of powers would encourage the lodgment of appeals across an endless range of matters. Ultimately, he observed, it was possible that the democratic rule of law could collapse, and the Constitutional Court could come to hold absolute power.[22]

With the Yingluck administration forced to abandon any attempt to introduce an amnesty law or revise the constitution, an unstoppable anti-government momentum was gathering force. In late October 2013, this erupted into large scale anti-Yingluck demonstrations led by former Democrat Party secretary-general Suthep Thaugsuban. By

---

22 See *Prachatai*, 24 November 2012. Available at: https://prachatai.com/journal/2013/11/49942 (accessed 2 September 2018).

the end of November, demonstrators had occupied the offices of the Ministry for Finance and Ministry for Foreign Affairs. In an attempt to calm an increasingly out-of-control situation, Prime Minister Yingluck dissolved the House of Representatives on 9 December and announced an election. On 21 December, the Democrat Party, the largest party in the opposition block, gave notice that it would boycott the election. Demonstrators then began a series of tactics, such as sabotaging early voting, in order to prevent the 2 February 2014 general election from going ahead.

Amid these heightened tensions, control was eventually wrested by the Constitutional Court and independent agencies, including the Election Commission, the National Anti-Corruption Commission and the National Ombudsman. On 7 January 2014, the National Anti-Corruption Commission voted to investigate 308 members of parliament on the grounds of proposing and endorsing constitutional revisions related to senate selection methods. After large scale demonstrations blockaded parts of Bangkok on 13 January, a State of Emergency (proposed for sixty days) was declared on 22 January. Two days later, following an approach from the Election Commission, the Constitutional Court ruled in favor of postponing the day of the election. The ruling also required the prime minister to consult with the Election Commission to determine a new date in the event of the election being postponed.[23] While the government's consistent position was to hold the election on the day originally scheduled, on 27 January the Election Commission recommended an extension of five months. In other words, by opposing the 2 February 2014 date on which the Yingluck administration planned to conduct the general election, both the Constitutional Court and the Election Commission gave their support to demonstrators seeking to obstruct this event.

The general election went ahead according to plan on 2 February. Interference by anti-government protesters, however, meant that in many constituencies voting could not proceed. This was particularly the case in Democrat Party strongholds in the southern regions. The Democrat Party therefore appealed to the National Ombudsman

---

23 There was no legal provision requiring a prime minister to consult with the Election Commission in the event of an election date change.

to declare the election null and void. On 7 February, however, the National Ombudsman refused to accept the appeal. The Democrat Party then turned directly to the Constitutional Court, which also declared the appeal to be without basis. At this point, the situation changed. On 17 March, a university lecturer requested that the National Ombudsman accept their appeal that the February general election was invalid. Although a Democratic Party approach on the same matter had been rejected, this case was accepted. On 13 March, moreover, the Constitutional Court announced that it would accept appeals simultaneously lodged on the same matter by the Election Commission and the National Ombudsman. A mere one week later, on 21 March, the court ruled the 2 February general election invalid.

With uncertainty surrounding the date of any forthcoming repeat election, the National Anti-Corruption Commission initiated proceedings against Prime Minister Yingluck. The agency began to seek a resolution to dismiss the government in the Senate against corruption in the rice-pledging scheme, which was the centerpiece policy of the Yingluck administration. At the same time, a group of senators appealed to the Constitutional Court claiming interference by the Yingluck government in 2011 high level civil service personnel matters. With a 7 May court ruling of unconstitutionality regarding the latter charge, the prime minister and nine other cabinet members lost their positions. A clear alliance formed by the country's 'independent' agencies saw Prime Minister Yingluck's administration surrounded on all sides. When the Yingluck government fell, Deputy Prime Minister Niwatthamrong Boonsongpaisan became the caretaker prime minister. Now, however, the new problem arose of whether a provisional cabinet had the power to conduct general elections. From a legal standpoint there was no way forward. This political paralysis created by the rulings of the Constitutional Court and independent agencies was abruptly alleviated on 22 May when the military seized power by means of a coup d'état.

The sequence of events leading to the 2014 coup was very similar to those that preceeded the 2006 military takeover. Both occurred when the Constitutional Court ruled invalid the intentions of a popularly elected government that sought to deflect criticism of its

Table 7.3 Brief summary of political rulings since 2013

Year of Ruling	Case	Accused	Relevant Court or Agency	Relevant Sections	Ruling
2013	Ruling on revisions to 2007 Constitution 1 (Constitutional Court ruling 15-18/2556)	Speaker of the parliament, vice-speaker of the parliament, 312 members of the Senate and House of Representatives	Constitutional Court	Section 68	Guilty
2014	Ruling on revisions to 2007 Constitution 2 (Constitutional Court ruling 1/2557)	Speaker of the parliament, vice-speaker of the parliament, 381 members of the Senate and House of Representatives	Constitutional Court	Section 68	Guilty
2014	Ruling on invalidity of the 2 February 2014 General Election (Constitutional Court ruling 5/2557)		Constitutional Court, Office of the National Ombudsman	Section 108, Paragraph 2	Declared invalid
2014	Ruling on unconstitutionality of high-ranking government official reshuffle (Constitutional Court ruling 9/2557)	Prime Minister Yingluck	Constitutional Court	Section 268; Section 266, paragraphs 2 and 3	Guilty

Source: Compiled by the author.

administration by holding a general election to gauge the will of the people. Although there was no such pattern in Thailand's previous coups d'état, both the 2006 and 2014 coups can be said to have occurred in order to circumvent a possible election outcome. A further common point is that on both occasions university faculty personnel lodged an appeal with the ombudsman (the Parliamentary Ombudsman in 2006 and the National Ombudsman in 2014) who then sent the case to the Constitutional Court. It is even possible to argue that this systemic alliance between Thailand's independent agencies, which enabled an individual to use the office of the National Ombudsman to lodge an appeal with the Constitutional Court, facilitiated the 2006 and 2014 coups. Furthermore, the construction of an integrated military and independent agencies network that led to those coups began as early as the 1997 Constitution.

By scrutinizing the selection procedures and roles of appointed Senate members, this chapter considered the hypothesis that the 2007 Constitution bestowed a new political 'mission' upon the Thai upper house. It becomes clear when considering the prior experiences of appointed senators in conjunction with shifts in Senate powers and interference in attempts at real constitutional reform, that the Senate was expected to act as a 'guardian of the constitution'.

It was noted how the process of personnel appointment resulted in close mutual connections between the courts, independent agencies and appointed members of the Senate. The 'package' created by the alliance between Thai courts and independent agencies was, in fact, examined in Chapter 6. Ultimately, appeals lodged by both appointed senators and independent agencies, in conjunction with the rulings of the Constitutional Court, created a structure that actually made it possible to prevent constitutional revision or reform. That is to say, a three-way alliance between non-elected officials was able to suppress the workings of the country's popularly elected law-making and governance procedures. This cannot be justified on the grounds of cracking down on politicians' corruption. It can lead to the denial of democracy. Given the powers of the Senate, the 2007 Constitution's appointed senators could be far more undemocratic and dangerous than the 1991 Constitution's elected senators.

Conclusion: Constitutional Reform – What Has It Achieved?

This final chapter revisits the influence that the enactment of two constitutions exerted on democratization in Thailand, the intent that underpinned the political background to these, and the relationship between constitutional reform and democratization. It concludes by considering the 2017 Constitution and the future of democratization in Thailand.

The impact of constitutional reform on the political thinking of the Thai people

Confidence in democracy

There is an extremely interesting data source examining the influence of the 1997 and 2007 constitutions on democratization in Thailand. This is the series of reports derived from opinion polls on the attitudes to democracy of people across all of Thailand conducted from 2001 to 2014 by the King Prajadhipok Institute.[1] On four occasions – 2001, 2006, 2010 and 2014 – institute staff under the direction of Thawilwadee Bureekul held face-to-face interviews with randomly selected subjects eighteen years old or above. They sought to determine confidence both in democratic systems generally and in specific administrations, including prime ministers, in power at the time.

Interviews focused on people's trust of the current government, given, it was argued, that this was important for democracy in general (Thawilwadee and Ratchawadee 2017: 8–9). The survey results appear below.

Various key facts emerged from these consecutive opinion surveys, conducted from 2001 by a conservative research institute effectively established as a government agency. The first election conducted

---

1 This research institute was established by law in 1998 and is an agency supervised by the chair of the parliament. The first director was Bowonsak Uwanno, who played a central role in drafting both the 2007 Constitution and one of the drafts produced following the 2014 coup d'état. Bowonsak was appointed director for a second term from December 2006 to December 2014. Information available at: https://www.kpi.ac.th/about/history (accessed 12 November 2022).

Table C.1 Survey period and sample numbers

Survey	Year	Period	Prime Minister	Sample Numbers
1	2001	October to November	Thaksin Shinawatra	1,546
2	2006	April to September	Thaksin Shinawatra	1,546
3	2010	August to December	Abhisit Vejjajiva	1,512
4	2014	August to October	Prayut Chan-o-cha	1,200

Source: Compiled from Thawilwadee and Ratchawadee (2017).

Table C.2 Satisfaction rating towards democracy and the government (%)

Opinion Surveyed	Year of Survey			
	2001	2006	2010	2014
I am largely satisfied with the workings of the democratic system	90.4	83.6	82.5	79.5
I am largely satisfied with the current government	89.7	81.4	68.4	90.2

Source: Compiled from Thawilwadee and Ratchawadee (2017).

Table C.3 Level of trust in the prime minister (%)

Opinion Surveyed	Year of Survey			
	2001	2006	2010	2014
I largely trust the current prime minister	*	69.9	64.7	75.5

Source: Compiled from Thawilwadee and Ratchawadee (2017). Note: *No survey in 2001.

Table C.4 Approval of non-democratic government (%)

Opinion Surveyed	Year of Survey			
	2001	2006	2010	2014
	Support/Oppose	Support/Oppose	Support/Oppose	Support/Oppose
Strong leader, no elections or parliament	22.9 / 77.1	23.9 / 76.1	25.6 / 74.4	37.6 / 62.4
Military government	18.4 / 81.6	21.5 / 78.5	20.3 / 79.7	54.3 / 45.7
Technocratic government	21.4 / 78.6	* / *	18.7 / 81.3	32.3 / 67.7

Source: Compiled from Thawilwadee and Ratchawadee (2017). Note: *No survey in 2006.

Table C.5 Disapproval of non-democratic government: entire nation

Opinion Surveyed	Year of Survey			
	2001	2006	2010	2014
No support for strong leader, no elections or parliament	3.15	3.00	3.15	2.83
No support for military government	3.27	3.11	3.30	2.42
No support for technocratic government	3.20	*	3.32	2.87
Support for democracy (16 points in total)	12.38	12.28	13.05	11.01

Source: Compiled from Thawilwadee and Ratchawadee (2017).
Notes: 1. A scale of 1–4 where 1 refers to support for, and 4 refers to no support for, a non-democratic government. 2. *The point relating to lack of support for a technocratic government was not administered in 2006.

Constitutional Reform

Table C.6 Disapproval of non-democratic government: Bangkok

Opinion Surveyed	Year of Survey			
	2001	2006	2010	2014
No support for strong leader, no elections or parliament	3.44	2.85	3.37	2.67
No support for military government	3.51	2.92	3.18	2.74
No support for technocratic government	3.25	*	3.44	2.69
Support for democracy (16 points in total)	13.43	11.67	13.09	9.98

Source: Compiled from Thawilwadee and Ratchawadee (2017).
Note: A scale of 1–4 where 1 refers to support for, and 4 refers to lack of support for, a non-democratic government.

Table C.7 Disapproval of non-democratic government: Central Region

Opinion Surveyed	Year of Survey			
	2001	2006	2010	2014
No support for strong leader, no elections or parliament	3.18	2.80	3.37	3.19
No support for military government	3.15	3.01	3.41	2.55
No support for technocratic government	3.10	*	3.47	3.20
Support for democracy (16 points in total)	11.93	11.81	13.12	11.55

Source: Compiled from Thawilwadee and Ratchawadee (2017).
Note: A scale of 1–4 where 1 refers to support for, and 4 refers to lack of support for, a non-democratic government.

Table C.8 Disapproval of non-democratic government: Northern Region

Opinion Surveyed	Year of Survey			
	2001	2006	2010	2014
Lack of support for strong leader, no elections or parliament	3.00	3.09	3.15	2.66
Lack of support for military government	3.24	3.17	3.21	2.59
Lack of support for technocratic government	3.23	*	3.35	2.74
Support for democracy (16 points in total)	12.23	12.32	12.08	9.77

Source: Compiled from Thawilwadee and Ratchawadee (2017).
Note: A scale of 1–4 where 1 refers to support for, and 4 refers to lack of support for, a non-democratic government.

Table C.9 Disapproval of non-democratic government: Northeastern Region

Opinion Surveyed	Year of Survey			
	2001	2006	2010	2014
No support for strong leader, no elections or parliament	3.20	3.13	3.12	2.81
No support for military government	3.28	3.11	3.50	2.16
No support for technocratic government	3.28	*	3.36	2.81
Support for democracy (16 points in total)	12.37	12.55	12.97	10.47

Source: Compiled from Thawilwadee and Ratchawadee (2017).
Note: A scale of 1–4 where 1 refers to support for, and 4 refers to lack of support for, a non-democratic government.

Table C.10 Disapproval of non-democratic government: Southern Region

Opinion Surveyed	Year of Survey			
	2001	2006	2010	2014
No support for strong leader, no elections or parliament	2.97	3.12	2.66	2.55
No support for military government	3.34	3.39	2.77	2.54
No support for technocratic government	3.12	*	2.82	2.67
Support for democracy (16 points in total)	12.14	13.12	10.84	10.29

Source: Compiled from Thawilwadee and Ratchawadee (2017).
Note: A scale of 1–4 where 1 refers to support for, and 4 refers to lack of support for, a non-democratic government.

under the 1997 Constitution was held in 2001. The period that followed, punctuated by the 2006 coup, records a steady decline in trust in democracy. This shift was especially notable in Bangkok where, notwithstanding 2001 as a high point in trust in the democratic process, the city ultimately came to have the second lowest level after the northern regions. In inverse proportion, there was growing support for non-elected, technocratic and military forms of government and growing approval for the absence of an elected parliament.

Although it cannot be said that Thai people have come to deny democratic systems based on these figures, they do confirm a rise in distrust of democratic processes such as elections. Through experiencing the 1990s political reform movement, the enactment of the 1997 Constitution, the 2006 coup d'état and then the enactment of the 2007 Constitution, people in Thailand became increasingly suspicious of Western-style democracy and the election process underpinning this. When comparing newspaper reports of the 1992 Bloody May Incident and the 2006 coup d'état in Chapter 1, a shift was noted during that time in points of contention from 'elected prime minister' to 'corruption'. While it is possible that small sample sizes skewed the results of the surveys conducted by Thawilwadee and her colleagues, to some extent the change in issues of concern referred to above seems to accurately reflect shifting understandings of democracy among the people of Thailand observed in the survey data.

Evaluation of former prime minister Thaksin

It is not possible to examine either the 1997 or 2007 constitutions without reference to Thaksin's presence in the political landscape of the time. This was discussed in Chapter 1, where it was pointed out that the demise of the 1997 Constitution, a mere nine years after being enacted, came from attempts to limit the excesses of the administration and parliament and thereby to manage corruption associated with Thaksin's millionaire populism (Pasuk and Baker 2009; Ginsburg 2009). There were certainly various problems associated with the Thaksin administration. This has been pointed out in the many studies conducted into both corruption in the Thaksin administration and human rights violations in the south (Sripan 2009; Pasuk and Baker 2009; Khien 2011; Toyama 2018). However, in addition to investigating the provisions enacted in both the 1997 and 2007 constitutions, it is important to examine the brake placed on Thaksin in order to make sense of the impact of these constitutions on democratization in Thailand and the political meaning and intent of this.

As discussed in Chapter 1, 'transparency', 'stability', 'consistency' and 'universality' were regarded as elements of the rule of law necessary to facilitate the accord of the general populace with the legal system. In contrast, 'ambiguity', 'class blockade' and 'retrospectivity' were factors that impeded the capacity of the law to lead or guide. This point was addressed in the third part of this book which considered how the courts and independent agencies used the stipulations of the 1997 and 2007 constitutions to crackdown on the Thaksin administration. Attention was also given to the struggles associated with the 2007 constitutional revisions. It became apparent that Thailand was beset by various problem regarding the rule of law. One of the problems was examined in Chapter 5 with a focus on the legal definition of 'corruption'. As a result, it became clear that the gray zone that can be recognized as corruption has been unnecessarily expanded due to the revision of the constitution and laws, and that the definition of politicians' corruption has become more ambiguous. It was further explained that, following the 2006 coup d'état, the judges who ruled to dissolve the Thai Rak Thai Party, which had formed the previous administration, drew on the coup group proclamation to rule retrospectively that the previous executives of that now dissolved party be stripped of voting rights for five years. Chapter 6 presented the system blueprint and rulings of the Constitutional Court and each of Thailand's independent agencies. The chapter discussed obvious problems in the application of the wording of the constitution in the court ruling on the eligibility of Red Shirts executive member, Jatuporn Prompan, to stand as a candidate for the parliament. It was further noted how rulings for dissolution were generally handed down against parties connected to the Thaksin faction while the opposition Democrat Party evaded dissolution, in spite of repeatedly being suspected of corruption. This raised doubts as to the neutrality of the rulings of the Constitutional Court.

The 'Red Shirts' (*suea daeng*), generally regarded as Thaksin supporters, strongly protested the overthrow of the democratically elected government in the 2006 coup d'état and the double standards of courts and independent rulings. In other words, they protested a failure to preserve democracy and protect the rule of law. This makes no claim that there were absolutely no problems with Thaksin. However, we cannot overlook the fact that ongoing protests by the pro-Thaksin faction arose from a failure to preserve the principle of democracy, that those who held government were chosen by popular election, and in terms of the rule of law, that people should be governed by laws with 'clarity', 'stability', 'consistency' and 'universality'.

The impact on rule of law and democracy

This book set out to examine the impact of political reforms grounded in constitutionalism through an analysis of successive Thai constitutions. As a result, it became apparent that Thai people's trust in democracy and the rule of law has been declining. As discussed in the introductory chapter, Thai style democracy was constructed by Thai intellectuals who drew on a discourse of 'the king as the font of high moral virtue contrasted against the bad politician, the morally inferior direct opposite of the king'. This discourse, which supported the notion of 'Thailand as a democratic regime of government with the king as head of state', was profiled in the activities of the 1990s political reform movement and repeatedly referenced during 2005 and 2006 by members of the movement opposing the Thaksin administration (Saichon 2021: 208). Since the beginning of the twenty-first century, this discourse of 'bad politicians' has permeated the Thai people widely and deeply, and the discourse has become more believable than before. In the background, the legal provisions and institutional design of the 1997 and 2007 constitutions also must have had a strong influence on such changes. In particular, as examined in Chapter 6 of this book, the scope of recognition of politicians' corruption has expanded significantly since the 1997 Constitution due to ambiguous regulations. As a result, a number of politicians, especially former Prime Minister Thaksin, have been convicted by courts of 'corruption'. It is undeniable that the fact that many politicians have been convicted of 'corruption' strengthened the discourse that 'politicians = corruption', which had been an impression until then. It can be argued that the 'bad politician' discourse that has been cultivated over time has been reinforced by the 1997 and 2007 constitutions and it has created a strong distrust of party politicians and Western-style democracy among the Thai people in the twenty-first century.

On the other hand, these two constitutions also created distrust in the rule of law among the Thai people. Oversight of the exercise of state power based on constitutionalism and the rule of law is a global trend, not limited to Thailand. Since the 1990s, the influence of judicial power on administrative and legislative power has been increasing worldwide. However, even in the debate over constitutionalism, in recent years, the value has been found in the promotion of dialogue between powers through the constitutional review system, and the judicial omnipotent approach has not been adopted. Thus, current forms of constitutionalism and rule of law in Thailand are quite distant from the original forms, which are expected to contribute to the progress of democratization. Of the three powers, the Thai Constitution excessively expanded that of the judiciary, thus initiating governance changes through the legal system. It was furthermore pointed out, as stated above, that legal 'transparency', 'stability', 'consistency' and 'universality' were necessary if people were to abide by the law. However, ambiguous rulings, which repeatedly dissolved political parties and found guilty large numbers of politicians indicted on charges of corruption, incited a deep distrust of rule of law among the people.

Political crisis and the king

The risk of political intervention

Reference to the country's monarch is an imperative in any discussion of the constitution in Thailand. As discussed above, the major characteristic of Thai democracy is the determination of the king as the source of political legitimacy. The political system called 'democratic regime of government with the king as head of state' suggests that the king is furthermore expected to play an important mediating role in times of national crisis. While usual conditions give no capacity for royal involvement, there are two situations when a response from the king is expected. The first is a failure of the governing mechanism of state; the second is the time when the king's intervention is regarded as absolutely vital to ensuring stability, prosperity and development for 'the nation and the people' (Katō 1995: 327–328). First appearing in the 1949 Constitution, the ideal that 'Thailand is a democratic regime of government, and the king is head of state' was clearly written also into the Thai constitutions of 1968, 1974 and 1978. This was modified slightly in the constitutions of 1991, 1997 and 2007 to a stipulation that read: 'Thailand is a democratic regime of government with the king as head of state'. Furthermore, the 1978, 1991, 1997 and 2007 constitutions determined that: 'Sovereignty resides with the people of Thailand. the king who is head of the state, executes that authority through the parliament, the cabinet and the courts in compliance with the provisions of the constitution'. In addition, a provision operating from 1991 stipulated that, in the absence of the provision of the constitution being applicable to a specific instance, any response should comply with the customary practice of the democratic regime of government with the king as head of state (Kōchū 2010: 68).

It is clear from this provision that, although promoted as the country's legislative apex, the Thai Constitution was subject to a norm above and beyond even itself, namely the 'customary practice of a democratic regime of government with the king as head of state'. Opinion is divided, however, on the value of King Bhumibol's role as a balancer in Thai politics. The king's political intervention in times of crisis has become a 'myth', but the king is by no means an all-powerful god. This was because, first, rather than protecting the rights of the people and the value of rule of law, the king's intervention aimed to maintain 'social order', and, second, the sphere to which the 'virtue' (*Barami*) of the king could extend its influence was regarded as not without limits.

King Bhumibol is said to have actually appointed an interim prime minister on three occasions. These prime ministers were Sanya Dharmasakti (1973–1974), Thanin Kraivichien (1976–1977) and Anand Panyarachun (1991, 1992). While Sanya and Thanin were former justices of the Supreme Court, Anand was a former diplomat. The king first exercised political leadership with the appointment of Prime Minister Sanya in October 1973. At the time, there were student protests against the military regime and many lives were lost on 14 October in clashes between security forces and the people and students. With the country in crisis, the king made an impression by assuming a political role and moving proactively to, for example, hold talks with student leaders, appoint Sanya as prime minister and order members of the military regime to seek exile overseas (Suehiro 1993: 64–68). Deaths occurred again in May 1992 when the military and the police clashed with groups of students and intellectuals who had demanded the resignation of Prime Minister Suchinda Kraprayoon and the appointment of a leader who had been subject to popular election. At that time, also, the king summoned the leaders of both groups to the royal palace, instructing them to resolve the conflict. After Suchinda stepped down, Anand was appointed interim prime minister through the direction of former prime minister and privy councilor, Prem Tinsulanonda, who spoke as the proxy of the king. It has been noted that, subsequent to these events, the king was regarded as an indispensable entity in terms of political and economic stability so that no group in Thailand criticized the country's political system with the king as head of state (Suehiro 1993: 208–214).

Of these administrations, however, the extremely right-wing and openly anti-Communist Thanin government is remembered for its harsh suppression of the freedom of the media and the people. Under that administration, furthermore, almost all criminal cases were tried in military courts with those accused having no right of appeal. Objections were accordingly lodged by politicians and human rights organizations from the United States and Japan (Cooper 1995: 254–255). Thanin, however, denied being a dictator and claimed to govern according to 'a democratic regime of government with the king as head of state' (Suthacai 2012: 33–34). With his administration deposed by the 1977 military coup d'état, Thanin was appointed to the Privy Council by the king. In addition, as noted in chapters 5 and 6, it is said that the Thai judiciary became effectively politicized since 2006 when the king delivered a 'Royal Statement' to the judges of three courts on whether or not to recognize the outcome of the April 2006 general election. During the debate around constitutional amendments in the early 1990s, King Bhumibol declared that Thailand should endeavor to produce a Thai-style democracy in accordance with Thai values and customs. The king also supported the view that the leader of the government (the prime minister) need not necessarily be chosen through popular election (Hewison and Kengkij 2010: 191). However, this was at odds with the point of view of the average person in Thailand at the time. In this way, looking back at the political history of Thailand, various problems emerge with respect to the relationship between the king and democracy.

A further point of importance was the sphere over which the king's 'virtue' could exert influence. As verified in chapters 1 and 2 of this book, it was already becoming difficult for King Bhumibol to directly intervene and mediate in political crises even at the time of the bloodshed in May 1992. Behind this change to the king's political intervention were socio-economic changes, rising political awareness among the general public, and the emergence of larger and more violent mass demonstrations than in the past. During the 1973 student uprising, the king was merely required to direct the military prime minister, Thanom Kittikachorn, to step down. However, while the 'myth' of the king's powers of arbitration remained active at the time of the

1992 Bloody May Incident, the scale of the demonstration was larger than before, and it was not possible for a specific group to control the entire demonstration. The situation was very difficult, but the two factions that were in conflict at this time, Prime Minister Suchinda and Chamlong Srimuang, who had instigated some of the demonstrations, were both ex-military men, so the king was barely able to conduct mediation after very careful pre-arrangement. On the other hand, the chaotic emergence of the anti-Thaksin movement in 2006 expanded the scale of protests even further. In addition, while Chamlong was once more a participant, the central figure was now Sondhi Limthongkul from the business sector, while Thaksin, the prime minister whom Sondhi opposed, was also a person from the business sector and a former member of the police. Moreover, the participating protestors' profiles were extremely diverse. Under these circumstances, there was a considerable risk for the king to intervene in politics. At the time of the 2006 anti-Thaksin movement, the king accordingly confined his involvement to directing the Supreme Court and other members of the judiciary to find a solution to the problem.

Much previous research regarding the political reform movement and the 1997 Constitution focused on the concerns over the issue of royal succession since the 1990s, and pointed out as follows: the evolution of the constitutional system has enabled the protection of a weak and unpopular king (Hewison 1997: 74). It is even possible to see the 1997 'people's constitution' as a 'palace constitution', a document drafted to help ensure the survival and future stability of the Chakri dynasty (McCargo 2001: 97–98). In short, it has been argued that political reform was in fact a response to fears regarding what might happen with the accession to the throne of an unpopular crown prince. In reality, however, changes to Thai society during the King Bhumibol era itself already limited the degree to which the royal 'myth' could endure. While the 1992 Bloody May Incident may have appeared to be a high point of the king's authority, intellectuals at this point – as discussed in Chapter 2 – already had a strong sense of a governance system in crisis.

'A democratic regime of government with the king as head of state' and the rule of law

There is a further point of emphasis concerning the relationship between the constitution and the king. As noted in a number of chapters, references to the king increased exponentially in the 1997 and 2007 constitutions, with a constant refrain being 'a democratic regime of government with the king as head of state' (*rabop prachathipatai an mi phramahakasat song pen pramuk*). The 'General Provisions' of Chapter 1 of the Constitution now included a section that read, 'Whenever no provision under this Constitution is applicable to any case, it shall be decided in accordance with the constitutional practice in the democratic regime of government with the King as Head of the State'.[2] As noted in Chapter 3 of this book, moreover, many provisions relating to the king also appeared in Chapter 5 of the Constitution, headed 'Directive Principles of Fundamental State Policies'. As discussed in chapters 6 and 7 of this book, the term 'democratic regime of government with the king as head of state' was also included in provisions related to the dissolution of political parties and to provisions obstructing political reform. Furthermore, more than just abstract provisions, the influence of the king also grew in the legislature. Section 178 of the 1997 Constitution, for example, read as follows: 'In the case where the term of the House of Representatives expires or the House of Representatives is dissolved, the draft Constitution Amendment, or all bills or organic law bills to which the King has refused His assent or which have not been returned by the King within ninety days, shall lapse'.[3] There is no doubt that constitutional statements related to the king gradually assumed greater weight and gravity.[4]

Furthermore, as noted in chapters 4 and 6, Section 63 of the 1997 Constitution and Section 68 of the 2007 Constitution stipulated that

---

2 Translator's note: This is a pre-existing translation available at: http://www.asianlii.org/th/legis/const/2007/1.html
3 Translator's note: This is a pre-existing translation, originally sourced on the site, ThaiLaws.com. While this seems to be no longer available, the same text can be found here: https://en.wikisource.org/wiki/Constitution_of_Thailand_(1997)#CHAPTER_VI:_The_National_Assembly
4 Attention has recently turned to the matter of lèse-majesté in Thailand. There is a movement largely centered on Red Shirt members and young

it was possible to dissolve a political party through a ruling of the Constitutional Court. The conditions for such dissolution, however, were merely as follows:

> No person shall exercise the rights and liberties prescribed in the Constitution to overthrow the democratic regime of government with the King as Head of the State under this Constitution or to acquire the power to rule the country by any means which is not in accordance with the modes provided in this Constitution [paragraph 1].
> [...]
> In the case where the Constitutional Court makes a decision compelling the political party to cease to commit the act under paragraph two, the Constitutional Court may order the dissolution of such political party [paragraph 3].

This opaque text made it difficult to determine precisely what infringements might lead to dissolution. A similar ambiguity characterized the provisions relating to Constitutional revisions, with both the 1997 and 2007 Constitutions determining that: 'A motion for [constitutional] amendment which has the effect of changing the democratic regime of government with the King as Head of the State or changing the form of the State shall be prohibited'.[5]

In this way, the provisions of both constitutions violated the fundamental principles of the rule of law with the result that the legal system was unable to play a guiding role not only for politicians but

---

activists campaigning for the repeal of Article 112 of the Criminal Code that determines this crime. The provision pertaining to lèse-majesté has operated from 1908 to the present, with more severe penalties introduced in 1978 (three to five years in prison). Initially, the number of indictments was negligible with an average of only five cases per year investigated between 1992 and 2005. After the 2006 coup d'état, however, there was a spike in cases so that between 2006 and 2009 the yearly average was 100 cases before the lower courts, nine before the Appellant Court and two before the Supreme Court (Streckfuss 2011: 111–112).

5 Translator's note: Existing translation available at: https://en.wikisource. org/wiki/Constitution_of_Thailand_(1997)#CHAPTER_XII:_Amendment_ of_the_Constitution

for the people generally. Ambivalent provisions, moreover, facilitated a comprehensive arbitrariness in the application of matters of law by judges and members of independent agencies. Since 2006, there has been mounting distrust in Thailand, particularly among members of the Thaksin faction, of the courts and independent agencies and this has been a major cause of ongoing political instability. We can say that the ambivalent provisions of the constitution and related statutes feed that distrust. The phrase 'the democratic regime of government with the king as head of state', which was originally supposed to refer to the royal prerogative not stipulated in the constitution, was written into many articles of the constitutions and the organic laws, and it often has been used to dissolve political parties and to obstruct law-making by immoderately expanding the breadth of arbitrary judicial interpretation. The application of such legal provisions not only undermines the rule of law but also damages the influence and prestige of the king and the monarchy as a whole.

The 2014 coup and enactment of the new constitution

Aims of the new constitution

On 22 May 2014, the military staged a thirteenth coup. After taking all state powers, the National Council for Peace and Order (NCPO; *khana raksa khwamsagop haeng chat*), headed by Army Commander-in-Chief Prayut Chan-o-cha, followed the template set in the past and abolished the 2007 Constitution. After Thailand functioned without a constitution for two months, an interim constitution was eventually promulgated on 22 July 2014.

The chapter now presents an overview of the battle over the drafting process of the 2017 Constitution and the future of democratization in Thailand. This is because the 2017 Constitution also inherited the trend of constitutional reform since the 1990s. Prime Minister Prayut took control of each of the three powers (administrative/executive, legislative and judicial) through Section 44 of the Interim Constitution and was installed as an absolute dictator. Since without the promulgation of the new constitution, a legal framework enabling elections could not be implemented, the first step in transition to civilian government was the implementation of a new permanent document. Prime Minister Prayut accordingly summoned Witsanu Khruea-ngam as a legal specialist to be one of the country's deputy prime ministers. The drafting process for the new constitution commenced in 2014, with the first version (the so-called Bowonsak draft) released in August 2015 rejected by the National Reform Council, and the second version (the so-called Meechai draft) released on 29 January 2016. Although the drawing-up and implementation of a permanent constitution had occurred under an interim military administration in the past, this was the first time that a council-like body had rejected a draft.[6] We will examine that process and contents in detail below.

The Constitution Drafting Committee was not entirely free to draft a new constitution. Rather, Article 35 of the 2014 Interim Constitution stipulated the fundamental policy framework for any new constitutional draft and required the committee to operate within those boundaries. Outlining the necessary framework for a draft of the new permanent constitution, Section 35 of the 2014 interim document stipulated six points: 1. democratic regime of government with the king as head of state appropriate for Thai societal conditions; 2. a governance administration structure that benefits the state and the people by ensuring the use of state power to protect against and effectively investigate and eliminate corruption and dishonest dealings by the state and the private sector; 3. a structure that decisively prevents the assumption of political office by people who had previously been subject to a ruling or order of corruption, dishonest dealing or electoral fraud; 4. a structure that provides effective long-term protection against state governance forms that might promote political preferences that damage the national economy and the people; 5. a structure that effectively prevents the destruction of the important principles of the constitution; and 6. a structure that adequately promotes reform concerning various matters of concern.

---

6 Many were of the view that, from the outset, the interim military administration sought to buy time in order to delay the conduct of a general election.

Summarizing the framework outlined above while referencing available public documents, we might conclude that the main objectives of the new constitution were maintaining a democratic regime of government with the king as head of state, controlling corruption, preventing populist policies or populist budget decisions, preventing politicians such as Thaksin and his colleagues who had been ruled guilty of corruption from returning to political office, and preventing significant constitutional reform. Furthermore, while not immediately clear from the text of Section 35, the repeated message resonating in speeches by Prime Minister Prayut and in government campaigns was the need to prevent the street clashes and divisions evident between the people over the past few years as expressed in the so-called 'Red Shirts vs Yellow Shirts' conflict. In other words, one important objective of the regime was 'resolving' antagonism among the people.

The Bowonsak draft (released August 2015)

As previously noted, Bowonsak Uwanno was a key figure in the drafting of the 1997 Constitution. We might then consider the nature of the draft he presented approximately twenty years later under the Prayut interim military administration. There were five characteristics to Bowonsak's constitutional draft: 1. a strong nuance of idealism through the introduction of wording that profiled the ideal 'citizen' (*phonlamueang*) and the 'virtuous political leader'; 2. a change in lower house voting to first past the post (300 seats) and party list proportional representation (150–170 seats) using an open list; 3. an upper house that was a mixture of elected and appointed members, with seventy-seven of the 200 seats being for one elected member each from the country's seventy-seven *changwat* (provinces) with the remainder appointed; 4. the option of prime ministerial appointments coming from outside elected members of the lower house; and 5. a stipulation establishing a national reform and harmony strategy committee and a reform implementation and harmony building council.

Three especially important points to emerge from Bowonsak's draft were the conditions of prime ministerial appointment, upper house membership by appointment and the National Reform and

Harmony Strategy Committee. Removing a need for the prime minister to be a member of the lower house was a return to provisions not seen for around the quarter-century since the 1992 revisions to the 1991 Constitution. Upper house appointments were to be made from expert representatives from, for example, bureaucrats (permanent under-secretary level), the military (such as Ministry of Defense permanent under-secretary, supreme commander of the armed forces), representatives from the agricultural sector, labor, academics and education, villages, and regional legal practitioners, and experts in sectors such as politics, security, governance, the legal system, the judiciary, finance, public health, the environment, natural resources, energy, science and technology, society and religion, the arts and culture, children and youth, women, disability and the self-employed. It was decided that the National Reform and Harmony Strategy Committee would consist of one chairperson and twenty-two members. As for members, the speaker of the parliament, the president of the Senate, the prime minister, supreme commander of the armed forces, each commander of the three armed forces, and the commander-in-chief of the police were supposed to be members as a matter of course. In addition, it was decided that one member each of the past speakers of the parliament, prime ministers, and chief justices of the Supreme Court would be elected from among themselves, and that experts (eleven or less) would also be included as members. While the draft provided for the National Reform and Harmony Strategy Committee remained active for only five years after the enactment of the new constitution, there were also exceptions that allowed the period to be extended. In addition, if, within five years of the entry into force of the constitution, the national security was disturbed and the constitutional agencies and cabinet were unable to control the situation, the National Reform and Harmony Strategy Committee was stipulated to be able to exert its power to regain order in concert with the Constitutional Court and the Supreme Administrative Court. It was furthermore determined that the committee chair could issue commands related to legislative and administrative governance and these commands would be regarded as in accord with the constitution.

The Bowonsak draft thus supported a non-elected prime minister, advocated an upper house with a majority of appointed members and provided for the military to have direct control of the running of national affairs through the National Reform and Harmony Strategy Committee. Bowonsak had played a role in drafting the 1997 Constitution, regarded as the most democratic in Thai history with its introduction of a popularly elected prime minister and an upper house in which all members were elected by the people. In this sense, it appeared that this draft and the 1997 Constitution seem to be quite different. At the same time, however, Bowonsak's emphasis on the ideal 'citizen' and the 'political leader of virtue' was fundamentally unchanged from the 1997 Constitution.

The Meechai draft – version 1 (released in January 2016)

The first version of the Meechai draft was made public on 29 January 2016. As noted previously, Meechai Ruchphan was the chairman of the Drafting Committee for the 1991 Constitution, which allowed a non-elected prime minister and resulted in the bloodshed of May 1992. There were seven points to check in the Meechai draft, as follows:

1. In addition to wording that strengthened the rights of the people, the repeated appearance of new text forbidding the damage of the rights of others.
2. Single-seat constituencies and proportional representation (350 electoral districts and 150 proportional representation) will be adopted for elections to the House of Representatives. The conventional method of casting one vote each in constituencies and proportional representation was changed to a new method in which voters cast only one vote, and in the case of proportional representation, the votes of candidates who lost in constituencies are also used to calculate the number of seats.
3. All 200 of the upper house seats to be by appointment.
4. Membership of the lower house no longer to be a prerequisite for a prime ministerial appointment, with each political party

required to submit the names of three prime ministerial candidates to the Election Commission prior to an election.
5. A heightening of the powers of the Constitutional Court.
6. A heightening of the powers of independent agencies especially the Election Commission and the National Anti-Corruption Commission.
7. An increase in the degree of difficulty of constitutional amendment.

Even in seminars held to explain the constitutional draft, there was an emphasis on prohibiting damage to others. This was possibly a response to the mass protests that had occurred on the streets in the previous few years. Recommended changes to the method of electing lower house members were designed to prevent an overwhelming win by a single political party. While upper house membership was determined by mutual selection from people possessing attributes such as knowledge, expertise and experience in various groups of society, the prime ministerial selection method outlined was quite complicated. From a list of prime ministerial candidates previously compiled by the political parties who had gained more that 5% of the overall number of seats in the lower house, those whose candidature was agreed upon by more than one tenth of the lower house membership were put forward for a ballot for prime minister. The candidate who gained a majority of votes would be appointed. This provision made it difficult for voters to anticipate who might become prime minister after an election.

The Meechai draft, on the other hand, had no provisions related to the 'National Reform and Harmony Strategy Committee' that was profiled in the Bowonsak draft. Instead, the Constitutional Court and the independent agencies were given important roles in the administration of the state and politics. Newly introduced provisions entitled 'Duties of the State' stipulated that a failure by the state to implement a matter for which it was determined responsible, such as education or public health, etc., would permit a citizen or citizens to bring an indictment to the Constitutional Court. A further provision enabled more than one tenth of the members of the House of Representatives to file a lawsuit with the Constitutional Court when a member of the house made changes to the budget proposal so that he or she could be involved. It was also stipulated that if the person concerned was a minister and the Constitutional Court rendered a guilty verdict, the cabinet must resign en masse. Furthermore, the cabinet in this situation was not permitted to conduct interim cabinet duties prior to the installation of new ministers. Cabinet roles would instead be assumed by the permanent undersecretaries of each ministry, with that group also choosing a proxy prime minister. It was moreover determined that, should a situation arise to which constitutional stipulations did not apply, the Constitutional Court must rule in accordance with the 'tradition of a democratic regime of government with the King as Head of state'.

The powers of independent agencies were also expanded, with these granted the legislative right to decide the 'ethical norms' that bound members of the upper house, lower house and cabinet. When election dishonesty was suspected, the Election Commission could issue orders to suspend the right of a candidate to hold office, to cancel an election result or to call for a new election, and to stop the ballot in an election or a national referendum. The commission was furthermore granted the power to order a second election within a year of the original ballot. The powers of the National Anti-Corruption Commission were also strengthened with targets now even including those who committed a serious violation of the previously mentioned 'ethical norms'. In addition, even with insufficient proof of corruption for a criminal charge, it became possible to lodge a case with the Constitutional Court to have the individual involved stripped of their status. This meant that the power to impeach which had previously resided with the upper house was now transferred to the Constitutional Court.

The Meechai document introduced provisions that made constitutional amendment even more difficult than in the past. It now became necessary in the third reading of a motion for constitutional amendment: 1. to be accepted by a majority of the total combined numbers of the upper and lower houses; 2. to be approved by all political parties that had more than ten members sitting in the lower house; 3. to be agreed upon by lower house members who exceeded more than 10% of each political party; 4. to be agreed upon by more than 10% of the group comprised of political parties in which the total number of attached lower house members was less than ten and when adding these together came to greater than ten; and 5. to be agreed upon by more than one third of the upper house. In addition, there was a special supplementary provision making a referendum necessary prior to the king being presented with a proposal for changes to Chapter 1 entitled 'General Provisions', Chapter 2 entitled 'The King' or Chapter 15 entitled 'Constitutional Amendment'. We might conclude that, under these provisions, substantive constitutional amendment became impossible.

Criticism from the people

Both the Bowonsak and Meechai drafts expressed overt distrust of a popularly elected prime minister and anticipated that the Constitutional Court and independent agencies would play a role in controlling politicians. Importantly, both proposals largely called for intervention in the case of mass protests or other political crises to come from the Constitutional Court rather than the government or, as had occurred during the 1973 student uprising, the king. Even from the time of the Bloody May Incident of 1992, intellectuals had expressed alarm at the fact that reconciliatory action by the king would become increasingly difficult. It was evident in both the Bowonsak and Meechai drafts, released in 2015 and 2016 respectively, that managing political crises was now a key role of both the Constitutional Court and independent agencies.

Strong criticism of both drafts came from the media, scholars and the people. Objections to Bowonsak's draft were: 1. qualification to become prime minister did not include membership of the lower house, 2. the Senate was not popularly elected, 3. the National Reform and Harmony Strategy Committee was undemocratic and could become a means by which the interim administration retained power, and 4. it was difficult to understand the meaning of the term used for 'citizen' (*phonlamueang*). Although almost impossible to confirm, rumors also circulated that members of the National Reform Council were lobbied to reject the Bowonsak draft at the time of the September 2015 vote. Criticisms levelled at the Meechai draft, on the other hand, included: 1. qualifications for prime ministerial appointments did not include membership of the lower house, 2. the Senate was not popularly elected, 3. too much power was concentrated in the hands of the Constitutional Court and independent agencies, 4. the draft made constitutional amendment extremely difficult, and 5. even after a new constitution was promulgated, the current interim administration would remain in place until a new administration was installed.[7]

A positive interpretation of the downgrading of democratic governance processes emphasized in both the Bowonsak and Meechai drafts was that this resulted from a perceived need to control crisis situations such as protests and violent clashes on the streets. The explanatory booklet distributed by the Constitution Drafting Committee also noted that, while not necessarily in the text of the constitutions of other countries, such provisions were necessary in Thailand to ensure that clashes did not occur.[8] However, it was also true that many Thai citizens, legal scholars and political scientists have criticized both draft constitutions and were fighting for election-based politics.

The Meechai Draft – version 2 (released in March 2016)

After listening to opinions from various quarters, the Meechai draft was revised in March of the same year. The most significant change was to Section 5, a revised version of Section 7 of both the 1997 and 2007 constitutions. According to this Section 5, any case or circumstances not covered in the constitution would be addressed by a joint meeting, convened by the chief justice of the Constitutional Court, composed of the chair of the lower house, the leader of the opposition in the lower house, the chair of the upper house, the prime minister, the chief justice of the Supreme Court, the chief justice of the Supreme Administrative Court, the chief justice of the Constitutional Court, and the chairs of the independent agencies. That is say, when the chief

---

7 This is according to the February 2016 edition of the magazine published by the 'New Democracy Movement' comprised mainly of staff and students of Thammasat University.

8 This is according to 'A Summary of Necessary Principles', published in January 2016 by the Constitution Drafting Committee.

justice of the Constitutional Court handed down a ruling declaring a state of emergency, the leadership of the state moved from the prime minister to the chief justice of the Constitutional Court. Determinations of the meeting so convened were to be regarded as final and binding on the parliament, the cabinet, the courts, the independent agencies and any other national agencies. Furthermore, the Constitutional Court was to be granted the power to rule on issues related to the power and duties of the lower house, upper house, parliament and independent agencies, with the Constitution Drafting Committee arguing that such articles would act as 'a pathway to resolving constitutional crises'. These proposed provisions could be seen as an attempt to unequivocally transfer any intervention and conciliation function of the king at times of political crisis to the Constitutional Court and independent agencies.

The 2017 Constitution and King Vajiralongkorn

The national referendum

Administered by Thailand's Election Commission and held between 8 am and 4 pm on 7 August 2016, a national referendum was held to determine whether or not the draft of the new constitution would be adopted. In order to take part in the referendum, voters were required to: 1. confirm their family names through either the electoral roll available at each polling booth or correspondence forwarded by post to their household heads, 2. display their identification, 3. put their fingerprint on the ballot paper received, 4. fill in the ballot paper, and 5. place the paper in the ballot box. In the referendum, two items were prepared for voters to answer. The first was 'Do you support or oppose the new constitutional draft?' while the second question asked 'Do you support or oppose the nomination of a prime minister by a joint meeting of both houses of the parliament within the first five years of the enactment of the new constitution?' This second, supplementary question was added during the referendum preparation process and was criticized by many scholars and the media. The layout of the ballot paper, furthermore, made it difficult to understand the key point of either question. This was especially the case with question two, the text for which was written in small font and broken into four lines so that voters needed some time to understand the meaning. The full text of question two, in fact, read as follows:

> Do you support or oppose that for contributing continuity of the country reform according to the national strategic plan, it should be stipulated in the Transitory Provisions of the Constitution of the Kingdom of Thailand that for the duration of 5 years from the first sitting of the Parliament under this constitution; the joint sitting of the two chambers of the Parliament shall convene to consider approving a person to be appointed as the Prime Minister?[9]

To understand the real intent of this question, voters needed considerable knowledge of both the Thai Constitution and the country's political landscape. This included being aware that this new constitution would mark the first time that the National Council for Peace and Order (NCPO) appointed members of the upper house, that the selection of the prime minister by a meeting of both houses of the parliament in fact meant granting the choice of prime minister to the upper house, which had been appointed by the NCPO, and that the qualifications for prime ministerial candidature were not limited to elected members of the lower house. In all likelihood, however, such knowledge was limited to voters who were students or those with political interests. There were accordingly predictions that many ballots would be cast without voters understanding the outcomes intended by the question.

This, however, was not the only problem associated with the 2016 referendum. Measures were also taken to limit the people's ability to engage in free discussion or to debate the constitutional draft. These measures were stipulated through the referendum law.

---

9 Translator's note: This wording is adapted from the Wikipedia page entitled '2016 Thai constitutional referendum'. It itself is a very slightly modified version taken from https://anfrel.org/wp-content/uploads/2016/06/The-voting-in-Referendum-booklet2016.pdf which appears to be an English language version of an explanatory pamphlet of the referendum produced by the Election Commission of Thailand. The pdf includes a section explaining why this supplementary question was addended.

The Referendum Law in 2016

Let us examine the provisions of the Referendum Law. While this law came into force in 2009 during the Abhisit administration, a second paragraph was added in 2016 to Section 61. That second pargraph read:

> Any person who disseminates texts, pictures or sound through newspaper, radio, television or other electronic media in a way that distorts the facts or has violent, aggressive, rude, inciting, or threatening characteristics aiming to induce eligible voters to refrain from voting or to vote in a certain way or to abstain from voting shall be regarded as causing disorder in the vote.[10]

Those found guilty of violating this provision could be sentenced to up to ten years imprisonment and fined up to 200,000 baht, with the court also able to revoke voting rights for up to five years. These inordinately severe penalties effectively meant that the government was able to close-down criticism of the draft of the new constitution. Concerned that the Referendum Law may have violated the constitution, the Office of the National Ombudsman sought a ruling on the new provision from the Constitutional Court. When the court handed down a unanimous ruling of constitutionality, the decision was released as a single-page media statement without any press conference or detailed judicial analysis explaining the ruling. With many concerned at the referendum outcome, the draft received a majority vote. Election Commission figures gave a turn-out rate of 59.40%, with 61.35% in support and 38.65% against. The matters outlined above, however, suggest that the outcome could not necessarily be read as a show of support for the Prayut administration.

---

10 Translator's note: This is a modified version of an unofficial English translation of the relevant extract from Section 61 prepared by the Asian Network for Free Elections. The pdf of that translation is available here: https://anfrel.org/wp-content/uploads/2016/06/Organic-Act-on-Referendum-for-the-Draft-Constitution-2016-part-1.pdf

The passing of King Bhumibol and amendment of the draft by the new King Vajiralongkorn

On 12 October 2016, news came of the serious decline in the health of King Bhumibol who had long been much loved and respected by the Thai people. Once the king was admitted to Siriraj Hospital, many, including media representatives, gathered outside. Holding aloft King Bhumibol's portrait, they chanted sutras and generally prayed for the monarch's recovery. In spite of an announcement that the king's condition had stabilized and that he was resting, news came during the night of 13 October that the monarch had passed away. Mourners outside Siriraj Hospital wept, while some women fainted from shock. As Crown Prince Vajiralongkorn and Princess Sirindhorn entered the hospital, the gathered crowds cried 'Long live the king'.

On the afternoon of 14 October, King Bhumibol's body was taken to the Grand Palace for funerary rites. With huge crowds of Thai people standing along the road in the blazing sun to farewell the king, the departure of the funeral cortege, scheduled for 1 pm, was delayed until after 4 pm. However, those assembled remained devotedly waiting without complaint for the procession to pass. I myself, the author, was among the crowd in front of the Supreme Court building opposite the Sanam Luang park area. When some remained standing as the procession approached, angry voices cried from the crowd: 'You're Thai, aren't you? Lower yourselves in the king's presence'. As the procession went by, there was a moment of utter silence as bystanders farewelled on his journey to the next life the man whom they had been proud to call king, the 'Father of Thailand', for the past seventy years. For many in Thailand, the possibility of King Bhumibol's demise had long been accompanied by fears of an outbreak of political unrest. The moment of that demise had now arrived.

Since King Bhumibol passed away before signing the new permanent constitution approved by the national referendum of August 2016, the new king's hand was required to ratify the constitution. Crown Prince Vajiralongkorn, however, did not immediately assume the Thai throne. While the official explanation was that he wished 'to share his sorrow with the people of Thailand', there was considerable speculation on his accession to the monarchy. On the evening of 1 December 2016, however, the crown prince accepted a request from the chair of the parliament to accede to the throne and was thus formally installed as King Rama X. While this was around a month and a half after the 13 October death of King Bhumibol, it was announced that the new king's reign would retrospectively begin from that date. This erased from history the time during which Thailand had no king. While there were rumors in the foreign press of discord between the crown prince and Prem Tinsulanonda, former chair of the Privy Council who became regent while the Thai throne was vacant, the new King Vajiralongkorn appointed Prem as Privy Council chair once more.

The first important duty of the new monarch was to adopt the new constitution. However, in a move unexpected by the Thai people – and perhaps even by Prime Minister Prayut – King Vajiralongkorn requested various revisions to the constitutional draft. While the new king exercised his authority in accordance with the interim constitution, such a development was unprecedented in Thailand. With Prime Minister Prayut explaining the request in terms of its applying to 'passages in the constitution related to the king', on 13 January 2017, the Thai Parliament approved a constitutional draft with the new king's revisions. The revised draft included a stipulation making it possible for the king to travel outside Thailand without a regent being appointed, among other amendments.

The key revision made by King Vajiralongkorn, however, related to Section 5 which, as noted above, was the new document's iteration of what had been Section 7 in the constitutions of 1997 and 2007. The old Section 7, which determined, 'When no provision under this constitution applies to a specific case, the matter shall be decided in accord with the conventions of a democratic regime of government with the king as head of the state', came to be understood among the Thai people as one of the powers held by the king.[11] The Meechai draft of the new constitution did not have such an abstract content,

---

11 Many protestors from the anti-Thaksin faction believed that Section 7 gave King Bhumibol the power to appoint an interim prime minister. According to Worachet Pakeerut, however, the understanding among public law scholars was that Section 7 could actually be read as meaning: 'When no applicable passage was found in the constitution, the Constitutional Court had the power to make a ruling based on that text'.

but specifically stipulated that a joint conference headed by the Constitutional Court would deal with political crises. It is possible that this text was articulated in the new constitution in response to a perceived need to manage political crises, something that had generated fear among conservatives and intellectuals from as long ago as the Bloody May Incident of 1992. However, depending on how to read this article, people could also read it as if the royal power was reduced. In the constitutional draft produced with the new king's revisions, the relevant passage in Section 5 accordingly returned to the original wording to read, as noted above: 'When no provision under this constitution applies to a specific case, the matter shall be decided in accord with the conventions of a democratic regime of government with the king as head of the state'.

This intervention in the wording of the constitution by the new king might be interpreted as the partial failure of a twenty-year project to construct a system of dealing with political crisis that gave ascendency to the Constitutional Court. Even in the amended version of the new constitution, however, the considerable power of that court and the independent agencies was, from a general perspective, preserved.

On the afternoon of 6 April 2017, King Vajiralongkorn signed the new constitution in the presence of Prime Minister Prayut and his cabinet and the ambassadors of countries with offices in Thailand. This brought into force the 2017 Constitution, the twentieth in Thailand. The constitution did not require the prime minister to be an elected member of the lower house, and neither was the upper house elected. Furthermore, the Prayut interim military administration in actuality had the power to appoint members of the upper house in the first term, for which period only the number of upper house members was increased by fifty to 250 (Section 269). In addition, the powers of the Constitutional Court and the independent agencies were so strong that even if a general election resulted in an administration led by a popularly elected prime minister, the determined framework could give the power of control to the bureaucracy, including the army. Thus, the Thai Constitution and democratization in Thailand effectively backtracked around a quarter of a century to a situation that had prevailed prior to the revisions to the 1991 Constitution. From the perspective of democratization, we might even say that conditions were now more challenging than when the 1991 Constitution was adopted. Meechai was the Chair of the 1991 Constitution Drafting Committee, and he also chaired the drafting committee for the 2017 Constitution. Like its 1991 iteration, the 2017 Constitution supported prime ministerial appointments from candidates not chosen by popular election. The re-emergence of a constitution advocating this possibility did not only result from the harsh restrictions on freedom of speech that operated under the interim Prayut military administration. We cannot discount the possibility also that, as previously noted, the excessive crackdown on political corruption evident in the constitutions of 1997 and 2007 fostered distrust among the people of Thailand towards both politicians and democratic systems. In other words, the brand of constitutionalism introduced into Thailand in the 1990s ultimately damaged the democratic systems that were grounded in the election process.

Constraints on future governance through a 'Twenty-Year National Strategy' and democratization in Thailand

After the coup d'état in May 2014, the general election was postponed several times. Although not described in detail in this book, the first general election after the 2014 coup was finally held in March 2019, and pro-military parties succeeded in establishing a coalition government. Then, in June 2019, Prayut returned to the prime minister's post after a popular election. Until that point, however, the interim military administration had gradually introduced a range of constraints against the operation of future non-military administrations. These 'restraints' were imposed through the development of a 'Twenty-Year National Strategy' that was largely overseen by Deputy Prime Minister Wissanu. That strategy was to apply also to future administrations that took office after elections and required those future administrations to govern according to what was outlined. The Twenty-Year National Strategy largely referred to six specific areas, namely: 1. security strategy, 2. competitiveness strategy, 3. development and empowerment, 4. equal opportunity and social equality, 5. a lifestyle valuing the environment, and 6. proportion and development of the bureaucratic system of government. To ensure the compliance of future governments, especially those chosen by election, the interim military administration appointed a National Strategy Committee and a National Anti-Corruption Commission with the power to determine sanctions – including terms of imprisonment – against the cabinet of a future administration that failed to follow what was required. Devised by the interim military administration, the strategy was an extremely powerful stipulation that also bound future administrations. While not articulated so overtly, we might argue that the 'Directive Principles for Fundamental State Policy' that were a feature of the 1997 and 2007 constitutions as discussed in Chapter 3 had a similar power to draw on both the constitution and a national strategy to prescribe limits on governance and government policy.

Given the restraints operating through the 2017 Constitution and the Twenty-Year National Strategy, it seems that the future of democratization in Thailand is precarious in the extreme. Not every aspect, however, has reverted to 1980s semi-democracy mode. Since the 2014 coup, the Prayut administration has used computer crime law and lèse-majesté legislation to clamp down on anti-government and anti-monarchy discourse, particularly as these appeared on social media and the internet. It is impossible, however, to drag the now awakened consciousness of the Thai people back to the past. Since 2020, not only anti-government and anti-coup d'état demonstrations, but also those calling for reform of the monarchy have been instigated mainly by young people. Many Thai adults were shocked by the youth movement that directly addressed the long taboo royal issue. Although there is a difference in opinion on the reform of the monarchy, many organizations such as student organizations, Red Shirts, other political activists and some political parties are loosely linked, and movements aiming for democratization have continued to spread on the streets and in cyberspace.

The development of the internet has made it difficult to monitor or control a resistance movement that for some time has been elusive and hard to pin down. Thai people note how, in comparison to the King Bhumibol era, the situation with King Vajiralongkorn is difficult for them to observe. And although as the movement for monarchy reform gathered force the new king toured the country to make a show of consulting with his people, he clearly did not intervene in protests. It is not merely that King Vajiralongkorn is unpopular among the Thai people, again, the difficulty and high risk of political intervention in a crisis seem to affect the behavior of the king. When a critical situation arises for conservatives, it will be necessary to pay close attention to how long the crisis management system with the Constitutional Court at the top can control it, or whether other new measures will be taken.

Bibliography

Acemoglu, Daron and James A. Robinson, 2001, 'A Theory of Political Transitions', *The American Economic Review*, 91(4): 938–963.

Albertus, Michael and Victor A. Menaldo 2013, 'Gaming Democracy: Elite Dominance during Transition and Prospects for Redistribution', *British Journal of Political Science*, 44(3): 1–29.

Amon Chantharasombun, 1994a, *Constitutionalism: Thang-ok khong Prathet Thai* (Constitutionalism: Way Out for Thailand), Bangkok: Institute of Public Policy Studies.

Amon Chantharasombun, 1994b, *Rang Ratthathammanun kaekhai phoemtoem phuea Kanpatirup thang Kanmueang tam Naeothang Constitutionalism* (Proposed Constitutional Amendment for Political Reform in Accordance with the Policy of Constitutionalism), Bangkok: Institute of Public Policy Studies.

Amon Chantharasombun, 1994c, *Khrongsang lae Konkai thang Kotmai khong Ratthathammanun* (Constitutional Legal Structure and Devices), Bangkok: Institute of Public Policy Studies.

Anek Laothamatas, 1996, *Business Associations the New Political Economy of Thailand: From Bureaucratic Polity to Liberal Corporatism*, Boulder: Westview.

Asami, Yasuhito, 1998, 'Chukanso no Zodai to Seiji Ishiki no Henka' (Growing Middle Class and Changing Political Consciousness), in Toshio Tasaka ed., *Ajia no Daitoshi (1) Bankoku* (Major Cities in Asia #1: Bangkok), Tokyo: Nippon Hyoron sha co., Ltd., pp. 305–328.

Aso, Tamon, 2006, 'Kenryoku Bunritsu Genri no Jyuyo to Tenkai' (Acceptance and Development of the Principle of Separation of Powers), in Naruto University of Education ed., *Naruto University of Education Kenkyu Kiyo* (Bulletin of Naruto University of Education), 21: 258–67.

Bellamy, Richard, 2007, *Political Constitutionalism: A Republican Defence of the Constitutionality of Democracy*, New York: Cambridge University Press.

Bertok, Janos, 2008, 'Conflict of Interest: The Challenge to Develop Tools for Implementation and Enforcement', in *Managing Conflict of Interest: Frameworks, Tools, and Instruments for Preventing, Detecting, and Managing Conflict of Interest*, Asian Development Bank, pp. 85–91. http://www.oecd.org/dataoecd/50/12/40838870.pdf (accessed December 1, 2011).

Bertrand, Jacques, 2013, *Political Change in Southeast Asia*, New York: Cambridge University Press.

Bidhya, Bowornwathana, 2010, 'Government Interference, Trust, and the Capacity to Perform: Comparing Governance Institutions in Thailand', *International Public Management Review*, 11(2): 64–77.

Boonsri Mewongukote, 1995, *Kanprapprung rabop phakkanmueang* (Improvement of the Political Party System), Samnakngan kongthun sanapsanun kanwichai.

Boonsri Mewongukote, 2014, 'Constitutionalism in Thailand: Problems and Perspectives', in Dirk Ehlers, Henning Glaser and Kittisak Prokati eds., *Constitutionalism and Good Governance: Eastern and Western Perspectives*, Baden: Nomos, pp. 217–242.

Bowonsak Uwanno, 1999, *Ratthathammanun naru* (An Interesting Constitution), Bangkok: Samnakphim Winyuchon.

Bowonsak Uwanno, 2001, *Chettanarom Ratthathammanun* (Spirit of the Constitution), Bangkok: Sathaban Phrapoklao.

Callahan, William A., 1998, *Imagining Democracy: Reading "The Events of May" in Thailand*, Singapore: Institute of Southeast Asian Studies.

Callahan, William A., 2005, 'The Discourse of Vote Buying and Political Reform in Thailand', *Pacific Affairs*, 78(1): 95–113.

Carothers, Thomas, 2002, 'The End of the Transition Paradigm', *Journal of Democracy*, 13(1): 5–21.

Case, William, 1996, 'Can the "Halfway House" Stand? Semidemocracy and Elite Theory in Three Southeast Asian Countries', *Comparative Politics*, 28(4): 437–464.

Case, William, 2002, *Politics in Southeast Asia: Democracy or Less*, London and New York: RoutledgeCurzon.

Chada Nonthawat, 2009, *Kabot Phaendin Yaengching Amnat* (National Treason, Power Struggle), Bangkok: YPSY.

Chai-Anan Samudavanija, 1982, *The Thai Young Turks*, Singapore: Institute of Southeast Asian Studies.

Chai-Anan Samudavanija, 1989, 'Thailand: A Stable Semi-democracy', in Larry Diamond, Juan J. Linz and Seymour Martin Lipset eds., *Democracy in Developing Countries, Volume 3: Asia*, Boulder: Lynne Rienner, pp. 305–346.

Chai-Anan Samudavanija, 1997, 'Old Soldiers Never Die. They Are Just Bypassed: The Military, Beaucracy and Globalisation', in Kevin Hewison ed., *Political Change in Thailand: Democracy and Participation*, London and New York: Routledge, pp. 42–57.

Chai-Anan Samudavanija, 2002, *Thailand: State-Building, Democracy and Globalization*, Bangkok, Institute for Public Policy Studies.

Chairat Charoensin-o-larn, 2009, 'Military Coup and Democracy in Thailand', in John Funston ed., *Divided over Thaksin: Thailand's Coup and Problematic Transition*, Singapore: Institute of Southeast Asian Studies, pp. 49–79.

Chairat Charoensin-o-larn, 2012, 'A New Politics of Desire and Disintegration in Thailand', in Michael J. Montesano, Pavin Chachavalpongpun and Aekapol Chongvilaivan eds., *Bangkok May 2010: Perspectives on a Divided Thailand*, Singapore: Institute of Southeast Asian Studies, pp. 87–96.

Chambers, Paul, 2009, 'Superfluous, Mischievous or Emancipating? Thailand's Evolving Senate Today', *Journal of Current Southeast Asian Affairs*, 28(3): 3–38.

Chaowana Traimat, 2008, *Kanmueang nai Ratthathammanun* (Politics in the Constitution), Bangkok: Institute of Public Policy Studies.

Chumphon Nimphanit, 2002, 'Panha Kanmueang Thai dan Rabop' (Thai Politics in Terms of the System), in Sakhawicha Rathasat Mahawitthayalai Sukhothaithammathirat eds., *Ekkasan Kanson Chutwicha: Panha Kanmueang Thai Patchuban Current Political Issues Nuai thi 1-8* (Current Thai Political Issues Chapters 1-8), Nonthaburi: Sukhothaithammathirat University Book Center, pp. 70–115.

Connors, Michael, 2002, 'Framing the "People's Constitution"', in Duncan McCargo ed., *Reforming Thai Politics*, Copenhagen: Nordic Institute of Asian Studies, pp. 37-55.

Connors, Michael, 2003, *Democracy and National Identity in Thailand*, London: Routledge Curzon.

Cooper, Donald F., 1995, *Thailand: Dictatorship or Democracy?*, Montreux, London, Washington: Minerva Press.

Croissant, Aurel, 2011, 'Types of Democracy in Southeast Asia and Democratic Consolidation', in Aurel Croissant and Marco Bunte eds., *The Crisis of Democratic Governance in Southeast Asia*, New York and Hampshire: Palgrave Macmillan, pp. 93-113.

Dahl, Robert A., 1971, *Polyarchy. Participation and Opposition*, New Haven: Yale University Press.

Diamond, Larry, 1999, *Developing Democracy: Toward Consolidation*, Baltimore: Johns Hopkins University Press.

Diamond, Larry and Leonardo Morlino eds., 2005, *Assessing the Quality of Democracy*, Baltimore: Johns Hopkins University Press.

Diamond, Larry, Marc F. Plattner and Christopher Walker, 2016, *Authoritarianism Goes Global*, Baltimore: Johns Hopkins University Press.

Dressel, Björn, 2009, 'Thailand's Elusive Quest for a Workable Constitution, 1997-2007', *Contemporary Southeast Asia*, 31(2): 296-325.

Dressel, Björn, 2010, 'Judicialization of Politics or Politicization of the Judiciary? Considerations from Recent Events in Thailand', *The Pacific Review*, 23(5): 671-691.

Dressel, Björn, 2014, 'Governance, Courts and Politics in Asia', *Journal of Contemporary Asia*, 44(2): 259-278.

Dressel, Björn and Khemthong Tonsakulrungruang, 2019, 'Judiciary and Judicialisation in Thailand', in Pavin Chachavalpongpun ed., *Routledge Handbook of Contemporary Thailand*, London: Routledge, pp. 165-176.

Dressel, Björn and Marcus Mietzner, 2012, 'A Tale of Two Courts: The Judicialization of Electoral Politics in Asia', *Governance*, 25(3): 391-414.

Edles, Laura Desfor, 1995, 'Rethinking Democratic Transition: A Culturalist, Critique and the Spanish Case', *Theory and Society*, 24(3): 355-384.

Endō, Satoshi, 2008, 'Tai Okoku Kenpo no Seitei Katei to Sono Seiritsu' (The Process of Enactment of the Constitution of Thailand and Its Formation), *Gaikoku no Rippo* (Foreign Legislation), no. 235, Research and Legislative Reference Bureau, National Diet Library, pp. 204-221.

Ferrara, Federico, Erik S. Herron and Misa Nishikawa, 2005, *Mixed Electoral Systems Contamination and its Consequences*, New York and Hampshire: Palgrave Macmillan.

Freedman, Amy L., 2007, 'Consolidation or Withering Away of Democracy? Political Changes in Thailand and Indonesia', *Asian Affairs: An American Review*, 33(4): 195-216.

Funston, John, 2000, 'Political Reform in Thailand: Real or Imagined?', *Asian Journal of Political Science*, 8(2): 89-108.

Gardiner, John, 1993, 'Defining Corruption', *Corruption and Reform*, 7(2): 111–124.

Gargarella, Roberto, 2004, 'In Search of Democratic Justice – What Courts Should Not Do: Argentina, 1983-2002', in Siri Gloppen, Roberto Gargarella and Elin Skaar eds., *Democratization and the Judiciary: The Accountability Function of Courts in New Democracies*, London and Portland: Frank Cass, pp. 181–197.

Ginsburg, Tom, 2003, *Judicial Review in New Democracies: Constitutional Courts in Asian Cases*, Cambridge: Cambridge University Press.

Ginsburg, Tom, 2009, 'Constitutional Afterlife: The Continuing Impact of Thailand's Postpolitical Constitution', *I·CON*, 7(1): 83–105.

Ginsburg, Tom, 2012, 'Courts and New Democracies: Recent Works', *Public Law Working Paper* No. 388, University of Chicago.

Girling, John, 1981, *Thailand: Society and Politics*, Ithaca: Cornell University Press.

Girling, John, 1997, *Corruption, Capitalism and Democracy*, London and New York: Routledge.

Guzzetta, Giovanni, 2008, 'Legal Standards and Ethical Norms Defining the Limits of Conflicts Regulations', in Christine Trost and Alison L. Gash eds., *Conflict of Interest and Public Life: Cross-National Perspectives*, New York: Cambridge University Press, pp. 21–34.

Hagino, Yoshio, Hiroyuki Hata and Kazuo Hatanaka, 2007, *Ajia Kneposhu Dai 2 han* (Asian Constitution Collection, 2nd edition), Tokyo: Akashi Shoten.

Handley, Paul, 1997, 'More of the Same? Politics and Business, 1987-96', in Kevin Hewison ed., *Political Change in Thailand: Democracy and Participation*, London and New York: Routledge, pp. 94–113.

Harding, Andrew, 2012, 'The Politics of Law and Development in Thailand: Seeking Rousseau, Finding Hobbes', in Gerald Paul McAlinn and Caslav Pejovic eds., *Law and Development in Asia*, London and New York: Routledge, pp. 109–136.

Harding, Andrew and Peter Leyland, 2011, *The Constitutional System of Thailand: A Contextual Analysis*, Oxford and Portland: Hart Publishing.

Heidenheimer, Arnold J., 1970, *Political Corruption: Readings in Comparative Analysis*, New York: Holt Rinehart and Winston, Inc.

Hewison, Kevin, 1996, 'Political Oppositions and Regime Change in Thailand', in Garry Rodan ed., *Political Oppositions in Industrialising Asia*, London and New York: Routledge.

Hewison, Kevin, 1997, 'The Monarchy and Democratization', in Kevin Hewison eds., *Political Change in Thailand: Democracy and Participation*, London: Routledge, pp. 58–74.

Hewison, Kevin and Kengkij Kitirianglarp, 2010, 'Thai-Style Democracy: The Royalist Struggle for Thailand's Politics', in Soren Ivarsson and Lotte Isager eds., *Saying the Unsayable: Monarchy and Democracy in Thailand*, Copenhagen: Nordic Institute of Asian Studies, pp. 179–202.

Hicken, Allen, 2006, 'Party Fabrication: Constitutional Reform and the Rise of Thai Rak Thai', *Journal of East Asian Studies*, 6: 381–407.

Hicken, Allen, 2009, *Building Party Systems in Developing Democracies*, New York: Cambridge University Press.

Higley, John and Michael G. Burton, 1989, 'The Elite Variable in Democratic Transitions and Breakdowns', *American Sociological Review*, 54(1): 17–32.

Higuchi, Yoichi, 1994, *Gendai Horitsugaku Zenshu 36, Hikaku Kenpo, Zentei Dai 3 Pan* (The Collected Edition of Modern Law 36, Comparative Constitutional Law, a Completely Revised Edition 3), Tokyo: Seirin Shoin.

Hirschl, Ran, 2006, 'The New Constitution and the Judicialization of Pure Politics Worldwide', *Fordham Law Review*, 75(2): 721–753.

Hirschl, Ran, 2008, 'The Judicialization of Mega-Politics and the Rise of Political Courts', *Annu. Rev. Polit. Sci.*, 11: 93–118.

Huntington, Samuel P., 1991, *The Third Wave: Democratization in the Late Twentieth Century*, Norman: University of Oklahoma Press.

Imaizumi, Shinya, 2003, 'Tai no Seiji Kaikaku to 1997 Nen Kenpo' (Political Reforms in Thailand and the 1997 Constitution), in Naoyuki Sakumoto and Shinya Imaizumi eds., *Ajia no Minshuka Katei to Ho: Firipin, Tai, Indoneshia no Hikaku* (Democratization Process and Law in Asia: Comparison of the Philippines, Thailand, and Indonesia), Tokyo: Institute of Developing Economies, Japan External Trade Organization (IDE-JETRO), pp. 41–68.

Imaizumi, Shinya, 2008, 'Saiban Seido Kaikaku: Tai Seiji no Shihoka to Sono Genkai' (Court Reform: Judicialization of Thai Politics and Its Limitations), in Yoshifumi Tamada and Tsuruyo Funatsu eds., *Tai Seiji Gyosei no Henkaku: 1991–2006* (Thailand in Motion: Political and Administrative Changes, 1991–2006), Tokyo: IDE-JETRO, pp. 67–116.

Imaizumi, Shinya, 2012, 'Tai no Rippo Katei no Kozo to Tokucho' (Structure and Characteristics of the Legislative Process in Thailand), in Shinya Imaizumi ed., *Tai no Rippo Katei: Kokumin no Seiji Sanka e no Mosaku* (The Legislative Process in Thailand: The Search for Political Participation of the People), Tokyo: IDE-JETRO, pp. 29–74.

Ji, Ungpakorn, 1997, *The Struggle for Democracy and Social Justice in Thailand*, Bangkok: Arom Pongpangan Foundation.

Ji, Giles Ungpakorn, 2002, 'From Tragedy to Comedy: Political Reform in Thailand', *Journal of Contemporary Asia*, 32(2): 191–205.

Juree, Vichit-Vadakan, 2011, 'Public Ethics and Corruption in Thailand', in Evan M. Berman ed., *Public Administration in Southeast Asia: Thailand, Philippines, Malaysia, Hong Kong, and Macao*, Boca Raton: CRC Press, pp. 79–137.

Kamonchai Rattanasakaowong, 1995, *San Ratthathammanun lae Withi Phicharana Kadhi Ratthathammanun* (Constitutional Courts and Methods of Hearing Constitutional Litigation), Bangkok: Samnakgan kongthun sanapsanun kanwichai.

Kanin Bunsuwan, 1999, *Prawat ratthathammanun Thai* (History of the Constitution of Thailand), Bangkok: Samnakphim Phumpanya.

Kanin Bunsuwan, 2008, *Ratthathammanun 2550: Thammai Tong Kae* (The 2007 Constitution: Why Should It Be Amended?), Bangkok: Prachathathat.

Kasit Piromya, 2012, 'Thailand's Rocky Path towards a Full-Fledged Democracy', in Michael J. Montesano, Pavin Chachavalpongpun and Aekapol Chongvilaivan eds., *Bangkok May 2010: Perspectives on a Divided Thailand*, Singapore: Institute of Southeast Asian Studies, pp. 161–170.

Katō, Kazuhide, 1995, *Tai Gendai Seijishi: Kokuo wo Genshu to suru Minshu Shugi* (Modern Thai Political History: Democracy with the King as Head of State), Tokyo: Kobundo.

Kawamura, Koichi, 2012, 'Shiho Seido' (Judicial System), in Masashi Nakamura ed., *Tonan Ajia no Hikaku Seijigaku* (Comparative Politics in Southeast Asia), Tokyo: IDE-JETRO, 77–102.

Kawanaka, Takeshi, 2018, *Kotai Suru Minshu Shugi: Kyoka Sareru Keni Shugi -Sairyo no Seiji Seido to wa Nani ka-* (Democracy in Retreat: Strengthening Authoritarianism - What is the Best Political System?), Tokyo: Minerva Shobo.

Khanakammakan phattana prachathipatai, 1995, *Khosanoe Krop Kwamkhit nai Kanpatirup Kanmueang Thai* (A Proposed Framework for Thinking in Thai Political Reform), Bangkok: Samnakngan kongthun sanapsanun kanwichai.

Khanakammakan Po. Po. Cho., 2010, *Phon-ngan Khanakammakan Po Po Cho nai rop3 pi (2550–2552)* (Three-Year Results of the National Anti-Corruption Commission: 2007–2009), Po Po Cho. http://www.nacc.go.th/ (accessed April 29, 2010).

Khanakammakansueksa Naeothang Kankaekhai Phuemtuem Ratthathammanun, 2006, *Naeothang Kaekhai Puemtuem Ratthatahammanun rueang San Ratthathammanun* (Constitutional Amendment Policy on the Constitutional Court), Bangkok: Samnakganlekhathikan sapaphuthaenratsadon.

Khanin Bunsuwan, 1999, *Prawat Ratthathammanun Thai* (History of the Constitution of Thailand), Bangkok: Samnakphim Phumipanya.

Khien Theeravit, 1997, *Thailand in Crisis: A Study of the Political Turmoil of May 1992*, the Thailand Research Fund and the Institute of Asian Studies, Chulalongkorn University.

Khien Theeravit, 2011, *Thaksin Shinawatra and the Political Turmoil in Thailand*, Bangkok: Thai World Affairs Center Institute of Asian Studies, Chulalongkorn University.

Klein, James R., 1998, 'The Constitution of the Kingdom of Thailand, 1997: A Blueprint for Participatory Democracy', *Working Paper #8*, Asia Foundation.

Kobayashi, Shozo, 1999, *Hikaku Kenpogaku: Josetsu* (Comparative Constitutional Law: An Introduction), Tokyo: Seibundo.

Kobkua Suwannathat-Pian, 2004, *King, Country and Constitution: Thailand's Political Development 1932-2000*, London and New York: RoutledgeCurzon.

Kochu, Nobuo, 2010, 'Tai Okoku no Kenpo' (Constitution of the Kingdom of Thailand), *Seisaku Sozo Kenkyu* (The Journal of Policy Studies), 3: 61–93.

Kowit Wongsurawat, 2010, *Kanmueang Kanpokrong Thai: Lai Miti* (Politics, Governing Thailand: Different Aspects), Bangkok: Krongkan Ratthasatsueksa Phakwicha Ratthasat lae Ratthaprasatsanamai Mahawitthayalai Kasetrasat.

Kriengsak Charoenwongsak, 2003, *Sapha thi Prueksa Setthakit lae Sangkhom haeng Chat kap Naeo nayobai phuenthan haeng chat* (Advisory Council of National Economic Development and National Basic Policy), Rat. Ratthasapasan, April, 2003, Bangkok. LIRT, 51-4. http://dl.parliament.go.th/handle/lirt/25481 (accessed July 10, 2012).

Kubo, Keiich, 2012, 'Posto shakai shugiken ni okeru minshu shugi no shitsu: Taisei tenkangono bunki no kitei yōin ni kansuru keiryō bunseki' (Quality of democracy in the post-socialist world: Econometric analysis of the determinants of divergence after regime change), *Gendai minshu shugi no saikentō: Nihon Hikaku Seiji Gakkai nenpō 14* (Reexamination of Modern Democracy: Annual Report of Japan Association for Comparative Politics, 14), Minerva Shobo, pp. 27–58

Kuhonta, Erik Martinez, 2008, 'The Paradox of Thailand's 1997 "People's Constitution": Be Careful What You Wish For', *Asian Survey*, 48(3): 373–392.

Levitsky, Steven and Daniel Ziblatt, 2018, *How Democracies Die - What History Reveals about Our Future*, London: Penguin Books.

Levitsky, Steven and Lucan A. Way, 2010, *Competitive Authoritarianism: Hybrid Regime after Cold War*, Cambridge: Cambridge University Press.

Likhit Thirawekhin, 2010, *Kanmueang Kanpokkhrong khong Thai Chabap Phim Krangthi8 Kaekhai Prapprung* (Political Administration in Thailand, 8th Revised Edition), Bangkok: Samnakphim Mahawitthayalai Thammasat.

Lipset, Seymour Martin, 1959, 'Some Social Requisites of Democracy: Economic Development and Political Legitimacy', *The American Political Science Review*, 53(1): 69–105.

Machidori, Satoshi, 2015, *Daigisei Minshu Shugi: 'Mini' to 'Seijika' wo Toinaosu* (Representative Democracy: Questioning the 'Will of the People' and 'Politicians'), Tokyo: Chuko Shinsho.

Manit Chumpa, 2008, *Khwamru Bueangton Kiaokap Ratthathammanun haeng Ratcha-anachakthai* (Basic Knowledge of the Constitution of Thailand), Bangkok: Samnakphim haeng Chulalongkon Mahawitthayalai.

Manit Chumpa, 2010, *Tham-Top Kotmai Ratthathammanun* (Questions and Answers, Legal Constitution), Bangkok: Samnakphim haeng Chulalongkon Mahawitthayalai.

McCargo, Duncan, 1998, 'Alternative Meanings of Political Reform in Contemporary Thailand', *The Copenhagen Journal of Asian Studies*, 13(98): 5–30.

McCargo, Duncan, 2000, *Politics and the Press in Thailand: Media Machinations*, London and New York: Routledge.

McCargo, Duncan, 2001, 'Populism and Reformism in Contemporary Thailand', *South East Asia Research*, 9(1): 89–107.

McCargo, Duncan, 2005, 'Network Monarchy and Legitimacy Crises in Thailand', *The Pacific Review*, 18(4): 499–519.

McCargo, Duncan, 2019, *Fighting for Virtue: Justice and Politics in Thailand*, Ithaca, N.Y.: Cornell University Press.

McCargo, Duncan and Ukrist Pathumanand, 2005, *The Thaksination of Thailand*, Copenhagen: NIAS Press.

Medhi Krongkaew, 2008, 'Private Gain from Public Loss: How Thailand Copes with Corruption from Conflict of Interest', in *Managing Conflict of Interest: Frameworks, Tools, and Instruments for Preventing, Detecting and Managing Conflict of Interest*, pp. 92–116, Asian Development Bank. http://www.oecd.org/dataoecd/50/12/40838870.pdf (accessed December 1, 2011).

Mérieau, Eugénie, 2016, 'Thailand's Deep State, Royal Power and the Constitutional Court (1997–2015)', *Journal of Contemporary Asia*, 46(3), 445–466.

Mérieau, Eugénie, 2021, *Constitutional Bricolage: Thailand's Sacred Monarchy vs. the Rule of Law (Constitutionalism in Asia)*, Oxford: Hart Publishing.

Messick, Richard E., 2008, 'Regulating Conflict of Interest: International Experience with Asset Declaration and Disclosure', *Managing Conflict of Interest: Frameworks Tools and Instruments for Preventing Detecting and Managing Conflict of Interest*, pp. 36–43, Asian Development Bank. http://www.oecd.org/dataoecd/50/12/40838870.pdf (accessed December 1, 2011)

Müller, Jan-Werner, 2017, *Kenpo Patoriotizumu* (Constitutional Patriotism), Kazuhisa Saito, Shinichi Tabata and Yohei Koike (trans.), Tokyo: Hosei University Press.

Murashima, Eiji, 1987, 'Tai ni okeru Seiji Taisei no Shukiteki Tenkan: Gikaisei Minshu Shugi to Gunbu no Seiji Kainyu' (Cyclical Transformation of the Political System in Thailand: Parliamentary Democracy and Military Intervention in Politics), in Yoshiyuki Hagiwara and Eiji Murashima eds., *ASEAN Shokoku no Seiji Taisei* (Political System of ASEAN Countries), Tokyo: IDE-JETRO.

Murray, David, 1996, *Angels and Devils: Thai Politics from February 1991 to September 1992: A Struggle for Democracy?*, Bangkok: White Orchid Press.

Mutebi, Alex M., 2008, 'Explaining the Failure of Thailand's Anti-Corruption Regime', *Development and Change*, 39(1): 147–171.

Neher, Clark D., 1977, 'Political Corruption in a Thai Province', *Journal of Developing Areas*, 11(4): 479–492.

Nelson, Michael H., 2008, 'Thaksin Overthrown: Thailand's "Well-intentioned" Coup', in Thang D. Nguyen ed., *The Thai Challenge: Unity, Stability and Democracy in Times of Uncertainty*, New York: Nova Science, pp. 11–22.

Nidhi Eoseewong, 2009, *Thang-ok khong "Phak Prachachon" nai Kansawaeng Chutruam Bon Wethi Kanmueang Yukmai Rakya Sang Ban Chonchanklang Sang mueang* (The Exit of the People in the Search for a Meeting Point in the Political Arena of the New Era: Grassroots People Build Communities, Middle Class Build Nations), Bangkok: Matichon.

Nidhi Eoseewong, 2010, *An Kanmueang Thai Lamdap thi 1: Kanmueang Rueang Phi Thaksin* (Thai Politics 1st: The Politics of Thaksin's Ghost Story), Bangkok: Open Books.

Niyom Rathamarit, 2006a, 'Corruption Inquiry and the Impeachment Process in Thailand', in Niyom Rathamarit, ed., *Eyes on Thai Democracy National and Local Issues*, Bangkok: King Prajadhipok's Institute, pp. 49–72.

Niyom Rathamarit, 2006b, *Re-Establishing Democracy: How Kriangsak and Prem Managed Political Parties*, Bangkok: King Prajadhipok's Institute.

Nualnoi Treerat, 2004, 'Controlling Corruption in Thailand: Transforming the Problems and Paradoxes', in Vinay Bhargava and Emil Bolongaita eds., *Challenging Corruption in Asia: Case Studies and a Framework for Action*, Washington: The World Bank, pp. 171–207.

Nualnoi Treerat, 2005, 'Combating Corruption in the Transformation of Thailand', in Nicholas Tarling ed., *Corruption and Good Governance in Asia*, New York: Routledge.

Ockey, James, 1992, 'Business Leaders, Gangsters and the Middle Class', PhD dissertation, Cornell University.
Ockey, James, 2004, *Making Democracy: Leadership, Class, Gender, and Political Participation in Thailand*, Chiang Mai: Silkworm Books.
Ockey, James, 2008, 'Thailand in 2007: The Struggle to Control Democracy', *Asian Survey*, 48(1): 20–28.
O'Donnell, Guillermo, 2005, 'Why the Rule of Law matters', in Larry Diamond and Leonardo Morlino eds., *Assessing the Quality of Democracy*, Baltimore: The Johns Hopkins University Press, pp. 3–17.
O'Donnell, Guillermo, Philippe C. Schmitter and Laurence Whitehead, 1986, *Transitions from Authoritarian Rule: Comparative Perspectives*, The Johns Hopkins University Press.
Ōtomo, Nao, 2003, 'Tai ni okeru Oshoku to Fusei: 1997 Nen Kenpo no Torikumi' (Corruption and Fraud in Thailand: The 1997 Constitution Enforcement), in Naoyuki Sakumoto and Shinya Imaizumi eds., *Ajia no Minshuka Katei to Ho: Firipin, Tai, Indoneshia no Hikaku* (Democratization Process and Law in Asia: Comparison of the Philippines, Thailand, and Indonesia), Tokyo: IDE-JETRO, pp. 129–165.
Ottaway, Marina, 2003, *Democracy Challenged: The Rise of Semi-Authoritarianism*, Washington DC: Carnegie Endowment for International Peace.
Pasuk Phongpaichit, 2004, 'Keynote Speech "People's Government, People's Rights, People's Justice"', in Nuannoi Trirat ed., *Prachathipatai Prachasit Prachatham* (Democracy, People's Rights, People's Justice), Bangkok: Political Economy Research Center, pp. 12–20.
Pasuk Phongpaichit and Chris Baker, 1996, *Thailand's Boom!*, Chiang Mai: Silkworm Books.
Pasuk Phongpaichit and Chris Baker, 2000, *Thailand's Crisis*. Chiang Mai: Silkworm Books.
Pasuk, Phongpaichit and Chris Baker, 2004, *Thaksin: The Business of Politics in Thailand*, Chiang Mai: Silkworm Books.
Pasuk Phongpaichit and Chris Baker, 2009, *Thaksin: The Business of Politics in Thailand*, second edition, Chiang Mai: Silkworm Books.
Pasuk Phongpaichit and Sungsidh Piriyarangsan, 1994, *Corruption and Democracy in Thailand*, Chiang Mai: Silkworm Books.
Peerenboom, Randall, 2004, 'Varieties of Rule of Law: An Introduction and Provisional Conclusion', in Randall Peerenboom ed., *Asian Discourses of Rule of Law*, London: Routledge, pp. 1–55.
Phaithun Bunwat, 1995, *Rabop Kanluaektang thi Lot Kansuesiang lae hai Okat Khondi Samak Luaektang phuea Thotthaen Rabop Kanlueaktang thi chai yu nai Patchuban* (An Alternative to the Current Electoral System that Reduces Vote Buying and Gives People of Good Moral Character the Opportunity to Run for Office), Bangkok: Samnakgan Kongthun Sanapsanun Kanwichai.
Phopu Khruba, 2010, *Thaksin phit, duai rue ?* (Is Thaksin Wrong?), Bangkok: Khe.Khe. plaplitching.
Piyabutr Saengkanokkul, 2016, *Ratthammanun-Prawathisat khokhwamkhit amnat sathapana lae kanplianphan* (History and Changes in the Concept of Sovereignty), Nonthaburi: Fa Diao kan.

Poonthep Sirinupong, 2016, *Talok Ratthathammanun* (The Ridiculous Constitution), Bangkok: Shine Publishing House.

Prajak Kongkirati, 2016, 'The Rise and Fall of Electoral Violence in Thailand: Changing Rules, Structures, and Power Landscapes', in Eugénie Mérieau ed., *The Politics of (No) Elections in Thailand: Lessons from the 2011 General Election*, Bangkok: White Lotus Press, pp. 15–44.

Prawase Wasi, 2002, 'An Overview of Political Reform', in Duncan McCargo ed., *Reforming Thai Politics*, Copenhagen: Nordic Institute of Asian Studies, pp. 21–35.

Pye, Lucian W., 1990, 'Political Science and the Crisis of Authoritarianism', *American Political Science Review*, 84.

Reilly, Benjamin, 2007, 'Democratization and Electoral Reform in the Asia-Pacific Region: Is There an "Asian Model" of Democracy?', *Comparative Political Studies*, 40(11): 1350–1371.

Riggs, Fred W., 1966, *Thailand: The Modernization of a Bureaucratic Polity*, Honolulu: East-West Center Press.

Saichon Sattayanurak, 2021, 'Historical Legacy and the Emergence of Judicialization in the Thai State', in Michael K. Conners and Ukrist Pathmanand eds., *Thai Politics Translation: Monarchy, Democracy and the Supraconstitution*, Copenhagen: NIAS Press, pp. 187–216.

Sakaguchi, Shojiro, 2001, *Rikken Shugi to Minshu Shugi* (Constitutionalism and Democracy), Tokyo: Nippon Hyoron sha.

Samnakgan Lekhathikan Sapha Phuthaenratsadon, 2006, *Naeothang Kankaekhai Phuemtuem Ratthathammanun rueang Khanaratthamontri lae Kankaekhai Phuemtuem Ratthathammanun rueang Ratthasapha* (Constitutional Reform Policy of the Cabinet and the Parliament), Bangkok: Samnakgan Lekhathikan Sapha Phuthaenratsadon.

Sampford, Charles, 2006, *Retrospectivity and the Rule of Law*, New York: Oxford University Press.

Sane Camarik, 1998, *Kanmuang thai kap phattanakan ratthathammanun* (Thai Politics and Constitutional Development), Bangkok: Munlanithi khrongkan tamra sangkhommasat lae manutsayasat.

Saneh Chamarik, 2006, *Kanmueang Thai kap Phattanakan Ratthathammanun* (Thai Politics and Constitutional Development), Bangkok: The Foundation for the Promotion of Social Sciences and Humanities Textbooks Project.

Sarakhadi (Future Magazine), 1998, *Ruam lueat nuea chat chuea Thai- Ruam sam hetkan samkhannu thang prawathisat kanmueang Thai* (Gathering the Blood and Flesh of the Thai Nation: Three Important Events in Thai Political History), Bangkok: *Sarakhadi* (Future Magazine).

Sathaban Phrapokklao, 2001, *Khrongkan chaluem Phrakiat Saranukrom Ratthathammanun haeng Ratchaanachak Thai* (Project in Honor of His Majesty the King, Encyclopedia of the Constitution of the Kingdom of Thailand, 1997) (Pho. So. 2540): Rabop Kanlueaktang. Nonthaburi: Sathaban Phrapokklao.

Sato, Koji, 2015, *Hoso Daigaku Sosho 028 Rikken Shugi ni tsuite: Seiritsu Katei to Gendai* (The Open University of Japan Series 028, On Constitutionalism: Establishment Process and the Present Day), Tokyo: Sayu sha.

Scott, James C., 1972, *Comparative Political Corruption*, Englewood Cliffs: Prentice-Hall.

Seksan Praseritkun, 2005, *Kanmueang Phak Prachachon nai Rabop Prachathipathai Thai* (National Sector Politics in Thailand's Democratic System), Bangkok: Wiphasa.

Shapiro, Martin, 2004, 'Judicial Review in Developed Democracies', in Siri Gloppen, Roberto Gargarella and Elin Skaar eds., *Democratization and the Judiciary: The Accountability Function of Courts in New Democracies*, London and Portland: Frank Cass, pp. 7–26.

Shimojo, Yoshiaki, 2000, '"Tai Shiki Rippo Shugi" ni okeru Jinken Hosho' (Human Rights Guarantees in 'Thai-Style Constitutionalism'), in Yasumi Doi ed., *Tonan Ajia Shokoku Kenpo ni okeru Jinken Hosho* (Human Rights Guarantees in the Constitutions of Southeast Asian Countries), Tokyo: Sagano Shoin, pp. 157–177.

Shimojo, Yoshiaki, 2004, 'Tai Okoku no Kenpo Seido: Tai no Minshuka to 1997 (Butsureki 2540) nen Okoku Kenpo no Tokushoku' (Constitutional System of the Kingdom of Thailand: Democratization of Thailand and Features of the Kingdom's 1997 Constitution [Buddhist Era 2540]), *Commerce and Business Review*, 45(1): 25–43, Kyushu Sangyo University.

Shimojo, Yoshiaki, 2010, 'Tai Kenposhi ni okeru Rikken Kunshusei no Tenkai to Oken no Kannen' (The Development of a Constitutional Monarchy and the Idea of Kingship in Thai Constitutional History), *Commerce and Business Review*, 50(2): 17–40, Kyushu Sangyo University.

Shimojo, Yoshiaki, 2013, 'Tai Kenpo Seiji no Tokushoku to Kokuo Gainen: Hikaku Bunmeiteki Shiten wo Majiete' (Features of Thai Constitutional Politics and the Concept of the King: With a Comparative Civilizational Perspective), *Bunmei Kyushu* (Civilization Studies in Kyushu), 7, 55–66

Shiyake, Masanori and Miyoko Tsujimura eds., 2010, *Shin Kaisetsu: Sekai Kenposhu Dai 2 han* (New Commentary: International Constitution Collection 2nd edition), Tokyo: Sanseido.

Sinpeng, Aim, 2021, *Opposing Democracy in the Digital Age: The Yellow Shirts in Thailand*, Ann Arbor: University of Michigan Press.

Siracha Charoenphanit and Somchat Thamsiri, 2002, 'Panha Kanmueang Thai kap Kotmai' (Thai Political Issues and Law), in Sakhawicha Ratthasat Mahawitthayalai Sukhothaithammathirat ed., *Ekkasan Kanson Chutwicha: Panha Kanmueang Thai Patchuban Current Political Issues Nuai thi 9-15* (Current Thai Political Issues: Chapters 9–15), Nonthaburi: Sukhothaithammathirat University Book Center, pp. 234–291.

Siripan Nogsuan Sawasdee, 2006, *Thai Political Parties in the Age of Reform*, Bangkok: Institute of Public Policy Studies.

Sombat Chantornvong, 2002, 'The 1997 Constitution and the Politics of Electoral Reform', in Duncan McCargo ed., *Reforming Thai Politics*, Copenhagen: Nordic Institute of Asian Studies, pp. 203–222.

Somkit Lertpaithoon, 2007, *Khwampenma lae Chettanarom khong Rattathammanun haeng Ratcha-anachakthai phuttasakarat 2550* (Origin and Spirit of the 1997 Constitution), Nonthaburi: King Prajadhipok's Institute.

Somkit Lertpaithoon, 2008, 'The Origins and Spirit of the 2007 Constitution', in Wutthisarn Tanchai ed., *KPI Yearbook4 Exploring the 2007 Constitution*, Nonthaburi: King Prajadhipok's Institute, pp. 1–42.

Sripan Rattikalchalakorn, 2009, 'Politics under Thaksin: Popular Support, Elite Concern', in John Funston ed., *Thaksin's Thailand: Populism and Polarisation*, Bangkok: Institute of Security & International Studies.

Streckfuss, David, 2011, *Truth on Trial in Thailand: Defamation, Treason, and Lese-majeste*, London and New York: Routledge.

Suchit Bunbongkan, 2002, 'Panha Kanmueang Thai kap Khorapchan' (Thai Political Issues and Corruption), in Sakhawicha Ratthasat Mahawitthayalai Sukhothaithammathirat ed., *Ekkasan Kanson Chutwicha: Panha Kanmueang Thai Patchuban Current Political Issues Nuai thi 1-8* (Current Thai Political Issues: Chapters 1–8), Nonthaburi: Sukhothaithammathirat University Book Center, pp. 180–210.

Suchit Bunbongkarn, 2006, 'A Reflection on the Role of a Justice of the Thai Constitutional Court', in Niyom Rathamarit ed., *Eyes on Thai Democracy National and Local Issues*, Bangkok: King Prajadhipok's Institute, pp. 41–48.

Suchit Bunbongkarn, 2009, 'Thailand's 2007 Constitution and Re-emerging Democracy: Will Political Polarization Continue?', in John Funston ed., *Divided over Thaksin: Thailand's Coup and Problematic Transition*, Singapore: Institute of Southeast Asian Studies, pp. 89–95.

Suchit Bunbongkarn and Prudhisan Jumbala, 2012, *Monarchy and Constitutional Rule in Democratizing Thailand*, Bangkok: Institute of Thai Studies, Chulalongkorn University.

Suehiro, Akira, 1993, *Tai: Kaihatsu to Minshu Shugi* (Thailand: Development and Democracy), Tokyo: Iwanami Shoten.

Suraphol Nitikraipot, 1995, *Rabop Khuapkumtruatsop Ratthaban thang Kanmueang thi mosom* (Politically Appropriate Inspection Systems for Government), Bangkok: Samnakngan Kongthun Sanapsanun Kanwichai.

Suraphon Traiwet, 2006, *Phramahakasat Ratthathammanun lae Prachathipatai* (King, Constitution and Democracy), Bangkok: Winyuchon Publication House.

Surin Maisrikrod, 1992, *Thailand's Two General Elections in 1992: Democracy Sustained*, Singapore: Institute of Southeast Asian Studies.

Surin Maisrikrod, 1997, 'The Making of Thai Democracy: A Study of Political Alliances among the State, the Capitalists, and the Middle Class', in Anek Laothamatas ed., *Democratization in Southeast Asia and East Asia 1997*, Singapore: Institute of Southeast Asian Studies.

Suthacai Impraserit, 2012, 'Prawatisat waduai Kanratthaprahan nai Prathet Thai', (History of Coups in Thailand), in Chetda Chotikitphiwat and Witthatakon Bunrueang eds., *Prachachon Tan Ratthaprahan*, Bangkok: Laisen, pp. 13–44.

Tamada, Yoshifumi, 1988, 'Tai no Jitsugyoka Seito to Gun' (Thai Businessmen's Parties and the Military), *Japanese Journal of Southeast Asian Studies*, 26(3): 293–307.

Tamada, Yoshifumi, 2003, *Minshuka no Kyozo to Jitsuzo: Tai Gendai Seiji Hendo no Mekanizumu* (False Images and Realities of Democratization: Mechanisms of Contemporary Political Change in Thailand), Kyoto: Kyoto University Press.

Tamada, Yoshifumi, 2005, 'Takkushin Seiken no Antei: Hossoku 3 nen me ni atatte' (Stability of the Thaksin Regime: On the Occasion of the 3rd Year Since Its Establishment), *Asian and African Area Studies*, 4(2): 167–194, Graduate School of Asian and African Area Studies, Kyoto University.

Tamada, Yoshifumi, 2006, 'Tai Seiji no Minshuka to Kaikaku' (Democratization and Reform of Thai Politics), in Yoshifumi Tamada and Kan Kimura eds., *Minshuka to Nashonarizumu no Genchiten* (Democratization and the Current Point of Nationalism), Tokyo: Minerva Shobo, pp. 78–102.

Tamada, Yoshifumi, 2009, 'Democracy and Populism in Thailand', in Kosuke Mizuno and Pasuk Phongpaichit eds., *Populism in Asia*, Singapore: NUS Press, pp. 94–111.

Tamada, Yoshifumi, 2010, 'Tai ni okeru Senkyo wo meguru Kobo: Minshuka to Datsu Minshuka' (The Offensive and Defense over Elections in Thailand: Democratization and De-democratization), in Yoko Yoshikawa ed., *Minshu Katei no Senkyo: Chiiki Kenkyu kara Mita Seito, Kohosha, Yukensha* (Elections in the Democratic Process: Political Parties, Candidates, and Voters from Regional Studies), Tokyo: Koro sha, pp. 223–244.

Tamada, Yoshifumi, 2014, '10 gatsu 14 ka Seihen kara 40 nen: Tai Seiji no Genchiten' (Forty Years after the October 14 Political Upheaval: The Current Point in Thai Politics), *Kokusai Josei: Kiyo* (International Affairs: Bulletin), vol. 84 (February), The Institute Of International Affairs, 239–262.

Tate, Neal C., 1994, 'The Judicialization of Politics in the Philippines and Southeast Asia', *International Political Science Review*, 15(2): 187–197.

Thak Chaloemtiarana, 2007, *Thailand: The Politics of Despotic Paternalism*, Ithaca: Cornell University Press.

Thawilwadee Bureekul and Ratchawadee Sangmahamad, 2017, 'Kansanapsunun Prachathipatai Thai: Phonkansamruat Asian Barometer Survey' (Promoting Thai Democracy: Asia Barometer Survey Results), in Amphon Thamronglak, Thampaphon Darayen and Napanat kaewket eds., *Kanprachum wichakanratprasasonsat radapchat khrang thi 5* (Fifth National Conference on Public Administration Proceeding), Bangkok: Samakhom ratprasasonsat haeng pratet Thai, pp. 2–27.

Thiradet Iamsamron and Ram Judaravichit, 2008, *Thot salak khadhi Prasert PhraWihan-Kan mueang mai: Wiwatha kuru sutyot haeng thotsawat* (Unraveling the Lawsuit of Temple Phra Wiharn: New Politics, the Best Guru Bickering in the Past Decade), Bangkok: Matichon Publishing.

Thiraphat Serirangsan, 2010, *Nakkanmueang Thai: Chariyatham, Phonprayotthapson, Kankhorapchan-Sapappanha, Sahet, Phonkrathop, Naeo thang Kaekhai Phim khrangthi 2* (Thai Politician: Ethics, Contrary Interests, Sewage – Status of the Problem, Causes, Effects, Directions for Solving the Problem, 2nd Edition), Bangkok: Saithran Publish.

Thitinan Pongsudhirak, 2009, 'The Tragedy of the 1997 Constitution', in John Funston ed., *Divided over Thaksin Thailand's Coup and Problematic Transition*, Singapore: Institute of Southeast Asian Studies, pp. 89–95.

Thongchai Winichakul, 2008, 'Toppling Democracy', *Journal of Contemporary Asia*, 38(1): 11–37.

Toyama, Ayako, 2016, 'Tai rikken kunshusei to wa nani ka: Fukusho kara no ichi kōsatsu' (What Is Thailand's Constitutional Monarchy?: A Thought from Countersignature), *Nenpō Tai kenkyū* (The journal of Thai studies), 16: 61–80.

Toyama, Ayako, 2018, '"Tai" Takkushin ha Naze Osorerare Tsuzukeru no ka: Horobinai Popyurizumu to Seiji Tairitsu Kozo no Henka' ('Thailand' Why is Thaksin Continuously Feared? Enduring Populism and the Changing Structure of Political Conflict), in Ayako Toyama, Wataru Kusaka, Tsukasa Iga and Ken Miichi eds., *21 seiki Tonan Ajia no Kyoken Seiji: "Sutorongu Man" Jidai no Torai* (Twenty-first Century Southeast Asian Coercive Politics: Coming of Age of the 'Strong Man'), Tokyo: Akashi Shoten, pp. 38–99.

Toyama, Ayako, Wataru Kusaka, Tsukasa Iga and Ken Miichi eds., 2018, *21 seiki Tonan Ajia no Kyoken Seiji: "Sutorongu Man" Jidai no Torai* (Twenty-first Century Southeast Asian Coercive Politics: Coming of Age of the 'Strong Man'), Tokyo: Akashi Shoten.

Tsujimura, Miyoko, 2010, 'Furansu Kyowa Koku' (French Republic), in Masanori Shiyake and Miyoko Tsujimua eds., *Shin Kaisetsu: Sekai Kenposhu Dai 2 han* (New Commentary: International Constitution Collection, 2nd edition), Tokyo: Sanseido, pp. 223–272.

van Roy, Edward, 1970, 'On the Theory of Corruption', *Economic Development and Cultural Change*, 19(1), October.

Vicha, Mahakun, 2007, 'Amnat Tulakan: Ongprakopmai puea Kandamrong Kwamyutitham nai Sangkhom' (Jurisdiction: A New Element for Maintaining Justice in Society), *Journal of King Prajadhipok's Institute*, 5(3): 24–36.

Vitit, Muntarbhorn, 2009, 'Deconstructing the 2007 Constitution', in John Funston ed., *Divided over Thaksin Thailand's Coup and Problematic Transition*, Singapore: Institute of Southeast Asian Studies, pp. 80–88.

Wannatham Kannachonsuwan, Seni Khamsuk and Thasothon Tuthongkham, 2002, 'Panha Kanmueang Thai dan Krabuankan thang Kanmueang' (Thai Political Issues in the Political Process), in Sakhawicha Ratthasat Mahawitthayalai and Sukhothaithammathirat, eds., *Ekkasan Kanson Chutwicha: Panha Kanmueang Thai Patchuban Current Political Issues Nuai thi 9-15* (Current Thai Political Issues Chapters 9–15), Nonthaburi: Sukhothaithammathirat University Book Center, pp. 2–58.

Wichitwong Na Pomphet, 2010, *Lakkhit nai Kan Pathirup Prathetthai* (Principles of Thought in Thai Reform), Bangkok: Vasira.

Wisanu Khrueagam, 2012, 'Witsanu chi Prachaniyom kae Panha mai dai Nae 5 lak chat tham Nayobai' (Populism Cannot Solve Problems, Present Five Principles of Policy Formation), ASTV, http://manager.co.th/Hom/Viewnews.aspx?NewsID=9550000062836 (accessed July 10, 2012).

Worachet Phakhirat, 2009, *Chut Fai nai Sailom* (Light a Fire in the Flow of the Wind), Bangkok: Open Books.

Worachet Phakhirat, 2012 (Download from http://www.enlightened-jurists.com/directory/60/Rechtstaat-vs-Rules-Of-Law.html, on August 20, 2012)

Worachet Phakhirat, 2015, *Duai Kotmai lae Udomkan* (Laws and Ideals), Bangkok: Shine Publishing House.

Yamamoto, Hajime, 2017, 'Dai 2 sho: Furansu Kenpogaku to "Rikken Shugi"' (Chapter 2: French Constitutional Law and 'Constitutionalism'), in Miyoko Tsujimura et al., ed., *Koza: Seiji Shakai no Hendo to Kenpo, Furansu Kenpo kara no Tenbo Dai 1 kan, Seiji Hendo to Rekken Shugi no Tenkai* (Lesson: Political and Social Change and the Constitution, Perspectives from the French Constitution vol.1, Political Change and the Development of Constitutionalism), Tokyo: Shinzan sha, pp. 39–80.

Administrative Documents

Constitution
Buddhist Era 2475 (1932 CE), Constitution of the Kingdom of Thailand
Buddhist Era 2489 (1946 CE), Constitution of the Kingdom of Thailand
Buddhist Era 2490 (1947 CE), Constitution of the Kingdom of Thailand
Buddhist Era 2492 (1949 CE), Constitution of the Kingdom of Thailand
Buddhist Era 2495 (1952 CE), Constitution of the Kingdom of Thailand
Buddhist Era 2511 (1968 CE), Constitution of the Kingdom of Thailand
Buddhist Era 2517 (1974 CE), Constitution of the Kingdom of Thailand
Buddhist Era 2521 (1978 CE), Constitution of the Kingdom of Thailand
Buddhist Era 2534 (1991 CE), Constitution of the Kingdom of Thailand
Buddhist Era 2540 (1997 CE), Constitution of the Kingdom of Thailand
Buddhist Era 2550 (2007 CE), Constitution of the Kingdom of Thailand
Buddhist Era 2560 (2017 CE), Constitution of the Kingdom of Thailand

Court decisions
Constitutional Court decisions
3/2543, 4/2543, 5/2543, 10/2543, 11/2543, 23/2543, 24/2543, 27/2543, 29/2543, 30/2543, 31/2543, 56/2543, 63/2543, 64/2543
1/2544, 2/2544, 5/2544, 6/2544, 7/2544, 8/2544, 19/2544, 20/2544, 21/2544, 22/2544, 23/2544, 24/2544, 25/2544, 26/2544, 28/2544, 30/2544, 31/2544, 32/2544, 34/2544, 51/2544
1/2545, 2/2545, 5/2545, 8/2545, 10/2545, 11/2545, 12/2545, 14/2545, 17/2545, 18/2545, 35/2545, 36/2545, 37/2545, 39/2545, 41/2545, 42/2545, 43/2545, 50/2545, 51/2545, 52/2545, 53/2545, 54/2545, 55/2545, 56/2545, 58/2545, 60/2545, 63/2545, 64/2545
7/2546, 12/2546, 13/2546, 15/2546, 23/2546, 25/2546, 29/2546, 31/2546, 33/2546, 38/2546, 39/2546, 42/2546, 46/2546, 47/2546, 48/2546, 50/2546, 51/2546
26/2547, 27/2547, 35/2547, 51/2547, 54/2547, 55/2547, 56/2547, 57/2547, 59/2547, 60/2547, 61/2547, 83/2547, 85/2547, 88/2547
1/2548, 2/2548, 3/2548, 31/2548, 42/2548, 46/2548, 47/2548, 48/2548, 52/2548, 57/2548, 59/2548
1/2549, 3/2549, 4/2549, 7/2549, 8/2549, 14/2549

1-2/2550, 3-5/2550, 6/2550, 7/2550, 12/2550, 13/2550, 14/2550, 15/2550, 16/2550, 17/2550, 18/2550, 19/2550, 20/2550, 21/2550, 22/2550, 23/2550, 24/2550, 25/2550, 26/2550
5/2551, 9/2551, 11/2551, 12-13/2551, 18/2551, 19/2551, 20/2551
15/2552
2/2553, 3/2553, 4-5/2553, 7/2553, 12-14/2553, 15/2553, 16/2553
22/2554, 25/2554
8-9/2555, 10-11/2555, 13/2555, 14/2555, 18-22/2555

Supreme Court decisions
Political Office Holders Criminal Litigation Division 6/2553, 1/2550, 1/2553, 10/2552, 1/2546, 3/2554, 2/2552, 2/2546, 6/2552, 8/2552, 9/2552
4/2555, 3/2555

Central Administrative Court decision
908/2552

Election Commission documents
Election Commission Resolution 66/2554, 67/2554, 69/2554, 70/2554, 72/2554, 74/2554, 75/2554, 76/2554, 77/2554, 78/2554,
79/2554, 80/2554, 83/2554, 84/2554, 88/2554, 90/2554, 92/2554, 93/2554, 95/2554

Election result statistics
General election (Year 2001, 2005, 2007, 2011)
Senate Election (Year 2000, 2008)
List of Senators

Interviews
Nakharin Mektrairat: held on 6 October 2013
Pramot Piphatana: held on 26 March 2017
Prinya Thaewanarumitkul: held on 13 June 2017
Sant Hathirat: held on 21 May 2017
Suraphol Nitikraipot: held on 8 June 2017
Vicha Mahakun: held on 2 and 5 October 2015

Bibliography

Laws
Buddhist Era 2522 (1979 CE), Election Law
Buddhist Era 2541 (1998 CE), Election Law
Buddhist Era 2550 (2007 CE), Election Law
Buddhist Era 2524 (1981 CE), Political Parties Law
Buddhist Era 2541 (1998 CE), Political Parties Law
Buddhist Era 2550 (2007 CE), Political Parties Law
Buddhist Era 2541 (1998 CE), Election Commission Law
Buddhist Era 2518 (1975 CE), Anti-corruption Law
Buddhist Era 2530 (1987 CE), Anti-corruption Law
Buddhist Era 2542 (1999 CE), Anti-corruption Law
Buddhist Era 2539 (1996 CE), Senator and Representative Assets and Liabilities Reporting Law
Buddhist Era 2543 (2000 CE), Law on the Management of the Minister's Joint Venture and Shareholding
*See Thiraphat (2010) pp. 441–448 for the conflict of interest bill drafted in 2006

Magazines
Far Eastern Economic Review

Minutes
Raingankanprachum khanakammathikan yokrang ratthathammanun 2540 (Minutes of the 1997 Constitution Drafting Committee).
Raingankanprachum khana-anukammathikan yokrang ratthathammanun 2550 kropthi2 (Minutes of the 2007 Constitution Drafting Subcommittee Group 2).
Raingankanprachum khana-anukammathikan yokrang ratthathammanun 2550 kropthi3 (Minutes of the 2007 Constitution Drafting Subcommittee Group 3).
Raingankanprachum sapha rang ratthathammanun 2550 (Minutes of the 2007 Constitution Drafting Assembly).

Newspapers
Thai: *Sayam Rat, Matichon*
English: *Bangkok Post, The Nation*

Other
Census data of Year 2000

Speech on Governance

Banharn Cabinet Policy Speech (July 26, 1995), *Official Gazette*, vol. 112–32 (July 26, 1995), 1–35

Chavalit Cabinet Policy Speech (December 11, 1996), *Official Gazette*, vol. 113–48 (December 11, 1996), 1–27

Chuan Cabinet Policy Speech (November 20, 1997), *Official Gazette*, vol. 114–112, (December 2, 1997), 1–37

Thaksin Cabinet Policy Speech (February 26, 2001), *Official Gazette*, vol. 118–21 (March 2, 2001), 1–44

Samak Cabinet Policy Speech (February 18, 2008), *Official Gazette*, vol. 125–64 (March 31, 2008), 1–41

Somchai Cabinet Policy Speech (October 7, 2008), *Official Gazette*, vol. 125–164 (October 10, 2008), 1–46

Abhisit Cabinet Policy Speech (December 30, 2008), *Official Gazette*, vol. 125–198 (December 30, 2008) 1–48

Websites

Constitutional Court: http://www.constitutionalcourt.or.th/
Election Commission: http://www.ect.go.th/
Human Rights Watch: https://www.hrw.org/ja
Office of the National Anti-Corruption Commission: http://www.nacc.go.th/
Official Gazette: http://www.ratchakitcha.soc.go.th/
Prachathai: https://prachatai.com/
Supreme Court: http://www.supremecourt.or.th/

Index

Personal Name Index

Amon Chantharasombun, 23, 27–30, 55–56, 59, 80–92, 94, 97–98, 101, 134–136, 145, 155, 170, 183, 266, 293

Anand Panyarachun, 9, 49–50, 54, 57–59, 70, 81, 339

Anek Laothamatas, 74, 112

Banharn Silpa-archa, 9, 54, 59, 86, 110, 160

Bhumibol Adulyadej (Rama IX), 33, 35, 45–47, 63, 68–71, 73, 76, 79, 139, 176, 288, 339–341, 356–357, 360

Bowonsak Uwanno, 23–24, 54, 56–60, 105–106, 109, 113–115, 140, 180, 184, 187, 331, 345–346, 348–349, 351–352

Chatchai Choonhavan, 9, 41, 43, 47, 101–102, 181

Chuan Leekpai, 9, 50, 52, 72, 160–162

De Gaulle, Charles, 19–20

Hitler, Adolph, 19, 102, 119, 135–136

Meechai Ruchuphan, 23–24, 345, 348–352, 357, 359

Montesquieu, Charles-Louis de, 125

Nakharin Mektrairat, xi, 104, 120, 126

Niwatthamrong Boonsongpaisan, 328

Piyabutr Saengkanokkul, xi, 26, 79

Potjaman Shinawatra, 251

Prasit Pivavatnapanich, 26

Prawase Wasi, 56, 59, 79, 92

Prayut Chan-o-cha, 3, 6, 9, 25, 332, 344–346, 355, 357–360

Prem Tinsulanonda, 9, 23, 47, 224, 339, 357

Samak Sundaravej, ix, 6, 9, 28, 161–162, 223, 227, 247, 251, 254, 257, 283–284, 289, 322–323

Sanya Dharmasakti, 8, 23, 69, 229, 339

Somkit, Lertpaithoon, 23, 25, 65–66, 108, 115–117, 119, 126, 180

Sondhi Limthongkul, 63, 75–76, 341

Suchinda Kraprayoon, 4, 9, 49–51, 54–56, 70–75, 81–83, 101, 138, 181, 262, 339, 341

Suraphol Nitikraipot, xi, 97–98, 101–102, 114–115, 136

Teera Suteewarangkurn, xi, 26

Thaksin Shinawatra, ix, 9, 24, 27, 31, 34, 60–63, 66, 68, 73–78, 91, 116–117, 122, 131, 180, 189, 212, 223, 243–244, 247, 249–254, 256–257, 260, 263–264, 283–286, 288–289, 291–293, 296, 313, 320–323, 325–326, 332, 335–337, 341, 344, 346, 357

Thapanan Nipithakul, 26

Thirayuth Boonmee, 45, 59, 68

Vajiralongkorn (Rama X), 33, 353, 356–358, 360–361

Vicha Mahakun, 115–117, 124, 127–129, 131–132, 134, 140

Wissanu Krea-ngam, 23–25, 148, 359

Worachet Pakeerut, xi, 25–27, 29, 79, 137, 146, 149, 263–264, 321, 326, 357

Yingluck Shinawatra, ix, 6, 9, 216, 263, 323–324, 326–329

Subject Index

14 October 1973 student uprising, 40–41, 45, 56, 68–73, 77, 227, 229, 340, 351

1992 Bloody May Incident (*pruetsapakhom tamin*), ix, 4–5, 23, 52, 68, 71, 75, 77–78, 82, 96, 101, 104, 106–107, 109, 112, 114, 134, 138, 141, 334, 341

absolute monarchy, 17, 40, 45
abuse of power, 10, 62, 66, 101, 287
accountability, *see* political reform, 10, 13, 54–55, 59, 292–293
actions associated with government designated policy, 28
administration
 change of government, 4, 7, 40
 military regime, 3, 24–25, 39–40, 43, 71–72, 76, 224, 339
 stable government, 180–181, 184–185, 187, 218
Administrative Court (*san pokkhrong*), *see* courts, 28, 63, 76, 128, 267, 270, 275, 287–288
 Central Administrative Court, 27–28, 174, 211
 Supreme Administrative Court, 76, 121, 126–127, 132–133, 189, 268–269, 271, 274–275, 277, 284, 301, 347, 352
administrative power, 83, 85, 89–90, 97, 113, 147, 171–172, 175, 187, 189, 191, 217–218, 275
advisory house, 95
anti-Communist, 40, 340
anti-corruption measures, 55, 61, 66, 81, 265
anti-majoritarianism, *see* majority decision-making, 15
Anti-Money Laundering Law (*phraratchabanyat pongkan lae prap pram kanfokngoen* Pho. So. 2542), 227

anti-Thaksin movement, *see* Thaksin administration, 34, 62–63, 68, 73–78, 341
assets
 assets and liabilities statement, 227, 229–230, 242–249, 262, 272–273
 Assets Examination Committee (*khana kammakan truatsop kankratham thi ko hai koet khwamsiahai kae rat*), 228, 253, 313
 assets of children under the age of majority, 230, 246
 expenditure report, 199, 200, 205, 208–209
 false assets and liabilities statement, 228, 242–245, 249–250, 271, 277, 282–284, 286
 unusual asset increase (*sappasin phuemkhuen phitpakati*), 228, 238–239, 250
 unusually wealthy (*ram ruai phitpakati*), 113, 225, 228–231, 233, 237–239, 241–242, 277
authoritarianism, 1, 11, 22, 41, 180
 competitive authoritarianism, 10
 semi-authoritarianism, 1, 2
 state authoritarianism, 66, 180
 strongmen, 4

bad man (*khon chua khon leu*), *see* good people (*khon di*), 60
Bangkok
 Bangkok citizen/residents, 4, 48, 262
Banharn administration, *see* Banharn Silpa-archa, 59
bicameral system, *see* parliament, 42–43, 95, 111, 118
Board of Audit (*sathaban kiaokap kantruatgoenphendin*) / National Audit Board, 74, 90, 189, 264, 301–302, 308, 310

Index 383

buffet [self-serving] cabinet, 53
bureaucrats, 10, 33, 40–41, 44–45, 47, 55, 62, 64, 74–75, 82, 179, 223–224, 241, 244, 255, 272, 305, 347
bureaucratic polity/system, 40–41, 140, 360

cabinet, 24, 27–29, 42–43, 48, 53–54, 57, 81–83, 85, 88, 91, 94, 97–98, 137, 146–149, 152, 156, 158–166, 169–170, 172–177, 179, 182, 186–187, 189, 191, 223, 228–229, 231, 233, 235, 238, 244, 246–249, 254, 257, 262, 273, 278, 284, 313, 315–316, 318, 328, 338, 347, 350, 353, 358, 360
cabinet policy speech, 160, 162, 164
cabinet appointment, 42, 187, 189
Campaign for Popular Democracy, 48, 62
Caravan of the Poor, 63
Central Administrative Court, 27–28, 174, 211
checks and balances, *see* political reform, 10, 16–17, 55, 66, 85–86, 91, 93, 97, 112–113, 117, 134–135, 165–166, 175, 326
Chuan Cabinet/Chuan Leekpai administration, *see* Chuan Leekpai, 52, 160–161
Chulalongkorn University, x, 24, 105
citizen, 13, 17, 20, 22, 27, 48, 71–72, 84, 137, 153, 170, 241, 261–263, 282, 295, 302, 324, 346, 348–349, 351–352
civil official, 8–9, 44
civil service commission, 90
civil servant, x, 42–43, 45, 64, 88, 93, 236–237, 259, 279, 296, 299–300, 302, 304–305
former civil servant, 302–304, 306–309, 311–312
class, 27, 93, 111, 119, 155, 241, 335
closed-class, 22
combativeness, *see* memory and combativeness, constitutional patriotism, 19

Committee on Developing Democracy (*khanakammakan phatthana prachathipatai*), 24, 55–56
communism, 7, 40, 48, 135, 340
competitive authoritarianism, *see* authoritarianism, 10
conflict of interest (*kankhatkan rawang prayotsuanbukkhon lae prayotsuanruam*), 166, 236, 239–242, 251–262, 272, 283, 289, 293, 323
consolidation phase, *see* democratization, 7
Constitution
  interim constitution, 25, 39, 41, 48, 64–65, 77, 124, 141, 146, 150, 229, 267, 283, 344, 357
People's Constitution (*ratthathammanun chabap prachachon*), 5, 60, 66, 116, 266, 341
Thailand constitution
  1991 Constitution, 4, 23, 32, 47, 49, 55, 70–72, 75, 80, 89, 91, 107, 115, 139, 155, 157–158, 160, 179, 181, 188–189, 227–228, 230–231, 234–235, 240, 262, 298, 313, 316, 318, 330, 338, 347–348, 358–359
  (amendment of) Section 211, 80, 158
  1997 Constitution, ix, 5–7, 24, 34–35, 43, 56, 58–62, 64–66, 75, 78, 80–81, 91–92, 102, 104–105, 109, 112, 114–117, 119, 123, 125, 127, 133–138, 140–141, 145–147, 150, 154–163, 165, 174–175, 179–181, 183–195, 197, 200, 204, 210–215, 217–218, 224–225, 227–236, 241, 243, 245, 250, 263–270, 275, 278–282, 284–285, 287, 291–293, 295, 297, 299–300, 313–314, 316–319, 329, 334–335, 337–338, 341–342, 346, 348, 352, 360
  2006 Interim Constitution, 5, 269, 284–285, 295, 309

2007 Constitution, ix, 5, 7, 25, 35, 39, 64–67, 78, 80, 91–92, 102–104, 115–118, 122–123, 125, 129, 133–134, 137, 140–141, 146–147, 149–151, 154–159, 161–162, 165, 167, 173, 175–176, 179–181, 189, 191–193, 203, 212, 214, 217, 223, 226–235, 241, 247–250, 252, 263–267, 269, 274–276, 279, 281–285, 289–290, 292, 295–297, 300–301, 303, 305, 309–311, 313–325, 329–331, 334–335, 337–338, 342–344, 352, 360

2007 Constitution Drafting Assembly (*sapha rang ratthathamnanun*), see Constitution Drafting Assembly, 92, 295, 309–310, 323

2007 Constitution Drafting Committee, see constitutional draft, 35, 92, 115

2014 Interim Constitution, 345

2017 Constitution, 23, 331, 344, 353, 358–360

Constitutions other than the Thai

Constitution of the Fifth Republic (France), 19–20, 163, 170–171

Fundamental Law for the Federal Republic of Germany, 17, 99, 163, 169

United States Constitution, 17, 86, 163, 171–172

Weimar Constitution, 94, 101

Constitution Drafting Assembly (*sapha rang ratthathammanu*), 57–60, 64–65, 80, 92, 104, 114–115, 295, 309–310, 312, 320–321, 323

2007 Constitution Drafting Assembly (*sapha rang ratthathamnanun*), 92, 295, 309–310, 323

Constitution of the Fifth Republic (France), 19–20, 163, 170–171

Constitutional Council (France, *Conseil Constitutionnel*), 20, 170

Constitutional Court (*san ratthathammanun*), see courts, 3, 6, 12, 18, 25, 30, 34, 63, 76, 78–79, 88, 90–91, 94, 98–104, 112, 117, 124, 127–132, 138, 140, 145, 147, 157, 173–174, 176–177, 192–194, 199, 202, 211–214, 231, 243, 245, 247–248, 252, 254, 258, 263–294, 310, 313, 315–317, 319–320, 323–330, 336, 343, 347, 349–353, 355, 357–358, 361

chief justice of the Constitutional Court, 121, 126, 132, 189, 269, 271, 274–275, 277, 352–353

Constitutional Court ruling, 6, 157, 174, 252, 254, 279, 281–282, 284, 286, 289–290, 323–326, 329

constitutional review committee/ constitutional tribunal committee, 90, 230

dissolution by the Constitutional Court, see dissolution of political parties, 101, 200, 279

justice of the Constitutional Court, 276, 280, 286, 293, 301, 353

constitutional draft, 23–24, 57–58, 66, 80, 86, 102, 105, 117, 141, 345–346, 349, 353–354, 357–358

2007 Constitution Drafting Committee, 35, 92, 115

Constitution Drafting Committee (*khanakammathikan yokrang ratthathammanun*), 23–24, 35, 57, 65, 104, 140, 190, 267, 289, 295, 320–321, 323, 345, 352–353, 359

constitutional tribunal (*khana tulakan ratthathammanun*), 212, 213, 214, 283–284, 289

Draft Amendment Committee (*khanakammathikan phitcharana rang ratthathammanun*), 57, 104, 114

sub-committees to the Constitution Drafting Committee (*khana anukammathikan rang ratthathammanun*), 65

constitutional monarchy, 40, 45–46, 69

Index   385

constitutional patriotism, *see* liberal democratic Constitution, 19
memory and combativeness, 19
constitutional reform, ix, 52, 55, 59, 75, 80, 86–88, 91, 95, 97, 112, 138, 145, 159, 181, 218, 226, 261, 264, 281–282, 285, 292, 321–322, 330–331, 344, 346
Constitutional Reform Committee, 24
constitutional revision, 4, 20, 50, 53, 86, 146, 151, 155, 159, 178, 182, 212, 231, 261, 298, 315, 318, 320, 322, 324, 326–327, 330, 335, 343
constitutional revolution (of 1932)/ Siamese Revolution, ix, 5, 39–40, 42, 45, 48, 69, 110
constitutionalism, ix, 1, 7, 10, 12–17, 20–21, 23, 25, 29–30, 35, 55, 59, 67, 78, 80, 84, 86–89, 91–92, 94, 134–137, 139, 141, 145, 147, 149, 165, 173, 174–177, 317, 336–337, 359
legal constitutionalism, 16, 92
modern constitutionalism, 16
political constitutionalism, 16
constitutionality, *see* constitution, 17–18, 100, 173, 252, 269, 272, 278, 293, 313, 317, 320, 322, 324, 326, 328–329, 355
constitutionality of laws, 18, 272, 278
contract with the nature of an economic monopoly, *see* matters forbidden, 231
corrupt government business (*kanthutcharit nai wongratchakan*) and illegal acts related to government business (*kanprapruettimichop nai wongratchakan*), 238
corruption, *see* money politics, 53, 55, 58, 61–62, 74, 77–78, 91, 93–94, 101, 105, 113, 117, 139, 151–152, 168, 176, 189, 200, 204, 211–212, 214–218, 223–230, 233, 237–238, 241–243, 246, 248–251, 255–258, 261–266, 271, 277, 279, 291–293, 312–313, 315, 328, 330, 334–335, 337–338, 345–346, 350

corruption in duties of employment (*thutcharit to nathi*), 238
criticism of corruption, 53, 261
electoral corruption, 179–180, 182–183, 218
legal definition of corruption, 225–227, 241–242, 261
policy corruption (*kankhorapchan choeng nayobai*), 256, 260
political corruption, 48, 53, 66, 94, 138, 184–185, 224, 241, 243, 359
suspicions of corruption, 57, 64, 117, 336
corruption in duties of employment (*thutcharit to nathi*), *see* corruption, 238
Council of National Security (CNS; *khana montri kwammankhong heang chat*), 64, 248
council of state (*samnakgan khanakammakan krisdika*), *see* quasi-legal functions, 24, 90, 140, 266, 310
Counter-Corruption Commission (*khanakanmakan po po po*), 90, 238, 259
coup (*ratthaprahan*), ix, 2–6, 11, 23–25, 39–41, 43–44, 46, 48–49, 53, 61, 63–64, 66–68, 70, 75, 77, 83–84, 91, 102, 104–106, 113, 116, 123, 135, 137–141, 146, 180–181, 189, 212–213, 223, 228–229, 245, 251, 253, 257–258, 261–262, 267, 269, 275, 282–284, 289, 293, 295, 305, 311–314, 318, 320–322, 324, 328–329, 331, 334–335, 340, 344, 359–360
2006 coup, 6–7, 23, 25–27, 73, 77, 79, 92, 115–116, 137, 141, 213, 224, 228, 248, 257–258, 262, 264, 267, 283, 285, 288, 295, 309, 320, 322, 324, 334–336, 343
failed coups (*kabots*), 39
legitimized by the consent of the king, 269

courts
  Administrative Court (san
    pokkhrong), 28, 63, 76, 128, 267,
    270, 275, 287–288
  Central Administrative Court,
    27–28, 174, 211
  Constitutional Court
    (san ratthathammanun), 3, 6,
    12, 18, 25, 30, 34, 63, 76, 78–79,
    88, 90–91, 94, 98–104, 112, 117,
    124, 127–132, 138, 140, 145, 147,
    157, 173–174, 176–177, 192–194,
    199, 202, 211–214, 231, 243, 245,
    247–248, 252, 254, 258, 263–294,
    310, 313, 315–317, 319–320,
    323–330, 336, 343, 347, 349–353,
    355, 357–358, 361
  Supreme Administrative Court,
    76, 121, 126–127, 132–133, 189,
    268–269, 271, 274–275, 277, 284,
    301, 347, 352
  Supreme Court, 4, 12, 63, 76, 96,
    113–115, 117, 125–127, 129–132,
    134, 140, 189, 205, 214, 218, 223,
    228, 231, 245, 252, 268, 271,
    274–275, 277–281, 284, 288, 292,
    301, 315, 339, 341, 343, 356
Criminalizing [Political]
  Tendering for State Agencies
  Law (phraratchabanyat waduai
  khwamphit kiaokap kansanoe
  rakha to nuaingan khong rat Pho.
  So. 2542), 226–227

democracy, 1, 4–6, 11–12, 15–16,
  18–20, 22–23, 25–26, 31, 40, 46, 48,
  50, 52–53, 55–56, 58, 70, 77, 81–83,
  86–87, 91, 93, 95, 98–99, 101, 105,
  109, 114, 118–119, 131, 135–137,
  141, 167, 174–175, 177–178, 181,
  201, 223–224, 263–265, 287, 316,
  330–332, 334, 336–338, 340
  participatory democracy, 59
  quality of a democracy, 10
Democrat Party, 8–9, 50, 72, 74, 76,
  212, 216, 283–285, 290, 325–328, 336
democratic government/democratic
  regime of government, 5, 18, 66–67,
  224

democratization, ix, 1–7, 10–11, 13–14,
  30, 35, 39–42, 52–53, 60, 68, 72, 82,
  86, 93, 101–102, 114, 136, 141, 145,
  147, 168, 180, 182, 224–225, 227, 255,
  261, 263, 291, 298, 318, 331, 335, 337,
  344, 358–360
  consolidation phase, 7
  democratization theory, 1, 7, 10
  institutional democratization, 4,
    11, 47
  third wave, 1, 13
  transition period/stage, 1, 7, 10, 14
demonstration, 4–6, 39–40, 50, 52,
  68, 74, 80, 137–139, 324, 326–327,
  340–341, 360
developed nations, 3, 15, 20, 85,
  136–137
dictatorship by law, 291, 294
Directive Principles of Fundamental
  State Policies (Directive
  Principles), see constitution,
  145–150, 152–153, 156, 159–161,
  164, 166, 169, 173, 342, 360
discretionary power, 15, 21, 123, 148,
  163, 174
dishonesty/wrong-doing, 74, 77, 87,
  204, 223, 236, 271, 277, 279, 350
dismissal, see regulating corruption,
  225, 236, 238, 248, 273, 279–281,
  286, 313
dissolution of political parties,
  100–101, 191, 196, 199, 213, 283,
  322, 342
  dissolution by the Constitutional
    Court's judgment, see
    Constitutional Court, 101, 199
  dissolution of opposition parties
    by the judiciary/dissolution of
    the Thai Rak Thai Party, 4, 6,
    213, 283
district head, 305
diversity, 50–51, 72, 74, 110, 122,
  133–134, 136, 269
diversity of (Thai) society, 109–111
double standards, 137, 336

Draft Amendment Committee (*khanakammathikan phitcharana rang ratthathammanun*), 57, 104, 114

dualist, *see* monist, 85, 97

efficiency, *see* efficiency of the political system, 54, 60, 66, 80, 93, 152, 154, 164, 166, 266–267

efficiency of the political system, 93

election boycott, 76, 286

Election Commission (*khana kammakan kanlueaktang*), 79, 89, 126, 131, 145, 184, 189, 194, 197, 201–212, 214–218, 263–264, 266–270, 272–276, 278–281, 283–288, 290, 301–308, 310, 312–313, 315, 321, 323, 327–328, 349–350, 353–355

Election Law, 181, 194, 203, 211, 218

1998 Election Law (1998 law, *phraratchabanyat prakop ratthathammanun waduai kanlueaktang samachik sapha phuthaen ratsadon lae samachik uthisapha* Pho. So. 2541), 197–200, 203–206, 209–210

2007 Election Law (2007 law, *phraratchabanyat prakop ratthathammanun waduai kanlueaktang samachik sapha phuthaen ratsadon lae kandaimasueng samachik uthisapha* Pho. So. 2550), 195, 200–204, 206, 210–211

encouragement of reports about election fraud, 210

electoral corruption, *see* corruption, 179–180, 182–183, 218

electoral system, 120, 179–180, 182–183, 188–189, 192, 218

electoral system reform, 179–182, 185, 189

eligibility to be elected, 228, 230

elimination of drugs, 61

elite, 7, 11, 30, 41, 46, 55, 85, 90, 135–136, 145, 300, 307

emergency powers, 124

employees of the state (*caonathi khong rat*) / officials of the nation (*chao nathi khong rat*), *see* corruption, 28, 152, 236, 258–259

encouragement of reports about election fraud, *see* regulating corruption, 210

ethics, 66, 167, 241, 279

executive, *see* party executive, 104, 187–188, 193–195, 197–198, 200–202, 211, 213–215, 218, 279, 289–290, 325, 336

farm worker/farmer, 63–64, 110, 151–153, 166, 174

fascism, 135

fear, 35, 129–130, 134, 341, 356, 358

fortified democracy, 18

France
 Constitution of the Fifth Republic, 19–20, 163, 170–171
 Constitutional Council (*Conseil Constitutionnel*), 20, 170
 higher court, the Parlement of the Ancien Régime, 19

Freedom House, 2

fundamental human rights, 163, 173

general election, *see* popular election, 3–6, 39, 47, 49, 52–53, 61–63, 68, 72–73, 75–76, 113, 183–184, 190, 192, 215–216, 284, 286–287, 289, 292, 295, 324, 327–329, 340, 345, 358–359

Germany
 Fundamental Law for the Federal Republic of Germany, 17, 99, 163, 169
 German Constitutional Court, 17
 Weimar Constitution, 94, 101

good governance, *see* political reform, 13, 59–60, 78, 148

good people (*khon di*) / virtuous political leader, *see* bad man (*khon chua khon leu*), 60, 85, 346, 348

government appointment
(kansanha), 42–43, 109, 120, 182,
189, 210, 258, 263, 275, 295–296,
301, 322, 346, 348
government appointed parliament
member, see parliament member,
179
guardian of the constitution, 320, 330

higher court of France, the Parlement
of the Ancien Régime, 19
Holocaust, 19
House of Representatives (lower
house), 3–4, 29, 39, 42–45, 47, 49–55,
63, 68, 72, 74–75, 81–83, 87–92,
95–98, 101, 107–113, 115, 119–123,
132, 135–136, 163, 179–186, 188–194,
199, 202, 205–206, 210–218, 223,
227–230, 232, 234, 244–245, 248,
262, 268–272, 274–277, 280–281,
286–290, 296–301, 303, 305, 309,
314–320, 325, 327, 329, 342,
346–354, 358
  chair of the lower house, 43, 51–52,
  352
  members of the House of
  Representatives, 47, 79, 108,
  181–182, 187–190, 193–194, 206,
  219, 228–230, 234, 237, 245, 247,
  259, 262, 315–318, 325, 349
House of Sages, see parliament
member, 95, 97
human rights violation, 19–20, 74,
105, 137, 335
hunger strikes, 50, 72

impeachment, 78, 88, 94, 111,
113–114, 119, 281
independent agencies, 30, 65, 79, 90,
94–95, 112, 115–118, 121, 125–134,
139, 141, 145–146, 197, 217, 226,
263–268, 270, 273–278, 280–283,
285–286, 288–294, 301, 310, 312–313,
315–316, 320, 322, 327–330, 335–336,
344, 349–353, 358
independent agency package,
265, 268, 273, 292, 294

institutional democratization,
see democratization, 4, 11, 47
intellectual, 31, 35, 53–56, 59–60, 65,
74, 77–79, 82–83, 123, 130, 136,
138, 165, 182–183, 228, 256, 261,
263–264, 269, 286–287, 292–293,
299, 336, 339, 341, 351, 358
intentionality, see regulating
corruption, 250
interim Anand administrations,
see Anand Panyarachun, 54
interim constitution, see
Constitution, 25, 39, 41, 48, 64–65,
77, 124, 141, 146, 150, 229, 267, 283,
344, 357

joint session, 314–315, 323
joint statement by the Thai and
Cambodian governments, 27–28
judges, 15, 30–31, 34, 67, 76, 98–99,
113, 132, 263, 335, 340, 344
  oath ceremony (for judges of
  the Supreme and Administrative
  courts), 76
judicial legal status, 155
judicial review, 10, 13–16, 18–20, 167,
175
judicial states, 177
judicialization of politics, 7, 12–14, 30
judiciary, ix, 3, 6–7, 9, 11, 13–20,
25, 28–31, 33–34, 76, 91, 112, 125,
132, 136–138, 140, 146, 157, 165,
168–169, 172, 177, 189, 227, 269,
275, 278, 293, 301, 306, 310, 316,
322, 337, 340–341, 347
  intervention by the judiciary into
  the political realm, 20, 29
judicial activism, 130
judicial independence, 12, 22, 31
judicial power, 67, 86, 90–91,
  112–113, 116–117, 124, 127, 131,
  134, 269, 273, 316, 337
quasi-legal functions, 90

kamnan (district head), 53, 110, 217–218, 236, 305, 308, 321

King

   Democratic regime of government with the King as Head of State (DKHS, *Prathetthai mi kan pokkhrong rabob prachathipatai an mi phramahakasat thong pen pramuk*), 31–32, 34, 35, 67, 80, 93–94, 100, 106–107, 140, 152, 160, 176–177, 199–201, 213, 269, 278, 281, 287, 319, 326, 336, 338–340, 342, 344–346, 350

   intervention by King, 69, 73, 76

   virtue (king's 'virtue' to directly intervene and mediate in political crises) (*phrabarami; barami*), 31–32, 34–35, 45, 59–60, 66, 70, 73, 84–85, 336, 339–340

King Prajadhipok Institute, 331

lack of transparency, 58

leadership, 6, 19, 41, 51, 63, 71, 75, 85, 93, 98, 170, 288, 339, 353

legal and judicial enforceability, 152

legal and judicial status, 155

legal constitutionalism, *see* constitutionalism, 16, 92

legal official, 8–9, 44, 303

Legal Reform Commission (*khana kammakan phatthana kotmai*), 267

legislative body, 316

legislative power, 29, 55, 85, 89–90, 92–93, 113, 158, 165, 167, 169, 171–175, 177, 186–187, 189, 191, 217–218, 320, 324, 337

legitimation, 26, 41

liberal democratic Constitution, *see* constitutional patriotism, 19

liberalism/liberalist, 135–137

majority decision-making, *see* antimajoritarianism, 86, 92, 147

majority group, 16, 91, 307

   dictatorship by majority, 54, 94, 101–102, 135, 176

majoritarian rule, 13

mass media, 50, 115, 147, 165, 232, 256, 308–309, 312

Matters forbidden to members of the House of Representatives, 231, 234

   entering into a monopoly contract, 232–234, 240

   not receiving special privilege, 240

mayor, 50, 237, 305

mega-politics, 14

memory and combativeness, *see* constitutional patriotism, 19

middle class, 31, 40–41, 54, 70, 93, 145, 262

   urban middle-class, 145, 266

military regime, *see* administration, 3, 24–25, 39–40, 43, 71–72, 76, 224, 339

military service, 308

military officer, 8–9, 40, 44

Ministry of the Interior, 179, 197, 204, 305, 308–309

minority group, 15–16, 18, 187

modern constitutionalism, *see* constitutionalism, 16

modernization (theory of modernization), 1, 7

monarchy, 31–33, 35, 44–47, 67, 70, 79–80, 93–95, 145, 269, 344, 360–361

money politics, *see* corruption, 66, 261, 266

monist, *see* dualist, 85, 97

multiple-seat constituency system, *see* single-seat constituency system, 188, 192

National Audit Commission (*khana kammakan truat guen phendin*), 267, 275–276, 280

National Counter-Corruption Commission (*khana kammakan pongkan lae prappram kanthucharit heang chat*), 74, 145, 224–225, 229, 231, 233, 235–237, 239, 241, 243, 245–247, 258–259, 266–270, 272–273, 276, 280, 283–284, 310

National Economic and Social Consultative Commission (*sapha thi prueksa setthakit lae sangkhom haeng chat*), 267

National Human Rights Commission (*khana kammakan sithi manutsayachon haeng chat*), 125, 127, 145, 166, 266–267, 276, 278

National Legislative Assembly (*sapha nitipanyat haeng chat*), 23–25, 48, 309, 312, 321

National Peace-Keeping Council (NPKC; *khana raksa khwamsagopriaproi haeng chat*), 41, 48

national referenda, 54, 162, 272, 315, 350, 353, 356

Referendum Law, 354, 355

National Reform and Harmony Strategy Committee, 346–349, 351

National Student Center of Thailand (NSCT; *Sunklang nisitnakusueksa haeng chat*), 45, 68–69, 71

Nazi, 19–20, 94, 99, 101–102, 135–138

new forms of 'corruption', 241–242

newly emerging nations, 1, 7, 59

NGO, 48–52, 55, 60, 62, 71–72, 74–75, 79, 286–287

Nitirat, 25–29, 326

non-democratic, 11, 42, 44, 93, 101, 332–334

non-elected prime minister, *see* prime minister, 40, 47, 49, 52, 72, 74–75, 81, 98, 102, 125, 138–139, 181, 348

northeastern region (in Thailand), 63, 82, 89, 138, 162, 183, 300, 333

North-East Farm Workers' Network, 63

oath ceremony (for judges of the Supreme and Administrative courts), 76

ombudsman, *see* Parliamentary Ombudsman, 55, 90, 125, 241, 272–273, 288, 310, 312, 329

opposition parties, 4, 50–52, 63, 72, 75–76, 132, 210–211, 274, 286–287

Organic Act on Elections (*phraratchabanyat kanlueaktang samachik sapha phuthaen ratsadon*), *see* Election Law, 181, 186, 194, 203

organic law, 32, 35, 88, 90, 93, 123, 140–141, 188, 193, 226, 228, 272, 301, 314–317, 319–321, 342, 344

organic law bill, 186, 188, 193, 342

package, *see* independent agency package, 155, 265–266, 268, 273–275, 282, 291–292, 294, 330

parliament, 12, 16, 19–20, 29, 32, 40–43, 46–52, 55–57, 60, 62–63, 65–67, 72, 74, 78, 80–85, 87–99, 101–102, 108–111, 116, 118–119, 121–122, 124, 126, 129, 132–139, 146, 149, 155, 159–161, 165–167, 169–173, 175, 177, 179, 181–182, 186, 219, 224, 226, 229, 235, 237, 246, 248–249, 257, 260–262, 272–273, 275, 279–280, 284, 290, 293–295, 297–298, 300, 309, 314, 317–318, 321, 323, 325–327, 329, 331–336, 338, 347, 353–354, 357

bicameral system, 42–43, 95, 111, 118

chair of the parliament, 42–43, 47, 49–52, 331, 357

dissolution of the parliament, 82–83

members of parliament, 43, 74, 81, 84, 98, 133, 135, 229, 246, 248, 279, 297, 300

power to dissolve the lower house, 82

rationalization of parliament (*rationalisation du parlement*), 20

tricameral, 95

parliament member, 43, 74, 81, 84, 98, 133, 135, 229, 246, 248, 297, 300

government appointed parliament member, *see* government appointment, 179

members of the House of Sages, 95, 97

Index 391

members of parliament, 43, 74, 81, 84, 98, 133, 135, 229, 246, 248, 279, 297, 300

popularly elected member, *see* popular election, 42–44, 51, 55, 108, 295, 303

provincial assembly members, 236, 259, 305

parliamentary democracy, 40, 82, 84–85, 136–137, 160–161, 219, 260–262, 293–294, 321

parliamentary dictatorship (*phadetkan thang ratthasapa*), 48–49, 53, 66, 84–86, 90, 92, 116, 134, 138

Parliamentary Ombudsman (*phu truat kanphendin khong ratthasapa*) / National Ombudsman (*phu truat kanphendin haeng chat*), 126–127, 145, 189, 266–267, 272, 275–276, 279–280, 282–284, 287, 290, 301, 315, 327–329, 355

parliamentary system, 56, 83, 85–86, 88–89, 91, 93, 97, 135, 169, 182

participation in state governance and politics, 58, 105

participatory democracy, *see* democracy, 59

Penal Code (*pramuan kotmai aya*), 226

People (citizen)

government by the people, 105

participation by the people, 57, 59, 67, 93, 116, 118, 266

representatives of the people, 85, 87, 121, 124, 172, 177

People's Assembly (*samatcha haeng chat khong prathet thai*), 64, 305, 309–310, 312, 320

People's Constitution (*ratthathammanun chabap prachachon*), *see* Constitution, 5, 60, 66, 116, 266, 341

People's Party (*khana rat*), 4, 8, 40, 46, 110

People's Power Party, 6, 9, 283, 322–323

Pheu Thai Party, 6, 9, 212, 216–217, 263, 284, 290, 323

Pheu Thai Party government, 323

policy, 5, 10, 12–13, 28–30, 54, 62, 79, 87, 94, 104–105, 108, 112, 118, 131, 137, 147–150, 153, 155–156, 158–177, 180, 184, 201, 251–252, 254, 256–257, 260, 299, 314, 322, 328, 345, 360

policy corruption (*kankhorapchan choeng nayobai*), *see* corruption, 256, 260

political constitutionalism, *see* constitutionalism, 16

political corruption, 48, 53, 66, 94, 138, 184–185, 224, 241, 243, 359

political crises, 33, 35, 116, 123, 130, 133, 139, 141, 287, 338, 340, 351, 353, 358

political intervention, 33–34, 78, 116–117, 130–131, 285, 338–340, 361

political office holders (*phu damrongtamnaeng thang kanmueang*), 66, 229, 236

political parties, 5, 19, 29–30, 43, 54, 58, 82, 89–90, 93, 99–101, 107, 109–110, 117, 135, 149, 179–188, 190–193, 195, 203, 211–215, 217–218, 232, 269, 271–272, 284–285, 289, 292, 315, 321, 337, 344, 349–350, 360

establishment of political parties, 195–196, 200

dissolution of political parties, 100–101, 191, 196, 199, 213, 283, 322, 342

party executive, 51, 187, 198, 201–203, 214–215, 218, 279, 289

party leader, 6, 51, 116, 184, 197–198, 200–201, 203, 209, 211, 214, 218, 279

party registration, 198, 203

political party dictatorship (*rabop phadetkan doi phakkanmuaeng*), 29

Political Party Establishment
Committee (*khana phuroem chattang phakkanmueang*), 195, 197
political party's regulations, 201
report of political party activities (annual), 198–200, 215
political party law
  1998 Political Party Law (*phraratchabanyat prakop ratthathammanun waduai phakkanmueang* Pho. So.2541), 195–196, 213, 215, 285
  2007 Political Party Law (*phraratchabanyat prakop ratthathammanun waduai phakkanmueang* Pho. So.2550), 195–196, 214–215
  (provision of) Organic Act on Political Parties (*phraratchabanyat phakkanmueang*), 181, 194, 209
political reform, 5, 7, 13, 55, 57–59, 61–62, 64–65, 79–82, 86–87, 89, 92–94, 116, 134–138, 148, 154–155, 165, 178, 187, 266, 336, 341–342
  accountability, 10, 13, 54–55, 59, 292–293
  checks and balances, 10, 16–17, 55, 66, 85–86, 91, 93, 97, 112–113, 117, 134–135, 165–166, 175, 326
  good governance, 13, 59–60, 78, 148
  rule of law, 10, 12–15, 21–23, 26–28, 30, 59–60, 67, 147–148, 150, 153, 156, 263, 265, 291, 326, 335–339, 342–344
  transparency, 59, 61, 66, 166, 335, 337
political reform movement, ix, 5, 7, 24, 27, 31–35, 47, 53, 55–60, 65–66, 78–81, 93, 101, 104, 114, 134–135, 141, 155, 170, 175, 183–184, 228, 263, 266, 334, 336, 341
political rights, 2

politician, 4–5, 10, 13, 17, 29–31, 33–35, 41, 45–48, 50, 53–55, 57–61, 65–66, 68, 71–72, 74–75, 82, 84, 86–89, 91, 93, 105, 108–110, 113, 122, 130–131, 134, 139, 141, 145, 155, 223–226, 228, 231–233, 237, 240–241, 243–244, 246–247, 249, 255, 260–267, 272, 279, 282, 294, 303–305, 308–309, 311–312, 330, 335–337, 340, 343, 346, 351, 359
  corruption among politicians, *see* corruption, 91, 224, 226, 261–262, 265
popular election, 3–4, 7, 43, 50–51, 53–54, 59, 85, 96, 104, 111, 114–115, 119–122, 133, 141, 145, 184, 189, 203, 210, 265, 275, 295–296, 299, 306–307, 310, 336, 339–340, 359
  2008 upper house election (2008 election), 303–304
democratic leadership, 56
election promises, 62, 177
general election, 3–6, 39, 47, 49, 52–53, 61–63, 68, 72–73, 75–76, 113, 183–184, 190, 192, 215–216, 284, 286–287, 289, 292, 295, 324, 327–329, 340, 345, 358–359
popularly elected member, *see* parliament member, 42–44, 51, 55, 108, 295, 303
popularly elected prime minister, 4, 42, 47, 49, 56, 101–102, 107, 122, 141, 145, 348, 351, 358
violating election regulations/ Electoral Law violations, 278, 126
popularly elected governments, ix, 6, 282, 284, 289
  demise of democratically elected administrations, 78
populism (*prachaniyom*), 62, 148, 256, 335, 346
Preah Vihear Temple, 27
Prem administration, *see* Prem Tinsulanonda, 23
presidential system, 85, 88–89

prime minister, 3–5, 8–9, 23, 25, 29, 42–45, 47, 49–58, 61–64, 69, 71–72, 74–77, 81–83, 87–93, 96–98, 101–102, 104, 107–110, 112, 114–115, 121–124, 126, 133–136, 138–139, 148, 159–160, 170–171, 180–182, 184, 186–187, 189, 191, 216, 229, 233, 235, 237, 241, 244, 251–254, 256–257, 259–260, 262–263, 283, 285–286, 317, 323, 325, 327–328, 331–332, 334–335, 339–341, 345–354, 357–359

popularly elected prime minister, see popular election, 4, 42, 47, 49, 56, 101–102, 107, 122, 141, 145, 348, 351, 358

private sector, 64, 105, 301–302, 306–310, 312, 345

Privy Council, 33, 81, 121, 339–340, 357

proportional representation system, 95, 108, 110–111, 183–184, 186, 188–190, 192

first past the post (300 seats) and party list proportional representation, 346

prosecutor, 100, 103, 252, 267, 270, 272–273, 276, 285, 324

provincial assembly members, see parliament member, 236, 259, 305

provincial governor, 204, 305

provision upholding the constitution, 106

provisions, see (provision of) Organic Act on Political Parties (Political Party Law), 6, 42–43, 47, 67, 72, 75, 88, 90, 93, 95, 99–100, 102, 105, 115, 134–135, 141, 146, 152–154, 156–157, 163, 168, 174, 179, 181–182, 186–188, 191–196, 203–204, 206–207, 226, 228–229, 231, 233–237, 239, 241, 254, 268, 279–281, 285, 287, 296–297, 301, 313, 316, 318, 325–326, 335, 337–338, 342–344, 347, 349, 350–353, 355

public law scholar, 18, 23–28, 32, 45, 54–55, 59, 105, 136, 148–149, 357

quasi-legal functions, 90

Board of Audit (*sathaban kiaokap kantruatgoenphendin*), 74, 90, 264, 302, 308, 310

Constitutional Court (*san ratthathammanun*), 3, 6, 12, 18, 25, 30, 34, 63, 76, 78–79, 88, 90–91, 94, 98–104, 112, 117, 124, 127–132, 138, 140, 145, 147, 157, 173–174, 176–177, 192–194, 199, 202, 211–214, 231, 243, 245, 247–248, 252, 254, 258, 263–294, 310, 313, 315–317, 319–320, 323–330, 336, 343, 347, 349–353, 355, 357–358, 361

council of state (*samnakgan khanakammakan krisdika*), 24, 90, 140, 266, 310

Counter-Corruption Commission (*khanakanmakan po po po*), 90, 238, 259

ombudsman, 55, 90, 125, 241, 272–273, 288, 310, 312, 329

Red Shirts (*suea daeng*), 25, 263, 289, 291, 336, 346, 360

re-election, 201, 204–205, 215–216

regional/local businessmen, 54, 79

regulating corruption, 227, 244, 256

1999 Counter Corruption Law, 237–239, 241, 246, 252

Counter Corruption Law (*phraratchabanyat prakop ratthathammanun waduai kanpongkan lae prappram kanthutcharit*), 226–227, 229, 236–237, 239–241, 250–252, 257

Regulation of Ministerial Equities and Shareholdings Law (*phraratchabanyat kanchatkan hunsuan lae hun khong ratthamontri Pho.So. 2543*), 227, 233, 247 representative, 3, 21, 23, 31, 43, 56, 59, 61, 64, 68, 82–83, 85, 87, 98, 105, 108–109, 111, 113–114, 117, 119–122, 124, 127, 132, 135–136, 138, 172, 176–177, 187, 198, 202, 218, 235, 240, 265, 268–269, 271, 276, 289–290, 295–296, 301, 313, 347, 356

representative democracy, 59, 105, 135

restrictions on freedom of speech, 359

retrospectively, 335, 357

revocation of the right to vote, 208, 210

revolution (*patiwat*), 11, 39, 41

revolutionary decree/Revolutionary Group Decree, 228, 284, 289, 335

right to submit draft laws, 78, 317

royal prerogative (*Praratchaamnat*), 83, 344

royalist, 40, 46, 165

rule of law, 10, 12–15, 21–23, 26–28, 30, 59–60, 67, 147–148, 150, 153, 156, 263, 265, 291, 326, 335–339, 342–344

rural voters, 81, 84

Samak administration, *see* Samak Sundaravej, ix, 28, 247, 251, 322–323

selection committee/Appointment Committee, 98, 109, 119–121, 126–127, 130–132, 189, 202, 268–269, 271, 274–275, 277, 281, 301

semi-authoritarianism, *see* authoritarianism, 1, 2

semi-democracy (*prachatipatai khrueng bai*), 40–42, 44, 181, 224, 227, 360

senate appointments introduced in the 2007 Constitution (*kansanha*), 301

appointed members, 120, 275, 295, 297, 306–307, 309–312, 317, 320, 323, 330, 346, 348, 354

separation of powers, 15, 17, 30, 134–135, 141, 145, 165, 172, 175, 177, 316

shareholding, *see* unusually wealthy and unusual asset increase, 232–233, 242, 244–246, 248–249, 257

upper limit for shareholding, 233, 245, 247–248

single party system, 85, 90, 92

single-seat constituency system, *see* multiple-seat constituency system, 185, 188, 192

Somchai administration, ix, 6

southern region (Thailand), 62, 74, 89, 183, 300, 327, 334–335

Southeast Asia, x, 2, 4, 12–13

specialization, 90, 301

spouse, 230, 232–235, 245–247, 259–260, 298

stable government, *see* administration, 180–181, 184–185, 187, 218

state authoritarianism, *see* authoritarianism, 66, 180

strongmen, *see* authoritarianism, 4

student uprising, *see* 14 October 1973 student uprising, 40, 45, 56, 68–73, 77, 229, 340, 351

succession (royal), 51, 70, 95, 314, 341, 356

Supreme Administrative Court, *see* Administrative Court, courts, 76, 121, 126–127, 132–133, 189, 268–269, 271, 274–275, 277, 284, 301, 347, 352

chief justice of the Supreme Administrative Court, 121, 126, 132, 269, 271, 274–275, 277, 284, 352

Supreme Court, *see* courts, 4, 12, 63, 76, 96, 113–115, 117, 125–127, 129–132, 134, 140, 189, 205, 214, 218, 223, 228, 231, 245, 252, 268, 271, 274–275, 277–281, 284, 288, 292, 301, 315, 339, 341, 343, 356

chief justice of the Supreme Court, 69, 121, 126, 132, 268, 271–275, 277, 284, 347, 352
full bench of the Supreme Court, 189, 268, 271, 274, 277
Supreme Court Political Criminal Litigation Bureau/ Supreme Court's Political Criminal Proceedings Division/ Criminal Division for Persons Holding Political Positions of the Supreme Court, 128, 130, 251–252, 278
Supreme Court chief justice, 269
Supreme Court of Japan, 29
supreme law, 10, 67, 87–88, 149, 157

technocrat, 54, 60, 79, 332–334
Thai Rak Thai Party, 6, 9, 61–62, 66, 74–75, 187, 210, 212–213, 223, 227, 283–285, 287, 289, 335
Thailand
  cyclic turnover of the Thai political system, 41
  double standards, 137, 336
  northeastern region, 63, 82, 89, 138, 162, 183, 300, 333
  rights and freedoms of the people, 10, 166
  southern region, 62, 74, 89, 183, 300, 327, 334–335
  vicious cycle, 5, 41, 140
Thaksin administration, see Thaksin Shinawatra, ix, 60–63, 73–74, 77, 122, 180, 223, 247, 252, 256, 260, 285, 289, 291, 293, 313, 335, 337
  anti-Thaksin movement, 34, 62–63, 68, 73–78, 341
Thaksin supporters, 27, 63, 223, 264, 320, 336
Thaksin system (*Rabop Thaksin*), 77
Thammasat University, x–xi, 23–25, 45, 51, 68–69, 71–72, 79, 97, 138, 326, 352
theories of democratic transitions, 7

thick theories, see thin theories, 21–22
thin theories, see thick theories, 21–22
third wave, see democratization, 1, 13
three powers (administrative/ executive, legislative and the judiciary), 10, 15, 17, 19–20, 28–29, 88, 91, 112, 114, 125, 128, 130, 133–134, 141, 172, 337, 344
division of the three powers/ separation of powers, 15, 17, 29–30, 125, 134–135, 141, 145, 165, 172, 175, 177, 316
transition period/stage, see democratization, 1, 7, 10, 14
transparency, see political reform, 59, 61, 66, 166, 335, 337
tricameral, see parliament, 95

United States
  United States Constitution, 17, 86, 163, 171–172
  United States Supreme Court, 15
unusual asset increase (*sappasin phuemkhuen phitpakati*), see shareholding, 228, 238–239, 250
unusually wealthy (*ram ruai phitpakati*), see shareholding, 113, 225, 228–231, 233, 237–239, 241–242, 277
upper house, 3, 30, 42–44, 49–52, 74, 78, 91, 95, 109, 111–112, 114, 118–122, 131, 133, 136, 163, 181, 184, 189, 203, 210, 266–271, 273, 275–282, 290, 292, 296–297, 299, 304, 307, 313, 318, 322, 324, 330, 346, 348–351, 353–354, 358
  chair of the upper house, 42–43, 47, 49, 352
  senator, 109, 112, 119–120, 184, 193–194, 206, 234, 237, 244–245, 247–248, 259, 263, 270–271, 275, 295–298, 300–305, 307, 309–310, 312–313, 316, 320, 323–325, 328, 330

urban elite, *see* elite, 64
urban middle-class, *see* middle class, 145, 266

village head (*phuyaiban*), 53, 236, 305
village subsidies, 62
virtue (king's 'virtue' to directly intervene and mediate in political crisis) (*phrabarami*; *barami*), 31–32, 34–35, 45, 59–60, 66, 70, 73, 84–85, 336, 339–340
vote-buying (*khai sitthi sue siang*), 53–54, 84, 88–89, 93, 100, 111, 119, 123, 180, 182, 184, 214, 217, 223, 266

Weimar Constitution, *see* Germany, 94, 101
worker, 62, 74, 151, 165, 168, 258–259, 302, 307–309, 313
World Heritage, 27
World War II, 17–18, 20, 97, 137, 170

Yellow Shirts, 346
Yingluck administration, *see* Yingluck Shinawatra, ix, 6, 323–324, 326–328